# 1930
# *Federal Population*
# CENSUS

CATALOG OF NATIONAL ARCHIVES MICROFILM

NATIONAL ARCHIVES TRUST FUND BOARD
WASHINGTON, DC
2002

PUBLISHED FOR THE NATIONAL ARCHIVES AND RECORDS ADMINISTRATION
BY THE NATIONAL ARCHIVES TRUST FUND BOARD
2002

Library of Congress Cataloging-in-Publication Data

United States. National Archives and Records Administration.
    The 1930 federal population census: catalog of National Archives mi-
crofilm.
        p. cm.
    "Published for the National Archives and Records Administration"—
T.p. verso.
    ISBN 1-880875-25-X
    1. United States—Population—Statistics—Bibliography—Microform
catalogs. 2. United States—Census, 15th, 1930—Bibliography—Microform
catalogs. 3. United States National Archives and Records Administration—
Microform catalogs. 4. Microforms—Catalogs. I. National Archives Trust
Fund Board. II. Title.

Z7553.C3 U48 2002
[HA201]
016.3046'2'097309043—dc21                               2001055875

THE PAPER USED IN THIS PUBLICATION MEETS THE MINIMUM REQUIREMENTS OF THE
AMERICAN NATIONAL STANDARD FOR PERMANENCE OF PAPER FOR PRINTED LIBRARY
MATERIALS Z39.48-1992.

COVER: *"Kansas Entomological Society, April 24, 1926"*
        *(7H-51B-1560).*

# FOREWORD

THE NATIONAL ARCHIVES AND RECORDS ADMINISTRATION (NARA) is the Federal agency that determines which of the wide-ranging records of the U.S. Government will be preserved and made accessible to the American people. Records are housed in 2 archival facilities in the Washington, DC, area, 19 regional records services facilities, and 10 Presidential libraries.

Archival holdings, now amounting to more than 2 million cubic feet, date from the First Continental Congress and consist of the records of the legislative, judicial, and executive branches. NARA has microfilmed over 2,000 series of Federal records that contain a wealth of valuable information. A comprehensive source of information about the holdings is the *Guide to Federal Records in the National Archives of the United States*. The text of that guide and other relevant material can be accessed through NARA's web site at *www.nara.gov*.

These research resources document significant events in our nation's history, but most of them are preserved because of their continuing practical use in the ordinary processes of government, for the protection of private rights, and for the use of researchers and the public. Although Federal records were not created for genealogists, the holdings of the National Archives of the United States contain valuable sources of genealogical information. Perhaps the richest source for genealogists is the information contained in the Federal decennial population census schedules.

---

SEE THE 1930 CENSUS MICROFILM LOCATOR AT
*http://1930census.archives.gov*

You can use this Locator to find the roll of film you need for a specific county, township, or enumeration district. You can also search by place or institution.

The Locator also guides you to specific Soundex microfilm rolls for the 12 Southern Soundexed states.

The Locator is not a family or name index, and it is not a digital version of the census.

# TABLE *of* CONTENTS

*"Loggers on a western red-cedar stump near Deming, Washington, 1925"*
*(95-G-195968).*

# 1930 Census
## *Introduction*

Article I, section 2, of the U.S. Constitution requires that a population census be taken at least every 10 years. Congress uses the census figures to reapportion seats in the House of Representatives. The census also determines each state's number of votes in the Electoral College, which selects the President and Vice President; affects apportionment in state and local legislatures; benchmarks demographic surveys such as the current population surveys (CPS); and influences the distribution of Federal grants to state and local governments.

The records described in this catalog are from Record Group 29, the Records of the Bureau of the Census (hereinafter referred to as the Bureau). To ensure the privacy of individuals, there is a 72-year restriction on access to Federal population schedules. This catalog lists the roll breaks for the 1930 population schedules, reproduced as microfilm publication T626, and the available 1930 census Soundex indexes. The National Archives and Records Administration (NARA) reproduced this microfilm from the highest quality master negatives available from the Bureau of the Census. The original film may have included defects that affect the legibility of some frames. The original schedules no longer exist.

The information in this catalog is current as of December 1, 2001.

This catalog supplements *The 1790–1890 Federal Population Censuses, The 1900 Federal Population Census, The 1910 Federal Population Census,* and *The 1920 Federal Population Census.* These catalogs are available for $3.50 each (plus shipping and handling) from the National Archives Trust Fund Board, Dept. 710, P.O. Box 100793, Atlanta, GA 30384. For orders up to $50, add a $3 shipping and handling fee; $50.01 to $100, add a $5 shipping and handling fee; orders more than $100, add 5% of merchandise total.

As with the 1880 through 1920 censuses, the 1930 census is arranged by census year, state, county, city or township, and enumeration district (ED). There are Soundex indexes for 12 states, which are described on page xix. To use the 1930 census records for unindexed states, it is essential to know as much specific information as possible about where a person lived.

To assist researchers, NARA also reproduced *Enumeration District Maps for the Fifteenth Census of the United States, 1930 Census* (National Archives Microfilm Publication M1930) (see page xxii) and an *Index to Selected City Streets and Enumeration Districts, 1930 Census* (National Archives Microfilm Publication M1931) (see page xxiii).

NARA also purchased many city directories on microfilm from Primary Source Microfilm, Inc. (See page xxv.)

## SCHEDULES

The official census day was April 1, 1930, except for Alaska. The Bureau, however, began taking the census on April 2, 1930. Because of anticipated severe weather in April, the Alaska census day was October 1, 1929.

For the 1930 census, the Bureau of the Census developed a new ED numbering system for 52 of the 56 jurisdictions. Within each state, each county has a distinct number that is followed by the specific enumeration district number. The county numbers were assigned based on the alphabetical order of the counties within each state. For example, Adams County, Washington, has EDs 1-1 to 1-22; Asotin has EDs 2-1 to 2-17; and Benton County has EDs 3-1 to 3-29. American Samoa, the Canal Zone, Guam, and the Virgin Islands, however, did not use this system.

Sometimes no one lived in an ED, in which case the enumerator wrote "no population" on the sheet. These EDs are noted in the catalog by "NP." Some of the EDs contain as few as one person. Care must be taken when viewing the film in order to not miss these small EDs.

In a few cases, the Bureau combined two EDs. The number that was not used is listed as "void." Occasionally a single page within an ED may be missing. These pages have not been noted in the catalog. In other cases, the enumerators transposed the ED number on the census schedule. For example, ED 34-71 might read 34-17.

The Bureau designated large institutions, such as prisons and hospitals, as separate EDs. In larger cities, apartment buildings having 100 or more apartments also were made separate EDs. In most cases, employees of the institution or building were the enumerators. On military and naval stations, officers and enlisted men were appointed enumerators.

### Questions on the 1930 Census

#### Place of abode
1. Street, avenue, road, etc.
2. House number
3. Number of dwelling house in order of visitation
4. Number of family in order of visitation

#### Name
5. Name of each person whose place of abode on April 1, 1930, was in this family. Enter surname first, then the given name, and middle initial, if any. Include every person living on April 1, 1930. Omit children born since April 1, 1930.

#### Relation
6. Relationship of this person to the head of the family

#### Home data
7. Home owned or rented
8. Value of home, if owned, or monthly rental, if rented
9. Radio set
10. Does this family own a farm?

#### Personal description
11. Sex
12. Color or race
13. Age at last birthday
14. Marital condition
15. Age at first marriage

#### Education
16. Attended school or college any time since Sept. 1, 1929
17. Whether able to read or write

#### Place of birth
Place of birth of each person enumerated and of his or her parents. If born in the United States, give State or Territory. If of foreign birth, give country in which birthplace is now situated. Distinguish Canada-French from Canada-English and Irish Free State from Northern Ireland.
18. Place of birth—person
19. Place of birth—father
20. Place of birth—mother

#### Mother tongue (or native language) of foreign born
21. Language spoken in home before coming to the United States

#### Citizenship, etc.
22. Year of immigration into the United States
23. Naturalization
24. Whether able to speak English

#### Occupation and industry
25. Trade, profession, or particular kind of work done
26. Industry or business
27. Class of worker

#### Employment: Whether actually at work yesterday (or the last regular working day)
28. Yes or no
29. If not, line number on Unemployment schedule. (These schedules no longer exist.)

#### Veterans: Whether a veteran of U.S. military or naval forces
30. Yes or no
31. What war or expedition?

#### Farm schedule
32. Number of farm schedule
There are general farm schedules and livestock schedules for 1930 for these territories:

*"Rev. Smith enumerating the 1930 Census in a Navajo Indian Camp" (29-NR-2S).*

Alaska
Guam
Hawaii
American Samoa
Virgin Islands

## *Alaska Schedules*

### Place of abode
1. Number of dwelling house in order of visitation
2. Number of family in order of visitation
3. Name of each person whose place of abode on October 1, 1929, was in this family

### Relation
4. Relationship of this person to the head of the family

### Personal Description
5. Sex
6. Color or race
7. Age at last birthday
8. Single, married, widowed, or divorced

### Education
9. Attended school any time since Jan. 1, 1929
10. Whether able to read and write

### Place of birth
11. Person
12. Father
13. Mother

### Citizenship
14. Year of immigration to the United States
15. Naturalized or alien
16. Whether able to speak English

### Occupation and industry
17. Trade, profession, or particular kind of work done
18. Industry or business in which at work

### Veterans: Whether a veteran of the U.S. military or naval forces. Mobilized for any war or expedition.
19. Yes or No
20. What war or expedition?

## *Merchant Seamen Schedules*

*1930 Census of Merchant Seamen* (National Archives Microfilm Publication M1932, 3 rolls). In 1930, for the first time, the Bureau took an enumeration of merchant seamen serving on U.S. flag merchant vessels. The Bureau created a new form, 15-202, *Crews of Vessels*, to gather this information. This microfilm publication will be released on April 1, 2002.

### Questions on *Crews of Vessels*
The following information is found across the top of the form:
Name and address of owner or operator of vessel
Name of vessel

Date of enumeration
Name of enumerator, usually his signature and/or typewritten name

### Questions on the schedule
1. Name of each person whose *place of abode* on April 1, 1930, was on board this ship
2. Sex
3. Color or race
4. Age at last birthday
5. Single, married, widowed, or divorced
6. Whether able to read or write
7. Place of birth. If born in the United States, give the State or Territory. If of foreign birth, give the country of birth.
8. Naturalized or alien
9. Whether able to speak English
10. Occupation—Trade, profession, or particular kind of work done, as *purser, electrician, machinist, seaman, stewardess, cook,* etc.

Whether a veteran of the U.S. military or naval forces mobilized for any war or expedition
11. Yes or No
12. What war or expedition
13. Address of wife or next of kin

### Codes
In addition to the 13 numbered columns described above, the Form 15-202 also contained three lettered columns "for office use only" into which a tabulation code was entered:
   A–state code
   B–country code
   C–occupation code
Subsequently, the data from the schedules were tabulated for statistical purposes, and this information was incorporated into the Bureau's published reports on the Fifteenth Census.

### Instructions to the Enumerators: Merchant Seamen
The instructions to the enumerator below are found in Form 15-203, *Instructions for Filling Out Schedules for Crews of Vessels* (1929).

3. Who is to be enumerated—All persons aboard ship are to be enumerated *except those officers who have regular or fixed places of abode ashore.* The census data for these persons will be obtained at their homes. Seamen and other persons who claim to be married or give on the crew lists the names of their next of kin should be included in the enumeration of the vessels on which they are employed or have secured employment on April 1, 1930, even though they may maintain fixed places of abode on shore in the intervals between employment on different vessels.

4. Heading of the schedule—Enter in the spaces provided at the top of the schedule the name and address of the owner or operator of the vessel, name of vessel, and home port of the vessel. If the vessel does not have any regularly established home port, enter the name of the port in which the vessel is anchored on the census day or from which it sailed last prior to April 1, 1930.

25. Column 13. Address of wife or next of kin—In this column give the address of the next of kin of each person enumerated, if

possible; the wife, in the case of a married man, or the parents or other near relatives in the case of others. Indicate at the right of the column whether wife (W), parent (P), or other relative (R).

Roll 1    Alabama, California, Connecticut, Florida, Georgia, Illinois, Indiana

Roll 2    Louisiana, Maine, Maryland, Massachusetts, Michigan, Minnesota, New Hampshire, New Jersey

Roll 3    New York, Ohio, Oregon, Pennsylvania, Rhode Island, Texas, Virginia, Washington, Wisconsin, and correspondence files

### *Instructions to the Enumerators: Population Schedules*

The following is a summary of the *Instructions to the Enumerators*. The number in front of each instruction refers to the corresponding numbered paragraph in the published instructions. See *Instructions to Enumerators: Population and Agriculture* (U.S. Department of Commerce, Bureau of the Census: GPO, Washington, DC, 1930, [C3.37/6:En8/rev.]). Copies should be available at Federal Depository Libraries.

### Summary of General Instructions

15. It is your duty *personally* to visit every family and farm within your territory.

16. You are cautioned not to mention or emphasize the compulsory feature of the enumeration unless it is necessary.

17. Many persons will give information after a night's reflection which they refuse to give when first visited.

32. Time allowed for enumeration. In any city or other incorporated place having 2,500 inhabitants or more (based on the 1920 census) the enumeration must be completed within two weeks from the commencement of the work, and in all other districts within 30 days.

### Population Schedule

49. The recopying of schedules should be avoided so far as possible.

52. Persons who move into your district after April 1, for permanent residence, however, should be enumerated by you, unless you find that they have already been enumerated in the district from which they came.

### Who are to be enumerated in your district?

54. In general, all persons are to be enumerated at their "usual place of abode" on April 1, 1930.

55. As a rule, the usual place of abode is the place where a person usually sleeps.

56. Residents absent on census day. There will be a certain number of persons having their usual place of abode in your district who are absent at the time of the enumeration. These you must include and enumerate, obtaining the facts regarding them from their families, relatives, acquaintances, or other persons able to give this information. A son or daughter permanently located elsewhere, however, or regularly employed elsewhere and not sleeping at home, should not be included with the family. Persons to be counted as members of the family include the following:

a. Members of the family temporarily absent on the census day, either in foreign countries or elsewhere in the United States on business or visiting.

b. Members of the family attending schools or colleges located in other districts, except cadets at Annapolis and West Point. (But a student nurse who receives even a nominal salary should be enumerated where she is in training.)

c. Members of the family who are ill in hospitals or sanitariums.

d. Servants, laborers, or other employees who live with the family, sleeping on the premises.

e. Boarders or lodgers who sleep in the house.

57. In the great majority of cases it is more than likely that the names of absent members of the family will not be given to you by the person furnishing the information, unless particular attention is called to them. Before finishing the enumeration of a family you should in all cases, therefore, specifically ask the question as to whether there are any absent members, as described above, who should be enumerated with the family.

58. Designation for absent person. After you have entered the name of such absent members of the family, write after the name in column 5, well toward the right-hand side of the column, the designation, "Ab," thus, "Smith, Robert B.—Ab."

59. Classes not to be enumerated.

a. Persons visiting with the family.

b. Transient boarders or lodgers who have some other usual or permanent place of abode where they are likely to be enumerated.

c. Persons from abroad temporarily visiting or traveling in the United States. (Persons from abroad who are *employed* here should be enumerated, even though they do not expect to remain here permanently.)

d. Students or children living or boarding with this family in order to attend some school, college, or other educational institution in the locality, but not regarding the place as their home.

e. Persons who take their meals with this family, but lodge or sleep elsewhere.

f. Servants, apprentices, or other persons employed by this family and working in the house or on the premises, but *not sleeping* there.

g. Any person who was formerly in this family, but has since become an inmate of an asylum, almshouse, home for the aged, reformatory, prison, or any other institution in which the inmates may remain for long periods of time.

70. Inmates of medical or surgical hospitals. Most inmates of medical and surgical hospitals are there only for temporary treatment and have other regular places of abode. Therefore, you should not enumerate as a resident of the hospital any patient unless it appears that he has no other usual place of abode from which he is likely to be reported. A list of persons having no permanent homes can usually be obtained from the hospital records.

71. Inmates of prisons, asylums, and institutions other than hospitals. If there is within your district a prison, reformatory, or jail, an almshouse, an asylum or hospital for the insane, a home for orphans, or for the blind, deaf, or incurable, an institution for the feeble-minded, a solders' home, a home for the aged, or any similar institution in which inmates usually remain for long periods of

time, all the inmates of such an institution should be enumerated as of your district. It is to be specially noted that in the case of jails the prisoners should be there enumerated, however short the term of sentence.

72. Persons engaged in railway services or traveling. Railway men, canal men, expressmen, railway mail clerks, traveling salesmen, and the like, usually have homes to which they return at intervals and which constitute their usual place of abode within the meaning of the census act. Therefore, any such person who may be in your district temporarily on April 1, 1930, are not be by enumerated by you unless they claim to have no other regular place of abode within the United States. But if any such persons have their homes in your district, they should be enumerated there, even though absent on April 1, 1930.

73. Soldiers, sailors, marines, and civilian employees of the United States. If, therefore, any family in your district reports that one of its members is a soldier, sailor, marine, or civilian employee of the United States with a post of duty or station elsewhere, you should not report him as a member of that family. Cadets at Annapolis and West Point are enumerated at those places.

75. Sailors on merchant vessels—The officers of merchant vessels under the United States flag should be enumerated at their homes on land, where they will be reported by some member of the family.

76. Special provision is made for the enumeration of the crews of vessels in foreign or intercoastal trade on the Great Lakes and of the crews of sea-going private vessels of all kinds, except yachts, under the American flag, even though these crews have homes on shore. You should omit such men from your enumeration, therefore, when they are returned as "absent members" by their families. You are to include, however, and report in the regular way, men employed on boats running on the inland waters (rivers, canals, etc.) of the United States, other than the Great Lakes.

77. Enumerate, where found, all persons usually employed on board ship who are out of employment on the census date. Crews of foreign vessels are not to be enumerated.

78. Citizens abroad at time of enumeration. Any citizen of the United States who is a member of a family living in your district, but abroad temporarily at the time of the enumeration, should be enumerated as of your district. It does not matter how long the absence abroad is continued, provided the person intends to return to the United States. These instructions apply only to *citizens* of the United States and not to aliens who have left this country.

## Method of canvassing a city block.

83. If your district is in a city or town having a system of house numbers, canvass one block or square at a time. Do not go back and forth across the street. Begin each block at one corner, keep to the right, turn the corner, and go in and out of any court, alley, or passage way that may be included in it until you reach the point of starting. Be sure that you have gone around and through the entire block before you leave it.

84. The arrows in the following diagram indicate the manner in which a block containing an interior court or place is to be canvassed:

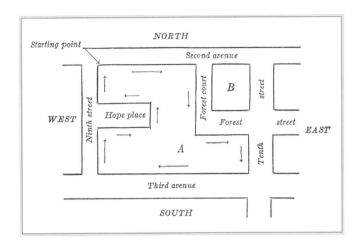

## Subdivisions of districts

101. In general, you should include as a part of the village population all families, which are locally considered to live in the village. Usually the opinion of the family, as to whether it is in the village or outside, may be accepted.

## The headings of the schedule

107. Township or other division of county. Write not only the name or number by which the division of the county is known, but also the name of the class (as township, town, precinct, district, ward, beat, etc.) to which it belongs.

110. Relation of incorporated place to township in which it is located. If any incorporated place forms a part of the township in which it is located, the name of the township as well as that of the incorporated place must be entered on the head of the sheet, each in the space indicated for it.

111. Ward of city, etc. If the city, or other incorporated place, is divided into wards, enter the number or name of the ward in the space provided at the head of each sheet. In this case of a block city, enter also the block number.

112. Name of institution. In case only a portion of the total number of persons enumerated on that sheet of the schedule are in the institution, indicate the lines on which the names of the inmates of the institution appears, as "Jefferson County Almshouse, lines 25 to 69, inclusive."

113. Date. If a page of the schedule is not completely filled at the end of a day's work, do not leave it blank but draw a line in the left-hand margin of the schedule just under the number of the line for the last person enumerated on that day, and on the following day enter the date in the margin under this line.

## Place of Abode

Column 1: Street, avenue, road, etc.

115. The places at which you begin and end work on any street are to be marked by a heavy line in ink (———) across the first and second columns.

Column 2. House number

116. If a house is in the rear of another one fronting on a street and has no number of its own, give it the same number as the front house and add the word "rear."

Column 3. Number of dwelling house in order of visitation

118. Dwelling house defined. A dwelling house, for census purposes, is a place in which, at the time of the census, one or more persons regularly sleep. It need not be a house in the usual sense of the word, but may be a room in a factory, store, or office building, a loft over a garage, a boat, a tent, a freight car, or the like. A building like a tenement or apartment house counts as only one dwelling house, no matter how many persons or families live in it.

Column 4. Number of family in order of visitation

120. Family defined. The word "family," for census purposes, has a somewhat different application from what it has in popular usage. It means a group of persons living together in the same dwelling place. The persons constituting this group may or may not be related by ties of kinship, but if they live together forming one household they should be considered as one family.

121. Two or more families may occupy the same dwelling house without living together. If they occupy separate portions of the dwelling house and their housekeeping is entirely separate, they should be returned as separate families.

124. Families in hotels. The distinction between an apartment house and an apartment hotel, and in turn between an apartment hotel and a hotel devoted mainly to transients, will often be difficult to establish.

125. Institutional families. The officials and inmates of an institution who live in the institution building or buildings form one family. But any officers or employees who sleep in detached houses or separate dwellings containing no inmates should be returned as separate families.

126. Persons living alone. The census family may likewise consist of a single person. Thus, an employee in a store who regularly sleeps there is to be returned as a family and the store as his dwelling place.

## Name and Relation

Column 5. Name of each person enumerated

128. Order of entering names. Enter the number of each family in the following order: (1) the head of the family; (2) his wife; (3) the children (whether sons or daughters) in the order of their ages, beginning with the oldest; and (4) all other persons living with the family, whether relatives, boarders, lodgers, or servants.

129. How names are to be written. Enter first the last name or surname, then the given name in full, and the initial of the middle name.

Column 6. Relationship to head of family

131. Designate the head of the family, whether husband or father, widow, or unmarried person of either sex, by the word *"head."* For other members of a family write *wife, father, mother, son, daughter, grandson, daughter-in-law, uncle, aunt, nephew, niece, boarder, lodger, servant,* etc., according to the particular relationship that the person bears to the head of the family.

132. Homemaker. Column 6 is to be used also to indicate which member of the family is the "homemaker," that is, which one is responsible for the care of the home and family. After the word "wife," "mother," or other term showing the relationship of such person to the head of the family, add the letter "H," thus "Wife—H." Only one person in each family should receive this designation.

133. Occupants of an institution or school, living under a common roof, should be designated as *officer, inmate, pupil, patient, prisoner,* etc.

134. If two or more persons share a common abode as partners, write *head* for one and *partner* for the other or others.

135. In the case of a hotel or boarding or lodging house family, the *head* of the family is usually the manager or the person who keeps the hotel or boarding or lodging house.

Column 7. **Home data**

136. Home owned or rented. Make no entries in this column for the other members of the family.

138. Home owned. It is not necessary that full payment for the property should have been made or that the family should be the sole owner.

139. Rented home. Every home not owned . . . should be returned as rented, whether rent is actually paid.

140. Where the owner of a house occupies a room or floor, but rents out the major portion of the house, including the first floor, the person hiring the house is to be entered as *"head,"* the home as *"rented,"* and the owner as a *"lodger."*

Column 8. Value of home, if owned, or monthly rental, if rented.

141. The current market value of the home as nearly as it can be ascertained. Unless the house has been recently purchased it will be necessary to estimate its value. . . . The assessor's value, on which taxation is based, is not generally a safe guide, being usually below the market value. Make it clear to your informant that the values returned on the census schedule are not to be used in any way in connection with taxation and are not open to public inspection.

142. The amount paid *each month* as rent, or one-twelfth of the annual rental, in case payment is not made monthly.

143. If no actual rental is paid, as where a workman receives the use of a house as a part of his wages, give in column 8 the estimated monthly rental value of the house. This estimate may be based on the amount of rent paid for similar houses in the neighborhood.

Column 9. Radio set

145. Radio set. If the family, or any member of the family, has a radio set, write "R" opposite the name of the head of the family. If the family has no radio set, leave this column blank.

Column 10. Does this family live on a farm?

146. This question is to be answered, "Yes" or "No," for every family, except that in a thickly settled city district a statement may be made on the first schedule to the effect that there are no farms in the district, and the column may then be left blank.

147. If the family lives on a farm, that is, a place for which a farm schedule is made out *and which is also locally regarded as a farm*, the answer should be "Yes," even though no member of the family works on the farm. It is a question here of residence, not of occupation.

148. Occasionally there will be a place for which a farm schedule is required, but which is not commonly regarded as a farm. A greenhouse establishment located in a city or village and having little land attached would be an example. For such a place the entry in column 10 would be "No." Likewise for a one-time farm on which no farming is now being done, the place being occupied as a residence only, the entry in column 10 should be "No," even though the place is still called a farm. Where the farmer and his family do not live on the farm, the entry should be "No."

**Personal description**

Column 11. Sex

149. Write "M" for male and "F" for female.

Column 12. Color or race

150. Write "W" for white; "Neg" for Negro; "Mex" for Mexican" "In" for Indian; "Ch" for Chinese; "Jp" for Japanese; "Fil" for Filipino; "Hin" for Hindu; and "Kor" for Korean. For a person of any other race, write the race in full.

151. Negroes. A person of mixed white and Negro blood should be returned as Negro, no matter how small the percentage of Negro blood. Both black and mulatto persons are to be returned as Negroes, without distinction. A person of mixed Indian and Negro blood should be returned a Negro unless the Indian blood predominates and the status as an Indian is generally accepted in the community.

152. Indians. A person of mixed white and Indian blood should be returned as Indian, except where the percentage of Indian blood is very small, or where he is regarded as a white person by those in the community where he lives.

153. For a person reported as Indian in column 12, report in column 19 whether "full blood" or "mixed blood," and columns 19 and 20 are thus to be used to indicate the degree of Indian blood and the tribe, instead of the birthplace of father and mother.

154. Mexicans. Practically all Mexican laborers are of a racial mixture difficult to classify, though usually well recognized in the localities where they are found. In order to obtain separate figures for this racial group, it has been decided that all persons born in Mexico, or having parents born in Mexico, who are not definitely white, Negro, Indian, Chinese, or Japanese, should be returned as Mexican ("Mex").

155. Other mixed races. Any mixture of white and nonwhite should be reported according to the nonwhite parents. Mixtures of colored races should be reported according to the race of the father, except Negro-Indian.

Column 13. Age at last birthday

156. This question calls for the age in completed years at last birthday. Remember, however, that age question, like all other questions on the schedule, relates to April 1, 1930. A person whose exact age on April 1, is 17 years, 11 months, and 25 days should be returned simply as 17, because that is his age at his last birthday prior to April 1, even though at the time of your visit he may have completed 18 years.

157. Age in round years. In many cases persons will report the age in round numbers, like 30 or 45, or "about 30" or "about 45," when that is not the exact age. Therefore, when an age ending in "0" or "5" is reported, you should inquire whether it is the exact age. If, however, it is impossible to get the exact age, enter the approximate age rather than return the age as unknown.

158. Ages of children. Take particular pains to get the exact ages of children. In the case of a child less than 5 years old, the age should be given in completed months, expressed as twelfths of a year.

159. Enumerators must make a special effort to obtain returns for all infants and young children. Children under 1 year of age, in particular, have frequently been omitted from the enumeration in past censuses.

Column 14. Marital condition

160. Write "S" for a single or unmarried person of whatever age, "M" for a married person, "Wd" for widowed (man or woman), and "D" for divorced.

Column 15. Age at first marriage

161. This question applies only to married persons; that is, those for whom the entry in column 14 is "M."

Column 16. **Education**

162. Include attendance at night school.

Column 17. Whether able to read or write

163. Write "Yes" for a person 10 years of age or over who can read and write in any language, whether English or some other, and "No" for such person who cannot both read and write in some language. Do not return any person as able to read and write simply because he can write his own name.

164. For a blind person, write "Yes" if he could read and write in any language before becoming blind or, if, being born blind, he has been taught to read and write in any language.

**Place of birth**

Column 18. Place of birth of person

165. If the person was born in the United States, give the State or Territory in which born. The words "United States" are not sufficiently definite. A person born in what is now North Dakota, South Dakota, or Oklahoma should be so reported, although at the time of his birth the particular regions had a different name. For a person born in Washington, D.C., write District of Columbia. Do not abbreviate the names of States or Territories.

166. If the person was born in a foreign country, enter the name of the country only, as *Belgium, Czechoslovakia, France, Italy, Yugoslavia, Norway, Poland, China*, etc., as the case may be, *except as noted in the following paragraphs.*

OPPOSITE: *"Sometimes the whole family gathered around the receiving set. This Hood River County, Oregon, farm family is listening to the radio,"* July 20, 1925 (33-SC-4849).

167. Since it is essential that each foreign-born person be credited to the country in which his birthplace is *now* located, special attention must be given to the six countries which lost a part of their territory in the readjustments following the World War. These six countries are as follows:

Austria, which lost territory to Czechoslovakia, Italy, Yugoslavia, Poland, and Rumania.

Hungary, which lost territory to Austria, Czechoslovakia, Italy, Poland, Rumania, and Yugoslavia.

Bulgaria, which lost territory to Greece and Yugoslavia.

Germany, which lost territory to Belgium, Czechoslovakia, Danzig, Denmark, France, Lithuania, and Poland.

Russia, which lost territory to Estonia, Finland, Latvia, Lithuania, Poland, and Turkey.

Turkey, which lost territory to Greece and Italy, and from which the following area became independent: Iraq (Mesopotamia); Palestine (including Transjordan), Syria (including Lebanon); and various States and Kingdoms in Arabia (Asir, Hejaz, and Yemen).

168. If the person reports one of these six counties as his place of birth or that of his parents, ask specially whether the birthplace is located within the present area of the country; and if not, find out to what country it has been transferred. If a person was born in the Province of Bohemia, for example, which was formerly in Austria but is now a part of Czechoslovakia, the proper return for country of birth is *Czechoslovakia.* If you can not ascertain with certainty the present location of the birthplace, enter *in addition to the name of the country,* the name of the province or state in which the person was born. (*Alsace-Lorraine, Bohemia, Croatia, Galacia, Moravia, Slovakia,* etc., or the city, as *Warsaw, Prague, Strasbourg,* etc.)

169. Do not return a person as born in Great Britain, but indicate the particular country, as *England, Scotland, Wales,* etc. Distinction must be made between *Northern Ireland* and *Irish Free State.* It is not sufficient to report that a person was born in Ireland.

170. French Canadian should be distinguished from other Canadians.

171. If a person was born in Cuba or Puerto Rico, so state, and do *not* write West Indies.

172. If a person was born abroad, but of American parents, write in column 18 both the birthplace and *"Am. Cit."* that is, American citizen. For a person born at sea, write *"At sea."*

173. Spell out the names of counties, provinces, etc., and *do not abbreviate* in any case.

Columns 19 and 20. Place of birth of parents

174. In case, however, a person does not know the State or Territory of birth of his father (or mother), but knows that he (or she) was born in the United States, write *United States* rather than *unknown."*

174a. For the Indian population, which is practically all of native parentage, these columns are to be used for a different purpose. In column 19 enter, in place of the country of birth of the father, the degree of Indian blood, as, "full blood" or "mixed blood." In column 20 enter, in place of the country of birth of the mother, the tribe to which the Indian belongs.

Column 21. **Mother Tongue**

175. Do not ask for the mother tongue of persons born in the United States.

177. The principal foreign languages are:

Albanian

Arabic

Armenian (spoken by Turkish Armenians and by the Armenians in Russia)

Basque

Breton (language of Lower Brittany)

Bulgarian

Czech

Chinese

Croatian

Dalmatian (language of a region of Yugoslavia bordering the Adriatic on the West)

Danish

Dutch

Egyptian

English

Estonian

Finnish

Flemish (a form of Dutch spoken in northern Belgium)

French

Frisian (a Germanic language spoken by the Frisian people)

Friulian (language of northeast Italy)

Gaelic (a language most commonly spoken in the western counties of Ireland)

Georgian

German

Great Russian (a member of the Russian-speaking people largely of the central and northeastern areas of Russia)

Greek

Gypsy

Hebrew (the national language of Israel)

Hindu

Icelandic

Irish

Italian

Japanese

Korean

Kurdish

Lappish (the language of Lapland in northwest Europe containing the Arctic sections of Norway, Sweden, and Finland)

Lettish (Latvian)

Lithuanian

Little Russian (the slavic language of the Belorussians, also called White Russian)

Macedonian

Magyar

Montenegrin

Norwegian

Persian (the official language of Iran and widely used in Afghanistan)

Polish

Portuguese

Romanish (language of the Romany gypsies)

Rumanian

Russian

Ruthenian (Ukranian)

Scotch (sic) (Scottish)

Serbian

Slovak

Slovenian

Spanish

Swedish

Syrian

Turkish

Ukrainian

Walloon (language of southern Belgium and adjacent parts of France)

Welsh

Wendish (a Slavic language of Saxony or Brandenburg)

White Russian (see Little Russian)

Yiddish (language spoken by Polish and Russian Jews)

## Citizenship, etc.

Column 22. Year of immigration to the United States

178. If the (immigrant) has come into the United States more than once, give the year of his first arrival.

Column 23. Naturalization

179. Prior to September 22, 1922, a foreign-born woman became a citizen when her husband was naturalized. Since that date, she must take out papers in her own name, and if she does not do this she remains an alien even though her husband becomes naturalized. The questions should be answered, therefore, for every person whose birthplace was in a foreign country, as follows:

180. For a foreign-born male 21 years of age and over, write "Na" (for "naturalized") if he has either (1) taken out second or final naturalization papers, or (2) become naturalized while under the age of 21 by the naturalization of either parent.

181. For a foreign-born female 21 years of age and over, write "Na" if she has either (1) taken out final papers, or (2) become naturalized through the naturalization of either parent while she was under the age of 21, or (3) if she became naturalized prior to 1922 by the naturalization of her husband.

182. For a foreign-born person under 21 years of age, write "Na" if either parent has been naturalized. This applies to infants and young children as well as to older persons under 21.

183. For all foreign-born persons who have not been naturalized but have taken out first papers write "Pa" (for "papers"). Note that a person must be at least 18 years of age in order to take out first papers. Minor children should not be returned "Pa" merely because their parents have taken out first papers.

184. For all foreign-born persons neither naturalized nor having first papers, write "Al" (for "alien").

Column 24. Whether able to speak English

185. Write "Yes" for a person 10 years of age and over who can speak English, and "No" for such a person who cannot speak English. For persons less than 10 years of age leave the column blank.

Column 25. **Occupation**

186. An entry should be made in this column for every person enumerated. The entry should be either (1) the gainful occupation pursued—that is, the word or words which most accurately indicated the particular kind of gainful work done, as *physician, carpenter, dressmaker, salesman, newsboy*; or (2) *none* (that is, no gainful occupation).

A "gainful occupation" in census usage is an occupation by which the person who pursues it earns money or a money equivalent, or in which he assists in the production of marketable goods. The term "gainful worker," as interpreted for census purposes, does not include women doing housework in their own homes, without wages, and having no other employment, or children working at home, merely on general household work, on chores, or at odd times on other work.

187. Unless a person spends at least the equivalent of one day per week at the occupation, he or she should not be returned as a gainful worker—that is, the entry in column 25 should be none.

188. Persons retired or incapacitated. Care should be taken in making the return for persons who on account of old age, permanent invalidism, or other reasons are no longer following any occupation. Such persons may desire to return the occupation formerly followed, which would be incorrect. If living on their own income, or if they are supported by other persons or institutions, or if they work only occasionally or only a short time each day, the return should be *none*.

189. Occupation of persons unemployed. On the other hand, persons out of employment . . . may state that they have no occupation, when the fact is that they usually have an occupation but happen to be idle or unemployed at the time of the visit. In such cases the return should be the occupation followed when the person is employed or the occupation in which last regularly employed, and the fact that the person was not at work should be recorded in column 28.

190. Persons having two occupations. If a person has two occupations, return only the more important one; that is, the one from which he gets the more money. If you cannot learn that, return the one at which he spends the more time. For example: Return a man as a farmer if he gets more of his income from farming, although he may also follow the occupation of a clergyman or preacher; but return him as a clergyman if he gets more of his income from that occupation.

Column 26. **Industry**

191. Make an entry in this column in all cases where an occupation is reported in column 25. But when the entry in column 25 is "none," leave column 26 blank. The entry in column 26, when made, should be the name of the industry, or the business, or the place in which this person works, as *cotton mill, coal mine, drygoods, insurance office, bank,* etc.

192. Never use the word "Company" in column 26. Never enter in column 26 such indefinite terms as "factory," "mill," "shop," or "store," without stating the kind of factory, etc., as soap factory, cotton mill, blacksmith shop, grocery store. Likewise, never enter a firm name in column 26, as "Jones & Co.," but state the industry or business in which the person works, as coal mine, real estate, etc. Avoid entering the word "Contractor" in column 26. Enter, instead, the name of the industry in which the person works, as building construction, street construction, etc.

194. Women doing housework. In the case of a woman doing housework in her own home and having no other employment, the entry in column 25 should be none. But a woman doing housework for wages should be returned in column 25 as housekeeper, servant, cook, or chambermaid, as the case may be; and the entry in column 26 should state the kind of place where she works, as private family, hotel, or boarding house.

195. Where a woman not only looks after her own home but also has employment outside or does work at home for which she receives payment, the outside work or gainful employment should originally be reported as her occupation, unless this takes only a very small fraction of the woman's time. For instance, a woman who regularly takes in washing should be reported as laundress or washerwoman, followed in column 26 by at home.

196. Farm workers. Return a person in charge of a farm as a farmer, whether he owns it or operates it as a tenant, renter, or cropper; but a person who manages a farm for someone else for wages or a salary should be reported as a farm manager. A man who directs farm labor under the supervision of the owner or manager should be reported as a farm foreman or farm overseer. A person who works on a farm for someone else, but not as a manager or foreman, should be reported as a farm laborer.

197. Women doing farm work. A woman who works only occasionally or only a short time each day at outdoor farm or garden work or in the dairy, or in caring for livestock or poultry should not be returned as a farm laborer, but for a woman who works regularly and most of the time at such work, the return in column 25 should be farm laborer. Of course, a woman who herself operates or runs a farm or plantation should be reported as a farmer and not as a farm laborer.

198. Unusual occupations for women. There are many occupations, such as carpenter and blacksmith, which women usually do not follow. Therefore, if you are told that a woman follows an occupation which is very peculiar or unusual for a woman, verify the statement.

199. Children on farms. In the case of children who work regularly for their own parents on a farm, in an orchard, on a truck farm, etc., the entry in column 25 should be farm laborer, orchard laborer, or garden laborer, as the case may be.

200. Children working for parents. Children who work for their parents at home merely on general household work, at chores, or at odd times on other work, should be reported having no occupation. Those, however, who somewhat regularly assist their parents in the performance of work other than household work or chores should be reported as having the occupation represented by this work.

201. Unusual occupations for children. Whenever you are told that a child is following an occupation usually followed only by adults, ask whether the child is not merely a helper or an apprentice in the occupation, and make the entry accordingly.

202. Keeping boarders. Keeping boarders or lodgers should be returned as an occupation if the person engaged in it relies upon it as his (or her) principal means of support or principal source of income. In that case the return should be boarding-house keeper or lodging-house keeper.

If, however, a family keeps a few boarders or roomers merely as a means of supplementing the earnings or income obtained from other occupations or from other sources, no one in the family should be returned as a boarding- or lodging-house keeper.

203. Officers, employees, and inmates of institutions or homes. For an officer or regular employee of an institution or home, such as an asylum, penitentiary, jail, reform school, or convict camp, return the occupation followed in the institution. For an inmate of such an institution, if regularly employed, return the occupation pursued in the institution, whether the employment is at productive labor or at other duties, such as cooking, scrubbing, laundry work, etc.; but if an inmate is not regularly employed—that is, has no

specific duties or work to perform—write "none" in column 25. Do not return the occupation pursued prior to commitment to the institution.

205. Builders and contractors. Craftsmen who usually work with their tools should be returned as carpenters, plasterers, etc., and not as contractors.

206. Doctors and physicians. In the case of a doctor or physician, enter the class to which he belongs, as medical, osteopathic, chiropractic, etc.

207. Engineers. Distinguish carefully the different kinds of engineers by stating the full descriptive titles, as civil engineer, electrical engineer, locomotive engineer, mechanical engineer, mining engineer, stationary engineer, etc.

208. Nurses. In the case of a nurse, always specify whether she is a trained nurse or a child's nurse.

209. Cooks and general house workers. Distinguish carefully between cooks and general house workers. Return a person who does general housework as a servant and not as a cook.

210. Workers attending school. In the case of a person who is at work and also attends a school or college, enter the occupation followed in columns 25 and 26, and indicate school or college attendance in column 16.

211. Avoid general or indefinite terms.

212. The term "laborer" should be avoided if any more precise statement of the occupation can be secured.

213. Avoid the use of the word "mechanic" whenever a more specific occupation can be given.

214. Distinguish carefully the different kinds of "agents" by stating in column 26 the line of business followed.

215. Distinguish carefully between retail and wholesale merchants, as retail merchant—dry goods; wholesale merchant—dry goods.

216. Avoid the use of the word "clerk" wherever a more definite occupation can be named. Do not return a stenographer as a "secretary."

217. Distinguish a traveling salesman from a salesman in a store; the former should be reported as a commercial traveler.

218. You need not give a person's occupation just as he expresses it. Always find out exactly the kind of work he does and the industry, business, or place in which he works.

Column 27. Class of worker

220. "E" for an employer

"W" for a wage or salary worker

"O" for a person working on his own account

"NP" for an unpaid family worker—that is, a member of the family employed without pay on work which contributes to the family income.

For all persons returned as having no gainful occupation, leave column 27 blank.

221. Employers ("E"). An employer is one who employs helpers, other than domestic servants, in transacting his own business. The

term "employer" does not include the superintendent, agent, manager, or other person employed to manage an establishment; and it does not include the foreman of a room, the boss of a gang, or the coal miner who hires his helper. All such should be returned as wage or salary workers, for while any one of these may employ persons, none of them does so in transacting his own business. In short, no person who himself works for wages or a salary is to be returned as an employer.

222. Wage or salary worker ("W"). Any person who works for wages or salary, at piece rates, or on commission, and is subject to the control and direction of an employer, is to be considered a wage or salary worker.

223. Working on own account ("O"). A person who has a gainful occupation and is neither an employer, nor a wage or salary worker, nor an unpaid family worker, is considered to be working on his own account; such persons are the independent workers. Include, generally speaking, hucksters, peddlers, newsboys, bootblacks, etc.

224. Unpaid family worker ("NP"). A wife, son, daughter, or other relative of the head of the family who works regularly and without wages or salary on the family's farm, in a shop or store from which the family obtains its support, or on other work that contributes to the family's income (not including housework or incidental chores) is to be returned as an unpaid family worker.

**Employment**

Column 28. Whether actually at work yesterday *("Yes" or "No.")*
225. In case "yesterday" was a holiday or the worker's "day off" or "rest day," the question should apply to his last regular working day.

226. In every such case the question "Whether actually at work," must apply to the last regular working day of the person enumerated.

228. In the case of men who run a business of their own it may not always be easy to determine whether the man is actually at work. In general, such men should be returned as "at work" if the business operates continuously under their orders, even though they may have been temporarily absent on the last regular working-day.

The same return should be made for the professional or business man who is the active manager of an office, store, or factory, although he may be absent or not occupied with matters for which he receives pay on the day in question. For example, a man operating a cobbler's shop or an automobile repair and service station should be returned as at work on a given day if he spends any part of that day at the shop, even though he may not make any sales or do any work for which he receives payment. Similarly doctors, lawyers, dentists, and other professional men, and proprietors and managers of retail stores, who put in time at their place of business should be returned as "at work."

229. Farmers and farm laborers, including the members of the farmer's family who usually work on the farm, are to be considered at work if they are doing anything whatever in connection with the farm or with any farming activities or supplemental occupation.

230. Teachers in schools and college professors and instructors, if they hold positions, will be regarded as "at work," even though the enumeration date falls within the Easter or spring vacation.

231. Persons who normally work only part time and who do not wish a full-time job are to be returned as "at work," unless such part-time employment itself fails. For example, the waitress who works three hours daily during the lunch period is to be returned as at work if she was employed for this period "yesterday;" and the seamstress or laundress who regularly works one or more days a week, either at her own home or elsewhere, is to be returned as at work if she worked on her last regular working-day preceding the enumerator's visit.

232. Persons not at work—Write "No" if the person enumerated worked no part of the last regular working day. Men and women temporarily absent because of sickness, accident, voluntary lay-offs, and all personal reasons are to be regarded as not at work, even though they continue to hold their position.

233. Men locked out or on strike are "not at work," although in receipt of trade-union strike benefits or occupied in the conduct of the strike.
Men who customarily work "by the job" are not at work if they have no job in process, even though actively seeking new contracts.
Retail dealers are not at work if their last business has been permanently closed, although they may be planning a new enterprise.

235. Men who busy themselves with repair jobs, gardening, and home duties in the intervals of their regular occupation are to be returned as "not at work."
Coal miners and longshoremen are to be returned as "not at work" if they are idle on the day to which the question applies, even though they get in as much time weekly as is usual at the mines or wharves where they are accustomed to labor.
In general the list of those "not at work" should include all who did not labor at their gainful occupation on their last regular working day preceding the enumerator's visit.

Column 30. **Veterans**
237. Write "Yes" for a man who is an ex-service veteran of the United States forces (Army, Navy, or Marine Corps) mobilized for any war or expedition, and "No" for a man who is not an ex-service veteran. No entry is to be made for males under 21 years of age nor for females of any age whatever.

Column 31. What war or expedition?
238. Where the answer in column 30 is "Yes," give the name of the war or expedition in which the man served:

| | |
|---|---|
| World War | WW |
| Spanish-American War | Sp |
| Civil War | Civ |
| Philippine Insurrection | Phil |
| Boxer Rebellion | Box |
| Mexican Expedition | Mex |

239. Those men are to be counted as "veterans" who were in the Army, Navy, or Marine Corps of the United States during the period of any United States war, even though they may not have gotten beyond the training camp. A World War veteran would have been

in the service between 1917 and 1921; a Spanish-American War veteran between 1898 and 1902; a Civil War veteran, between 1861 and 1866.

240. Persons are not veterans of an expedition, however, unless they actually took part in the expedition. For example, veterans of the Mexican Expedition must have been in Mexico or Mexican waters at the time of the expedition; veterans of the Boxer Rebellion, in China or Chinese waters at the time of the rebellion, etc.

241. Persons in the military or naval service of the United States during peace times only are not be to listed as veterans.

### Instructions to the Enumerators: American Indians

Indians both on and off reservations are enumerated on the population schedules. The Bureau published separate instructions to enumerators for completing the census for the Indian population. See *Supplemental Instructions to Enumerators Regarding Indian Population* (Government Printing Office, Washington, DC 1930 (C3.37/6:En8/rev./pars. 457–488).)

The following summarizes the supplemental instructions. The number in front of each instruction refers to the corresponding numbered paragraph in the published instructions.

457. These instructions supplement but do not supersede those given in the book of "Instructions to Enumerators." They are intended to give additional information regarding conditions peculiar to Indian reservations or to Indians who live on land formerly included in an Indian reservation.

461. Where the term "Show separately" is applied to an unincorporated town or village having 500 inhabitants or more, you are to begin the enumeration of this unincorporated place on a new sheet. You should do the same for an Indian village which has an estimated population of 100 or over. Note that an Indian village will include only those persons who live there permanently; Indians who live on their allotments in the summer should be reported from their allotments.

468. Place of Abode. Attention is particularly called to the fact that the place of abode is the place where the person ordinarily sleeps. It has nothing to do with ownership of land or place of allotment. Thus an Indian may have an allotment in one township and may live in another township. He should be enumerated in the enumeration district where he actually has his residence. But it should be noted that if an Indian lives on his allotment during the summer and farms the allotment and moves to the neighborhood of the agency or school during the winter, he should be enumerated in the enumeration district where his allotment is located.

469. In the case of nomadic Indians who are not permanently domiciled in any place, the residence or place of abode for census purposes is the tent or other shelter occupied at the time they are enumerated. Every effort should be made to enumerate all these Indians, but at the same time care should be taken not to enumerate the same Indians twice.

470. Absent persons. Persons temporarily absent should be enumerated from their permanent homes; this applied particularly to children at boarding schools and persons temporarily in

hospitals. But note that persons in jail on April 1 should be enumerated from the jail regardless of length of term or sentence, and not from their permanent homes. In the case of every Indian family the question should be asked whether there are any children at boarding school or persons temporarily absent. Complete data should be obtained for every absent person, except those in jail.

473. Home ownership (column 7 of population schedule). It may happen that Indians will be found living in houses which are neither owned nor rented. Under the Census rule (par. 139) all such homes should be reported as rented. Where no rent is actually paid the enumerator should report in column 8 of the schedule the amount the house would ordinarily rent for. If the house has no marketable rental value, the enumerator should insert "0" in column 8. Some return must be made in column 8.

474. In the case of nomadic Indians who have no fixed domicile, the entry under column 7 should be rented; as these residences have no market value the entry in column 8 should be "0."

476. Color or race (column 12 of the population schedule). In New Mexico, Arizona, and California, enumerators should take special care to differentiate between Mexican laborers and Indians. Some Mexican laborers may endeavor to pass themselves as Indians. Persons residing in this region should have no difficulty in differentiating between the two types.

477. Degree of blood and name of tribe (columns 19 and 20 of population schedule). For every person reported as an Indian, column 19 should be used to indicate whether the person is a full blood or a mixed blood; column 20 is to be used to indicate the tribe. (See par. 174a. on page xiv.)

478. Citizenship, etc. (columns 22 to 24 of the population schedule). Columns 22 and 23 apply only to the foreign born, and therefore no answer is required from Indians born in the United States, but column 24 (where able to speak English) applies to all persons over 10 years of age, and the enumerator should not fail to ask this question of all Indians 10 years of age and over.

479. Occupation (column 25, 26, and 27 of population schedule). Particular efforts should be made to obtain correct reports on the occupation of Indians. An Indian who works regularly on a farm in summer should be reported as a farmer or farm laborer, as the case may be, even though he is living at the agency or school at the time the enumeration is made. The Indian who lives off his lease money or is supported by other members of this family should be reported as having no occupation even though he may work occasionally at gardening, hunting, or fishing. However, an Indian who has an appreciable income from trapping or fishing or who acts as a guide or teamster should be reported as occupied. In other words, if the Indian is engaged in a seasonal occupation and works at that occupation regularly during the season, he should be returned as so occupied. (See pars. 186 to 224 on pages iv–xvii.)

480. Unemployment. No return should be made on the unemployment schedule for Indians reported as engaged in agriculture, even though they are not at work at the time of the enumeration.

The Bureau extrapolated this information onto a *Supplemental Schedule for Indian Population*, however, these forms have not survived.

## Codes

After the Bureau collected the census schedules, staff went through and coded the nativity and occupation information using codes established for the 1930 census. The Bureau staff tabulated this data and created the statistical summaries. The data came directly from the census schedules.

### Nativity codes

These codes were derived from the information reported in columns 18, 19, and 20. The Bureau staff, not the census enumerators, assigned the codes after the enumerators returned the schedules to the Bureau. The Bureau used these codes when compiling the statistical summaries for its report to Congress.

The coding used in columns A, B, and C of the schedules may be summarized as follows:

| Individual | Column A | Column B | Column C |
|---|---|---|---|
| *Person Native* | | | |
| Both parents native | State of birth of person | Leave blank | Leave blank |
| Both parents foreign born | State of birth of person | Country of birth of father | Code "0" |
| Father foreign born, mother native | State of birth of person | Country of birth of father | Code "1" |
| Father native, mother foreign born | State of birth of person | Country of birth of *mother* | Code "2" |
| Father foreign-born, mother born at sea | State of birth of person | Country of birth of father | Code "0" |
| Father born at sea, mother foreign born | State of birth of person | Code "V9" | Code "0" |
| One parent native, one parent born at sea | State of birth of person | Leave blank | Leave blank |
| Person foreign born | Mother tongue of person | Country of birth of person | Code "V" |
| | | | |
| *American citizen born abroad* | | | |
| Parents native | Code "XO" | Leave blank | Leave blank |
| Father native, mother foreign born | "Code "XO" | Country of birth of mother | Code "2" |
| | | | |
| *Person born at sea* | | | |
| Parents native | Code "X9" | Leave blank | Leave blank |
| Father native, mother foreign born | Code "X9" | Country of birth of mother | Code "2" |
| Father foreign born | Mother tongue | Code "V9" | Code "V" |

For detailed legislative history pertaining to American citizens born abroad, see INS Interpretations, 320.1 or *www.ins.usdoj. gov/graphics/index.html.*

For a complete list of the codes, see U.S. Department of Commerce, Bureau of the Census, *Coding Instructions for the Population Schedule (Except Occupations), Fifteenth Census of the United States,* U.S. Government Printing Office: Washington, DC, 1930, (C3.37/6:C64/1-3).

### Occupation codes

The codes in column 26D of the schedules reflect the occupation reports in column 25. The Bureau staff, not the enumerators, assigned the codes after the enumerators returned the schedules to the Bureau. The Bureau used these codes when compiling the statistical summaries for its report to Congress. For a complete list of these codes, see U.S. Department of Commerce, Bureau of the Census, Classified Index of Occupations, Fifteenth Census of the United States, U.S. Government Printing Office: Washington, DC, 1930, (C3.37/2:Oc1/2-2).

## FINDING AIDS

Several finding aids are described below to assist researchers in locating a specific person or family.

### Soundex

The Works Progress Administration created complete indexes for 10 states, and partial indexes for 2 states. Complete indexes exist for Alabama (National Archives Microfilm Publication M2049), Arkansas (National Archives Microfilm Publication M2050), Florida (National Archives Microfilm Publication M2051), Georgia (National Archives Microfilm Publication M2052), Louisiana (National Archives Microfilm Publication (M2054), Mississippi (National Archives Microfilm Publication M2055), North Carolina (National Archives Microfilm Publication M2056), South Carolina (National Archives Microfilm Publication M2057), Tennessee (National Archives Microfilm Publication M2058), and Virginia (National Archives Microfilm Publication M2059).

The following counties were Soundexed for Kentucky (National Archives Microfilm Publication M2053): Bell, Floyd, Harlan, Kenton, Muhlenberg, Perry, and Pike. The following counties were Soundexed for West Virginia (National Archives Microfilm Publication M2060): Fayette, Harrison, Kanawha, Logan, McDowell, Mercer, and Raleigh.

Rolls 128 through 198 of Alabama comprise Jefferson, Mobile, and Montgomery counties. All of the other Alabama counties are on rolls 1 to 127. Researchers may need to check both parts of the Alabama Soundex.

All of the Soundex records are in the traditional format with a list of institutions on the last roll, with the exception of Georgia. Georgia is in Miracode and does not list the institutions. The Soundex does not appear to have "mixed codes," that is where two or more small groups of Soundex codes are interfiled. In some cases, however, the Soundex are not in straight order.

### The Soundex Indexing System

To use the census Soundex to locate information about a person, you must know his or her full name and the state or territory in which he or she lived at the time of the census. It is also helpful to know the full name of the head of the household in which the person lived because census takers recorded information under that name.

The Soundex is a coded surname (last name) index based on the way a surname sounds rather than the way it is spelled. Surnames that sound the same, but are spelled differently, like SMITH and SMYTH, have the same code and are filed together. The Soundex coding system was developed so that you can find a surname even though it may have been recorded under various spellings.

To search for a particular surname, you must first work out its code.

## Basic Soundex Coding Rules

Every Soundex code consists of a letter and three numbers, such as W-252. The letter is always the first letter of the surname. The numbers are assigned to the remaining letters of the surname according to the Soundex guide shown below. Zeroes are added at the end, if necessary, to produce a four-character code. Additional letters are disregarded. Examples:

Washington is coded W-252 (W, 2 for the S, 5 for the N, 2 for the G, remaining letters disregarded).

Lee is coded L-000 (L, 000 added).

## Soundex Coding Guide

Number represents the letters as follows:

1    B, F, P, V
2    C, G, J, K, Q, S, X, Z
3    D, T
4    L
5    M, N
6    R

Disregard the letters A, E, I, O, U, H, W, and Y.

## Additional Soundex Coding Rules

### 1. Names with double letters

If the surname has any double letters, they should be treated as one letter. For example, Gutierrez is coded G-362 (G, 3 for the T, 6 for the first R, second R ignored, 2 for the Z).

### 2. Names with letters side-by-side that have the same Soundex code number

If the surname has different letters side-by-side that have the same number in the Soundex coding guide, they should be treated as one letter.

Examples:

Pfister is coded as P-236 (P, F ignored, 2 for the S, 3 for the T, 6 for the R).

Jackson is coded as J-250 (J, 2 for the C, K ignored, S ignored, 5 for the N, 0 added).

Tymczak is coded as T-522 (T, 5 for the M, 2 for the C, Z ignored, 2 for the K). Since the vowel "A" separates the Z and K, the K is coded.

### 3. Names with prefixes

If a surname has a prefix, such as Van, Con, De, Di, La, or Le, code both with and without the prefix because the surname might be listed under either code. Note, however, that Mc and Mac are not considered prefixes.

For example, VanDeusen might be coded two ways:

V-532 (V, 5 for N, 3 for D, 2 for S)

or

D-250 (D, 2 for the S, 5 for the N, 0 added).

### 4. Consonant separators

If a vowel (A, E, I, O, U) separates two consonants that have the same Soundex code, the consonant to the right of the vowel is coded.

---

FAMILY CARD

Soundex Code          1930

| TEXAS | | | | |
|---|---|---|---|---|
| HEAD OF FAMILY | | | E.D. | SHEET |
| COLOR | AGE | BIRTHPLACE | VOL. | |
| COUNTY | | CITY | | |
| (OTHER MEMBERS OF FAMILY) | | | | |

| NAME | RELATION-SHIP | AGE | BIRTHPLACE |
|---|---|---|---|
| | | | |
| | | | |
| | | | |
| | | | |

INDIVIDUAL CARD

Soundex Code          1930

| TEXAS | | | | |
|---|---|---|---|---|
| NAME OF INDIVIDUAL | | | E.D. | SHEET |
| COLOR | AGE | BIRTHPLACE | VOL. | |
| COUNTY | | CITY | | |
| ENUMERATED WITH | | | | |
| RELATIONSHIP TO ABOVE | | | | |

- ☐ SON
- ☐ DAUGHTER
- ☐ BROTHER
- ☐ SISTER
- ☐ FATHER
- ☐ MOTHER
- ☐ GRANDSON
- ☐ GRANDDAUGHTER
- ☐ GRANDCHILD
- ☐ NEPHEW
- ☐ NIECE
- ☐ FATHER-IN-LAW
- ☐ MOTHER-IN-LAW
- ☐ SON-IN-LAW ☐ ROOMER
- ☐ DAUGHTER-IN-LAW
- ☐ BROTHER-IN-LAW
- ☐ SISTER-IN-LAW
- ☐ ORPHAN
- ☐ STEPSON
- ☐ STEP DAUGHTER
- ☐ COUSIN
- ☐ HIRED MAN
- ☐ SERVANT
- ☐ OTHER (SPECIFY)

VIRGINIA SOUNDEX

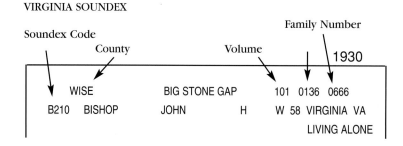

Example: Tymczak is coded as T-522 (T, 5 for the M, 2 for the C, Z ignored (see "Side-by-Side" rule above), 2 for the K). Since the vowel "A" separates the Z and K, the K is coded.

5. "H" and "W" as consonant separators
"H" or "W" are completely disregarded *except* as initial letters. In any other part of the surname, the letters "H" and "W" are treated as if they are not there. If "H" and "W" separate two consonants that have the same Soundex code, the consonant to the right of the "H" or "W" should *not* be coded. Examples:
Ashcraft is coded A-261 (A, 2 for S, C ignored, 6 for the R, 1 for the F)
Burroughs is coded B-620 (B, 6 is for R, 2 for G, S is ignored, 0 because there are no more letters to code)

It is very important to remember that not all Bureau of the Census employees Soundexed a name strictly according to the rules. As a result, Ashcraft may be found under A226 and Burroughs under B622.

## Enumeration District Descriptions

*(See page viii for a description of the 1930 ED numbering system.)*
Geographic descriptions of 1930 census EDs are reproduced on rolls 61–90 of *Descriptions of Census Enumeration Districts, 1830–1950* (National Archives Microfilm Publication T1224, 156 rolls). The descriptions of the 120,105 separate EDs for the 1930

census are arranged by state, by county, and then numerically by ED number. (The 1930 census is not arranged according to the supervisor's district.) A list of institutions appears at the end of the county. For the 1930 census, the enumeration district for 1920 is also listed.

| | |
|---|---|
| Roll 61 | Alabama, Arizona, Arkansas |
| Roll 62 | California: Alameda County through Los Angeles County (part) |
| Roll 63 | California: Los Angeles County (part) through Yuba County |
| Roll 64 | Colorado, Connecticut, Delaware, District of Columbia |
| Roll 65 | Florida, Georgia |
| Roll 66 | Idaho, Illinois: Adams County through Cook County |
| Roll 67 | Illinois: Crawford County through Woodford County |
| Roll 68 | Indiana, Iowa |
| Roll 69 | Kansas, Kentucky |
| Roll 70 | Louisiana, Maine, Maryland |
| Roll 71 | Massachusetts |
| Roll 72 | Michigan |
| Roll 73 | Minnesota, Mississippi |
| Roll 74 | Missouri |
| Roll 75 | Montana, Nebraska, Nevada, New Hampshire |
| Roll 76 | New Jersey, New Mexico |
| Roll 77 | New York: Bronx, Kings (Brooklyn), New York (Manhattan), and Richmond Counties. |

Descriptions of Census Enumeration Districts, 1830–1950 *(National Archives Microfilm Publication T1224), roll 68. ED 2-34 is bounded by the Wabash Railroad, Beuter Road, Pontiac (Pennsylvania Lines), and Anthony Boulevard.*

Roll 78   New York: Queens County; then Albany County through Jefferson County

Roll 79   New York: Lewis County through Yates County

Roll 80   North Carolina, North Dakota

Roll 81   Ohio: Adams County through Lorain County

Roll 82   Ohio: Lucas County through Wyandot County

Roll 83   Oklahoma, Oregon

Roll 84   Pennsylvania: Adams County through Perry County

Roll 85   Pennsylvania: Philadelphia County through York County, Rhode Island

Roll 86   South Carolina, South Dakota, Tennessee

Roll 87   Texas

Roll 88   Utah, Vermont, Virginia

Roll 89   Washington, West Virginia

Roll 90   Wisconsin, Wyoming, Alaska, American Samoa, Hawaii, Panama Canal Zone, Guam, Puerto Rico, Virgin Island

## Enumeration District Description Maps

*Enumeration District Description Maps for the Fifteenth Census of the United States, 1930* (National Archives Microfilm Publication M1930) reproduced some 8,345 separate map sheets used in preparing the 1930 census. These maps are part of the Records of the Bureau of the Census (Record Group 29). The Cartographic Branch at College Park, MD, holds the original paper maps.

An enumeration district is an area that could be covered by a single census taker in one census period (2 to 4 weeks for the 1930 census). EDs varied in size from several city blocks in densely populated urban areas to an entire county in sparsely populated rural areas.

The Bureau acquired maps of each county and of many of the towns and cities. For some of the largest cities, the Bureau made its own maps. Due to the wide variety of sources from which these maps originated, they vary from state to state and even

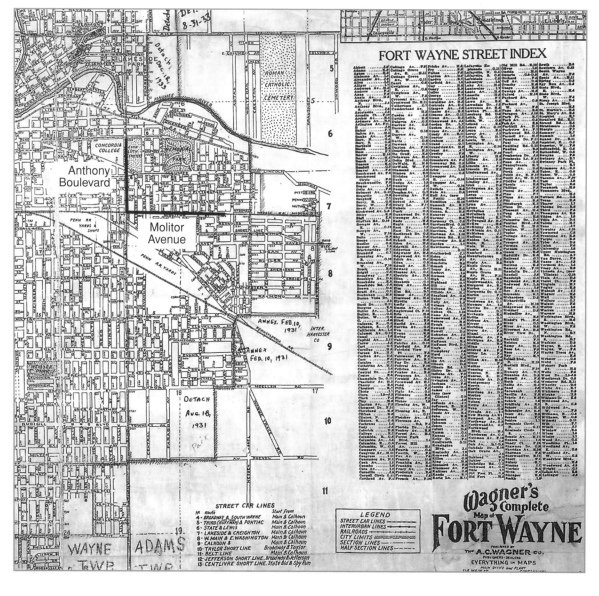

Enumeration District Maps for the Fifteenth Census of the United States *(National Archives Microfilm Publication M1930), roll ll. Anthony Boulevard and Molitor Avenue are in ED 2-34.*

among counties in the same state. There is little uniformity in map scale, size, or the number of sheets. The unifying feature of this series of maps is the annotations added by the Bureau. These annotations include the boundaries and numbers of the individual EDs, usually added in an orange grease or wax pencil.

The National Archives filmed the ED maps alphabetically by state, thereunder alphabetically by county, and thereunder alphabetically by minor civil divisions if such maps were used for that county. Maps of territories follow the maps of the states.

For additional information on this microfilm publication and a list of the maps, see the accompanying descriptive pamphlet. Copies of the descriptive pamphlet can be ordered from the Archives I Customer Service Center (NWCC1), National Archives, 700 Pennsylvania Avenue NW, Washington, DC 20408-001. (Telephone 202-501-5235 or 1-866-325-7208, fax 202-501-7170.)

## Roll List of M1930

### *Index to Selected City Streets and Enumeration Districts*

The *Index to Selected City Streets and Enumeration Districts, 1930 Census* (National Archives Microfilm Publication M1931) reproduces a 57-volume index to selected city streets and enumeration districts for the 1930 census. Most of the volumes contain all or part of a major U.S. city; a few also contain smaller cities. Each of the volumes generally contains the following information:

The list of named streets (roads, boulevards, avenues, lanes, etc.) arranged alphabetically shows the EDs in which the street is located. Streets with a prefix such as North, East, South, or West may be listed either under the prefix or under the street name. For example, East Archwood Avenue might be listed as "E. Archwood Ave." or as "Archwood Ave. E."

The list of numbered streets (roads, boulevards, avenues, lanes, etc.) arranged numerically indicates the EDs in which the street is located. Prefixes such as North, East, South, or West do not affect the arrangement. Thus, E. 26th and W. 26th will both be found together.

The list of institutions and named apartments gives the ED in which the institution or apartment will be found. The list of unnamed apartments indicates the ED in which the apartment will be found. Only a few of the larger cities have this list. The Bureau made handwritten corrections on these lists, presumably after the census was completed.

## North Carolina

The Bureau created special finding aids for North Carolina. The index to 22 cities with a population over 10,000 is arranged alphabetically. For each city, the volume gives the street name, house range, and ED number.

The index to named places with a population under 10,000 is arranged alphabetically by name, and, for each, the following information is given: county in which located, ED number, and adjacent ED numbers (if any). For example:

| PLACE | COUNTY | ED | ADJACENT |
|---|---|---|---|
| Rominger | Watauga | 95-10 | 95-13; 15 |
| Ronda | Wilkes | 97-5 | 97-6; 16; 8 |
| Rooks | Pender | 71-5 | 71-4 |
| Roosevelt | Henderson | 45-5 | — |

| STREETS | HOUSE NOS. | E.D. |
|---|---|---|
| Minalpen | -------- | 2-34 |
| Miner | (0-2100) | 2-19 |
| | (2200-2500) | 2-25 |
| Molitor | -------- | 2-34 |
| Mondamin Pass | -------- | 2-23 |
| Morning | -------- | 2-76 |
| Monroe, N. | -------- | 2-13 |
| Monroe, S. | (0-1100) | 2-10 |
| | (1100-1400) | 2-11 |
| | (1800-1900) | 2-78 |
| | (2800-4800) | 2-80 |
| Montclair Ave. | -------- | 2-21 |
| Montgomery (changed to E. Douglas Ave) | | |
| Montrose Ave. | -------- | 2-30 |
| Morrell | -------- | 2-24 |
| Morris | (0-1900) | 2-76 |
| | (2000-2500) | 2-23 |
| Morrison | -------- | 2-22 |
| Morton | -------- | 2-8 |
| Mulberry Road | -------- | 2-76 |
| Murray | -------- | 2-28 |
| Muskoday Ave. | -------- | 2-23 |
| Mutual Drive | -------- | 2-34 |
| Nelson | (0-900) | 2-20 |
| | (1000-1200) | 2-21 |
| | (1200-2100) | 2-24 |
| Nettie Ave. | -------- | 2-4 |
| Neuhaus Drive (outside city) | | |
| NEVA Ave. | -------- | 2-12 |
| Nevada Ave. | (0-1100) | 2-7 |
| | (1200-1400) | 2-6 |
| | (1500-1600) | 2-3 |
| New Haven Ave. | -------- | 2-34 |
| Newport Ave. (outside city) | | |
| Niagara Drive | -------- | 2-2 |
| Nokomis Road | -------- | 2-23 |
| Norfolk Ave. | -------- | 2-12 |
| Northway Ave. | -------- | 2-12 |
| Northwood Ave. (changed to Norfolk Ave., | | |
| Northwood Blvd. | -------- | even (outside city) |
| | | odd 2-12 |
| Nussbaum Ave. | -------- | 2-12 |
| Nuttman Ave. | (0-600) | 2-48 |
| | (700-1200) | 2-26 |
| | (1800) | 2-23 |
| Sts. Minalpen to Nuttman Ave. | Ft. Wayne | Page 19 |

Index to Selected City Streets and Enumeration Districts, 1930 Census *(National Archives Microfilm Publication M1931), Ft. Wayne, Allen County, Indiana, roll 3. Molitor is in ED 2-34.*

The index to townships is arranged alphabetically by name of the township and includes the county in which the township is located and its ED number(s). The index to institutions is listed alphabetically by name and lists the county and ED.

The county maps consist of hand-drawn rough sketches of each county that show the ED numbers and their approximate boundaries.

## Philadelphia

For many streets listed in the Philadelphia index, the name of the neighborhood in which the street is located is also listed. Some of the neighborhoods include Blue Bell Hill, Bridesburg, Bustleton, Chestnut Hill, Fox Chase, Falls of Schuylkill, Frankford, Germantown, Holmesburg, Manayunk, Olney, Palm West Philadelphia, Roxborough, Somerton, Tacony, and West Philadelphia.

For additional information on this microfilm publication and a list of the maps, see the accompanying descriptive pamphlet. Copies of the descriptive pamphlet can be order from the Archives I Customer Service Center (NWCC1), National Archives, 700 Pennsylvania Avenue NW, Washington, DC 20408-001. (Telephone 202-501-5235 or 1-866-325-7208, fax 202-501-7170.)

Roll List for M1931

Roll 1   Arizona: Phoenix
California:
Berkeley
Long Beach
Los Angeles County (6 vols.) includes Los Angeles City and Alhambra, Arcadia, Avalon, Azusa, Bell, Beverly Hills, Burbank, Claremont, Compton, Covina, Culver, Davidson, El Monte, El Segundo, Glendale, Glendora, Hawthorne, Hermosa Beach, Hollywood, Huntington Park, Inglewood, La Verne, Lynwood, Manhattan Beach, Maywood, Monrovia, Montebello, Monterey Park, Pasadena, Pomona, Redondo Beach, San Fernando, San Gabriel, San Marino, San Pedro, Santa Monica, Sierra Madre, Signal Hill, South Gate, South Pasadena, Temple, Torrance, Tujunga, Verdugo, Vernon, West Covina, Whittier, and Wilmington

     Vol. 1:   A-Colon
     Vol. 2:   Colonial-Harkins
     Vol. 3:   Harkness-Mayfield
     Vol. 4:   Mayflower-Romney

Roll 2      Vol. 5:   Romona-Wheeler
     Vol. 6:   Wheeler-Z
            1st-263rd (St., Ave., Rd., Pl., etc.)
            Ave. 16-Ave. 67
            Institutions and Apartments
            Minor Civil Divisions
San Diego
San Francisco
Colorado: Denver
District of Columbia
Florida: Miami, also includes Miami Beach and South Miami; Tampa
Georgia: Atlanta

Roll 3   Illinois:
    Chicago
       Vol. 1:   Abbott–Nutt
       Vol. 2:   Oak–York
                5th–138th
                Institutions and Apartments
    Peoria
    Indiana: Fort Wayne; Gary; Indianapolis; South Bend
    Kansas: Kansas City, Wichita
    Maryland: Baltimore

Roll 4   Michigan: Detroit; also includes Hamtramck and Highland
       Park; Grand Rapids
    Nebraska: Omaha
    New Jersey: Elizabeth, Newark, Paterson
    New York:
    Bronx and Manhattan (interfiled)
    Brooklyn
       Vol. 1:   A–Oxford
       Vol. 2:   Pacific–York
                1st–108th
                Institutions and Apartments

Roll 5   Queens
       Vol. 1:   Aberdeen–Zoller
                1st–43rd
       Vol. 2:   44th–271st
                Institutions and Apartments
    Richmond
    North Carolina:
    Cities over 10,000 Population
       Vol. 1:   Asheville, Charlotte, Concord, Durham,
                Elizabeth City, Fayetteville, Gastonia, Golds-
                boro, Greensboro

Roll 6       Vol. 2:   High Point, Kinston, Lexington, New Bern,
                Raleigh, Rocky Mount, Salisbury, Shelby,
                Statesville, Thomasville, Wilmington, Wilson,
                Winston-Salem
    Named Places Under 10,000 Population
       Vol. 1:   Aaron–Parker Crossroads
       Vol. 2:   Parker Ferry–Zorah
    Townships: Abbotts–Youngsville
    Institutions: A–Z
    County Maps: Alamance–Yancey
    Ohio: Akron, Canton, Cincinnati

Roll 7   Ohio: Cleveland, Dayton, Youngstown
    Oklahoma: Oklahoma City, Tulsa
    Pennsylvania:
    Erie
    Philadelphia
       Vol. 1:   A–Myrtlewood
       Vol. 2:   N–Zerelda
                1st St.–80th St.
                64th Ave.–80th Ave.
                23d N.–35th N.
                Institutions and Apartments

    Reading
    Tennessee: Memphis
    Texas: San Antonio
    Virginia: Richmond

### City Directories

NARA purchased microfilm copies of many city directories for 1929–31 from Primary Source Media. These films are available at the National Archives in Washington, DC, and in all of the National Archives regional facilities. For a complete list of the cities, see *www.nara.gov/genealogy/1930cen.html.*

These are not National Archives microfilm. For information on purchasing copies of this film, contact Primary Source Media at 1-800-444-0799.

## AVAILABILITY AND ACCESS

Microfilmed copies of the census records are available at the National Archives Building in Washington, DC; at NARA's 13 regional facilities; through the National Archives Microfilm Rental Program; at many large libraries and genealogical societies that have purchased all or some of the microfilm; and through purchase.

### National Archives Microfilm Rental Program

The National Archives Microfilm Rental Program rents microfilm of Federal population schedules from 1790 through 1930 and Soundex indexes from 1880 through 1930. The program also rents microfilm of American Revolutionary War military service records and indexes as well as pensions and bounty land warrant files. For a free brochure write to the National Archives, Census Microfilm Rental Program, P.O. Box 30, Annapolis Junction, MD 20701-0030 (301-604-3699).

### Ordering Copies by Mail

The National Archives in Washington, DC, can provide paper copies of specifically identified pages of Federal population census schedules through the mail. To receive this photocopying service, use NATF Form 82 (rev. 2000), and provide the following information: census year, state or territory, county, township or other subdivision, name of head of household, and page number. For the 1880 through 1930 censuses, the enumeration district is also necessary.

Frequently it is possible to use a census index to locate this information. Many private firms have produced statewide indexes to census records for specific years. These generally are available throughout the country in National Archives regional offices and in libraries that have genealogical collections.

### Buying the Microfilm

Microfilm copies of census records are also available for purchase. The schedules are on 35mm microfilm; the Soundex is on 16mm. Schedules for an entire county or enumeration district may be on one or more rolls of microfilm.

All microfilm publications of National Archives records are for sale. You can buy either individual rolls or a complete set (all rolls).

The prices, as of December 1, 2001, are $34 a roll for domestic orders, but these prices are subject to change without advance notice. The prices for foreign orders are $39 a roll. ED maps (M1930) are on 35mm color microfilm. The price for this color microfilm is $51 a roll for domestic orders and $56 a roll for foreign orders. Shipping is included in these prices.

A check or money order made payable to the "National Archives Trust Fund (NATF)" must accompany each order. Orders may also be charged to VISA, MasterCard, American Express, and Discover (Novus) accounts. Government agencies, educational institutions, and businesses may purchase microfilm on an accounts-receivable basis but must submit purchase orders. Mail orders to the National Archives Trust Fund (NAT), P.O. Box 100793, Atlanta, GA 30384-0793.

When ordering microfilm, please state the microfilm publication number; if you are not buying a complete set, also state the specific roll(s) you wish to purchase.

If you need more information on how to order, details of specific shipping charges, or help identifying which rolls of a publication you wish to purchase, please contact the National Archives and Records Administration, Research Support Branch (NWCC2), Room 1000, 8601 Adelphi Rd, College Park, MD 20740-6001 (telephone 301-713-6800 or 1-800-234-8861; fax 301-713-6169).

Copies of National Archives microfilm publications may also be purchased from Scholarly Resources, Inc., 104 Greenhill Avenue, Wilmington, DE 19805 (telephone 302-654-7713; fax 302-654-3871; email *sales@scholarly.com*). Copies available for sale from other sources have not been authorized or duplicated by the National Archives and may be one or more generations removed from the master materials adversely affecting the quality and legibility of each image.

"Mechanics, Air Mail Service, Omaha, Neb.," 1924 (28-MS-2B-8).

## ACKNOWLEDGMENTS

The following is a list of people without whose help the 1930 census microfilm and catalog could not have been produced. We express our thanks and acknowledge our debt.

### Office of Records Services

Dorinda Jean Cartwright, Katherine V. Coram, Diane Dimkoff, L.J. Divine, Anne Eales, Sandra Glasser, Nicole Gilkison, Benjamin Guterman, Janice Hargett, Dr. Kenneth Heger, Allan Hunt, Dr. David Kepley, Claire Kluskens, Maureen MacDonald, Sue McDonough, Cliff Macwha, Nancy Mottershaw, Charles Ponders, Constance Potter, Steve Puglia, Bob Richardson, Barry Roginski, Jack Saunders, Clarence Simmons, Richard Smith, Linda Tapscott, Judith Z. Thorne, Katherine Vollen, Heather Whewell, Kristen Wilhelm, Jo Ann Williamson, Rita Wolfinger
*Volunteers* - James P. Collins, Fred Matthies, Linda Faye Mora, Brittany Suzanne Smith, William Grant Stewart, and Lorenzo Vallone.

### Office of the General Counsel

Kevin Jessar
Christopher Runkel

### Office of Human Resources and Information Services

Steve Bern
Dr. Kenneth Hawkins

### Office of Regional Records Services

Nancy Malan
Greg Pomicter
Diane Voht-O'Conner

### NARA's Northeast Region (Boston)

Walter V. Hickey
James K. Owens
Bill Read
Erica Reece
George Sermuksnis

### NARA's Northeast Region (Pittsfield)

Mary Bazinet (volunteer)
Charlotte Davis (volunteer)
Arlene Jennings (volunteer)
Jean Kubica
Jean Nudd
Viola Sivik (volunteer)
Kathleen Stottle (volunteer)

### NARA's Northeast Region (New York)

John Celardo
Richard Gelbke
Greg Plunges
Martin Rosenberg
Carol Savo
Joan Young

### NARA's Mid Atlantic Region (Center City Philadelphia)

Kellee Blake
Patrick Connelly
Matthew DiBiase
Gail Farr
Jefferson Moak
Robert Plowman
Rebecca Warlow

*NARA's Southeast Region (Atlanta)*
Gary Fulton
Fred Munguia (volunteer)
Susana Munguia (volunteer)
Arlene Royer
Phyllis Dale Schiwal (volunteer)
Henry E. Trippe (volunteer)

*NARA's Southwest Region (Fort Worth)*
Barbara Crow (volunteer)
Nakita Gore
Meg Hacker
Aaron Holt
Rodney Krajca
Darla McFarland (volunteer)
Patsy Miller (volunteer)
Beverly Moody
Laverne Owens
Nigel Parker
Barbara Rust
Ruth Tipton Smith (volunteer)
Cindy Smolovik
Joyce Terrana (volunteer)
Jim Wendell (volunteer)

*NARA's Central Plains Region (Kansas City)*
Evie Bresette
Mary Burtzloff
Gloria Coleman (volunteer)
Marilyn Finke
Arline Hahn (volunteer)
Louis Hahn (volunteer)
Don Ireland (volunteer)
Carrie Kirk (volunteer)
Debbie Koenigsdorf (volunteer)
Judy Oakley (volunteer)
Tim Rives
Clara Rolen (volunteer)

*NARA's Great Lakes Region (Chicago)*
Sue Browne (volunteer)
Peter Bunce
Michael Cross
Bill Eilers (volunteer)
Betty Furimsky
Joan Kimpell (volunteer)
Barbara Principali (volunteer)
Martin Tuohy

*NARA's Rocky Mountain Region (Denver)*
Kathy Anderson
Eileen Bolger
Eric Bittner
Rick Martinez
Julie Miller (volunteer)
Darlene Romero
Jerry Sander (volunteer)
Marene Sweeney

*NARA's Pacific Alaska Region (Anchorage)*
Tammy Carlisle
Caroline Daugherty
Diana Kodiak
Bruce Parham
Judy Petersen
Tom Wiltsey

*NARA's Pacific Alaska Region (Seattle)*
Gretchen Brezarich (volunteer)
Celia Ceffalo
Susan Karren
Karl Kumm (volunteer)
Patty McNamee
LaVola Schrum (volunteer)
Helen Wick (volunteer)

*NARA's Pacific Region (San Francisco)*
Audrey Becker (volunteer)
Teria Brewer (volunteer)
Helen Crisman (volunteer)
Gloria Le Gaspi
John Hedger
Claude Hopkins
Sharleen Jerome (volunteer)
Harvey Jerome (volunteer)
Jackie Johnson (volunteer)
Bill Jordan (volunteer)
Catherine Kaminski (volunteer)
Rose Mary Kennedy
Carolyn Kennison (volunteer)
Joseph Sanchez

*NARA's Pacific Region (Laguna Niguel)*
Ed Brockett (volunteer)
Bill Doty
Lisa Gezelter
Karen Langer
Cathie Mauzey (volunteer)
Wendy Simpson
Randy Thompson
Pat Weeks (volunteer)

*Bureau of the Census, Jeffersonville, Indiana*
Betty Altman
Mary Lee Eldridge
Jean Hardin
Carole Hickerson
Nikki Merchant
Tina Pelsor

*Bureau of the Census, Suitland, Maryland*
David Pemberton
David Hendricks

*IBM Corporate Headquarters*
Laurie Wessner

*Signal Corp*
Ronald Thomas

*Science Applications International Corporation (SAIC)*
Dr. Richard Klobuchar
Brian A. Storeide

*"Children's story hour, Poplar Bluff, Missouri Library, ca. 1920s"*
*(83-ML-15022).*

# 1930 Census
## *Soundex*

M2049–M2060
1587 ROLLS

The Works Progress Administration created complete indexes for 10 states and partial indexes for 2 other states.

Complete indexes exist for Alabama (M2049), Arkansas (M2050), Florida (M2051), Georgia (M2052), Louisiana (M2054), Mississippi (M2055), North Carolina (M2056), South Carolina (M2057), Tennessee (M2058), and Virginia (M2059).

Partial indexes exist for Kentucky (M2053—Bell, Floyd, Harlan, Kenton, Muhlenberg, Perry, and Pike counties) and West Virginia (M2060—Fayette, Harrison, Kanawha, Logan, McDowell, Mercer, and Raleigh counties).

For addition information on the Soundex coding system, see page xix of the catalog.

The National Archives reproduced this microfilm from the highest quality master negatives available from the Bureau of the Census. The original film includes defects that affect the legibility of some frames.

**Alabama (M2049)**

For Jefferson, Mobile, and Montgomery counties, see rolls 128 to 198. All of the other Alabama counties are on rolls 1 to 127.

1. A-000—A-322 J.
2. A-322 K.—A-436
3. A-442—A-536 Joel B.
4. A-536 John—B-165
5. B-200—B-240 R.
6. B-240 S.—B-300
7. B-310—B-400 D.
8. B-400 E.—B-425 G.
9. B-425 H.—B-463 E.
10. B-463 F.—B-545
11. B-546—B-620 James W.
12. B-620 Jane—B-630 I.
13. B-630 J.—B-635 N.
14. B-635 O.—B-650 L.
15. B-650 M.—B-652
16. B-653—C-136
17. C-140—C-200 G.
18. C-200 H.—C-264
19. C-265—C-414
20. C-415—C-452 M.
21. C-452 N.—C-462
22. C-463—C-534
23. C-535—C-600 L.
24. C-600 M.—C-626
25. C-630—C-640 K.
26. C-640 L.—D-120 C.
27. D-120 D.—D-120 Z.
28. D-123—D-250 N.
29. D-250 O.—D-451
30. D-452—D-540 I.
31. D-540 J.—D-652
32. D-653—E-325
33. E-326—E-462
34. E-463—F-260 E.
35. F-260 F.—F-456
36. F-460—F-620 K.
37. F-620 L.—F-655 F.
38. F-655 G.—G-252 G.
39. G-252 H.—G-416
40. G-420—G-516
41. G-520—G-615
42. G-616—G-635 Maucy
43. G-635 Maud—G-653
44. G-654—H-200 Gotfie
45. H-200 Grace—H-240
46. H-241—H-320 C.
47. H-320 D—H-400 C.
48. H-400 D.—H-400 R.
49. H-400 S.—H-452 K.
50. H-452 L.—H-520 V.
51. H-520 W.—H-536 O.
52. H-536 P.—H-616
53. H-620—H-625 J.
54. H-625 K.—H-635 E.
55. H-635 F.—I-525
56. I-526—J-250 Jodie
57. J-520 Joe—J-520 C.
58. J-520 D.—J-520 Maxine
59. J-520 May—J-525 Charles W.
60. J-525 Charley—J-525 Marshall
61. J-525 Mat—J-635
62. J-636—K-420
63. K-421—K-523 I.
64. K-523 J.—K-665
65. L-000—L-155
66. L-156—L-236 I.
67. L-236 J.—L-360
68. L-361—L-520
69. L-521—L-650

70. L-652—M-200 Mezzie
71. M-200 Mike—M-235
72. M-236—M-245 L.
73. M-245 M—M252
74. M-253—M-262
75. M-263—M-322
76. M-323—M420 L.
77. M-420 M.—M-465
78. M-500—M-560
79. M-561—M-610
80. M-612—M-625 Jewel
81. M-625 Jim—M-642
82. M-643—N-350
83. N-351—N-631
84. N-632—O-505
85. O-520—P-200 I.
86. P-200 J.—P-350 J.
87. P-350 K.—P-400 R.
88. P-400 S.—P-500 I.
89. P-500 J.—P-620 Jace
90. P-620 Jack—P-626 I.
91. P-626 J.—P-651
92. P-652—R-151
93. R-152—R-163 I.
94. R-163 J.—R-220
95. R-223—R-263 K.
96. R-263 L.—R-350 Zel
97. R-350—R-523
98. R-524—S-151
99. S-152—S-241
100. S-242—S-315 L.
101. S-315 M.—S-346
102. S-350—S-363 F.
103. S-363 G.—S-420 Jordon
104. S-420 Joseph—S-514
105. S-515—S-530 Delia
106. S-530 Dell—S-530 Manzo
107. S-530 Maple—S-536 C.
108. S-536 D.—S-561
109. S-562—T-140
110. T-142—T-415
111. T-416—T-512 A.
112. T-512 B.—T-520 K.
113. T-520 L.—T-612
114. T-613—T-656 C.
115. T-656 D.—V-462
116. V-500—W-230 R.
117. W-230 S.—W-300 Henry
118. W-300 Henry A.—W-320 P.
119. W-320 Q.—W-352
120. W-353—W-420 Leck M.
121. W-420 Lee—W-425 V.
122. W-425 W.—W-436 R.
123. W-436 S.—W-452 Jeems
124. W-452 Jeff—W-460 L.
125. W-460 M.—W-623 S.
126. W-623 T.—Y520-L.
127. Y-520 M.—Institutions

Jefferson, Mobile, and Montgomery Counties
128. A-000 Elizabeth G.—A-450 Fred
129. A-450 Fred D.—A-663 Scott
130. B-000 Ada—B-300 Hykel
131. B-300 Ida—B-423 Curtis
132. B-423 David—B-550 Ill
133. B-550 Irene—B-626 Tom A.
134. B-626 Tyson—B-650 James S.
135. B-650 James T.—B-665 Willie G.

136. NO ROLL 136
137. C-000 Birdis—C-265 Fate
138. C-265 Foney—C-452 Richard
139. C-452 Richard H.—C-534 Raymond
140. C-534-Robert A.—C-630 Harry
141. C-630 Hattie M.—C-665 William
142. D-000 A.L.—D-200 Robert
143. D-200 Robert—D-520 Floyd Fl.
144. D-520 Forest—D-665 Willie
145. E-100 Clarence B.—E-524 Alery
146. E-524 Alfonse—E-663 Nettie M.
147. F-000 Albert—F-514 Orion
148. F-514 Robert—F-666 Arthur
149. NO ROLL 149
150. G-000 Abe—G-426 Mary
151. G-426—G-620 Louise C.
152. G-620 Lucie G.—G-665 Willie
153. H-000 Ada—H-252 Gertrude A.
154. H-252 Gloria—H-400 John
155. H-400 John—H-520 Herman H.
156. H-520 Horace—H-620 Alonza
157. H-620 Alonzo—H-632 James R.
158. H-632 James T.—H-656 V.G.
159. I-100 Ada—I-660 Luther C.
160. J-000 Alberta—J-520 Charles O.
161. J-520 Charles P.—J-525 Amma
162. J-525 Amos—J-660 Mary
163. NO ROLL 163
164. K-000 Albert—K-530 Horace M.
165. K-530 Hubert—K-662 Jese
166. L-000 A.C.—L-200 Viola
167. L-200 Viola H.—L-520 Jennie
168. L-520 Jeraldine—L-663 George
169. M-000 A. Dewey—M-235 Sam
170. M-235 Samuel—M-252 Willie
171. M-252 Willie—M-324 Josephine
172. M-325 Josephine—M-522 Arthur
173. M-522 Artino—M-620 Harry
174. M-620 Harry H.—M-665 Mike
175. N-000 Charle—N-663 Paralee
176. O-100 Ila—O-662 Thomas
177. P-000 Adam—P-362 William
178. P-362 William—P-612 James
179. P-612 James F.—Q-650 Jack
180. R-000 A.T.—R-200 Carlotta
181. R-200 Caroline—R-300 Jerome
182. R-300 Jerry A.—R-660 Edward L.
183. S-000 A.T.—S-300 Samuel
184. S-300 Samuel—S-362 Georgia
185. S-362 Geraldine—S-462 John
186. S-462 John H.—S-530 James
187. S-530 James—S-550 Lucille
188. S-550 Lushie—S-665 L. Gordon
189. T-000 Alice—T-550 Jesse
190. T-500 Jessie—T-560 Cleve C.
191. T-560 Crawford—U-653 John H. Jr.
192. V-120 Albert—V-660 Pete
193. W-000 Bill—W-300 Pearl
194. W-300 Pearl—W-410 Isaiah W.
195. W-410 Jack—W-426 Marium
196. W-426 Mark—W-452 Joseph F.
197. W-452 Joseph H.—W-623 James E.
198. W-623 James F.—Z-653 Margaret

## Arkansas (M2050)

1. A-000—A-352 M.
2. A-352 N.—A-536 B.
3. A-536 C.—B-164 Willie
4. B-200—B-260 B.
5. B-260 C.—~~C-346~~ Zeola B346 *correct* dee
6. B-350—B-420 William W. correct
7. B-420 Willie—B-500 L.
8. B-500 M.—B-600 R.
9. B-600 S.—B-624 Woodrow
10. B-625—B-635 John
11. B-635 John A.—B-650 Osbourn A.
12. B-650 Osca B.—B-653 Millage
13. B-653 Milton—C-160 Nichols
14. C-160 Noah—C-264
15. C-265—C-425 William R.
16. C-430—C-462 C.W.
17. C-462—C-516
18. C-520—C-615
19. C-616—C-636 Guy
20. C-636 H.—D-000 Ruth
21. D-000 S.—D-132
22. D-140—D-300 Doris
23. D-300 E.—E-520 K.
24. D-520 L.—D-652
25. D-653—E-363 H.
26. E-363 I.—F-165
27. F-200—F-435
28. F-436—F-623
29. F-624—F-664
30. G-000—G-355 D.
31. G-355 E.—G-500
32. G-510—G-620
33. G-621—G-650 O.
34. G-650 P.—H-156
35. H-160—H-235
36. H-236—H-324
37. H-325—H-400 Mary E.
38. H-400 Mary F.—H-453 E.
39. H-453 F.—H-526
40. H-530—H-560 J.
41. H-560 K.—H-624
42. H-625—H-650 F.
43. H-650 G.—J-250 Claude E.
44. J-250 Clay—J-520 C.
45. J-520 D.—J-520 Venson
46. J-520 Vera—J-525 John W.
47. J-525 Johney—J-660
48. K-000—K-500 D.
49. K-500 E.—K-620 R.
50. K-620 S.—L-200 D.
51. L-200 E.—L-313 H.
52. L-313 J.—L-520 V.
53. L-520 W.—M-000
54. M-100—M-216 John W.
55. M-216 Johnie—M-245 B.
56. M-245 C.—M-254 I.
57. M-254 J.—M-320 Travis L.
58. M-320 Troy—M-450 Burl
59. M-450 C.—M-532 G.
60. M-532 H.—M-600
61. M-610—M-625 William A.
62. M-625 Will B.—N-216
63. N-220—N-520 R.
64. N-520 S.—O-512
65. O-516—P-263
66. P-264—P-400 S.
67. P-400 T.—P-526 Jim
68. P-526 Jo Ely—P-623 C.
69. P-623 D.—P-636 S.
70. P-636 T.—R-152 G.
71. R-152 H.—R-200 E.
72. R-200 F.—R-260 I.
73. R-260 J.—R-320 K.
74. R-320 L.—R-500
75. R-510—S-133
76. S-134—S-235
77. S-236—S-320 C.
78. S-320 D.—S-353 P.
79. S-353 R.—S-365 L.
80. S-365 M.—S-500 D.
81. S-500 E.—S-530 Cly
82. S-530 Clyde—S-530 O.
83. S-530 P.—S-541
84. S-542—S-640 Riley
85. S-640 Rober—T-400 E.
86. T-400 F.—T-512 A.
87. T-512 B.—T-522
88. T-523—T-652 C.
89. T-652 D.—V-353
90. V-356—W-215
91. W-216—W-300-Frankie
92. W-300 Fred—W-325 C.
93. W-325 D.—W-363 K.
94. W-363 L.—W-422
95. W-423—W-426 K.
96. W-426 L.—W-452 E.
97. W-452 F.—W-452 W.W.
98. W-452 Waco—W-623 J.
99. W-623 K.—Y-520 H.
100. Y-520 I.—Institutions

## Florida (M2051)

1. A-000—A-415
2. A-416—A535
3. A-536—A-663
4. B-000—B-254
5. B-255—B-346
6. B-350—B-424
7. B-425—B-520
8. B-521—B-616
9. B-620—B626
10. B-630—B-646
11. B-650—B-650 Z.
12. B-651—B-665
13. C-000—C-200
14. C-210—C-400
15. C-410—C-454
16. C-455—C-513
17. C-514—C-566
18. C-600—C-622
19. C-623—C-646
20. C-650—D-116
21. D-120—D-125
22. D-126—D-216
23. D-252—D-516
24. D-520—D-626
25. D-630—E-356
26. E-360—E-663
27. F-000—F-434
28. F-435—F-623
29. F-624—F665
30. G-000—G-346
31. G-350—G-451
32. G-452—G-610
33. G-612—G-634
34. G-635—G-652
35. G-653—H-200
36. H-210—H-300
37. H-314—H-366
38. H-400—H-420
39. H-421—H-520
40. H-521—H-555
41. H-560—H-624
42. H-625—H646
43. H-650—J-212
44. J-213—J-516
45. J-520—J-520 John H.
46. J-520 John H.—J-524
47. J-525—J-525 Lysle
48. J-525, M.C.—J-663
49. K-000—K-514
50. K-515—K-616
51. K-620—L-136
52. L-140—L-236
53. L-240—L-516
54. L-520—L-565
55. L-600—M-200
56. M-210—M-240
57. M-241—M-251
58. M-252—M264 T.
59. M-264 T.—M-365
60. M-400—M-460
61. M-461—M-565
62. M-600—M-620
63. M-621—M-634
64. M-635—N-246
65. N-250—N-665
66. O-000—O-663
67. P-000—P-355
68. P-356—P-426
69. P-430—P-616
70. P-620—P-626
71. P-630—R-125
72. R-130—R-162
73. R-163—R-220
74. R-222—R-316
75. R-320—R-465
76. R-500—S-116
77. S-120—S-216
78. S-220—S-316
79. S-320—S-362
80. S-363—S-426
81. S-430—S-526
82. S-530—S-530 M.
83. S-530 N.—S-540
84. S-541—S-652
85. S-653—T-456
86. T-460—T-512
87. T-514—T-565
88. T-600—U-652
89. V-000—W-160
90. W-162—W-265
91. W-300—W-324
92. W-325—W-363
93. W-364—W-424
94. W-425—W-426
95. W-430—W-452 Henry A.
96. W-452 Henry C.—W-452 Z.
97. W-453—W-630
98. W-631—Institutions

## Georgia (M2052)
Georgia Soundex is in Miracode.

1. A-000 Carl R.—A-240 Lee
2. A-240 Lenora—A-350 Susie
3. A-350 Tabatha—A-364 Owen C.
4. A-364 Pearl—A-450 B. Fred
5. A-450 B.L.—A-512 George H.
6. A-512 J.W.—A-536 John H.
7. A-536 John H.—A-650 Harmon
8. A-650 Henry—A-664 James C.
9. B-000 A. Eloise—B-200 Louise
10. B-200 Louise—B-236 W. Frank
11. B-236 W.H.—B-255 Sallie
12. B-255 Sam—B-300 Frank
13. B-300 Frank—B-346 Accenia

14. B-346 Ada—B-400 Bakes
15. B-400 Balaly—B-400 Patsy
16. B-400 Patsy—B-421 Stella
17. B-421 Stephen—B-436 James
18. B-436 James—B-463 Lena
19. B-463 Leon—B-520 Pat L.
20. B-520 Patrick—B-530 William
21. B-530 William—B-600 Francis
22. B-600 Francis P.—B-620 Dora
23. B-620 Dora—B-620 Rosa
24. B-620 Rosa—B-624 Wade H.
25. B-624 Walace—B-630 Larry
26. B-630 Larua—B-634 Charlotte
27. B-634 Chas.—B-640 Misah
28. B-640 Mose—B-650 Ernest
29. B-650 Ernest A.—B-650 Johnnie
30. B-650 Johnnie—B-650 S. Allington
31. B-650 S.B.—B-652 George
32. B-652 George—B-653 Florence
33. B-653 Florence—B-654 Ruby M.
34. B-654 Ruth J.—B-666 Lem S.
35. C-000 Albert—C-155 Annie
36. C-155 Annie—C-200 Bernice F.
37. C-200 Berry—C-200 Roy H.
38. C-200 Rufus A.—C-250 Robert
39. C-250 Robert—C-350 Rosie L.
40. C-350 Roy—C-411 Rosser
41. C-411 Roy—C-434 Edward
42. C-434 Edward—C-452 Jno F.
43. C-452 Jodie—C-455 William
44. C-455 William—C-462 Maybel
45. C-462 Maybelle—C-510 Mary
46. C-510 Mary—C-520 William
47. C-520 William A.—C-552 Albert
48. C-552 Albert—C-600 Mattie
49. C-600 Mattie—C-616 Robert
50. C-616 Robert—C-624 Lillie M.
51. C-624 Lily—C-636 Columbus
52. C-636 Columbus—C-640 Herbert C.
53. C-640 Herbert L.—C-654 Benjamin H.
54. C-654 Benjamin—C-665 George W.
55. D-000 A.L.—D-120 Felton A.
56. D-120 Ferd D.—D-120 Mattie
57. D-120 Mattie—D-142 Lizzie M.
58. D-142 Pearlie—D-220 John L.
59. D-220 John M.—D-250 R.E.
60. D-250 R.F.—D-340 Jim
61. D-340 Jim—D-463 Edward T.
62. D-463 Elda L.—D-520 Julian E.
63. D-520 Julian J.—D-540 Gordon
64. D-540 Gordon—D-560 Richard
65. D-560 Richard—D-635 Enoch E.
66. D-635 Ernest—D-665 Willie
67. E-000 Helen L.—E-163 Jean
68. E-163 Jean E.—E-351 John A.
69. E-351 John C.—E-420 Charles Jr.
70. E-420 Charles L.—E-463 Chesly
71. E-463 Cicero W.—E-665 J.C.
72. F-000 Addie—F-300 Lawrence W.
73. F-300 Leona—F-430 William
74. F-430 William—F-455 Roberta
75. F-455 Robet—F-520 Amanda
76. F-520 Andrew—F-622 Richard
77. F-622 Richard—F-635 Jefferson I.
78. F-635 Jennie—F-655 John
79. F-655 John—F-665 William E.
80. G-000 (n.f.i.)—G-200 Columbus G.
81. G-200 Connie—G-341 Moses
82. G-341 Nellie—G-416 Francis M.
83. G-416 Frank—G-435 Callie M.
84. G-435 Calvin—G-520 Annie
85. G-520 Annie—G-600 Sam
86. G-600 Sam—G-615 Westley F.
87. G-615 Weyman—G-626 Thomas

88. G-626 Thomas—G-645 Johnnie L.
89. G-645 Johny—G-650 Louise
90. G-650 Louise—G-653 James
91. G-653 James—G-666 Ollie
92. H-000 A. Jack—H-163 John F.
93. H-163 John F.—H-200 Nettie B.
94. H-200 Nettie—H-235 Max
95. H-235 Maybelle—H-252 Harry
96. H-252 Harry—H-300 Minola
97. H-300 Minus—H-325 Jim L.
98. H-325 Jim M.—H-400 Carl
99. H-400 Carl—H-400 Joe G.
100. H-400 Joe H.—H-400 Thomas H.
101. H-400 Thomas H.—H-430 George
102. H-430 George—H-452 Victoria
103. H-452 Victoria—H-513 Mitch
104. H-513 Moah—H-522 Tolly
105. H-522 Tom—H-536 Annie
106. H-536 Annie—H-540 Horace L.
107. H-540 Horace L.—H-600 I. Murry
108. H-600 Ike—H-620 Burt
109. H-620 Burt—H-620 Pink L.
110. H-620 PinkeyH-630 Allievan
111. H-630 Alline—H-630 Nettie L.
112. H-630 Nettie M.—H-635 Nina
113. H-635 N.R.[followed by Noah]—H-665 James C.
114. I-000 Arnon—I-660 Mary
115. J-000 A.T.—J-250 Colonel
116. J-250 Colonel—J-250 Luther
117. J-250 Luther—J-452 Iad
118. J-452 Iraiah—J-520 Ella M.
119. J-520 Ella M.—J-520 John A.
120. J-520 John A.—J-520 Racksey
121. J-520 Rae—J-523 John
122. J-523 John—J-525 Elena
123. J-525 Elena—J-525 Jim
124. J-525 Jim—J-525 Ocy P.
125. J-525 Odel—J-525 Willis B.
126. J-525 Willis C.—J.663 Zora
127. K-000 A.—K-400 Arthur
128. K-400 Arthur J.—K-500 Joseph V.
129. K-500 Joseph W.—K-520 Lee
130. K-520 Lee—K-530 James
131. K-530 James—K-665 Rupeato
132. L-000 A.—L-000 Wash
133. L-000 Wash—L-163 Oscar
134. L-163 Oscar—L-200 Mose
135. L-200 Mose—L-240 Fred
136. L-240 Fred—L-316 G. Hughes
137. L-316 G. Hughes—L-460 James
138. L-460 James—L-520 Exir
139. L-520 Ezekiel—L-530 Emry F.
140. L-530 Ennis—L-563 J.C.
141. L-563 J.C.—L-665 Shavina
142. M-000 (n.f.n.)—M-200 Demery
143. M-200 Dennis—M-200 Sallie
144. M-200 Sallie—M-224 Malcolm
145. M-224 Marion—M-240 Caroline
146. M-240 Caroline A.—M-243 Ida B.
147. M-243 Ida M.—M-246 Noah L.
148. M-246 Norman—M-252 Merrill
149. M-252 Mildred—M-260 Cashiuos
150. M-260 Castoria—M-265 Johnnie L.
151. N-265 Johnnie—M-320 James H.
152. M-320 James H.—M-324 Jack
153. M-324 Jack—M-400 Florence
154. M-400 Fordie—M-435 Luther

155. M-435 Luther J.—M-460 Joanna
156. M-460 Joe—M-500 William
157. M-500 William—M-536 Luta
158. M-536 Luther—M-600 George
159. M-600 George—M-600 W.A.
160. M-600 W.B.—M-620 John
161. M-620 John—M-625 Elsie
162. M-625 Elsie—M-635 Carl
163. M-635 Carl—M-640 Charlie L.
164. M-640 Chas E.—M-666 Tommy
165. N-000 A. Cora—N-250 Dorothy A.
166. N-250 Dortha—N-420 Richard
167. N-420 Richard D.—N-630 Mary
168. N-630 Mary—N-663 Sudie
169. O-000 Albert—O-350 Joe S.
170. O-350 Joe S.—O-540 Edward
171. O-540 Edward—P-200 Margery
172. P-200 Margetta—P-320 Edd
173. P-320 Edd—P-362 Charles
174. P-362 Charles—P-400 Homer P.
175. P-400 Homer R.—P-412 Maderie A.
176. P-412 Madison—P-456 Eugene
177. P-456 Eugene—P-536 Henry C.
178. P-536 Henry R.—P-620 Collie
179. P-620 Collis—P-620 Willie V.
180. P-620 Willie W.—P-626 Charlie
181. P-626 Charlie—P-633 William L.
182. P-633 William L.—Q-653 Della
183. R-000 (n.f.n.) Thomas A.—R-140 Thomas A.
184. R-140 Thomas J.—R-162 Allen
185. R-162 Allen—R-163 James
186. R-163 James—R-200 Floyd A.
187. R-200 Floyd C.—R-212 Mary F.
188. R-212 Mike—R-252 Renie
189. R-252 Richard—R-263 Charlis
190. R-263 Charly—R-300 Ruby
191. R-300 Ruby L.—R-352 Jim
192. R-352 Jim—R-453 Linton
193. R-453 Lizzie—R-534 Eunice
194. R-534 Eunice—R-660 Helen A.
195. S-000 A.—S-143 Annie
196. S-143 Annie—S-162 Martin
197. S-162 Martin M.—S-236 Doloris
198. S-236 Donald R.—S-300 Joseph
199. S-300 Joseph—S-315 Harret S.
200. S-315 Harrett C.—S-322 Thurman
201. S-322 Tom—S-350 Essie C.
202. S-350 Essie M.—S-355 Fred W.
203. S-355 Garfield—S-362 Speak
204. S-362 Spencer—S-365 Homer Thorntog
205. S-365 Hood—S-420 Thomas
206. S-420 Thomas—S-460 Milton J.
207. S-460 Minnie—S-516 William O.
208. S-516 Willie—S-525 William
209. S-525 William—S-530 E.M.
210. S-530 E.M.—S-530 Isodore
211. S-530 Isom—S-530 Lula
212. S-530 Lula—S-530 Samues
213. S-530 Samuel—S-536 Earl
214. S-536 Earl—S-550 Jim
215. S-550 Jim—S-563 Jennie
216. S-563 Jesse—S-630 Myers H.
217. S-630 Myrtle—S-665 Gene
218. T-000 (N.R.) (followed by Abraham)—T-260 J.C.
219. T-260 J.D.—T-416 George
220. T-416 George—T-460 Jno.

221. T-460 Jno. J.—T-512 Floy
222. T-512 Floy—T-520 Chance
223. T-520 Chancey—T-520 Mary
224. T-520 Mary—T-540 Sarah
225. T-540 Spencer—T-616 William
226. T-616 William B.—T-653 James
227. T-653 James—T-656 R.T.
228. T-656 R.T.—U-660 Wealthy
229. V-000 Franklin—V-536 Rosa
230. V-536 Ross—W-214 Jim
231. W-214 Joe—W-252 Ed
232. W-252 Ed—W-300 Eddie
233. W-300 Eddie—W-300 Mitchell
234. W-300 Mitchell R.—W-320 Leona
235. W-320 Leonard—W-325 William D.
236. W-325 William E.—W-352 John T.
237. W-352 John W.—W-400 Grace
238. W-400 Grady—W-420 George J.
239. W-420 George Jr.—W-422 George M.
240. W-422 George M.—W-425 Lawton
241. W-425 Lazaras—W-426 Florence
242. W-426 Florence—W-426 William S.
243. W-426 William S.—W-450 John
244. W-450 John A.—W-452 Earnest F.
245. W-452 Earnestine—W-452 James
246. W-452 James—W-452 Mattie
247. W-452 Mattie—W-452 Will
248. W-452 Will—W-516 Georgia
249. W-516 Georgia M.—W-623 Arhur
250. W-623 Arillm B.—W-630 Edith
251. W-630 Edith—W-663 Ruth
252. Y-000 Addie—Y-550 Julia A.
253. Y-550 Kathaleene—Z-662 Joseph A.

### Kentucky (M2053)
Includes the following counties: Bell, Floyd, Harlan, Kenton, Muhlenberg, Perry, and Pike. Other Kentucky counties have **not** been Soundexed.

1. A-123—B-256
2. B-260—B-563
3. B-600—B-665
4. C-000—C-465
5. C-500—C-665
6. D-000—D-662
7. E-000—F-465
8. F-500—G-620
9. G-621—H-345
10. H-350—H-565
11. H-600—J-524
12. J-525—L-000
13. L-100—M-200
14. M-210—M-465
15. M-500—N-152
16. N-160—P-400
17. P-410—R-165
18. R-200—R-660
19. S-000—S-362
20. S-363—S-530
21. S-531—T-563
22. T-600—W-326
23. W-330—W-646
24. W-650—Institutions

### Louisiana (M2054)

1. A-000—A-2352
2. A-236—A-352 A.
3. A-352 B.—A-425 B.
4. A-425 C.—A-450 N.
5. A-450 O.—A-536 A.
6. A-536 B.—A-613
7. A-614—A-655
8. A-656—B-200 B.
9. B-200 C.—B-240 C.
10. B-240 D.—B-260 L.
11. B-260 M.—B-332
12. B-340—B-400 Annie Mae
13. B-400 Anthony—B-426 Funnie
14. B-426 Garfield—B-460 Edward H.
15. B-460 Edwin D.—B-530 Hypolite
16. B-530 I.C.—B-614 Ottis
17. B-614 Percy—B-620 Symonet
18. B-620 T.—B-626 Alprome
19. B-626 Alta—B-632 Duncon
20. B-632 E.L.—B-636
21. B-64—B-650 John
22. B-650 John A.—B-651 Joe S.
23. B-651 John—B-656 Claire
24. B-656 Clara—C-155 Norman
25. C-155 O.C.—C-234 Louie B.
26. C-234 Louis—C-346
27. C-350—C-430 Anita
28. C-430 Anna—C-453 Wilson L.
29. C-454—C-500 Johny Belle
30. C-500 Jonas—C-535
31. C-536—C-613 Hugh
32. C-613 Ida—C-632 Maurice A.
33. C-632 May—C-642 Fred
34. C-642 Gabriel—D-120 Butler
35. D-120 C.A.—D-120 Wilfred
36. D-120 Will—D-200 Burese
37. D-200 C.C.—D-240 Frank
38. D-240 Fred—D-300
39. D-310—D-451
40. D-452—D-530 Hyfolite
41. D-530 Ida—D-610 Grace
42. D-610 H.B.—E-152 Gertrude
43. E-152 Glen—E-355 Jim
44. E-355 Joe—E-552
45. E-553—F-250
46. F-251—F-446
47. F-450—F-535 N.
48. F-535 O.Z.—F-630 N.
49. F-630 O.J.—F-652 Perk
50. F-652 Peter—G-200 J.
51. G-200 K.—G-355 John W.
52. G-355 Joseph—G-425
53. G-426—G-500 Frank S.
54. G-500 Fred—G-612 B.
55. G-612 C.—G-625 Martin J.
56. G-625 Mary—G-650 Marvly
57. G-650 Mary—G-664
58. G-665—H-200 E.
59. H-200 F.—H-250 R.
60. H-250 S.—H-352
61. H-353—H-400 Wilfred
62. H-400 Will—H-513 L.
63. H-513 M.C.—H-535
64. H-536—H-560
65. H-561—H-620 Marie A.
66. H-620 Marion—H-635 Frank P.
67. H-635 Fread—I-526 M.
68. I-526 N.—J-250 Clexon
69. J-250 Clide—J-250
70. J-252—J-520 Henry
71. J-520 Henry A.—J-520 Tim
72. J-520 Tobe—J-525 Graddie
73. J-525 Grady—J-525 Pauline
74. J-525 Pearl—K-140
75. K-142—K-450 F.
76. K-450 G.C.—K-530 Goldie
77. K-530 Grace—L-000 E.
78. L-000 F.—L-143
79. L-144—L-200 A.
80. L-200 B.—L-200 Will S.
81. L-200 Willard—L-255
82. L-256—L-426
83. L-430—L-523 I.
84. L-523 J.—L-553
85. L-554—M-000
86. M-100—M-210
87. M-211—M-240 I.
88. M-240 J.—M-252 H.
89. M-252 I.—M-265 C.
90. M-265 D.—M-343
91. M-345—M-430 Paul
92. M-430 Pearl—M-460
93. M-462—M-540 Anise
94. M-540 Ann—M-600 O.
95. M-600 P.—M-620 Patrick
96. M-620 Paul—M-635 D.
97. M-635 E.—N-000
98. N-100—N-400 Jethro
99. N-400 Jim—N-635 E.
100. N-635 F.—O-520 H.
101. O-520 I.—P-200 Myuel
102. P-200 Nancy—P-360 O.
103. P-360 Paul—P-412 L.
104. P-412 M.—P-526
105. P-530—P-620 James
106. P-620 James A.—P-626 Q.
107. P-626 R.—P-653
108. P-654—R-151
109. R-152—R-163 Elizah
110. R-163 Ella—R-200 R.
111. R-200 S.—R-253
112. R-254—R-266
113. R-300—R-360
114. R-361—R-532
115. R-533—S-100 P.
116. S-100 R.—S-164
117. S-165—S-300 J.
118. S-300 K.—S-336
119. S-340—S-363 L.
120. S-363 M.—S-420 O.
121. S-420 P.—S-516
122. S-520—S-530 B.
123. S-530 C.—S-530 Marvin W.
124. S-530 Mary—S-535
125. S-536—S-560 C.
126. S-560 D.—S-636
127. S-640—T-260 F.
128. T-260 G.—T-460 Elliot
129. T-460 Ellis—T-515
130. T-516—T-520 S.
131. T-520 T.—T-630 R.
132. T-630 S.—T-656 L.
133. T-656 M.—V-450
134. V-451—V-653
135. V-654—W-252 E.
136. W-252 F.—W-300 F.
137. W-300 G.—W-320 V.
138. W-320 W.—W-400 T.
139. W-400 V.—W-425 C.
140. W-425 D.—W-426 K.
141. W-426 L.—W-451
142. W-452—W-452 Jodeen
143. W-452 Joe—W-452
144. W-453—W-623 I.
145. W-623 J.—Y-520 Jimmie
146. Y-520 Joe—Institutions

### Mississippi (M2055)

1. A-000—A-325 L.
2. A-325 M.—A-422
3. A-423—A-450 Sally

4. A-450 Sam—A-536 Henry
5. A-536 Henry C.—B-000 L.
6. B-000 M.—B-230 I.
7. B-230 J.—B-260 F.
8. B-260 G.—B-335
9. B-340—B-400 L.
10. B-400 M.—B-424
11. B-425—B-463
12. B-500—B-530 I.
13. B-530 J.—B-616
14. B-620—B-621
15. B-622—B-630
16. B-631—B-636
17. B-640—B-650 I.
18. B-650 J.—B-650 S.
19. B-650 T.—B-652
20. B-653—B-663
21. C-000—C-165
22. C-200—C-245
23. C-246—C-400 K.
24. C-400 L.—C-435
25. C-436—C-455 L.
26. C-455 M.—C-462
27. C-463—C-534
28. C-535—C-600
29. C-610—C-624
30. C-625—C-636 L.
31. C-636 M.—C-663
32. D-000—D-120 K.
33. D-120 L.—D-151
34. D-152—D-250
35. D-251—D-450
36. D-452—D-525
37. D-526—D-620
38. D-621—E-162
39. E-163—E-362
40. E-363—E-435
41. E-436—F-236
42. F-240—F-434
43. F-435—F-536
44. F-540—F-630
45. F-631—F-655
46. F-656—G-230
47. G-231—G-416
48. G-420—G-500
49. G-510—G-600
50. G-610—G-625
51. G-626—G-650 D.
52. G-650 E.—G-653 Q.
53. G-653 R.—H-160
54. H-161—H-216
55. H-220—H-252 L.
56. H-252 M.—H-324
57. H-325—H-400 Damsey
58. H-400 Dan—H-400 S.
59. H-400 T.—H-452 H.
60. H-452 I.—H-514
61. H-515—H-535 K.
62. H-535 L.—H-543
63. H-544—H-616
64. H-620—H-620 V.
65. H-620 W.—H-630 Q.
66. H-630 R.—H-651
67. H-652—I-615
68. I-620—J-250 G.
69. J-250 H.—J-400
70. J-410—J-520 F.
71. J-520 G.—J-520 Master
72. J-520 Mat—J-522
73. J-523—J-525 E.
74. J-525 F.—J-525 L.
75. J-525 M.—J-525 Wille B.
76. J-525 Willie—K-162
77. K-200—K-452

78. K-453—K-523 L.
79. K-523 M.—L-000 E.
80. L-000 F.—L-134
81. L-135—L-200 K.
82. L-200 L.—L-246
83. L-250—L-355
84. L-356—L-520 I.
85. L-520 J.—L-560
86. L-561—M-162
87. M-163—M-200 N.
88. M-200 O.—M-231
89. M-232—M-240
90. M-241—M-246
91. M-250—M-252
92. M-253—M261
93. M-262—M323
94. M-324—M-416
95. M-420—M-456
96. M-460—M-516
97. M-520—M-565
98. M-600—M-600 O.
99. M-600 P.—M-620 Joel T.
100. M-620 John—M-625
101. M-626—M-640
102. M-641—N-242
103. N-243—N-425
104. N-426—O-242
105. O-243—O-540
106. O-544—P-200
107. P-210—P-353
108. P-355—P-400
109. P-410—P-465
110. P-500—P-620 F.
111. P-620 G.—P-625 R.
112. P-625 S.—P-636 M.
113. P-636 N.—R-000
114. R-100—R-152 U.
115. R-152 V.—R-163
116. R-165—R-216
117. R-220—R-262 I.
118. R-262 J.—R-300
119. R-310—R-400
120. R-410—R-540
121. R-541—S-151
122. S-152—S-216
123. S-220—S-300
124. S-310—S-324
125. S-325—S-353
126. S-354—S-363 R.
127. S-363 S.—S-416
128. S-420—S-500
129. S-510—S-526
130. S-530—S-530 G.
131. S-530 H.—S-530 Marvin
132. S-530 Mary—S-530
133. S-531—S-550
134. S-551—S-626
135. S-630—T-260
136. T-261—T-460 C.
137. T-460 D.—T-500
138. T-510—T-520 D.
139. T-520 E.—T-524
140. T-525—T-626
141. T-630—T-656 K.
142. T-656 L.—V-465
143. V-500—W-200
144. W-210—W-252
145. W-253—W-300 M.

146. W-300 N.—W-324
147. W-325—W-350
148. W-352—W-416
149. W-420—W-420
150. W-421—W-425
151. W-426—W-435
152. W-436—W-452 Elgern
153. W-452 Eli—W-452 K.
154. W-452 L.—W-452 V.
155. W-452 W.—W-564
156. W-600—W-634
157. W-635—Y-520 L.
158. Y-520 M.—Institutions

### North Carolina (M2056)

1. A-100—A-260
2. A-261—A-416 J.
3. A-416 K.—A-450 H.
4. A-450 I.—A-536 I.
5. A-536 J.—A-654 F.
6. A-654 G.—B-210 P.
7. B-210 R.—B-251
8. B-252—B-300 E.
9. B-300 F.—B-350 E.
10. B-350 F.—B-400 U.
11. B-400 V.—B-424 E.
12. B-424 F.—B-453 C.
13. B-453 D.—B-500
14. B-510—B-534 E.
15. B-534 F.—B-616 B.
16. B-616 C.—B-620 Wilime
17. B-620 Will—B-630
18. B-630 C.—B-632 V.
19. B-632 W.—B-645
20. B-650—B-650 Knox
21. B-650 L.—B-652 Clarence
22. B-652 Clarence A.—B-653 Furestine
23. B-653 G.—B-660 V.
24. B-660 W.—C-152 E.
25. C-152 F.—C-200 Ivy
26. C-200 J.—C-244
27. C-245—C-400 B.
28. C-400 C.—C-434 T.
29. C-434 U.—C-455 J.
30. C-455 K.—C-500 Ramson
31. C-500 Ray—C-530 M.
32. C-530 N.—C-600 George
33. C-600 George A.—C-616 R.
34. C-616 S.—C-626 E.
35. C-626 F.—C-636 Willest
36. C-636 William—C-655 F.
37. C-655 G.—D-120 James
38. D-120 James A.—D-140
39. D-141—D-250 G.
40. D-250 H.—D-350
41. D-352—D-500 Q.
42. D-500 R.—D-542 I.
43. D-542 J.—E-145
44. E-146—E-250 L.
45. E-250 M.—E-363 Maxwell
46. E-363 May—E-456
47. E-460—F-200
48. F-210—F-416
49. F-420—F-460 C.
50. F-460 D.—F-612 I.
51. F-612 J.—F-640 L.

52. F-640 M.—G-000 F.
53. G-000 G.—G-300 H.
54. G-300 I.—G-400 V.
55. G-400 W.—G-466
56. G-500—G-600
57. G-610—G-625 F.
58. G-625 G.—G-650 A.
59. G-650 B.—G-652 C.
60. G-652 D.—H-125 J.
61. H-125 K.—H-200 James
62. H-200 James A.—H-235 R.
63. H-235 S.—H-263
64. H-265—H-325 Jettie
65. H-325 Jim—H-400 Ezra
66. H-400 F.—H-400 S.
67. H-400 T.—H-436 V.
68. H-436 W.—H-500 P.
69. H-500 R.—H-523 Z.
70. H-524—H-536 F.
71. H-536-G.—H-562 I.
72. H-562 J.—H-620 K.
73. H-620 L.—H-630 B.
74. H-630 C.—H-635 I.
75. H-635 J.—H-652 R.
76. H-652 S.—J-160
77. J-162—J-250 P.
78. J-250 R.—J-520 F.
79. J-520 G.—J-520 O.
80. J-520 P.—J-525 Chessly
81. J-525 Chester—J-525 L.
82. J-525 M.—J-560 M.
83. J-560 N.—K-260 M.
84. K-260 N.—K-520 A.
85. K-520 B.—K-530 V.
86. K-530 W.—L-000 F.
87. L-000 G.—L-152 M.
88. L-152 N.—L-200 V.
89. L-200 W.—L-250 V.
90. L-250 W.—L-346
91. L-350—L-510
92. L-512—L-522 F.
93. L-522 G.—L-500 E.
94. L-600 F.—M-200 B.
95. M-200 C.—M-213
96. M-214—M-235 K.
97. M-235 L.—M-243 K.
98. M-243 L.—M250 D.
99. M-250 E.—M-254 D.
100. M-254 E.—M-260 R.
101. M-260 S.—M-320 P.
102. M-320 Q.—M-400 I.
103. M-400 J.—M-456
104. M-460—M-500 V.
105. M-500 W.—M-562
106. M-563—M-600 Mary
107. M-600 Mary A.—M-620 G.
108. M-620 H.—M-625 L.
109. M-625 M.—M-635 S.
110. M-635 T.—N-250 H.
111. N-250 I.—N-520 F.
112. N-520 G.—O-216
113. O-220—O-520
114. O-521—P-200 L.
115. P-200 M.—P-322
116. P-323—P-362 R.
117. P-362 S.—P-412 I.
118. P-412 J.—P-500 Q.
119. P-500 R.—P-600 V.
120. P-600 W.—P-620 Q.
121. P-620 R.—P-626 Charles
122. P-626 Charles A.—P-635
123. P-636—R-100 K.
124. R-100 L.—R-152
125. R-153—R-200 C.

126. R-200 D.—R-233
127. R-234—R-262 V.
128. R-262 W.—R-320 H.
129. R-320 I.—R-420 J.
130. R-420 K.—R-543 L
131. R-543 M.—S-136
132. S-140—S-163 Jerry
133. S-163 Jess—S-255 L.
134. S-255 M.—S-315 R.
135. S-315 S.—S-340 L.
136. S-340 M.—S-352 M.
137. S-352 N.—S-363 James
138. S-363 James A.—S-416 V.
139. S-416 W.—S-500 E.
140. S-500 F.—S-525 M.
141. S-525 N.—S-530 Gracy
142. S-530 Gradie—S-530 Marjorie
143. S-530 Mark—S-534
144. S-535—S-552 J.
145. S-552 K.—S-620 S.
146. S-620 T.—T-232
147. T-233—T-400 I.
148. T-400 J.—T-460 Marth
149. T-460 Martha—T-512 S.
150. T-512 T.—T-532
151. T-534—T-640 R.
152. T-640 S.—U-536 M.
153. U-536 N.—W-100 A.
154. W-100 B.—W-235
155. W-236—W-300 F.
156. W-300 G.—W-314 J.
157. W-314 K.—W-326 F.
158. W-326 G.—W-362 A.
159. W-362-B—W-420 Charles
160. W-420 Charles A.—W-424
161. W-425—W-425 William
162. W-425 William A.—W-446
163. W-450—W-452 Herbert
164. W-452 Herma—W-452 Romie
165. W-452 Roney—W-523 F.
166. W-523 G.—W-630 E.
167. W-630 F.—Y-230
168. Y-240—Z-563
169. Z-565—Institutions

### South Carolina (M2057)

1. A-000—A-346
2. A-350—A-450 Eber C.
3. A-450 Ed—A-550
4. A-552—B-210 Wilford
5. B-210 Will—B-260 R.
6. B-260 S.—B-361
7. B-362—B-424 H.
8. B-424 I.—B-456
9. B-460—B-530
10. B-531—B-620 Hickman Sr.
11. B-620 Hiram—B-625 O.
12. B-625 P.—B-635 F.
13. B-635 G.—B-650 Henrietta
14. B-650 Henry—B-650 Toby
15. B-650 Tom—B-653-V.
16. B-653 W.—C-160 F.
17. C-160 G.—C-235 P.
18. C-235 R.—C-400 R.
19. C-400 S.—C-452 L.
20. C-452 M.—C-510 O.
21. C-510 P.—C-550
22. C-552—C-616
23. C-620—C-636 R.
24. C-636 S.—D-120 Clearous
25. D-120 Clede—D-125
26. D-130—D-250 L.

27. D-250 M.—D-500
28. D-510—D-612
29. D-613—E-152 O.
30. E-152 P.—E-420 M.
31. E-420 N.—F-236 L.
32. F-236 M.—F-436 G.
33. F-436 H.—F-600 L.
34. F-600 M.—F-652 E.
35. F-652 F.—G-220
36. G-230—G-360
37. G-362—G-451
38. G-452—G-600 E.
39. G-600 F.—G-626 S.
40. G-626 T.—G-650 Jasper
41. G-650 Jeff—G-654
42. G-655—H-200 S.
43. H-200 T.—H-300 D.
44. H-300 E.—H-400 Ell
45. H-400 Ella—H-435 P.
46. H-435 R.—H-520 Jhne
47. H-520 Jim—H-542
48. H-543—H-620 L.
49. H-620 M.—H-635 M.
50. H-635 N.—J-123
51. J-125—J-300
52. J-320—J-520 J.
53. J-520 K.—J-525 Clare
54. J-525 Clark—J-525 Marvin
55. J-525 Mary—J-635 L.
56. J-635 M.—K-500
57. K-510—K-600
58. K-610—L-152
59. L-153—L-250 M
60. L-250 N.—L-512
61. L-513—L-600 E.
62. L-600 F.—M-200 K.
63. M-200 L.—M-233
64. M-234—M-242
65. M-243—M-252 G.
66. M-252 H.—M-263 L.
67. M-263 M—M-342
68. M-343—M-460 C.
69. M-460 D.—M-532
70. M-533—M-600
71. M-610—M-630
72. M-631—N-242 C.
73. N-242 D.—N-620
74. N-621—O-520 S.
75. O-520 T.—P-300 M.
76. P-300 N.—P-400 V.
77. P-400 W.—P-536 I.
78. P-536 J.—P-625 D.
79. P-625 E.—P-653
80. P-654—R-152 I.
81. R-152 J.—R-163 S.
82. R-163 T.—R-250 L.
83. R-250 M.—R-300 Jobe
84. R-300 Joe—R-453 I.
85. R-453 J.—S-130
86. S-131—S-250
87. S-252—S-320 I.
88. S-320 J.—S-361 L.
89. S-361 M.—S-414
90. S-415—S-512 S.
91. S-512 T.—S-530 C.
92. S-530 D.—S-530 Q.
93. S-530 R.—S-540 G.
94. S-540 H.—S-500 E.
95. S-600 F.—T-265
96. T-300—T-460 V.
97. T-460 W.—T-520 John
98. T-520 John A.—T-641
99. T-642—V-536
100. V-540—W-252 D.

101. W-252 E.—W-300 M.
102. W-300 N.—W-340 K.
103. W-340 L.—W-420 F.
104. W-420 G.—W-425 R.
105. W-425 S.—W-452 A.
106. W-452 B.—W-452 L.
107. W-452 M.—W-552
108. W-553—W-655
109. W-656—Institutions

### Tennessee (M2058)

Rolls 7, 8, and 9 have the wrong targets.
Roll 7 reads roll 6, roll 8 reads roll 7, and
roll 9 reads roll 8. Roll 6 has no target.

1. A-000—A-321
2. A-322—A-416 V.
3. A-416 W.—A-450 R.
4. A-450 S.—A-536 R.
5. A-536 S.—A-666
6. B-000—B-210 L.
7. B-210 M.—B-255 J.
8. B-255 K.—B-300 L.
9. B-300 M.—M-364
10. B-365—B-415 M.
11. B-415 N.—B-435 A.
12. B-435 B.—B-460
13. B-461—B-530 E.
14. B-530 F.—B-600 H.
15. B-600 I.—B-620 J.
16. B-620 K.—B-625 E.
17. B-625 F.—B-631 Jody
18. B-631 Joe—B-635
19. B-636—B-650 H.
20. B-650 I.—B-650 William
21. B-650 William A.—B-653 G.
22. B-653 H.—B-660
23. B-661—C-160 E.
24. C-160 F.—C-200 Q.
25. C-200 R.—C-300 I.
26. C-300 J.—C-400 N.
27. C-400 O.—C-434
28. C-435—C-455 Jim T.
29. C-455 Joe—C-500 A.
30. C-500 B.—C-516 Q.
31. C-516 R.—C-552 J.
32. C-552 K.—C-615 D.
33. C-615 E.—C-621 H.
34. C-621 I.—C-635 R.
35. C-635 S.—C-640 V.
36. C-640 W.—D-100 L.
37. D-100 M.—D-120 M.
38. D-120 N.—D-200 E.
39. D-200 F.—D-250 Wiley
40. D-250 Will—D-400 C.
41. D-400 D.—D-500 R.
42. D-500 S.—D-541 N.
43. D-541 O.—D-646
44. D-650—E-232 I.
45. E-232 J.—E-363 M.
46. E-363 N.—E-516
47. E-520—F 230 R.
48. F-230 S.—F-420 M.
49. F-420 N.—F-460 H.
50. F-460 I.—F-620
51. F-621—F-640 F.
52. F-640 G.—F-662 I.
53. F-662 J.—G-243
54. G-245—G-412
55. G-413—G-452
56. G-453—G-600 A.
57. G-600 B.—G-616
58. G-620—G-635 B.

59. G-635-C.—G-650 M.
60. G-650 N.—G-665
61. H-000—H-200 B.
62. H-200 C.—H-200
63. H-210—H-250-O.
64. H-250 P.—H-300 Wiley
65. H-300 Will—H-340 M.
66. H-340 N.—H-400 Hershell W.
67. H-400 Hessie—H-400 Willianett
68. H-400 Willie—H-452-G.
69. H-452 H.—H-516 Jay
70. H-516 Jean—H-526
71. H-530—H-540 F.
72. H-540 G—H-614 L.
73. H-614 M.—H-620 Wiley
74. H-620 Will—H-630 P.
75. H-630 Q.—H-650 K.
76. H-650 L.—I-650
77. I-652—J-250 R.
78. J-250 S.—J-520 E.
79. J-520 F.—J-520 O.
80. J-520 P.—J-525 Cling
81. J-525 Clint—J-525 L.
82. J-525 M.—J-560 L.
83. J-560 M.—K-300 G.
84. K-300 H.—K-460 G.
85. K-460 H.—K-523 C.
86. K-523 D.—K-621 L.
87. K-621 M.—L-100 L.
88. L-100 M.—L-200 H.
89. L-200 I.—L-250 C.
90. L-250 D.—L-350 G.
91. L-350 H.—L-510 L.
92. L-510 M.—L-524
93. L-525—L-645
94. L-650—M-200 G.
95. M-200 H.—M-216 I.
96. M-216 J.—M-240 F.
97. M-240 G.—M-245 R.
98. M-245 S.—M252 G.
99. M-252 H.—M260 M.
100. M-260 N.—M-320 I.
101. M-320 J.—M-350 S.
102. M-350 T.—M-450
103. M-451.—M-465 J.
104. M-465 K.—M-550 I.
105. M-550 J.—M-600 J.
106. M-600 K.—M-620 E.
107. M-620 F.—M-625 Jimmy
108. M-625 Jo—M-635 P.
109. M-635 Q.—N-200 L.
110. N-200 M.—N-400 Q.
111. N-400 R.—N-630 B.
112. N-630 C.—O-256
113. O-260—O-540 O.
114. O-540 P.—P-200 Wiley
115. P-200 Will—P-350 B.
116. P-350 C.—P-400 G.
117. P-400 H.—P-425 L.
118. P-425 M.—P-536 J.
119. P-536 K.—P-620 H.
120. P-620 I.—P-625 Joe
121. P-625 John—P-632 M.
122. P-632 N.—Q-653
123. R-000—R-152 H.
124. R-152 I.—R-163 L.
125. R-163 M.—R-200 Rex
126. R-200 Rhea—R-250

127. R-251—R-263 Q.
128. R-263—R-326 L.
129. R-326 M.—R-453 C.
130. R-453 D.—R-541
131. R-542—S-130 K.
132. S-130 L.—S-163 L.
133. S-163 M.—S-300 Hassey
134. S-300 Hattie—S-316 M.
135. S-316 N.—S-346 H.
136. S-346 I.—S-361 E.
137. S-361 F.—S-365 O.
138. S-365 P.—S-432 C.
139. S-432 D.—S-500
140. S-510—S-530 A.
141. S-530 B.—S-530 I.
142. S-530 J.—S-530 Rastus
143. S-530 Ray—S-536 E.
144. S-536 F.—S-560 P.
145. S-560 R.—S-630 V.
146. S-630 W.—T-260 D.
147. T-260 E.—T-416 R.
148. T-416 S.—T 460 O.
149. T-460 P.—T-513
150. T-514—T-525
151. T-525 N.—T-631
152. T-632—T-656 R.
153. T-656 S.—V-543 C.
154. V-453 D.—W-100 V.
155. W-100 W.—W-250 C.
156. W-250 D.—W-300 Jake
157. W-300 James—W-320 G.
158. W-320 H.—W-326 J.
159. W-326 K.—W-363 L.
160. W-363 M.—W-420 Jiles
161. W-420 Jim—W-425 James
162. W-425 James A.—W-426 John
163. W-426 John A.—W-452 A.
164. W-452 B.—W-452 Loy
165. W-452 Loyd—W-513
166. W-514—W-623 H.
167. W-623 I.—W-650 M.
168. W-650 N.—Y-616 M.
169. Y-616 N.—Institutions

### Virginia (M2059)

1. A-000—A-235
2. A-236—A-415
3. A-416—A-530
4. A-532—A-650
5. A-651—B-200
6. B-210—B-260 G.
7. B-260 H.—B-346 E.
8. B-346 F.—B-400 William
9. B-400 William A.—B-435
10. B-436—B-500 V.
11. B-500 W.—B-556
12. B-560—B-620 J.
13. B-620 K.—B-626 D.
14. B-626 E.—B-635 E.
15. B-635 F.—B-650 G.
16. B-650 H.—B-652 C.
17. B-652 D.—B-656 F.
18. B-656 G.—C-160 T.
19. C-160 U.—C-240 H.
20. C-240 I.—C-412
21. C-413—C-452 G.

22. C-452 H.—C-462 I.
23. C 462 J.—C-516 D.
24. C-516 E.—C-600 G.
25. C-600 H.—C-620 R.
26. C-620 S.—C-636 Clemmie
27. C-636 Cleo—C-650 L.
28. C-650 M.—D-120 G.
29. D-120 H.—D-162
30. D-163—D-262 P.
31. D-262 R.—D-450 B.
32. D-450 C.—D-534
33. D-535—D-656
34. D-660—E-322
35. E-324—E-430 J.
36. E-430 K.—F-236 I.
37. F-236 J.—F-430 E.
38. F-430 F.—F-516
39. F-520—F-626
40. F-630—F-656 R.
41. F-656 S—G-324
42. G-325—G-430 I.
43. G-430 J.—G-600 F.
44. G-600 G.—G-625 C.
45. G-625 D.—G-650 Jim
46. G-650 Joan—H-125 G.
47. H-125 H.—H-200 L.
48. H-200 M.—H-252 H.
49. H-252 I.—H-325 I.
50. H-325 J.—H-400 Giles
51. H-400 Gillie—H-424
52. H-425—H-510
53. H-512—H-534
54. H-535—H-610
55. H-612—H-622
56. H-623—H-635 B.
57. H-635 C.—I 600
58. I-610—J-250 L.
59. J-250 M.—J-520 F.
60. J-520 G.—J-520 Snowden
61. J-520 Sol—J-525 G.
62. J-525 H.—J-525 Tolliver
63. J-525 Tom—K-200 M.
64. K-200 N.—K-460 N.
65. K-460 O.—K-542
66. K-543—L-125 G.
67. L-125 H.—L-200 M.
68. L-200 N.—L-262
69. L-263—L-516 D.
70. L-516 E.—L-550 I.
71. L-550 J.—M-200 E.
72. M-200 F.—M-235 R.
73. M-235 S.—M-250 V.
74. M-250 W.—M-320 B.
75. M-320 C.—M-414
76. M-415—M-460 I.
77. M-460 J.—M-532
78. M-533—M-600 R.
79. M-600 S.—M-620 William
80. M-620 William A.—M-635 H.
81. M-635 I.—N-241
82. N-242—N-532
83. N-540—O-415
84. O-416—P-200 C.
85. P-200 D.—P-355
86. P-356—P-412 J.
87. P-412 K.—P-500 V.
88. P-500 W.—P-620 E.
89. P-620 F.—P-626 M.
90. P-626 N—Q-426
91. Q-450—R-152 Marvin
92. R-152 Mary—R-200 C.
93. R-200 D.—R-245 M.
94. R-245 N.—R-300 I.
95. R-300 J.—R-360 K.

96. R-360 L.—R-534 J.
97. R-534 K.—S-142
98. S-143—S-163 N.
99. S-163 O.—S-300 M.
100. S-300 N.—S-330 I.
101. S-330 J.—S-354 I.
102. S-354 J.—S-365 P.
103. S-365 R.—S-446
104. S-450—S-525
105. S-526—S-530 Jasper
106. S-530 Jay—S-530 Williard
107. S-530 Willie—S-552 O.
108. S-552 P.—S-636
109. S-640—T-340
110. T-341—T-460 John
111. T-460 John A.—T-512 R.
112. T-512 S.—T-525 P.
113. T-525 R.—T-651
114. T-652—U-536 J.
115. U-536 K.—V-565
116. V-600—W-246
117. W-250—W-300 H.
118. W-300 I.—W-320 K.
119. W-320 L.—W-346
120. W-350—W-420 I.
121. W-420 J.—W-425 R.
122. W-425 S.—W-436 L.
123. W-436 M.—W-452 L.
124. W-452 M.—W-520 K.
125. W-520 L.—W-623
126. W-624—Y-520 Jettie
127. Y-520 Jim—Institutions

35. T-420—T-655
36. T-656—W-300
37. W-310—W-426
38. W-430—W-656
39. X-522—Institutions

### West Virginia (M2060)

Includes the following counties: Fayette, Harrison, Kanawha, Logan, McDowell, Mercer, and Raleigh. The other West Virginia counties have **not** been Soundexed.

1. A-100—A-325
2. A-650—B-400
3. B-410—B-560
4. B-600—B-646
5. B-650—C-166
6. C-200—C-445
7. C-450—C-560
8. C-600—C-663
9. D-000—D-256
10. D-260—D-660
11. E-000—F-263
12. F-300—F-630
13. F-631—G-450
14. G-452—G-663
15. H-000—H-326
16. H-330—H-452
17. H-453—H-620
18. H-621—J-463
19. J-500—J-654
20. K-000—K-665
21. L-000—L-366
22. L-400—M-200
23. M-210—M-300
24. M-312—M-460
25. M-462—M-625
26. M-626—O-265
27. O-300—P-440
28. P-450—P-636
29. P-640—R-246
30. R-250—R-660
31. S-000—S-316
32. S-320—S-432
33. S-435—S-532
34. S-533—T-416

*"Sorting and Packing Shed of American Fruit Growers, Inc., Wenatchee, Wash., 1922"*
*(86-G-1D-5).*

# 1930 Census
## *Schedules*

### T626
### 2,667 ROLLS

The 1930 census schedules are arranged by state or territory and thereunder by county. The counties are not necessarily listed in alphabetical order. Be sure to review the listings for the entire state or territory before placing your order.

For the 1930 census, the Bureau of the Census developed a new ED numbering system. Within each state, each county has a distinct number that is followed by the specific enumeration district number. The county numbers were assigned based on the alphabetical order of the counties. For example, Adams County, Washington, has counties 1-1 to 1-22.

This microfilm has been reproduced by the National Archives and Records Administration from the highest quality master negatives available from the Bureau of the Census. The original film includes defects that affect the legibility of some frames; the original schedules no longer exits.

## *Alabama*

1. Autauga   EDs 1-1 to 1-16
   Barbour   EDs 3-1 to 3-26
2. Baldwin   EDs 2-1 to 2-8, 2-22, 2-9 to 2-10, 2-23, 2-11 to 2-14, 2-24, 2-15 to 2-21
   Bibb   EDs 4-1 to 4-20
   Bullock   EDs 6-5 to 6-11
3. Bullock   EDs 6-1 to 6-4, 6-12 to 6-24
   Chambers   EDs 9-1, 9-5, 9-10, 9-13, 9-2 to 9-4, 9-6 to 9-9, 9-11 to 9-12, 9-14 to 9-31
4. Blount   EDs 5-1 to 5-41
   Butler   EDs 7-1 to 7-28
5. Calhoun   EDs 8-1 to 8-21, 8-43 to 8-46, 8-22 to 8-24, 8-47, 8-25 to 8-33, 8-48 to 8-49, 8-34, 8-50, 8-35 to 8-42
6. Cherokee   EDs 10-1 to 10-25
   Choctaw   EDs 12-1 to 12-5, 12-19, 12-6 to 12-18
   Clay   EDs 14-1 to 14-19
7. Chilton   EDs 11-1 to 11-22
   Clarke   EDs 13-1 to 13-27
8. Cleburne   EDs 15-1 to 15-18
   Coffee   EDs 16-1 to 16-32
9. Colbert   EDs 17-1 to 17-7, 17-8 (NP), 17-9 to 17-34
   Conecuh   EDs 18-1 to 18-21
10. Coosa   EDs 19-1 to 19-24
    Covington   EDs 20-1 to 20-28, 20-29 (NP), 20-30 to 20-35
11. Crenshaw   EDs 21-1 to 21-23
    Cullman   EDs 22-1 to 22-22
12. Cullman   EDs 22-23 to 22-33
    De Kalb   EDs 25-1 to 25-24, 25-39, 25-25 to 25-38
13. Dale   EDs 23-1 to 23-20
    Elmore   EDs 26-3 to 26-5, 26-1 to 26-2, 26-6 to 26-10, 26-26, 26-11 to 26-25, 26-27 to 26-29
14. Dallas   EDs 24-1 to 24-41
15. Escambia   EDs 27-1 to 27-11, 27-18, 27-12 to 27-17
16. Etowah   EDs 28-1 to 28-5, 28-59, 28-6, 28-63, 28-7, 28-60, 28-8 to 28-12, 28-61, 28-13 to 28-15, 28-44, 28-51, 28-16 to 28-43, 28-45 to 28-46, 28-52 to 28-58
17. Etowah   EDs 28-47 to 28-50, 28-62
    Fayette   EDs 29-1 to 29-24
    Franklin   EDs 30-1 to 30-24
18. Geneva   EDs 31-1 to 31-24
    Greene   EDs 32-1 to 32-16
    Henry   EDs 34-1 to 34-8
19. Henry   EDs 34-9 to 34-19
    Houston   EDs 35-3 to 35-8, 35-1 to 35-2, 35-9 to 35-29
20. Hale   EDs 33-1 to 33-22
    Jackson   EDs 36-1 to 36-30
21. Jackson   EDs 36-31 to 36-46
    Lamar   EDs 38-1 to 38-26
    Jefferson   EDs 37-109 to 37-119
22. Jefferson   EDs 37-108, 37-120 to 37-130, 37-136 to 37-137, 37-142 to 37-144, 37-1 to 37-6
23. Jefferson, Birmingham City   EDs 37-7 to 37-8, 37-219, 37-9, 37-147, 37-10 to 37-17, 37-198
24. Jefferson, Birmingham City   EDs 37-18 to 37-22
25. Jefferson, Birmingham City   EDs 37-23 to 37-43
26. Jefferson, Birmingham City   EDs 37-44 to 37-58
27. Jefferson, Birmingham City   EDs 37-59 to 37-73
28. Jefferson, Birmingham City   EDs 37-74 to 37-87
29. Jefferson, Birmingham City   EDs 37-88 to 37-97
30. Jefferson, Birmingham City   EDs 37-98 to 37-107
31. Jefferson   EDs 37-131 to 37-135, 37-138, 37-140, 37-139, 37-141, 37-145 to 37-146, 37-148 to 37-170
32. Jefferson   EDs 37-171 to 37-175, 37-176 (void), 37-177 to 37-181, 37-182 (NP), 37-183 to 37-197, 37-199 to 37-203, 37-215 to 37-216
33. Jefferson   EDs 37-204 to 37-214, 37-217 to 37-218
    Lauderdale   EDs 39-1 to 39-13, 39-24 to 39-33
34. Lauderdale   EDs 39-14 to 39-23
    Lee   EDs 41-1 to 41-8, 41-28, 41-9 to 41-27
35. Lawrence   EDs 40-1 to 40-24
    Limestone   EDs 42-1 to 42-22
36. Limestone   EDs 42-23 to 42-27
    Lowndes   EDs 43-1 to 43-22
    Macon   EDs 44-1 to 44-2, 44-4, 44-20, 44-5, 44-3, 44-6 to 44-19
37. Madison   EDs 45-1 to 45-39
38. Madison   EDs 45-40 to 45-45
    Marengo   EDs 46-1 to 46-31
39. Marion   EDs 47-1 to 47-27
    Marshall   EDs 48-1 to 48-24
40. Marshall   EDs 48-25 to 48-34
    Mobile   EDs 49-1 to 49-10, 49-19 to 49-21, 49-11 to 49-18, 49-22 to 49-31
41. Mobile   EDs 49-32 to 49-40, 49-41 (void), 49-42 to 49-72, 49-73 (NP)
42. Mobile   EDs 49-74 to 49-93
    Monroe   EDs 50-1 to 50-23
43. Montgomery   EDs 51-1 to 51-14, 51-36 to 51-38, 51-15 to 51-26, 51-30 to 51-35
44. Montgomery   EDs 51-27 to 51-29, 51-39 to 51-63
    Morgan   EDs 52-1 to 52-10
45. Morgan   EDs 52-11 to 52-37
    Perry   EDs 53-1 to 53-11, 53-13, 53-12, 53-14 to 53-19
46. Pickens   EDs 54-1 to 54-29
    Pike   EDs 55-9 to 55-14, 55-1 to 55-8, 55-15 to 55-30
47. Randolph   EDs 56-1 to 56-22
    Russell   EDs 57-1 to 57-17, 57-18 (NP), 57-19 to 57-21
48. St. Clair   EDs 58-1 to 58-33
    Shelby   EDs 59-1 to 59-8, 59-9 (NP), 59-10 to 59-17, 59-24, 59-18 to 59-23, 59-25 to 59-30
49. Sumter   EDs 60-1 to 60-27
    Talladega   EDs 61-1 to 61-22
50. Talladega   EDs 61-23 to 61-37
    Tallapoosa   EDs 62-8 to 62-13, 62-1 to 62-7, 62-14 to 62-29

51. Tuscaloosa   EDs 63-1 to 63-39
52. Tuscaloosa   EDs 63-40 to 63-52
    Walker   EDs 64-1 to 64-23
53. Walker   EDs 64-24 to 64-46
    Washington   EDs 65-1 to 65-16
    Winston   EDs 67-1 to 67-14
54. Wilcox   EDs 66-1 to 66-30

*Arizona*

55. Apache   EDs 1-1 to 1-23
    Mohave   EDs 8-1 to 8-6, 8-43 (NP), 8-7 to 8-39, 8-40 (NP), 8-41 to 8-42
    Cochise   EDs 2-1 to 2-39, 2-40 (NP), 2-78 (void), 2-41 (NP), 2-42 to 2-44
56. Cochise   EDs 2-45 to 2-77
    Greenlee   EDs 6-1 to 6-9
    Coconino   EDs 3-1, 3-2 (NP), 3-3 to 3-39, 3-40 (NP)
    Graham   EDs 5-1 to 5-10, 5-11 (NP), 5-12 to 5-17, 5-18 (NP), 5-19 to 5-21, 5-22 (NP), 5-23 to 5-24, 5-25 (NP), 5-26 to 5-31
57. Gila   EDs 4-1 to 4-45, 4-46 (NP), 4-47 to 4-55
    Maricopa   EDs 7-1 to 7-16
58. Maricopa   EDs 7-17 to 7-43, 7-44 (NP), 7-45 to 7-58
59. Maricopa   EDs 7-59 to 7-68, 7-69 (NP), 7-70 to 7-96, 7-97 (NP), 7-98 to 7-108
60. Maricopa   EDs 7-109 to 7-133
    Navajo   EDs 9-1 to 9-21
61. Pima   EDs 10-1 to 10-2, 10-71, 10-3 to 10-4, 10-69 to 10-70, 10-5 to 10-12, 10-72 to 10-75, 10-13 (NP), 10-14 to 10-20, 10-76 to 10-79, 10-21 to 10-24, 10-25 to 10-26 (NP), 10-27 to 10-44, 10-63 to 10-68
62. Pima   EDs 10-45 (NP), 10-46 to 10-62
    Santa Cruz   EDs 12-1 to 12-3, 12-5, 12-4, 12-6 to 12-18
    Pinal   EDs 11-1 to 11-29, 11-30 (NP), 11-31 to 11-35
63. Yavapai   EDs 13-1 to 13-4, 13-7 to 13-28, 13-5 to 13-6
    Yuma   EDs 14-1 to 14-11, 14-28, 14-12, 14-29, 14-13 to 14-27

*Arkansas*

64. Arkansas   EDs 1-1 to 1-27
    Ashley   EDs 2-1 to 2-27
65. Baxter   EDs 3-1 to 3-20
    Boone   EDs 5-1 to 5-32
    Benton   EDs 4-1 to 4-33, 4-38 to 4-43
66. Benton   EDs 4-34 to 4-37, 4-44 to 4-57
    Bradley   EDs 6-1 to 6-14, 6-19, 6-15 to 6-18
    Calhoun   EDs 7-1 to 7-15
    Carroll   EDs 8-1 to 8-25
67. Chicot   EDs 9-1 to 9-22
    Clark   EDs 10-1 to 10-26
68. Clay   EDs 11-1 to 11-35
    Cleburne   EDs 12-1 to 12-13, 12-28, 12-14 to 12-27
    Cleveland   EDs 13-1 to 13-17
69. Columbia   EDs 14-1 to 14-27
    Conway   EDs 15-1 to 15-29

70. Craighead   EDs 16-1 to 16-15, 16-25 to 16-34, 16-16 to 16-24, 16-35 to 16-38
    Grant   EDs 27-1 to 27-14
71. Crawford   EDs 17-1 to 17-36
    Crittenden   EDs 18-1 to 18-23
72. Crittenden   EDs 18-24 to 18-32
    Dallas   EDs 20-1 to 20-21
    Cross   EDs 19-1 to 19-18
73. Desha   EDs 21-1 to 21-24
    Drew   EDs 22-1 to 22-9, 22-21, 22-10 to 22-20, 22-22 to 22-26
    Izard   EDs 33-1 to 33-28
74. Faulkner   EDs 23-1 to 23-31
    Franklin   EDs 24-1 to 24-35
    Fulton   EDs 25-1 to 25-19
75. Garland   EDs 26-11 to 26-17, 26-42, 26-18, 26-43, 26-19 to 26-25, 26-1 to 26-10, 26-26 to 26-41
    Howard   EDs 31-1 to 31-31
76. Greene   EDs 28-1 to 28-30
    Hempstead   EDs 29-1 to 29-3, 29-31, 29-4 to 29-23
77. Hempstead   EDs 29-24 to 29-30
    Hot Spring   EDs 30-1 to 30-26
    Independence   EDs 32-1 to 32-42
78. Jackson   EDs 34-1 to 34-25
    Jefferson   EDs 35-1 to 35-5, 35-7, 35-6, 35-66, 35-8 to 35-9, 35-67 to 35-68, 35-10, 35-12 to 35-26, 35-29 to 35-31, 35-65
79. Jefferson   EDs 35-33 to 35-60, 35-27 to 35-28, 35-32, 35-61, 35-11, 35-62 to 35-64
    Johnson   EDs 36-1 to 36-29
80. Lafayette   EDs 37-1 to 37-9, 37-10 (NP), 37-11 to 37-18
    Marion   EDs 45-1 to 45-30
    Lawrence   EDs 38-1 to 38-30
81. Lee   EDs 39-1 to 39-19, 39-28, 39-20 to 39-27
    Lincoln   EDs 40-1 to 40-23
    Little River   EDs 41-1 to 41-8
82. Little River   EDs 41-9 to 41-21
    Madison   EDs 44-1 to 44-30
    Logan   EDs 42-1 to 42-37
83. Lonoke   EDs 43-1 to 43-41
    Monroe   EDs 48-1 to 48-25
84. Miller   EDs 46-1 to 46-23
    Nevada   EDs 50-1 to 50-23
85. Mississippi   EDs 47-1 to 47-30, 47-46, 47-31 to 47-34
86. Mississippi   EDs 47-35 to 47-45
    Montgomery   EDs 49-1 to 49-25
    Newton   EDs 51-1 to 51-29
    Ouachita   EDs 52-1 to 52-13
87. Ouachita   EDs 52-14 to 52-30
    Perry   EDs 53-1 to 53-37
    Phillips   EDs 54-1 to 54-18, 54-26 to 54-28
88. Phillips   EDs 54-19 to 54-25, 54-29 to 54-31
    Pike   EDs 55-1 to 55-22
    Poinsett   EDs 56-1 to 56-25

89. Polk   EDs 57-1 to 57-25

   Searcy   EDs 65-1 to 65-23

   Pope   EDs 58-1 to 58-14, 58-36, 58-15 to 58-28, 58-37, 58-29 to 58-35

90. Prairie   EDs 59-1 to 59-20

   Scott   EDs 64-1 to 64-30

   Pulaski   EDs 60-1 to 60-6, 60-42, 60-43 to 60-44 (NP), 60-45 to 60-57, 60-68 to 60-71

91. Pulaski   EDs 60-7 to 60-32

92. Pulaski   EDs 60-33 to 60-41, 60-58 to 60-67, 60-77, 60-72 to 60-76

93. Randolph   EDs 61-1 to 61-33

   St. Francis   EDs 62-1 to 62-28

94. Saline   EDs 63-1 to 63-31

   Sharp   EDs 68-1 to 68-23

   Sebastian   EDs 66-1 to 66-31, 66-52 to 66-55

95. Sebastian   EDs 66-32 to 66-51

   Sevier   EDs 67-1 to 67-20

   Stone   EDs 69-1 to 69-29

96. Union   EDs 70-1 to 70-2, 70-3 (NP), 70-4, 70-44, 70-5, 70-45, 70-6, 70-46, 70-7, 70-47, 70-8 to 70-14, 70-41 to 70-42, 70-15 to 70-40, 70-43

97. Van Buren   EDs 71-1 to 71-25

   Washington   EDs 72-1 to 72-49

98. White   EDs 73-1 to 73-37, 73-39 to 73-42, 73-38, 73-43 to 73-59

   Woodruff   EDs 74-1 to 74-16

99. Woodruff   EDs 74-17 to 74-21

   Yell   EDs 75-1 to 75-39

## California

100. Alameda   EDs 1-208 to 1-233

101. Alameda, Oakland City   EDs 1-1 to 1-22

102. Alameda, Oakland City   EDs 1-23 to 1-51

103. Alameda, Oakland City   EDs 1-52 to 1-89, 1-90 (void), 1-91 to 1-92

104. Alameda, Oakland City   EDs 1-108 to 1-126, 1-93 to 1-100

105. Alameda, Oakland City   EDs 1-101 to 1-107, 1-127 to 1-135

106. Alameda, Oakland City   EDs 1-136 to 1-156

107. Alameda, Oakland City   EDs 1-157 to 1-181

108. Alameda, Oakland City   EDs 1-182 to 1-207

109. Alameda   EDs 1-234 to 1-271

110. Alameda   EDs 1-331 to 1-339, 1-272 to 1-292

111. Alameda   EDs 1-293 to 1-326

112. Alameda   EDs 1-327 to 1-330, 1-340 to 1-353

   Alpine   EDs 2-1

   Calaveras   EDs 5-1 to 5-10

   Amador   EDs 3-1 to 3-11

   Butte   EDs 4-1 to 4-17

113. Butte   EDs 4-18 to 4-42

   Colusa   EDs 6-1 to 6-11

   Contra Costa   EDs 7-1 to 7-10, 7-60 to 7-61, 7-11 to 7-15, 7-22 to 7-23, 7-62, 7-24

114. Contra Costa   EDs 7-16 to 7-21, 7-25 to 7-37, 7-38 to 7-46, 7-63 to 7-67, 7-47 to 7-59

115. Del Norte   EDs 8-1 to 8-5

El Dorado   EDs 9-1 to 9-10, 9-15, 9-11 to 9-14

   Glenn   EDs 11-1 to 11-16

   Fresno   EDs 10-1 to 10-6, 10-9 to 10-13, 10-66 to 10-77, 10-97 to 10-99

116. Fresno   EDs 10-14 to 10-36

117. Fresno   EDs 10-37 to 10-52, 10-7 to 10-8, 10-53 to 10-65, 10-100 to 10-101

118. Fresno   EDs 10-78 to 10-90, 10-92 to 10-96, 10-102 to 10-107, 10-91, 10-108 (NP), 10-109, 10-111 to 10-122, 10-110 (NP)

   Imperial   EDs 13-1 to 13-9

119. Imperial   EDs 13-11 to 13-17, 13-18 (NP), 13-19 to 13-31, 13-33, 13-32, 13-34 to 13-42, 13-10, 13-43, 13-45 (NP), 13-44, 13-46 to 13-47, 13-50, 13-48 to 13-49, 13-51

   Inyo   EDs 14-1 to 14-4, 14-9, 14-5, 14-10, 14-6 to 14-8

120. Humboldt   EDs 12-1 to 12-25, 12-59, 12-26 to 12-58

   Lake   EDs 17-1 to 17-7

121. Kern   EDs 15-1 to 15-6, 15-31 to 15-47, 15-56 to 15-59, 15-61 to 15-62, 15-7 to 15-16, 15-18 to 15-28, 15-60

122. Kern   EDs 15-29 to 15-30, 15-17, 15-48 to 15-55, 15-63 to 15-67

   Kings   EDs 16-1 to 16-6, 16-15 to 16-26, 16-7 to 16-14

123. Lassen   EDs 18-1 to 18-3, 18-18, 18-4 to 18-13, 18-19, 18-14 to 18-15, 18-16 to 18-17 (NP)

   Los Angeles   EDs 19-796 to 19-803, 19-805 to 19-813, 19-804, 19-814 to 19-818, 19-1561 to 19-1573

124. Los Angeles   EDs 19-1574 to 19-1578, 19-819 to 19-843, 19-860 to 19-862, 19-866, 19-898 to 19-910

125. Los Angeles   EDs 19-844 to 19-859, 19-863 to 19-865, 19-879 to 19-883, 19-867 to 19-878, 19-884 to 19-889, 19-891 to 19-897

126. Los Angeles   EDs 19-911, 19-890, 19-912 to 19-927, 19-935 to 19-938, 19-1037, 19-1051, 19-928 to 19-934, 19-939 to 19-952

127. Los Angeles   EDs 19-953 to 19-989

128. Los Angeles   EDs 19-990 to 19-995, 19-996 (NP), 19-1002 to 19-1025

   Los Angeles, Long Beach City   EDs 19-997 to 19-1001, 19-1026 to 19-1036, 19-1060 to 19-1068

129. Los Angeles, Long Beach City   EDs 19-1069 to 19-1112

130. Los Angeles, Long Beach City   EDs 19-1113 to 19-1142

131. Los Angeles, Long Beach City   EDs 19-1143 to 19-1153, 19-1154 (NP), 19-1155, 19-1188

   Los Angeles   EDs 19-1038 to 19-1046, 19-1047 (NP), 19-1048 to 19-1050, 19-1052 to 19-1059

132. Los Angeles, Los Angeles City   EDs 19-1 to 19-23

133. Los Angeles, Los Angeles City   EDs 19-24 to 19-53

134. Los Angeles, Los Angeles City   EDs 19-54 to 19-68, 19-1594, 19-69 to 19-75, 19-1604 to 19-1606, 19-76

135. Los Angeles, Los Angeles City   EDs 19-1588, 19-77, 19-1602, 19-78, 19-1592, 19-79 to 19-94

136. Los Angeles, Los Angeles City   EDs 19-95 to 19-114

137. Los Angeles, Los Angeles City   EDs 19-115 to 19-131

138. Los Angeles, Los Angeles City   EDs 19-132 to 19-145, 19-1593, 19-146 to 19-150

139. Los Angeles, Los Angeles City   EDs 19-151 to 19-174

140. Los Angeles, Los Angeles City   EDs 19-175 to 19-199

141. Los Angeles, Los Angeles City   EDs 19-200 to 19-211, 19-212 (NP), 19-213, 19-214 (NP), 19-215 to 19-230

142. Los Angeles, Los Angeles City   EDs 19-231 to 19-260

143. Los Angeles, Los Angeles City   EDs 19-261 to 19-290

144. Los Angeles, Los Angeles City   EDs 19-291 to 19-313

145. Los Angeles, Los Angeles City   EDs 19-314 to 19-340

146. Los Angeles, Los Angeles City   EDs 19-341 to 19-374

147. Los Angeles, Los Angeles City   EDs 19-375 to 19-380, 19-1590, 19-381 to 19-386, 19-1591, 19-387 to 19-388, 19-1589, 19-389 to 19-401

148. Los Angeles, Los Angeles City   EDs 19-402 to 19-433

149. Los Angeles, Los Angeles City   EDs 19-434 to 19-461

150. Los Angeles, Los Angeles City   EDs 19-462 to 19-493

151. Los Angeles, Los Angeles City   EDs 19-494 to 19-516

152. Los Angeles, Los Angeles City   EDs 19-517 to 19-542

153. Los Angeles, Los Angeles City   EDs 19-543 to 19-560, 19-562

154. Los Angeles, Los Angeles City   EDs 19-561, 19-563 to 19-578

155. Los Angeles, Los Angeles City   EDs 19-579 to 19-585, 19-1599, 19-586 to 19-595

156. Los Angeles, Los Angeles City   EDs 19-596, 19-1603, 19-597 to 19-607

157. Los Angeles, Los Angeles City   EDs 19-1601, 19-608, 19-1595, 19-1600, 19-609, 19-1596, 19-612, 19-610 to 19-611, 19-613 to 19-614

158. Los Angeles, Los Angeles City   EDs 19-615 to 19-618, 19-621, 19-620, 19-1598, 19-622 to 19-623, 19-1597

159. Los Angeles, Los Angeles City   EDs 19-624, 19-626, 19-629, 19-625, 19-627 to 19-628, 19-619, 19-630 to 19-632

160. Los Angeles, Los Angeles City   EDs 19-633 to 19-650

161. Los Angeles, Los Angeles City   EDs 19-651 to 19-677

162. Los Angeles, Los Angeles City   EDs 19-678 to 19-689, 19-1579, 19-690 to 19-703

163. Los Angeles, Los Angeles City   EDs 19-704 to 19-711, 19-715, 19-712 to 19-714, 19-716 to 19-726

164. Los Angeles, Los Angeles City   EDs 19-727 to 19-736, 19-743, 19-740 to 19-742, 19-756, 19-737 to 19-739, 19-744 to 19-755, 19-757 to 19-758

165. Los Angeles, Los Angeles City   EDs 19-759 to 19-765, 19-1580, 19-766, 19-1581, 19-767 to 19-774, 19-1582, 19-775 to 19-778

166. Los Angeles, Los Angeles City   EDs 19-779 to 19-782, 19-1583, 19-783, 19-1584, 19-784 to 19-791, 19-1585, 19-792 to 19-795, 19-1586 to 19-1587

167. Los Angeles, Los Angeles City   EDs 19-1156 to 19-1166, 19-1189 to 19-1196, 19-1167 to 19-1184

168. Los Angeles   EDs 19-1185 to 19-1187, 19-1202 to 19-1238

169. Los Angeles   EDs 19-1239 to 19-1257, 19-1197 to 19-1201, 19-1258 to 19-1263, 19-1264 (void), 19-1265 to 19-1273

170. Los Angeles   EDs 19-1274 to 19-1284, 19-1305 to 19-1307, 19-1391 to 19-1395, 19-1285 to 19-1304, 19-1387 to 19-1390

171. Los Angeles   EDs 19-1308 to 19-1314, 19-1343 to 19-1357, 19-1315 to 19-1337, 19-1358

172. Los Angeles   EDs 19-1338 to 19-1342, 19-1359 to 19-1362, 19-1365 to 19-1373, 19-1363 to 19-1364, 19-1374 to 19-1386, 19-1510 to 19-1515

173. Los Angeles   EDs 19-1396 to 19-1442

174. Los Angeles   EDs 19-1443 to 19-1498

175. Los Angeles   EDs 19-1499 to 19-1509, 19-1516 to 19-1529, 19-1539 to 19-1560

176. Los Angeles   EDs 19-1530 to 19-1538

Madera   EDs 20-1 to 20-13, 20-14 to 20-15 (NP)

Marin   EDs 21-8 to 21-12, 21-47 to 21-48, 21-13 to 21-21, 21-49, 21-22 to 21-26

177. Marin   EDs 21-1 to 21-7, 21-27 to 21-46

Modoc   EDs 25-1 to 25-3, 25-14, 25-4 to 25-13

Mariposa   EDs 22-1 to 22-12

Mendocino   EDs 23-1 to 23-13, 23-15 to 23-16, 23-29, 23-17 to 23-19, 23-30, 23-20, 23-28, 23-21 to 23-23, 23-14, 23-24 to 23-27

178. Merced   EDs 24-1 to 24-15, 24-22 to 24-24, 24-16 to 24-21, 24-25 to 24-29

Mono   EDs 26-1 to 26-5

Nevada   EDs 29-1 to 29-11, 29-17, 29-12 to 29-16

179. Monterey   EDs 27-1 to 27-21, 27-44, 27-22 to 27-28, 27-31, 27-29, 27-30 (NP), 27-32 to 27-43

180. Napa   EDs 28-1 to 28-24

Orange   EDs 30-47 to 30-48, 30-1 to 30-20, 30-49 to 30-51

181. Orange   EDs 30-21 to 30-38, 30-87 to 30-89, 30-39 to 30-46, 30-52 to 30-59, 30-85 to 30-86

182. Orange   EDs 30-62 to 30-84, 30-60 to 30-61

Placer   EDs 31-1 to 31-29

183. Plumas   EDs 32-1 to 32-9, 32-10 to 32-11 (NP)

Riverside   EDs 33-1 to 33-5, 33-6 (NP), 33-7 to 33-27, 33-89 (NP), 33-28 to 33-43

184. Riverside   EDs 33-44 to 33-72, 33-85 to 33-88, 33-73 to 33-82, 33-83 (NP), 33-84

Sacramento   EDs 34-1 to 34-12, 34-106

185. Sacramento   EDs 34-13 to 34-27, 34-100 to 34-105, 34-28 to 34-50

186. Sacramento   EDs 34-51 to 34-87

187. Sacramento   EDs 34-88 to 34-99

San Benito   EDs 35-1 to 35-11

San Bernardino   EDs 36-1 to 36-10, 36-132, 36-11 to 36-22, 36-75, 36-23 to 36-24

188. San Bernardino   EDs 36-25, 36-117, 36-133 to 36-135, 36-26 to 36-29, 36-37 to 36-46, 36-30 to 36-36, 36-47 to 36-73

189. San Bernardino   EDs 36-76 to 36-116, 36-118, 36-74, 36-119 to 36-131

190. San Diego   EDs 37-1 to 37-24

San Diego, San Diego City   EDs 37-25 to 37-37, 37-39 to 37-48, 37-224, 37-49, 37-225

191. San Diego, San Diego City   EDs 37-50 to 37-51, 37-226, 37-52 to 37-64, 37-227, 37-65, 37-228, 37-66 to 37-67, 37-229, 37-68 to 37-70, 37-38, 37-71, 37-230, 37-72 to 37-73, 37-231, 37-74 to 37-75, 37-232, 37-76 to 37-82

192. San Diego, San Diego City   EDs 37-83 to 37-100, 37-233, 37-101 to 37-110, 37-234, 37-111 to 37-146

193. San Diego, San Diego City   EDs 37-147 to 37-218, 37-220, 37-219, 37-221 to 37-223

194. San Francisco, San Francisco City   EDs 38-1 to 38-26

195. San Francisco, San Francisco City   EDs 38-27 to 38-48

196. San Francisco, San Francisco City   EDs 38-49 to 38-66

197. San Francisco, San Francisco City   EDs 38-67 to 38-89

198. San Francisco, San Francisco City   EDs 38-90 to 38-111

199. San Francisco, San Francisco City   EDs 38-112 to 38-142

200. San Francisco, San Francisco City   EDs 38-143 to 38-171

201. San Francisco, San Francisco City   EDs 38-172 to 38-197

202. San Francisco, San Francisco City   EDs 38-198 to 38-222

203. San Francisco, San Francisco City   EDs 38-223 to 38-252

204. San Francisco, San Francisco City   EDs 38-253 to 38-278
205. San Francisco, San Francisco City   EDs 38-279 to 38-303
206. San Francisco, San Francisco City   EDs 38-304 to 38-325
207. San Francisco, San Francisco City   EDs 38-326 to 38-350
208. San Francisco, San Francisco City   EDs 38-351 to 38-374
209. San Francisco, San Francisco City   EDs 38-375 to 38-398
210. San Francisco, San Francisco City   EDs 38-399 to 38-409
     San Joaquin   EDs 39-1 to 39-23
211. San Joaquin   EDs 39-24 to 39-39, 39-57 to 39-69
212. San Joaquin   EDs 39-40 to 39-56, 39-70 to 39-91
213. San Luis Obispo   EDs 40-1 to 40-12, 40-19 to 40-28, 40-13 to 40-18, 40-29 to 40-36
     Santa Barbara   EDs 42-1 to 42-2, 42-54, 42-3 to 42-6
214. Santa Barbara   EDs 42-7 to 42-43, 42-51 to 42-53
215. Santa Barbara   EDs 42-44 to 42-50
     Santa Cruz   EDs 44-1 to 44-36
     Sierra   EDs 46-1 to 46-7
216. San Mateo   EDs 41-1 to 41-25, 41-62, 41-57, 41-61, 41-26, 41-28 to 41-36
217. San Mateo   EDs 41-27, 41-37 to 41-38, 41-39 (NP), 41-40 to 41-43, 41-45 to 41-52, 41-58 to 41-60, 41-44, 41-53 to 41-56
     Santa Clara   EDs 43-1 to 43-3, 43-18 to 43-25, 43-27, 43-26, 43-28 to 43-31, 43-32 (NP), 43-37, 43-33 to 43-36, 43-38
218. Santa Clara   EDs 43-4 to 43-6, 43-39, 43-78 to 43-101, 43-40, 43-42 to 43-58
219. Santa Clara   EDs 43-59 to 43-77, 43-7 to 43-11, 43-121, 43-102 to 43-110, 43-41, 43-111 to 43-115
220. Santa Clara   EDs 43-12 to 43-17, 43-116 to 43-120
     Shasta   EDs 45-1, 45-24, 45-2 to 45-22, 45-23 (NP)
     Siskiyou   EDs 47-1 to 47-4, 47-37, 47-5 to 47-36
221. Solano   EDs 48-1 to 48-8, 48-24 to 48-42, 48-9 to 48-23
     Sonoma   EDs 49-1 to 49-17
222. Sonoma   EDs 49-18 to 49-43, 49-74 to 49-76, 49-44 to 49-73, 49-77
223. Stanislaus   EDs 50-1 to 50-6, 50-25 to 50-28, 50-42 to 50-49, 50-7 to 50-24
224. Stanislaus   EDs 50-29 to 50-41, 50-50 to 50-51
     Sutter   EDs 51-1 to 51-14
     Tehama   EDs 52-1 to 52-24
     Tuolumne   EDs 55-1 to 55-4, 55-5 (void), 55-6 to 55-10, 55-14, 55-11 (NP), 55-12 to 55-13
225. Trinity   EDs 53-1 to 53-10
     Yolo   EDs 57-1 to 57-25
     Tulare   EDs 54-1 to 54-21, 54-41 to 54-54
226. Tulare   EDs 54-22 to 54-30, 54-33 (NP), 54-34 to 54-37, 54-62 to 54-74, 54-38 to 54-40, 54-57, 54-56 (NP), 54-58 to 54-61, 54-75 to 54-91, 54-31 to 54-32, 54-55 (NP)
227. Ventura   EDs 56-1 to 56-2, 56-34, 56-3 to 56-4, 56-35, 56-5 to 56-9, 56-36, 56-10 to 56-13, 56-20 to 56-33
228. Ventura   EDs 56-14 to 56-19
     Yuba   EDs 58-1 to 58-15

## Colorado

229. Adams   EDs 1-1 to 1-10, 1-11 (NP), 1-30, 1-12 to 1-13, 1-28, 1-14 to 1-23, 1-40, 1-24 to 1-27, 1-29, 1-31 to 1-39
     Archuleta   EDs 4-1, 4-6, 4-11, 4-2 to 4-5, 4-7 to 4-10, 4-12
     Alamosa   EDs 2-1 to 2-16

Baca   EDs 5-20, 5-1 to 5-13, 5-19, 5-14 to 5-18
Cheyenne   EDs 9-1 to 9-2, 9-4, 9-3, 9-5 to 9-9
Clear Creek   EDs 10-1, 10-2 (NP), 10-3, 10-5, 10-4, 10-6 to 10-12, 10-14, 10-16, 10-13, 10-15, 10-17 to 10-18
230. Arapahoe   EDs 3-1, 3-4, 3-2 to 3-3, 3-5 to 3-7, 3-22, 3-27, 3-8 to 3-21, 3-23 to 3-26, 3-28 to 3-40
     Bent   EDs 6-1 to 6-2, 6-16, 6-3 to 6-15
     Boulder   EDs 7-1 to 7-8, 7-39, 7-9 to 7-13, 7-43, 7-15, 7-14, 7-16 to 7-20, 7-28, 7-21 to 7-23, 7-31, 7-24 to 7-27, 7-29 to 7-30, 7-32 to 7-38, 7-40 to 7-42
231. Boulder   EDs 7-44 to 7-53, 7-56, 7-54, 7-55 (NP)
     Chaffee   EDs 8-1 to 8-3, 8-5, 8-4, 8-6 to 8-31
     Conejos   EDs 11-1 to 11-16, 11-20, 11-17 to 11-19
     Costilla   EDs 12-1 to 12-13
     Crowley   EDs 13-1 to 13-3, 13-5, 13-4, 13-6 to 13-13
     Custer   EDs 14-1 to 14-13
232. Delta   EDs 15-1 to 15-5, 15-21, 15-6 to 15-10, 15-17, 15-23, 15-11 to 15-12, 15-25, 15-13 to 15-16, 15-18 to 15-20, 15-22, 15-24, 15-26 to 15-30
     Dolores   EDs 17-1 to 17-7
     Douglas   EDs 18-1 to 18-4, 18-8, 18-5 to 18-7, 18-9 to 18-17
     Eagle   EDs 19-1 to 19-13, 19-15, 19-14, 19-16 to 19-21
     Denver, Denver City   EDs 16-1, 16-216, 16-2, 16-217, 16-3 to 16-5, 16-218, 16-6 to 16-8, 16-219, 16-9 to 16-11, 16-220, 16-12 to 16-14
233. Denver, Denver City   EDs 16-221, 16-15 to 16-17, 16-222 to 16-223, 16-18 to 16-28, 16-224, 16-29 to 16-30, 16-225, 16-31 to 16-36
234. Denver, Denver City   EDs 16-37 to 16-39, 16-226, 16-40 to 16-54, 16-239, 16-55 to 16-63
235. Denver, Denver City   EDs 16-64 to 16-69, 16-227, 16-70 to 16-73, 16-228, 16-74 to 16-76, 16-229, 16-77 to 16-80, 16-230
236. Denver, Denver City   EDs 16-81 to 16-85, 16-231, 16-86, 16-232, 16-87 to 16-88, 16-233, 16-89 to 16-90, 16-234, 16-91 to 16-97, 16-235, 16-98 to 16-99
237. Denver, Denver City   EDs 16-236, 16-100 to 16-105, 16-237, 16-106 to 16-112, 16-238, 16-113 to 16-117, 16-240 to 16-242, 16-118
238. Denver, Denver City   EDs 16-243, 16-119 to 16-123, 16-244, 16-124 to 16-136, 16-245, 16-137 to 16-140, 16-160 to 16-168
239. Denver, Denver City   EDs 16-141 to 16-159, 16-169 to 16-194
240. Denver, Denver City   EDs 16-195 to 16-207, 16-246, 16-208 to 16-212, 16-247, 16-213, 16-248, 16-214 to 16-215
241. Elbert   EDs 20-1 to 20-18
     Fremont   EDs 22-1 to 22-10, 22-12, 22-11, 22-13 to 22-18, 22-20, 22-19, 22-21 to 22-55
     El Paso   EDs 21-1 to 21-35
242. El Paso   EDs 21-36 to 21-47, 21-48 (NP), 21-49 to 21-53, 21-55, 21-54, 21-56 to 21-68, 21-70, 21-69, 21-71 to 21-86, 21-88, 21-87, 21-89 to 21-92
     Garfield   EDs 23-1, 23-3, 23-2, 23-4 to 23-7, 23-9, 23-11, 23-13, 23-8, 23-10, 23-12, 23-14 to 23-15, 23-17, 23-16, 23-18 to 23-22, 23-24, 23-31, 23-23, 23-25 to 23-27, 23-33, 23-28 to 23-30, 23-32, 23-34 to 23-38
     Gilpin   EDs 24-1 to 24-8

Grand    EDs 25-1 to 25-11, 25-12 (NP), 25-13 to 25-14

Gunnison    EDs 26-1, 26-3, 26-5, 26-2, 26-4, 26-6 to 26-9, 26-11, 26-10, 26-12 to 26-28

Hinsdale    EDs 27-1 to 27-5

Jackson    EDs 29-1 to 29-6

243.  Huerfano    EDs 28-1 to 28-5, 28-38, 28-6 to 28-37, 28-39 to 28-44

Kit Carson    EDs 32-1 to 32-16, 32-18, 32-17, 32-19 to 32-25

Jefferson    EDs 30-1 to 30-11, 30-13, 30-16, 30-18, 30-12, 30-14 to 30-15, 30-17, 30-19 to 30-21, 30-46, 30-27, 30-35, 30-41, 30-47, 30-22 to 30-26, 30-28 to 30-29, 30-39, 30-31, 30-30, 30-32 to 30-33, 30-50, 30-34, 30-36 to 30-38, 30-48, 30-40, 30-49, 30-42 to 30-45

Kiowa    EDs 31-1 to 31-11

244.  Lake    EDs 33-1 to 33-16

La Plata    EDs 34-1 to 34-18, 34-34, 34-19, 34-31, 34-20, 34-32, 34-21, 34-33, 34-22 to 34-30, 34-35

Larimer    EDs 35-1 to 35-27, 35-29, 35-28, 35-30, 35-52, 35-31 to 35-40

245.  Larimer    EDs 35-41 to 35-44, 35-51, 35-45 to 35-48, 35-49 (NP), 35-50

Las Animas    EDs 36-1 to 36-9, 36-35, 36-10 to 36-34, 36-36 to 36-67, 36-68 (NP), 36-69

Moffat    EDs 41-1, 41-17, 41-31, 41-2 to 41-16, 41-18 to 41-30, 41-32 to 41-33

246.  Lincoln    EDs 37-1 to 37-3, 37-5 to 37-18, 37-4, 37-19

Morgan    EDs 44-1 to 44-17, 44-19, 44-21, 44-23, 44-18, 44-20, 44-22, 44-24 to 44-26

Logan    EDs 38-1 to 38-10, 38-11, 38-12 (NP), 38-13 to 38-40, 38-45, 38-41 to 38-44, 38-46 to 38-48, 38-49 (void), 38-50 to 38-51

Mineral    EDs 40-1, 40-3, 40-2, 40-4

Ouray    EDs 46-1 to 46-2, 46-4, 46-3, 46-5, 46-12, 46-6 to 46-11

247.  Mesa    EDs 39-1 to 39-19, 39-26, 39-20 to 39-25, 39-27 to 39-32

Montezuma    EDs 42-1, 42-9, 42-2 to 42-3, 42-12, 42-4 to 42-5, 42-14, 42-6 to 42-8, 42-10 to 42-11, 42-13, 42-15 to 42-24

Montrose    EDs 43-1 to 43-11, 43-13, 43-12, 43-14 to 43-26

248.  Otero    EDs 45-1 to 45-40, 45-42, 45-41, 45-43 to 45-45

Park    EDs 47-1 to 47-21

Phillips    EDs 48-1 to 48-3, 48-5, 48-4, 48-6 to 48-8, 48-10, 48-9, 48-11 to 48-14

Pitkin    EDs 49-1, 49-3, 49-2, 49-4 to 49-8

Prowers    EDs 50-1 to 50-6, 50-19, 50-7 to 50-18, 50-20 to 50-23

249.  Pueblo    EDs 51-1 to 51-10, 51-11 (NP), 51-12 to 51-43

250.  Pueblo    EDs 51-44 to 51-59, 51-60 (NP), 51-61 to 51-62, 51-63 to 51-65 (NP), 51-66 to 51-91

San Juan    EDs 56-1, 56-3, 56-2, 56-4 to 56-7

Sedgwick    EDs 58-1 to 58-12

Rio Blanco    EDs 52-1 to 52-4, 52-10, 52-5 to 52-9, 52-11 to 52-17

Routt    EDs 54-1, 54-13, 54-2 to 54-12, 54-14 to 54-18, 54-24, 54-19 to 54-23, 54-25 to 54-30

Saguache    EDs 55-1 to 55-21

San Miguel    EDs 57-1, 57-3, 57-2, 57-4 to 57-18

251.  Rio Grande    EDs 53-1 to 53-4, 53-12, 53-5 to 53-11, 53-13 to 53-16

Summit    EDs 59-1, 59-3, 59-2 (NP), 59-4 to 59-11, 59-12 (NP), 59-13 to 59-15

Teller    EDs 60-1 to 60-7, 60-9, 60-8, 60-10, 60-12, 60-11, 60-13, 60-15, 60-14

Washington    EDs 61-1, 61-18, 61-3 to 61-17, 61-19 to 61-23, 61-2

Weld    EDs 62-1, 62-59, 62-96, 62-2 to 62-6, 62-23, 62-61, 62-7 to 62-8, 62-63, 62-9 to 62-10, 62-46, 62-11 to 62-16, 62-51, 62-17 to 62-21, 62-25, 62-35, 62-22, 62-24, 62-26 to 62-34, 62-36 to 62-38

252.  Weld    EDs 62-39 to 62-45, 62-47 to 62-50, 62-52 to 62-55, 62-72, 62-56 to 62-58, 62-60, 62-62, 62-64 to 62-71, 62-73 to 62-95, 62-97, 62-98 to 62-103

Yuma    EDs 63-1 to 63-2, 63-9, 63-23, 63-25, 63-3 to 63-6, 63-19, 63-21, 63-7 to 63-8, 63-10 to 63-18, 63-20, 63-22, 63-24, 63-26 to 63-29

## Connecticut

253.  Fairfield, Bridgeport City    EDs 1-98 to 1-99, 1-1 to 1-3, 1-10 to 1-17, 1-4 to 1-9, 1-69 to 1-75, 1-81

254.  Fairfield, Bridgeport City    EDs 1-82 to 1-97, 1-18 to 1-31

255.  Fairfield, Bridgeport City    EDs 1-32 to 1-38, 1-226, 1-39 to 1-56

256.  Fairfield    EDs 1-57 to 1-68, 1-76 to 1-80, 1-100, 1-116 to 1-125

257.  Fairfield    EDs 1-101 to 1-115, 1-130 to 1-140

258.  Fairfield    EDs 1-126 to 1-129, 1-141 to 1-171

259.  Fairfield    EDs 1-172 to 1-202

260.  Fairfield    EDs 1-203 to 1-209, 1-217 to 1-219, 1-210 to 1-216, 1-220 to 1-225

261.  Hartford    EDs 2-88 to 2-93, 2-109 to 2-111, 2-128 to 2-135, 2-94 to 2-108

262.  Hartford    EDs 2-112 to 2-127, 2-136 to 2-138

Hartford, Hartford City    EDs 2-139 to 2-143, 2-1 to 2-10

263.  Hartford, Hartford City    EDs 2-11 to 2-37

264.  Hartford, Hartford City    EDs 2-38 to 2-60

265.  Hartford, Hartford City    EDs 2-61 to 2-84

266.  Hartford    EDs 2-85 to 2-87, 2-158 to 2-174, 2-181 to 2-190

267.  Hartford    EDs 2-175 to 2-180, 2-191 to 2-199, 2-144 to 2-157, 2-200 to 2-203

268.  Hartford    EDs 2-204 to 2-209, 2-212 to 2-216, 2-210 to 2-211, 2-217 to 2-219, 2-235 to 2-244

269.  Hartford    EDs 2-220 to 2-234

Litchfield    EDs 3-1 to 3-11, 3-12 (void), 3-13 to 3-23, 3-44

270.  Litchfield    EDs 3-24 to 3-28, 3-47 to 3-58, 3-29 to 3-43, 3-45 to 3-46

271.  Middlesex    EDs 4-1 to 4-12, 4-30 to 4-33, 4-13 to 4-29

272.  New Haven    EDs 5-103 to 5-116, 5-121 to 5-123, 5-117 to 5-120, 5-124 to 5-133

273.  New Haven    EDs 5-134 to 5-164

274.  New Haven    EDs 5-165 to 5-177

New Haven, New Haven City    EDs 5-178 to 5-186, 5-1 to 5-8

275.  New Haven, New Haven City    EDs 5-9 to 5-20, 5-32 to 5-35, 5-21 to 5-31, 5-36 to 5-40

276.  New Haven, New Haven City    EDs 5-41 to 5-51, 5-54 to 5-56, 5-52 to 5-53, 5-57 to 5-62, 5-66 to 5-73

277.  New Haven, New Haven City    EDs 5-63 to 5-65, 5-74 to 5-75, 5-78 to 5-84, 5-76 to 5-77, 5-85 to 5-91, 5-98 to 5-99

278.  New Haven    EDs 5-92 to 5-97, 5-100 to 5-102, 5-187 to 5-193, 5-196 to 5-206

279.  New Haven    EDs 5-194 to 5-195, 5-207 to 5-236

280.  New Haven    EDs 5-237 to 5-268, 5-282

281.  New Haven    EDs 5-269 to 5-281

New London    EDs 6-1 to 6-13, 6-76, 6-14 to 6-17

282.  New London    EDs 6-18 to 6-25, 6-77, 6-26 to 6-38, 6-66 to 6-71

283.  New London    EDs 6-39 to 6-65, 6-72 to 6-75

284.  Tolland    EDs 7-1 to 7-25

Windham   EDs 8-1 to 8-13, 8-26 to 8-28

285.   Windham   EDs 8-14 to 8-25, 8-29 to 8-40

## Delaware

286.   Kent   EDs 1-1 to 1-41

New Castle   EDs 2-96 to 2-101, 2-122

287.   New Castle   EDs 2-80 to 2-85, 2-102 to 2-109, 2-111 to 2-115, 2-86 to 2-95, 2-110, 2-116 to 2-121

288.   New Castle, Wilmington City EDs 2-1 to 2-6, 2-67 to 2-71, 2-7 to 2-12, 2-22 to 2-27, 2-48 to 2-50, 2-52

* 289.   New Castle, Wilmington City   EDs 2-51, 2-53 to 2-60, 2-13 to 2-21, 2-61 to 2-66

290.   New Castle, Wilmington City   EDs 2-28 to 2-47, 2-72 to 2-79

291.   Sussex   EDs 3-1 to 3-43

## District of Columbia

292.   District of Columbia   EDs 1-1 to 1-34

293.   District of Columbia   EDs 1-35 to 1-67

294.   District of Columbia   EDs 1-68 to 1-83, 1-401, 1-84 to 1-85, 1-400, 1-86 to 1-109

295.   District of Columbia   EDs 1-110 to 1-112, 1-146 to 1-161, 1-113 to 1-131

296.   District of Columbia   EDs 1-132 to 1-145, 1-162 to 1-180

297.   District of Columbia   EDs 1-181 to 1-184, 1-397, 1-185 to 1-190, 1-399, 1-191 to 1-213

298.   District of Columbia   EDs 1-214 to 1-231, 1-404, 1-232 to 1-247

299.   District of Columbia   EDs 1-248 to 1-281

300.   District of Columbia   EDs 1-282 to 1-317

301.   District of Columbia   EDs 1-318 to 1-334

302.   District of Columbia   EDs 1-335 to 1-354

303.   District of Columbia   EDs 1-355 to 1-372

304.   District of Columbia   EDs 1-373 to 1-379, 1-403, 1-380 to 1-384, 1-398, 1-385, 1-402, 1-386 to 1-388

305.   District of Columbia   EDs 1-389 to 1-396

## Florida

306.   Alachua   EDs 1-1 to 1-39

Baker   EDs 2-1 to 2-8

Bay   EDs 3-1 to 3-5, 3-6 (NP), 3-7 to 3-22

307.   Bay   EDs 3-23 to 3-30

Bradford   EDs 4-1 to 4-12

Brevard   EDs 5-1 to 5-37

Broward   EDs 6-1 to 6-3, 6-16, 6-4 to 6-15, 6-17, 6-18 (NP), 6-19 to 6-33

308.   Calhoun   EDs 7-1 to 7-13

Charlotte   EDs 8-1 to 8-8, 8-10, 8-9, 8-11

Citrus   EDs 9-1 to 9-19

Clay   EDs 10-1 to 10-2, 10-5, 10-3 to 10-4, 10-6 to 10-15

Collier   EDs 11-1 to 11-4, 11-6, 11-5, 11-7 to 11-12

Columbia   EDs 12-1 to 12-20

Dade   EDs 13-1, 13-3, 13-2, 13-4 to 13-6, 13-8, 13-86, 13-7 (NP), 13-9 to 13-12

309.   Dade, Miami City   EDs 13-13 to 13-36

310.   Dade, Miami City   EDs 13-37 to 13-67

311.   Dade, Miami City   EDs 13-68 to 13-80, 13-81 (NP), 13-82 to 13-84, 13-122, 13-85, 13-87 to 13-92, 13-93 (NP), 13-94 to 13-101, 13-123 to 13-124 (NP), 13-125, 13-102 to 13-105, 13-107, 13-109, 13-106, 13-108, 13-110 to 13-115, 13-116 (NP), 13-120, 13-117 to 13-119, 13-121

DeSoto   EDs 14-1 to 14-6, 14-7 (NP), 14-8 to 14-11, 14-12 (NP), 14-13, 14-14 (NP), 14-15 to 14-16

312.   Dixie   EDs 15-1 to 15-10

Duval, Jacksonville City   EDs 16-1 to 16-20

313.   Duval, Jacksonville City   EDs 16-21 to 16-30, 16-31 (NP), 16-32 to 16-39

314.   Duval, Jacksonville City   EDs 16-43 to 16-48, 16-52 to 16-57, 16-40 to 16-42, 16-49 to 16-51, 16-58 to 16-72

315.   Duval   EDs 16-73 to 16-91

Escambia   EDs 17-1 to 17-2, 17-51, 17-3 to 17-30

316.   Escambia   EDs 17-31 to 17-50

Franklin   EDs 19-1 to 19-8, 19-9 (NP), 19-10 to 19-12

Flagler   EDs 18-1 to 18-9

Gadsden   EDs 20-1 to 20-18

317.   Gadsden   EDs 20-19 to 20-24

Gilchrist   EDs 21-1 to 21-8

Glades   EDs 22-1, 22-4, 22-8, 22-2 to 22-3, 22-5 to 22-7, 22-9 to 22-11, 22-12 (NP), 22-13 to 22-16

Gulf   EDs 23-1 to 23-9

Hamilton   EDs 24-1 to 24-7, 24-8 to 24-13

Hardee   EDs 25-1 to 25-23

Hendry   EDs 26-1 to 26-2, 26-4, 26-3, 26-5 to 26-8

Hernando   EDs 27-1 to 27-4, 27-6, 27-5, 27-7 to 27-12

318.   Highlands   EDs 28-1 to 28-15

Holmes   EDs 30-1 to 30-13, 30-27, 30-14 to 30-26, 30-28

Hillsborough   EDs 29-1 to 29-32

319.   Hillsborough, Tampa City   EDs 29-33 to 29-65, 29-81 to 29-97

320.   Hillsborough   EDs 29-66 to 29-80, 29-98 to 29-133

321.   Hillsborough   EDs 29-134 to 29-166

Indian River   EDs 31-1 to 31-7, 31-9, 31-8, 31-10, 31-11 to 31-13

Jackson   EDs 32-1 to 32-8, 32-40, 32-9 to 32-20

322.   Jackson   EDs 32-21 to 32-39, 32-41

Jefferson   EDs 33-1 to 33-13

Lake   EDs 35-1 to 35-23, 35-24 (NP), 35-25 to 35-42

323.   Leon   EDs 37-1 to 37-28

Lafayette   EDs 34-1 to 34-6

Lee   EDs 36-1 to 36-27

Levy   EDs 38-1 to 38-8

324.   Levy   EDs 38-9 to 38-22

Liberty   EDs 39-1 to 39-9

Madison   EDs 40-1 to 40-16

Manatee   EDs 41-1 to 41-33

325.   Marion   EDs 42-1 to 42-44

Martin   EDs 43-1 to 43-4, 43-5 (NP), 43-7, 43-9, 43-6, 43-8, 43-10 to 43-17

---

* Roll 289, New Castle, Wilmington City—There appears to be no ED 2-123 or 2-124.

Monroe EDs 44-1 to 44-9, 44-10 (NP), 44-11 to 44-13, 44-14 (NP), 44-15 to 44-29

326. Nassau EDs 45-1 to 45-16

Okaloosa EDs 46-1 to 46-25, 46-26 (NP), 46-27, 46-28 (NP)

Okeechobee EDs 47-1 to 47-4, 47-8, 47-5 to 47-7, 47-9

Orange EDs 48-1 to 48-19

327. Orange EDs 48-20 to 48-62

Osceola EDs 49-1 to 49-6, 49-14, 49-7 to 49-13, 49-15 to 49-16

Pasco EDs 51-1 to 51-9, 51-31, 51-10 to 51-30, 51-32 to 51-34

328. Palm Beach EDs 50-1 to 50-7, 50-25 (NP), 50-26 to 50-50, 50-52, 50-51, 50-53 to 50-59, 50-8 to 50-24

329. Pinellas EDs 52-1 to 52-33, 52-45 to 52-51

330. Pinellas EDs 52-34, 52-72, 52-35 to 52-40, 52-43, 52-76, 52-41 to 52-42, 52-44, 52-52 to 52-56, 52-58, 52-57, 52-59 to 52-71, 52-73 to 52-75, 52-77, 52-78 (NP), 52-79 to 52-81

Polk EDs 53-1 to 53-4, 53-80, 53-5 to 53-13, 53-74, 53-14, 53-75, 53-15 to 53-22, 53-33 to 53-35, 53-36 (NP), 53-37 to 53-40, 53-79, 53-41 to 53-47

331. Polk EDs 53-23, 53-76, 53-24 to 53-27, 53-77, 53-28 to 53-30, 53-78, 53-31 to 53-32, 53-48 to 53-55, 53-81, 53-56 to 53-61, 53-82, 53-62 to 53-73

Putnam EDs 54-1 to 54-22

332. Putnam EDs 54-23 to 54-34

St. Johns EDs 55-1 to 55-22, 55-28, 55-23 to 55-27

St. Lucie EDs 56-1 to 56-12

Seminole EDs 59-1 to 59-22

333. Santa Rosa EDs 57-1 to 57-24

Sarasota EDs 58-1, 58-18, 58-4, 58-13, 58-15, 58-2 to 58-3, 58-5 (NP), 58-6 to 58-8, 58-10, 58-9, 58-17, 58-11, 58-12, 58-14, 58-16

Sumter EDs 60-1 to 60-18

Suwannee EDs 61-1 to 61-27

334. Taylor EDs 62-1 to 62-15

Union EDs 63-1 to 63-8

Wakulla EDs 65-1 to 65-14

Volusia EDs 64-1 to 64-23, 64-36 to 64-42, 64-43 to 64-44 (NP), 64-45 to 64-50

335. Volusia EDs 64-24 to 64-35, 64-51 to 64-64, 64-65 (NP), 64-66 to 64-69

Walton EDs 66-1 to 66-15, 66-22, 66-16 to 66-21, 66-23 to 66-27, 66-28 (NP)

Washington EDs 67-1 to 67-9, 67-16, 67-10 to 67-15, 67-17 to 67-21

## Georgia

336. Appling EDs 1-1 to 1-13

Atkinson EDs 2-1 to 2-6

Bacon EDs 3-1 to 3-8

Baker EDs 4-1 to 4-7

Baldwin EDs 5-1 to 5-11

337. Baldwin EDs 5-12 to 5-13

Banks EDs 6-1 to 6-18

Barrow EDs 7-1 to 7-18

Bartow EDs 8-1 to 8-3, 8-22 to 8-23, 8-4 to 8-21

338. Ben Hill EDs 9-1 to 9-11

Berrien EDs 10-1 to 10-15

Bibb EDs 11-1 to 11-9, 11-19 to 11-31

339. Bibb EDs 11-10 to 11-18, 11-32 to 11-58, 11-61, 11-59 to 11-60

340. Bleckley EDs 12-1 to 12-9

Brantley EDs 13-1 to 13-11

Butts EDs 18-1 to 18-12

Brooks EDs 14-1 to 14-21

Bryan EDs 15-1 to 15-5

341. Bulloch EDs 16-1 to 16-14, 16-21, 16-15 to 16-20

Burke EDs 17-1 to 17-11, 17-26, 17-12 to 17-25

342. Calhoun EDs 19-1 to 19-11

Camden EDs 20-1 to 20-10

Campbell EDs 21-1 to 21-12

Candler EDs 22-1 to 22-7

Carroll EDs 23-1 to 23-10, 23-19 to 23-29

343. Carroll EDs 23-11 to 23-18, 23-30 to 23-38

Catoosa EDs 24-1 to 24-11

Charlton EDs 25-1 to 25-8

Chatham EDs 26-1 to 26-5, 26-61, 26-6 to 26-11

344. Chatham EDs 26-12 to 26-37, 26-62, 26-38 to 26-39, 26-63, 26-40, 26-64, 26-41, 26-65

345. Chatham EDs 26-42, 26-66, 26-43, 26-67, 26-44 to 26-48, 26-60, 26-49 to 26-59

Chattahoochee EDs 27-1 to 27-7

Chattooga EDs 28-1 to 28-17

346. Cherokee EDs 29-1 to 29-18, 29-22, 29-19 to 29-21

Clay EDs 31-1 to 31-7

Clarke EDs 30-1 to 30-22

347. Clayton EDs 32-1 to 32-8, 32-14, 32-9 to 32-13

Clinch EDs 33-1 to 33-12

Cobb EDs 34-1 to 34-35

348. Coffee EDs 35-1 to 35-16

Colquitt EDs 36-1 to 36-3, 36-12 to 36-15, 36-4 to 36-11, 36-16 to 36-31

349. Columbia EDs 37-1 to 37-10

Cook EDs 38-1 to 38-11

Crawford EDs 40-1 to 40-10

Coweta EDs 39-1 to 39-27

350. Crisp EDs 41-1 to 41-13

Dade EDs 42-1 to 42-12

Dawson EDs 43-1 to 43-13

Decatur EDs 44-1 to 44-5, 44-20, 44-6 to 44-19

DeKalb EDs 45-13 to 45-14

351. DeKalb EDs 45-15 to 45-25, 45-48, 45-26 to 45-44, 45-45 (NP), 45-46, 45-2 to 45-5

352. DeKalb EDs 45-6 to 45-12, 45-1, 45-47

Dodge EDs 46-1 to 46-22

Dooly EDs 47-5 to 47-7

353. Dooly EDs 47-1 to 47-4, 47-8 to 47-17

Douglas EDs 49-1 to 49-4, 49-12, 49-5 to 49-11

Dougherty EDs 48-1 to 48-15

Echols EDs 51-1 to 51-6

354. Early EDs 50-1 to 50-16

Effingham EDs 52-1 to 52-4, 52-9, 52-8, 52-5 to 52-6, 52-10, 52-7, 52-11

Elbert EDs 53-1 to 53-24

355. Emanuel EDs 54-1 to 54-26

Evans EDs 55-1 to 55-8

Fannin   EDs 56-1 to 56-19

Fayette   EDs 57-1 to 57-13

356.   Floyd   EDs 58-1 to 58-4, 58-7 to 58-17, 58-42, 58-18 to 58-20, 58-5 to 58-6, 58-21 to 58-41

357.   Forsyth   EDs 59-1 to 59-15

Franklin   EDs 60-1 to 60-19

Fulton   EDs 61-139 to 61-153, 61-167 to 61-169

358.   Fulton   EDs 61-154 to 61-155, 61-178, 61-182, 61-179, 61-183, 61-180, 61-184, 61-156 to 61-166, 61-170 to 61-177, 61-181

359.   Fulton, Atlanta City   EDs 61-1 to 61-25

360.   Fulton, Atlanta City   EDs 61-26 to 61-48

361.   Fulton, Atlanta City   EDs 61-49 to 61-70

362.   Fulton, Atlanta City   EDs 61-71 to 61-98

363.   Fulton, Atlanta City   EDs 61-99 to 61-109, 61-111 to 61-113

364.   Fulton, Atlanta City   EDs 61-114 to 61-118, 61-121 to 61-133

365.   Fulton, Atlanta City   EDs 61-134 to 61-138, 61-110, 61-185, 61-119 to 61-120, 61-186

Gilmer   EDs 62-1 to 62-17

Glascock   EDs 63-1 to 63-6

Greene   EDs 67-1 to 67-6, 67-8, 67-7, 67-9 to 67-23

366.   Glynn   EDs 64-1 (NP), 64-2 to 64-18

Gordon   EDs 65-1 to 65-19

Grady   EDs 66-1 to 66-18

367.   Gwinnett   EDs 68-1 to 68-30

Habersham   EDs 69-1 to 69-21

Hancock   EDs 71-1 to 71-2, 71-12, 71-3 to 71-11, 71-13 to 71-17

368.   Haralson   EDs 72-1 to 72-17

Harris   EDs 73-1 to 73-17

Hall   EDs 70-1 to 70-37

369.   Hart   EDs 74-1 to 74-16

Heard   EDs 75-1 to 75-16

Henry   EDs 76-1 to 76-19

Houston   EDs 77-1 to 77-6, 77-12, 77-7 to 77-11, 77-13 to 77-14

370.   Irwin   EDs 78-1 to 78-14

Jasper   EDs 80-1 to 80-24

Jackson   EDs 79-21 to 79-25, 79-1 to 79-20

Jeff Davis   EDs 81-1 to 81-4

371.   Jeff Davis   EDs 81-5 to 81-7

Jefferson   EDs 82-1, 82-22, 82-2 to 82-21

Jenkins   EDs 83-1 to 83-10

Johnson   EDs 84-1 to 84-17

372.   Jones   EDs 85-1 to 85-18

Lamar   EDs 86-1 to 86-10

Lanier   EDs 87-1 to 87-4

Laurens   EDs 88-1 to 88-22

373.   Laurens   EDs 88-23 to 88-32

Lee   EDs 89-1 to 89-8

Liberty   EDs 90-1 to 90-12

Lincoln   EDs 91-1 to 91-9

Long   EDs 92-1 to 92-9

Lowndes   EDs 93-1 to 93-3, 93-14 to 93-21

374.   Lowndes   EDs 93-4 to 93-13

McDuffie   EDs 95-1 to 95-9

Lumpkin   EDs 94-1 to 94-17

McIntosh   EDs 96-1 to 96-7

Madison   EDs 98-1 to 98-18

375.   Macon   EDs 97-1 to 97-13

Marion   EDs 99-1 to 99-9

Meriwether   EDs 100-1 to 100-22, 100-34, 100-23 to 100-33

Milton   EDs 102-1 to 102-2, 102-3 (NP), 102-4 to 102-9

376.   Miller   EDs 101-1 to 101-9

Mitchell   EDs 103-1 to 103-19

Monroe   EDs 104-1 to 104-17

Montgomery   EDs 105-1 to 105-13

377.   Morgan   EDs 106-1 to 106-23

Murray   EDs 107-1 to 107-16

Muscogee   EDs 108-26, 108-32 to 108-35, 108-1 to 108-13

378.   Muscogee   EDs 108-14 to 108-25, 108-27 to 108-31

379.   Newton   EDs 109-1 to 109-24

Oconee   EDs 110-1 to 110-16

Oglethorpe   EDs 111-1 to 111-18

Paulding   EDs 112-1 to 112-20

380.   Peach   EDs 113-1 to 113-10

Pickens   EDs 114-1 to 114-17

Pierce   EDs 115-1 to 115-12

Pike   EDs 116-1 to 116-13

Pulaski   EDs 118-1 to 118-9

381.   Polk   EDs 117-1 to 117-21

Putnam   EDs 119-1 to 119-17

Quitman   EDs 120-1 to 120-5

Rabun   EDs 121-1 to 121-5, 121-8, 121-6 to 121-7, 121-9 to 121-15

Rockdale   EDs 124-1 to 124-7

382.   Randolph   EDs 122-1, 122-17, 122-2 to 122-16

Richmond   EDs 123-42 to 123-46, 123-47 (NP), 123-48 to 123-53, 123-15 to 123-31

383.   Richmond   EDs 123-1 to 123-7, 123-32 to 123-41, 123-8 to 123-14

Schley   EDs 125-1 to 125-5

Stephens   EDs 129-1 to 129-11

384.   Screven   EDs 126-1 to 126-17, 126-22, 126-18 to 126-21

Seminole   EDs 127-1 to 127-8

Spalding   EDs 128-1 to 128-4, 128-15, 128-5 to 128-14

385.   Sumter   EDs 131-1 to 131-22

Stewart   EDs 130-1 to 130-13

Talbot   EDs 132-1 to 132-5, 132-19, 132-6 to 132-18

Taliaferro   EDs 133-1 to 133-12

386.   Tattnall   EDs 134-1 to 134-12, 134-18, 134-13 to 134-17

Taylor   EDs 135-1 to 135-13

Telfair   EDs 136-1 to 136-19

Terrell   EDs 137-1 to 137-7, 137-13 to 137-17

387.   Terrell   EDs 137-8 to 137-12

Thomas   EDs 138-1 to 138-8, 138-23 to 138-27, 138-9 to 138-22

Tift   EDs 139-1 to 139-10

388. Tift   EDs 139-11 to 139-15
    Toombs   EDs 140-1 to 140-14
    Towns   EDs 141-1 to 141-10
    Treutlen   EDs 142-1 to 142-7
    Twiggs   EDs 145-1 to 145-13
    Troup   EDs 143-18 to 143-27
389. Troup   EDs 143-1 to 143-17
    Turner   EDs 144-1 to 144-13
    Union   EDs 146-1 to 146-15
    Upson   EDs 147-1 to 147-4, 147-10 to 147-16
390. Upson   EDs 147-5 to 147-9
    Warren   EDs 151-1 to 151-4, 151-10, 151-5 to 151-9, 151-11 to 151-12
    Webster   EDs 154-1 to 154-8
    Walker   EDs 148-1 to 148-20
391. Ware   EDs 150-1 to 150-23
    Washington   EDs 152-1 to 152-29
392. Walton   EDs 149-1 to 149-27
    Wayne   EDs 153-1 to 153-11
    Wheeler   EDs 155-1 to 155-8
    White   EDs 156-1 to 156-12
393. Whitfield   EDs 157-1 to 157-20
    Wilcox   EDs 158-1 to 158-7, 158-10 to 158-11, 158-8 to 158-9, 158-12 to 158-18
    Worth   EDs 161-1 to 161-21
394. Wilkes   EDs 159-1 to 159-20
    Wilkinson   EDs 160-1 to 160-15

### Idaho

395. Ada   EDs 1-1 to 1-50
    Adams   EDs 2-1 to 2-12
    Bear Lake   EDs 4-1 to 4-27
396. Bannock   EDs 3-1 to 3-53
    Boise   EDs 8-1 to 8-14
    Bonner   EDs 9-1 to 9-45
397. Benewah   EDs 5-1 to 5-8, 5-9 (NP), 5-10, 5-11 (NP), 5-12 to 5-19, 5-20 (NP), 5-21 to 5-26
    Bingham   EDs 6-1 to 6-17, 6-34, 6-18 to 6-33
    Blaine   EDs 7-1 to 7-16
    Bonneville   EDs 10-1 to 10-34
398. Boundary   EDs 11-1 to 11-13
    Butte   EDs 12-1 to 12-10
    Camas   EDs 13-1 to 13-6
    Cassia   EDs 16-1 to 16-42
    Clark   EDs 17-1 to 17-13
    Canyon   EDs 14-1 to 14-26, 14-27 (NP), 14-28 to 14-45
399. Canyon   EDs 14-46 to 14-59
    Caribou   EDs 15-1 to 15-10
    Clearwater   EDs 18-1 to 18-30
    Custer   EDs 19-1 to 19-11
    Elmore   EDs 20-1 to 20-18
    Franklin   EDs 21-1 to 21-29
    Gem   EDs 23-1 to 23-15
    Gooding   EDs 24-1 to 24-11

* 400. Fremont   EDs 22-1 to 22-35, 22-36 to 22-40 (NP), 22-41, 22-42 to 22-46 (NP), 22-47 to 22-48, 22-49 to 22-50 (NP)
    Idaho   EDs 25-1 to 25-30, 25-31 (NP), 25-32 to 25-62
    Jefferson   EDs 26-1 to 26-22
    Jerome   EDs 27-1 to 27-15
    Madison   EDs 33-1 to 33-18
401. Kootenai   EDs 28-1 to 28-19, 28-20 to 28-21 (NP), 28-22, 28-23 (NP), 28-24 to 28-37, 28-38 (NP), 28-39 to 28-52, 28-53 (NP), 28-54 to 28-62
    Lemhi   EDs 30-1 to 30-25
    Latah   EDs 29-1 to 29-41
    Lewis   EDs 31-1 to 31-21
402. Lincoln   EDs 32-1 to 32-7
    Minidoka   EDs 34-1 to 34-16
    Oneida   EDs 36-1 to 36-20
    Owyhee   EDs 37-1 to 37-19, 37-24, 37-20 to 37-23
    Nez Perce   EDs 35-1, 35-2 (NP), 35-3 to 35-35, 35-37 to 35-41, 35-42 (NP), 35-43 to 35-51, 35-36
    Power   EDs 39-1 to 39-2, 39-15 to 39-16, 39-3 to 39-14
403. Payette   EDs 38-1 to 38-15
    Shoshone   EDs 40-1 to 40-34
    Teton   EDs 41-1 to 41-15
    Twin Falls   EDs 42-1 to 42-23
** 404. Twin Falls   EDs 42-24 to 42-36
    Fremont, Yellowstone National Park   EDs 22-51
    Valley   EDs 43-1 to 43-14
    Washington   EDs 44-1 to 44-21, 44-23, 44-22

### Illinois

405. Adams   EDs 1-1 to 1-7, 1-12, 1-8 to 1-11, 1-13 to 1-32, 1-60 to 1-63, 1-33 to 1-49
406. Adams   EDs 1-50 to 1-59
    Boone   EDs 4-1 to 4-16
    Alexander   EDs 2-1 to 2-24
407. Bond   EDs 3-1 to 3-22
    Brown   EDs 5-1 to 5-13
    Bureau   EDs 6-1, 6-25, 6-2 to 6-3, 6-11, 6-4 to 6-10, 6-58, 6-12 to 6-24, 6-26 to 6-36
408. Bureau   EDs 6-37 to 6-57
    Calhoun   EDs 7-1 to 7-13
    Carroll   EDs 8-1 to 8-3, 8-11, 8-4 to 8-7, 8-12, 8-8 to 8-10, 8-13 to 8-26
    Cass   EDs 9-1 to 9-10
409. Cass   EDs 9-11 to 9-12, 9-16, 9-13 to 9-15, 9-17 to 9-21
    Clark   EDs 12-1 to 12-20
    Champaign   EDs 10-1 to 10-4, 10-28, 10-31, 10-41 (NP), 10-5 to 10-9, 10-79 (NP), 10-10 to 10-27
410. Champaign   EDs 10-29 to 10-30, 10-32 to 10-37, 10-49, 10-38 to 10-40, 10-42 to 10-48, 10-50 to 10-73, 10-80 (NP), 10-74 to 10-78
    Christian   EDs 11-1 to 11-16
411. Christian   EDs 11-17 to 11-39
    Clay   EDs 13-1 to 13-7, 13-21, 13-8 to 13-15, 13-9 to 13-14, 13-16 to 13-20

---

* Roll 400, Fremont County—See roll 404 for 22-51, Yellowstone National Park.
** Roll 404, Yellowstone National Park—See roll 400, Fremont County for 22-1 to 22-50.

Coles   EDs 15-1 to 15-8

412.   Coles   EDs 15-9 to 15-31

Clinton   EDs 14-1 to 14-29

413.   Cook   EDs 16-1977 to 16-1979, 16-2910 (void), 16-1980 to 16-1983, 16-2911, 16-1984 to 16-1989, 16-2912, 16-1990 to 16-1996

414.   Cook   EDs 16-1997 to 16-2005, 16-2913 (void), 16-2026, 16-2332, 16-2027, 16-2014 to 16-2025

415.   Cook   EDs 16-2006 to 16-2013, 16-2029, 16-2334, 16-2030 to 16-2031, 16-2028, 16-2032 to 16-2033, 16-2067, 16-2065 to 16-2066, 16-2068, 16-2034 to 16-2047, 16-2058, 16-2359, 16-2059, 16-2360, 16-2063 to 16-2064

416.   Cook   EDs 16-2048 (NP), 16-2049 to 16-2055, 16-2060, 16-2056 to 16-2057, 16-2061 to 16-2062, 16-1, 16-2377 to 16-2378, 16-2, 16-2379, 16-3 to 16-5, 16-2380, 16-6 to 16-8, 16-2381, 16-9 to 16-10, 16-2382, 16-11, 16-2383, 16-12 to 16-15

417.   Cook, Chicago City   EDs 16-16 to 16-19, 16-2384, 16-20, 16-2385, 16-21 to 16-23, 16-2386, 16-24 to 16-25, 16-2387, 16-26, 16-2388, 16-27 (NP), 16-2389 to 16-2390, 16-28, 16-2391, 16-29, 16-2392 to 16-2393, 16-30 to 16-34, 16-2394, 16-35 to 16-36, 16-2395, 16-37, 16-2396, 16-38, 16-2397, 16-39 to 16-41, 16-2398, 16-42 to 16-45, 16-2399, 16-46, 16-2400, 16-47 to 16-48, 16-2401, 16-49 to 16-50, 16-2402, 16-51, 16-2403

418.   Cook, Chicago City   EDs 16-52, 16-2404 to 16-2405, 16-53 to 16-54, 16-2406, 16-55 to 16-56, 16-2407, 16-57 to 16-69, 16-2408, 16-70, 16-2409, 16-71 to 16-75, 16-2410, 16-76, 16-2411, 16-77 to 16-78, 16-2412, 16-79, 16-2413, 16-80, 16-2414, 16-81 to 16-83

419.   Cook, Chicago City   EDs 16-84 to 16-87, 16-2415, 16-88 to 16-90, 16-2416 (NP), 16-91 to 16-94, 16-2417, 16-95 to 16-96, 16-2418, 16-97 to 16-100, 16-2419, 16-101, 16-2420, 16-102, 16-2421, 16-103 to 16-104, 16-2422, 16-105, 16-2423 (NP), 16-2424, 16-106, 16-2425, 16-107 to 16-112, 16-2426

420.   Cook, Chicago City   EDs 16-113 to 16-126, 16-2427, 16-127 to 16-128, 16-2428, 16-129 to 16-131, 16-2429, 16-132 to 16-137, 16-2430, 16-138 to 16-141, 16-2431, 16-142 to 16-143

421.   Cook, Chicago City   EDs 16-144 to 16-145, 16-2432, 16-146 to 16-150, 16-2433, 16-151 to 16-180

422.   Cook, Chicago City   EDs 16-181 to 16-207

423.   Cook, Chicago City   EDs 16-208 to 16-236

424.   Cook, Chicago City   EDs 16-237 to 16-268

425.   Cook, Chicago City   EDs 16-269 to 16-296

426.   Cook, Chicago City   EDs 16-297 to 16-316

427.   Cook, Chicago City   EDs 16-317 to 16-322, 16-323 (NP), 16-2434, 16-324 to 16-331, 16-2435, 16-332 to 16-338, 16-339 (NP), 16-340

428.   Cook, Chicago City   EDs 16-341 to 16-344, 16-2436, 16-345 to 16-362, 16-364

429.   Cook, Chicago City   EDs 16-363, 16-365 to 16-367, 16-368 (NP), 16-2437 to 16-2438, 16-369 to 16-372, 16-2439, 16-373, 16-2440 to 16-2444, 16-374, 16-2445 to 16-2446, 16-375, 16-2447 to 16-2449, 16-376 to 16-379

430.   Cook, Chicago City   EDs 16-380 to 16-381, 16-2450, 16-382 to 16-398, 16-399 (NP), 16-2451, 16-400

431.   Cook, Chicago City   EDs 16-401 to 16-413, 16-2452 to 16-2453, 16-2454 (NP), 16-414, 16-2455

432.   Cook, Chicago City   EDs 16-415 to 16-417, 16-2456 to 16-2457, 16-418, 16-2458 to 16-2459, 16-419, 16-2460 to 16-2461, 16-420, 16-2462, 16-421 to 16-423, 16-2463, 16-424, 16-2464, 16-425, 16-2465, 16-426, 16-2466, 16-428, 16-2467, 16-429

433.   Cook, Chicago City   EDs 16-427, 16-430, 16-2468, 16-431, 16-2469, 16-432 to 16-433, 16-2470, 16-434 to 16-435, 16-2471 to 16-2472, 16-436, 16-2473, 16-437, 16-2474, 16-438 to 16-439, 16-2475 to 16-2476, 16-440, 16-2477 to 16-2481, 16-441,

16-2482, 16-2483 (NP), 16-442, 16-2484, 16-443, 16-2485, 16-444, 16-2486, 16-445, 16-2487 (NP), 16-2488, 16-446

434.   Cook, Chicago City   EDs 16-447 to 16-450, 16-2489, 16-451, 16-2490, 16-452, 16-2491, 16-453 to 16-454, 16-2492, 16-455, 16-2493, 16-456 to 16-457, 16-2494, 16-458 to 16-459, 16-2495 to 16-2496, 16-460, 16-2497, 16-461, 16-2498, 16-462, 16-2499, 16-463 to 16-464, 16-2500, 16-465 to 16-466, 16-2501, 16-467

435.   Cook, Chicago City   EDs 16-468 to 16-470, 16-2502, 16-471, 16-2503 to 16-2504, 16-472, 16-2505 to 16-2506, 16-473 (NP), 16-2507 to 16-2508, 16-2509 (NP), 16-474 to 16-481, 16-2510 (NP), 16-2511, 16-482, 16-2512, 16-483, 16-2513

436.   Cook, Chicago City   EDs 16-2514 to 16-2515, 16-484, 16-2516 to 16-2517 (NP), 16-485, 16-2518, 16-2519 (NP), 16-2520, 16-486, 16-2521, 16-487 to 16-490, 16-2522, 16-491 to 16-492, 16-2523, 16-493, 16-2524, 16-494, 16-2525, 16-495 to 16-496, 16-2526, 16-497, 16-2527, 16-498, 16-2528, 16-499, 16-2529, 16-500, 16-2530

437.   Cook, Chicago City   EDs 16-501 to 16-502, 16-2531, 16-503 (NP), 16-2532 to 16-2533 (NP), 16-504 (NP), 16-2534, 16-505, 16-2535, 16-506 to 16-508, 16-2536, 16-509 to 16-525

438   Cook, Chicago City   EDs 16-526 to 16-527, 16-2537, 16-528, 16-2538, 16-529 to 16-530, 16-2539, 16-531 to 16-535, 16-2907, 16-536 to 16-546, 16-2540, 16-547, 16-2541

439.   Cook, Chicago City   EDs 16-548, 16-2542, 16-549, 16-2543, 16-550, 16-2544, 16-551 to 16-552, 16-2545, 16-553 to 16-554, 16-2546, 16-555 to 16-556, 16-2547, 16-557 to 16-559, 16-2548, 16-560 to 16-565

440.   Cook, Chicago City   EDs 16-566 to 16-568, 16-2549, 16-569, 16-570 (NP), 16-2550, 16-571, 16-2551 to 16-2552, 16-572, 16-2553, 16-573, 16-2554, 16-574, 16-2555, 16-575, 16-2556 to 16-2558, 16-576, 16-2559 to 16-2561, 16-577 to 16-579

441.   Cook, Chicago City   EDs 16-2562, 16-580 to 16-587, 16-590, 16-588 to 16-589, 16-591 to 16-592, 16-2563, 16-593 to 16-600

442.   Cook, Chicago City   EDs 16-601 to 16-620, 16-2564, 16-621 to 16-622, 16-2565, 16-623 to 16-625

443.   Cook, Chicago City   EDs 16-626 to 16-631, 16-2908, 16-632 to 16-649, 16-2566

444.   Cook, Chicago City   EDs 16-650 to 16-671

445.   Cook, Chicago City   EDs 16-672 to 16-673, 16-2567, 16-674 to 16-675, 16-2568, 16-676 to 16-682, 16-2569, 16-683, 16-2570, 16-684, 16-2571, 16-685 to 16-689, 16-691

446.   Cook, Chicago City   EDs 16-690, 16-692 to 16-698, 16-2572 (NP), 16-699 to 16-712

447.   Cook, Chicago City   EDs 16-713 to 16-735, 16-736 (NP)

448.   Cook, Chicago City   EDs 16-737, 16-2573, 16-738 to 16-740, 16-2574, 16-741 to 16-750, 16-2575, 16-751, 16-2576, 16-752 to 16-753, 16-2577

449.   Cook, Chicago City   EDs 16-754 to 16-756, 16-2578, 16-757, 16-2579 to 16-2581, 16-758 to 16-760, 16-2582, 16-761 to 16-765, 16-2583, 16-766 to 16-771

450.   Cook, Chicago City   EDs 16-772 to 16-774, 16-2584, 16-775, 16-2585, 16-776, 16-2586, 16-777, 16-2587 to 16-2588, 16-778, 16-2589, 16-779, 16-2590, 16-780 to 16-781, 16-2591, 16-782, 16-2592, 16-783 to 16-784, 16-2593, 16-785, 16-2594 (NP), 16-786, 16-2595, 16-787 to 16-788, 16-2596, 16-789, 16-2597 to  16-2598 (NP), 16-790, 16-2599, 16-791

451.   Cook, Chicago City   EDs 16-792 to 16-804, 16-2600 (NP), 16-805, 16-2601, 16-806, 16-2602, 16-807, 16-2603 to 16-2604,

16-808, 16-2605, 16-809 to 16-811, 16-2606, 16-812, 16-2607 to 16-2608, 16-813, 16-2609

452. Cook, Chicago City   EDs 16-814, 16-2610 (NP), 16-815, 16-2611, 16-816, 16-2612, 16-817, 16-2613, 16-818 to 16-821, 16-2614, 16-822, 16-2615, 16-823 to 16-827, 16-2616, 16-828 to 16-835

453. Cook, Chicago City   EDs 16-836 to 16-846, 16-2617 (NP), 16-847 to 16-860, 16-2618 to 16-2619

454. Cook, Chicago City   EDs 16-861, 16-2620, 16-2621 (NP), 16-862 to 16-871, 16-873, 16-872, 16-874 to 16-882, 16-2622

455. Cook, Chicago City   EDs 16-883 to 16-886, 16-2623, 16-887 to 16-888, 16-2624, 16-889 to 16-890, 16-2625, 16-891 to 16-893, 16-2626, 16-894, 16-2627, 16-895 to 16-896, 16-2628, 16-897, 16-2629 to 16-2630, 16-898 to 16-899, 16-2631, 16-900 to 16-901, 16-2632, 16-902, 16-2633, 16-903 to 16-904, 16-2634

456. Cook, Chicago City   EDs 16-905, 16-2635, 16-906, 16-2636 to 16-2637, 16-907 to 16-908, 16-2638, 16-909 to 16-910, 16-2639, 16-911, 16-2640, 16-912 to 16-913, 16-2641, 16-914, 16-2642, 16-915, 16-2643, 16-916, 16-2644, 16-917 to 16-919, 16-2645, 16-920, 16-2646, 16-921, 16-2647, 16-922 to 16-927, 16-2648 to 16-2649

457. Cook, Chicago City   EDs 16-928 to 16-932, 16-2650 to 16-2651, 16-933 to 16-934, 16-2652, 16-935 to 16-937, 16-2653, 16-938 to 16-947, 16-2654, 16-948 to 16-953, 16-2655

458. Cook, Chicago City   EDs 16-954 to 16-959, 16-2656, 16-960 to 16-961, 16-2657, 16-1062 to 16-1065, 16-2672, 16-1066 to 16-1074, 16-2673, 16-1075 to 16-1077

459. Cook, Chicago City   EDs 16-1078 to 16-1080, 16-2674, 16-1081 to 16-1082, 16-2675, 16-1083 to 16-1085, 16-2676, 16-1086 to 16-1090, 16-2677 to 16-2679, 16-1091, 16-2680, 16-1092 to 16-1095, 16-962, 16-2658, 16-963 to 16-967, 16-2659, 16-968 to 16-974

460. Cook, Chicago City   EDs 16-975 to 16-989, 16-2660, 16-990 to 16-991, 16-2661, 16-992 to 16-996, 16-2662, 16-997 to 16-999, 16-2663, 16-1000 to 16-1001, 16-2664, 16-1002 to 16-1003

461. Cook, Chicago City   EDs 16-1004 to 16-1005, 16-2665, 16-1006 to 16-1018, 16-2666, 16-1019, 16-2667, 16-1020 to 16-1026

462. Cook, Chicago City   EDs 16-1027 to 16-1051, 16-2668, 16-1052 to 16-1053, 16-2669

463. Cook, Chicago City   EDs 16-1054 to 16-1058, 16-2670, 16-1059 (NP), 16-2671, 16-1060 to 16-1061, 16-1096 to 16-1098, 16-2681 to 16-2682, 16-1099 to 16-1101, 16-2683, 16-1102 to 16-1103, 16-2684, 16-1104 to 16-1109, 16-2685

464. Cook, Chicago City   EDs 16-1110 to 16-1111, 16-2686, 16-1112, 16-2687, 16-1113, 16-2688 (NP), 16-1114, 16-2689, 16-1115 to 16-1126, 16-2690, 16-1127, 16-2691, 16-1128 to 16-1129, 16-2692, 16-1130, 16-2693

465. Cook, Chicago City   EDs 16-1131 to 16-1134, 16-2694, 16-1135 (NP), 16-2695, 16-1136 to 16-1137, 16-2696, 16-1138, 16-2697, 16-1139, 16-2698, 16-1141 to 16-1142, 16-1140, 16-1143, 16-2699, 16-1144, 16-2700, 16-1145, 16-2701, 16-1146 to 16-1147, 16-2702 (NP), 16-1148, 16-2703, 16-1149 to 16-1154

466. Cook, Chicago City   EDs 16-1155 to 16-1156, 16-2704, 16-1157 to 16-1163, 16-2705, 16-1164 to 16-1170, 16-2706, 16-1171 to 16-1175, 16-2707, 16-1176 to 16-1177

467. Cook, Chicago City   EDs 16-1178 to 16-1182, 16-2708, 16-1183 to 16-1191, 16-2709, 16-1192, 16-2710, 16-1193 to 16-1194, 16-2711, 16-1195 to 16-1198, 16-2712, 16-1199

468. Cook, Chicago City   EDs 16-1200 to 16-1204, 16-2713, 16-1205 to 16-1206, 16-2714, 16-1207, 16-2715, 16-1208, 16-2716, 16-1209 to 16-1222, 16-2717, 16-1223 to 16-1224

469. Cook, Chicago City   EDs 16-1225 to 16-1229, 16-2718, 16-1230, 16-2719, 16-1231, 16-2720, 16-1232 to 16-1234, 16-2721, 16-1235 to 16-1236, 16-2722, 16-1237, 16-2723 (NP), 16-1238 to

16-1240, 16-2724, 16-1241 to 16-1244, 16-2725, 16-1245 to 16-1253, 16-2726

470. Cook, Chicago City   EDs 16-1254 to 16-1255, 16-2727, 16-1256 to 16-1257, 16-2728, 16-1258, 16-2729, 16-1259, 16-2730 to 16-2731, 16-1260 to 16-1263, 16-2732, 16-1264 to 16-1269, 16-2733, 16-1270 to 16-1274, 16-2734, 16-1275 to 16-1278, 16-2735, 16-1279 to 16-1282

471. Cook, Chicago City   EDs 16-1283, 16-2736, 16-1284 to 16-1286, 16-2737, 16-1287 to 16-1289, 16-2738, 16-1290 to 16-1291, 16-2739, 16-1292 to 16-1293, 16-2740, 16-1294 to 16-1295, 16-2741, 16-1296 to 16-1299, 16-2742, 16-1300 to 16-1312

472. Cook, Chicago City   EDs 16-1313, 16-2743, 16-1314, 16-2744, 16-1315 to 16-1327, 16-2745, 16-1328, 16-2746, 16-1329, 16-2747, 16-1330 to 16-1331, 16-2748, 16-1332 to 16-1333, 16-2749, 16-1334

473. Cook, Chicago City   EDs 16-1335 to 16-1347, 16-2750 to 16-2751, 16-1348 to 16-1358, 16-2752, 16-1359

474. Cook, Chicago City   EDs 16-1360 to 16-1364, 16-2753, 16-1365, 16-2754, 16-1366, 16-2755, 16-1367 to 16-1368, 16-2756, 16-1369, 16-2757, 16-1370, 16-2758, 16-1371 to 16-1377, 16-2759, 16-1378 to 16-1379, 16-2760, 16-1380 to 16-1381, 16-2761, 16-1382

475. Cook, Chicago City   EDs 16-1383, 16-2762, 16-1384, 16-2763 to 16-2765, 16-1385 to 16-1386, 16-2766, 16-1387 to 16-1388, 16-2767, 16-1389, 16-2768, 16-1390, 16-2769, 16-1391, 16-2770, 16-1392 to 16-1393, 16-2771, 16-1394, 16-2772, 16-1395 to 16-1396

476. Cook, Chicago City   EDs 16-2773, 16-1397 to 16-1400, 16-2774, 16-1401 to 16-1405, 16-2775, 16-1406, 16-2776 to 16-2777, 16-1407 to 16-1409, 16-2778, 16-1410 to 16-1411, 16-2779, 16-1412, 16-2780, 16-1413 to 16-1416, 16-2781

477. Cook, Chicago City   EDs 16-1417 to 16-1422, 16-2782, 16-1423 to 16-1430, 16-2783, 16-1431 to 16-1435, 16-2784, 16-1436 to 16-1437, 16-2785, 16-1438 to 16-1439, 16-2786

478. Cook, Chicago City   EDs 16-1440, 16-2787, 16-1441 to 16-1444, 16-2788, 16-1445 to 16-1451, 16-2789, 16-1452, 16-2790, 16-1453 to 16-1460, 16-2791, 16-1461 to 16-1464

479. Cook, Chicago City   EDs 16-1465, 16-2792, 16-1466 to 16-1468, 16-2793, 16-1469, 16-2794, 16-1470, 16-2795 to 16-2796, 16-1471 to 16-1475, 16-2797, 16-1476 to 16-1477, 16-2798, 16-1478 to 16-1481, 16-2799

480. Cook, Chicago City   EDs 16-1482, 16-2800 to 16-2801, 16-1483, 16-2802, 16-1484 (NP), 16-2803 to 16-2805, 16-1485, 16-2806 to 16-2807, 16-1486 to 16-1491, 16-2808, 16-1492 to 16-1497, 16-2809

481. Cook, Chicago City   EDs 16-1498 to 16-1500, 16-2810, 16-1501 to 16-1502, 16-2811, 16-1503, 16-2812, 16-1504, 16-2813, 16-1505, 16-2814, 16-1506, 16-2815 (NP), 16-1507 to 16-1508, 16-2816, 16-1509 to 16-1511, 16-2817, 16-1512 to 16-1513, 16-2818, 16-1514 to 16-1519

482. Cook, Chicago City   EDs 16-1520, 16-2819, 16-1521, 16-2820, 16-1522 to 16-1523, 16-2821, 16-1524 to 16-1526, 16-2822, 16-1527, 16-2823, 16-1528, 16-2824, 16-1529 to 16-1532, 16-2825, 16-1533, 16-2826, 16-1534 to 16-1536, 16-2827 to 16-2828

483. Cook, Chicago City   EDs 16-1537 to 16-1538, 16-2829, 16-1539, 16-2830, 16-1540, 16-2831, 16-1541, 16-2832, 16-1542, 16-2833, 16-1543, 16-2834, 16-1544, 16-2835, 16-1545 to 16-1546, 16-2836, 16-1547 to 16-1555, 16-2837, 16-1556 to 16-1559, 16-2838, 16-1560 to 16-1569, 16-2839, 16-1570, 16-2840 to 16-2841, 16-1571 to 16-1572, 16-2842

484. Cook, Chicago City   EDs 16-1573 to 16-1574, 16-2843, 16-1575 to 16-1576, 16-2844, 16-1577 to 16-1584, 16-2845, 16-1585 to 16-1595, 16-2846, 16-1596 to 16-1601, 16-2847

485. Cook, Chicago City   EDs 16-1602 to 16-1624, 16-1625 (void), 16-1626 to 16-1630, 16-2848, 16-1631 to 16-1633, 16-2849, 16-1634

486. Cook, Chicago City   EDs 16-1635 to 16-1667, 16-2850 to 16-2851, 16-1668

487. Cook, Chicago City   EDs 16-1669, 16-2852, 16-1670 to 16-1671, 16-2853, 16-1672 to 16-1674, 16-2854, 16-1675 to 16-1677, 16-2855, 16-1678 to 16-1681, 16-2856, 16-1682 to 16-1685, 16-2857, 16-1686 to 16-1688, 16-2858, 16-1689 to 16-1690, 16-2859, 16-1691 to 16-1692, 16-2860, 16-1693, 16-2861 to 16-2862, 16-1694

488. Cook, Chicago City   EDs 16-1695 to 16-1696, 16-2863, 16-1697 to 16-1698, 16-2864, 16-1699, 16-2865, 16-1700 to 16-1702, 16-2866, 16-1703, 16-2867, 16-1704 to 16-1715, 16-2868, 16-1716 to 16-1719, 16-2869

489. Cook, Chicago City   EDs 16-1720 to 16-1725, 16-2870, 16-1726 (void), 16-2871, 16-1727 to 16-1740, 16-2872, 16-1741 to 16-1742, 16-2873, 16-1743 to 16-1745, 16-2874, 16-1746 to 16-1753

* 490. Cook, Chicago City   EDs 16-1754 to 16-1756, 16-2875, 16-1757 to 16-1760, 16-2876, 16-1761, 16-2877, 16-1762 to 16-1765, 16-2878, 16-1766 to 16-1768, 16-2879, 16-1769 to 16-1770, 16-2880, 16-1771, 16-2881 to 16-2882, 16-1772, 16-2883, 16-1773 to 16-1774, 16-2884, 16-1775, 16-2885, 16-1776 to 16-1780

491. Cook, Chicago City   EDs 16-1781 to 16-1786, 16-1787 (NP), 16-1788 to 16-1806, 16-1807 (NP), 16-2887, 16-1808 to 16-1812

492. Cook, Chicago City   EDs 16-1813 to 16-1815, 16-2888, 16-1816 to 16-1830, 16-2889, 16-1831, 16-2890 (NP), 16-1832 to 16-1833, 16-2891, 16-1834 to 16-1847

493. Cook, Chicago City   EDs 16-1848 to 16-1861, 16-2892, 16-1862 to 16-1865, 16-2893, 16-1866, 16-2894, 16-1867 to 16-1876

494. Cook, Chicago City   EDs 16-1877 to 16-1884, 16-2895, 16-1885 to 16-1887, 16-2896, 16-1888 to 16-1895, 16-2897, 16-1896 to 16-1906, 16-1907 (NP), 16-1908 to 16-1910

495. Cook, Chicago City   EDs 16-1911 to 16-1921, 16-2898, 16-1922 to 16-1926, 16-1927 (void), 16-1928 to 16-1930, 16-2899, 16-1931 to 16-1934, 16-2900, 16-1935 to 16-1937

496. Cook, Chicago City   EDs 16-1938, 16-2901, 16-1939, 16-2902, 16-1940 to 16-1948, 16-2903, 16-1949 to 16-1953, 16-2904, 16-1954 to 16-1956, 16-2905, 16-1957 to 16-1964

497. Cook, Chicago City   EDs 16-1965 to 16-1973, 16-2906, 16-1974 to 16-1976, 16-2069 to 16-2074, 16-2914 (void), 16-2075 to 16-2077, 16-2915, 16-2078

498. Cook   EDs 16-2079 to 16-2103

499. Cook   EDs 16-2104 to 16-2107, 16-2367, 16-2108 to 16-2125

500. Cook   EDs 16-2126 to 16-2131, 16-2137 to 16-2140, 16-2132 to 16-2136, 16-2141, 16-2143, 16-2142, 16-2144 to 16-2146

501. Cook   EDs 16-2155 to 16-2159, 16-2909, 16-2147 to 16-2154, 16-2160 to 16-2165, 16-2196 to 16-2201, 16-2217, 16-2227, 16-2236, 16-2202, 16-2230 to 16-2231, 16-2203 to 16-2204

502. Cook   EDs 16-2166 to 16-2169, 16-2181 to 16-2189, 16-2170 to 16-2173, 16-2190, 16-2174 to 16-2176, 16-2916, 16-2177, 16-2191 to 16-2193, 16-2178 to 16-2180

503. Cook   EDs 16-2194, 16-2292, 16-2195, 16-2205 to 16-2207, 16-2208 (NP), 16-2220 to 16-2224, 16-2218 to 16-2219, 16-2238, 16-2209 to 16-2216, 16-2225 to 16-2226

504. Cook   EDs 16-2228 to 16-2229, 16-2232 to 16-2234, 16-2235 (NP), 16-2237, 16-2239 to 16-2245, 16-2286 to 16-2291, 16-2293, 16-2375, 16-2294, 16-2246 to 16-2259, 16-2260 (NP), 16-2261 to 16-2262

505. Cook   EDs 16-2263 to 16-2285, 16-2333, 16-2335 to 16-2336, 16-2368 to 16-2370

506. Cook   EDs 16-2295 to 16-2298, 16-2324 to 16-2328, 16-2299 to 16-2308, 16-2310 to 16-2311

507. Cook   EDs 16-2309, 16-2312, 16-2917, 16-2313, 16-2918, 16-2314, 16-2919, 16-2315, 16-2920, 16-2316, 16-2921, 16-2317, 16-2922, 16-2318, 16-2923, 16-2319, 16-2924, 16-2320, 16-2925, 16-2321, 16-2926, 16-2322, 16-2927, 16-2323, 16-2928, 16-2329, 16-2341, 16-2330 to 16-2331, 16-2343 to 16-2347

508. Cook   EDs 16-2337 to 16-2340, 16-2342, 16-2348, 16-2356 to 16-2358, 16-2361 to 16-2362, 16-2349 to 16-2355, 16-2364, 16-2363, 16-2365 to 16-2366, 16-2371 to 16-2374, 16-2376

509. Crawford   EDs 17-1, 17-9, 17-2, 17-21, 17-3 to 17-4, 17-22, 17-5 to 17-8, 17-10, 17-23, 17-11 to 17-13, 17-24, 17-14 to 17-19, 17-25, 17-20

Cumberland   EDs 18-1 to 18-12

De Witt   EDs 20-1 to 20-23

510. De Kalb   EDs 19-1 to 19-3, 19-9, 19-4 to 19-8, 19-10 to 19-40

Douglas   EDs 21-1 to 21-18

511. DuPage   EDs 22-8 to 22-12, 22-1 to 22-7, 22-13, 22-72, 22-14, 22-66 to 22-70, 22-15 to 22-17, 22-47 to 22-49, 22-44 to 22-46, 22-50 to 22-57

512. DuPage   EDs 22-18 to 22-30, 22-71, 22-58 to 22-59, 22-31 to 22-39, 22-40 to 22-41 (void), 22-42 to 22-43, 22-60 to 22-64, 22-65 (NP)

Edwards   EDs 24-1 to 24-13

513. Edgar   EDs 23-1 to 23-2, 23-8, 23-3 to 23-5, 23-24, 23-6 to 23-7, 23-9 to 23-23, 23-25 to 23-29

Effingham   EDs 25-1 to 25-9, 25-31, 25-10 to 25-21, 25-24 to 25-25, 25-22 to 25-23, 25-26 to 25-30

Fulton   EDs 29-1 to 29-7

514. Fulton   EDs 29-8 to 29-15, 29-27, 29-16 to 29-24, 29-45, 29-25 to 29-26, 29-28 to 29-44, 29-46 to 29-51

Hamilton   EDs 33-1 to 33-19

515. Fayette   EDs 26-1 to 26-31

Ford   EDs 27-1 to 27-10, 27-21, 27-11 to 27-20, 27-22 to 27-25

Gallatin   EDs 30-1 to 30-10, 30-14, 30-11 to 30-13, 30-15 to 30-17

516. Franklin   EDs 28-1 to 28-15, 28-35 to 28-40, 28-25, 28-16 to 28-24, 28-26 to 28-34

517. Franklin   EDs 28-41 to 28-47

Greene   EDs 31-1 to 31-18, 31-21 to 31-22, 31-19 to 31-20

Grundy   EDs 32-1 to 32-5, 32-12, 32-6, 32-13, 32-7 to 32-11, 32-14 to 32-37

518. Hancock   EDs 34-1 to 34-19, 34-27, 34-20 to 34-22, 34-37, 34-23 to 34-26, 34-28, 34-30, 34-29, 34-31 to 34-36, 34-38 to 34-42

Hardin   EDs 35-1 to 35-5, 35-11, 35-6 to 35-10, 35-12

Henderson   EDs 36-1 to 36-4, 36-7, 36-5 to 36-6, 36-8 to 36-13, 36-19, 36-14 to 36-18, 36-20 to 36-21

Johnson   EDs 44-1 to 44-16

519. Henry   EDs 37-1 to 37-17, 37-52, 37-18 to 37-24, 37-38 to 37-51, 37-25 to 37-37

Iroquois   EDs 38-1 to 38-9, 38-11 to 38-12

520. Iroquois   EDs 38-10, 38-33, 38-13 to 38-15, 38-51, 38-16 to 38-18, 38-25, 38-19 to 38-24, 38-26 to 38-32, 38-34 to 38-50

Jackson   EDs 39-1 to 39-23, 39-33 to 39-36, 39-38 to 39-39

---

*Roll 490, Chicago, Cook County—There appears to be no ED 16-2886.

521. Jackson   EDs 39-24 to 39-32, 39-37

Jasper   EDs 40-1 to 40-3, 40-18, 40-4, 40-21, 40-5 to 40-9, 40-19, 40-10 to 40-15, 40-20, 40-16 to 40-17

Jefferson   EDs 41-1, 41-3, 41-9, 41-14, 41-2, 41-4 to 41-5, 41-28, 41-6 to 41-8, 41-10 to 41-13, 41-15 to 41-27, 41-29 to 41-33

522. Jersey   EDs 42-1 to 42-21

Jo Daviess   EDs 43-1 to 43-35

Kendall   EDs 47-1, 47-10, 47-2 to 47-9, 47-11 to 47-17

Lee   EDs 52-1 to 52-10

523. Lee   EDs 52-11 to 52-40

Kane   EDs 45-1 to 45-17

524. Kane   EDs 45-18 to 45-31, 45-38, 45-32 to 45-37, 45-39 to 45-50, 45-78 to 45-85

525. Kane   EDs 45-51 to 45-77, 45-86, 45-89, 45-87 to 45-88, 45-90 to 45-100

526. Kankakee   EDs 46-1 to 46-4, 46-51, 46-5, 46-52, 46-6 to 46-9, 46-31, 46-10, 46-28 to 46-30, 46-32 to 46-50, 46-11, 46-53, 46-12, 46-54, 46-13, 46-55, 46-14 to 46-18, 46-56, 46-19 to 46-21, 46-57, 46-22, 46-58, 46-23, 46-59, 46-24 to 46-27, 46-60

527. Knox   EDs 48-1 to 48-10, 48-55, 48-11 to 48-54, 48-56 to 48-58

528. Lake   EDs 49-1 to 49-15, 49-37 to 49-40, 49-16 to 49-36

529. Lake   EDs 49-41 to 49-43, 49-53, 49-44, 49-46 to 49-50, 49-61 to 49-62, 49-56 to 49-60, 49-63 to 49-65, 49-51 to 49-52, 49-54, 49-45, 49-55, 49-66 to 49-69, 49-87, 49-86, 49-70 to 49-77

530. Lake   EDs 49-78 to 49-85

La Salle   EDs 50-1 to 50-25

531. La Salle   EDs 50-26 to 50-47, 50-93 to 50-95, 50-50, 50-48 to 50-49, 50-51 to 50-65, 50-78 to 50-83

532. La Salle   EDs 50-66 to 50-77, 50-84 to 50-92

Lawrence   EDs 51-1 to 51-9, 51-20, 51-10 to 51-17, 51-21, 51-18 to 51-19

McDonough   EDs 55-1 to 55-2, 55-13, 55-3

533. McDonough   EDs 55-4 to 55-12, 55-14 to 55-17, 55-22, 55-24, 55-23, 55-18 to 55-21, 55-25 to 55-29, 55-35, 55-30 to 55-34, 55-36

Livingston   EDs 53-1 to 53-5, 53-42, 53-6, 53-51, 53-7 to 53-32, 53-46 to 53-50, 53-52 to 53-53

534. Livingston   EDs 53-33 to 53-41, 53-43 to 53-45

Marshall   EDs 62-1 to 62-20

Logan   EDs 54-1 to 54-22, 54-25, 54-23 to 54-24, 54-26 to 54-32

535. Logan   EDs 54-33, 54-36, 54-34 to 54-35, 54-37 to 54-41

McLean   EDs 57-1 to 57-11, 57-18 to 57-23, 57-12 to 57-17, 57-24 to 57-36, 57-67, 57-37 to 57-38

536. McLean   EDs 57-39 to 57-66

McHenry   EDs 56-1, 56-6 to 56-7, 56-2 to 56-5, 56-8 to 56-10, 56-37, 56-11 to 56-16, 56-40, 56-17 to 56-30

537. McHenry   EDs 56-31 to 56-36, 56-38 to 56-39, 56-41

Mason   EDs 63-1 to 63-24

Macon   EDs 58-1 to 58-16

538. Macon   EDs 58-17 to 58-41, 58-64, 58-42 to 58-52

539. Macon   EDs 58-53 to 58-63

Mercer   EDs 66-1 to 66-15, 66-26, 66-16 to 66-25, 66-27

Macoupin   EDs 59-1, 59-60, 59-2 to 59-9, 59-16 to 59-18, 59-10 to 59-15, 59-19 to 59-27, 59-55, 59-28 to 59-29, 59-32, 59-30 to 59-31, 59-33

540. Macoupin   EDs 59-34 to 59-45, 59-58, 59-46 to 59-49, 59-61, 59-50 to 59-54, 59-56 to 59-57, 59-59, 59-62 to 59-73

Madison   EDs 60-1 to 60-17

541. Madison   EDs 60-18 to 60-28, 60-55 to 60-57, 60-77 to 60-83, 60-29 to 60-37, 60-94, 60-38 to 60-53, 60-87, 60-54

542. Madison   EDs 60-58 to 60-70, 60-76, 60-71 to 60-75, 60-84 to 60-86, 60-88 to 60-93, 60-99 to 60-102

543. Madison   EDs 60-95 to 60-98, 60-103 to 60-105

Marion   EDs 61-1 to 61-3, 61-14 to 61-28, 61-4 to 61-13, 61-29 to 61-39

544. Massac   EDs 64-1 to 64-16

Menard   EDs 65-1 to 65-18

Monroe   EDs 67-1 to 67-18

Montgomery   EDs 68-1 to 68-7, 68-12, 68-8 to 68-11, 68-13 to 68-16, 68-46 to 68-47, 68-49 to 68-50

545. Montgomery   EDs 68-17 to 68-31, 68-48, 68-32 to 68-35, 68-35 to 68-40, 68-33 to 68-34, 68-41 to 68-45

Morgan   EDs 69-1 to 69-21

546. Morgan   EDs 69-22 to 69-37

Moultrie   EDs 70-1 to 70-17

Ogle   EDs 71-1 to 71-36

547. Peoria   EDs 72-1, 72-88, 72-2 to 72-23, 72-99, 72-24, 72-25 (NP)

Peoria, Peoria City   EDs 72-26 to 72-32, 72-70 to 72-79

548. Peoria, Peoria City   EDs 72-33 to 72-38, 72-80 to 72-87, 72-39 to 72-53

549. Peoria, Peoria City   EDs 72-54 to 72-69, 72-89 to 72-98

Piatt   EDs 74-1 to 74-17

550. Perry   EDs 73-1 to 73-22

Pope   EDs 76-1 to 76-16

Pulaski   EDs 77-1 to 77-18

Putnam   EDs 78-1 to 78-9

551. Pike   EDs 75-1 to 75-41

Randolph   EDs 79-1 to 79-37

552. Randolph   EDs 79-38 to 79-43

Rock Island   EDs 81-1 to 81-5, 81-15, 81-6 to 81-14, 81-16, 81-26, 81-17 to 81-25, 81-98, 81-27 to 81-28, 81-65 (NP), 81-32 to 81-33, 81-29 to 81-31, 81-34 to 81-55

553. Rock Island   EDs 81-56 to 81-63, 81-93, 81-64, 81-66 to 81-92, 81-94 to 81-95, 81-99, 81-96 to 81-97

554. Richland   EDs 80-1 to 80-18

Saline   EDs 83-1, 83-5 to 83-11, 83-2 to 83-4, 83-13 to 83-20, 83-12, 83-21 to 83-31

555. St. Clair   EDs 82-1 to 82-18, 82-21 to 82-23, 82-19 to 82-20, 82-24 to 82-34, 82-78 to 82-85

556. St. Clair   EDs 82-35 to 82-59

557. St. Clair   EDs 82-60 to 82-70, 82-71 (NP), 82-72 to 82-77, 82-86 to 82-111

558. Sangamon   EDs 84-1 to 84-5, 84-54 to 84-84, 84-6 to 84-24

559. Sangamon   EDs 84-25 to 84-53

560. Sangamon   EDs 84-85 to 84-93

Schuyler   EDs 85-1 to 85-21

Scott   EDs 86-1 to 86-3, 86-16, 86-23, 86-4 to 86-14, 86-21, 86-15, 86-17 to 86-20, 86-22, 86-24

Stephenson   EDs 89-1, 89-21, 89-25, 89-2 to 89-6, 89-26 to 89-43

561. Stephenson   EDs 89-7 to 89-18, 89-19 (void), 89-20, 89-22 to 89-24

Shelby   EDs 87-1 to 87-16, 87-37, 87-17 to 87-36, 87-38 to 87-42

562. Stark   EDs 88-1 to 88-2, 88-11, 88-3 to 88-5, 88-10, 88-6 to 88-9, 88-12 to 88-14

Tazewell   EDs 90-1 to 90-9, 90-41, 90-10 to 90-14, 90-27, 90-15 to 90-26, 90-28 to 90-39

563. Tazewell   EDs 90-40, 90-42 to 90-44

Union   EDs 91-1 to 91-24

Vermilion   EDs 92-1 to 92-11, 92-40 to 92-41, 92-44 to 92-50, 92-43, 92-51 to 92-56

564. Vermilion   EDs 92-33, 92-42, 92-12 to 92-15, 92-75, 92-16 to 92-19, 92-76, 92-26 to 92-29, 92-20, 92-77, 92-21 to 92-25, 92-34, 92-30 to 92-32, 92-35 to 92-39

565. Vermilion   EDs 92-57 to 92-74

Wabash   EDs 93-1 to 93-16

Warren   EDs 94-1 to 94-7, 94-19, 94-8 to 94-18, 94-20 to 94-25

Washington   EDs 95-1 to 95-4

566. Washington   EDs 95-5, 95-10, 95-6 to 95-9, 95-11 to 95-22, 95-26, 95-23 to 95-25, 95-27 to 95-31

Whiteside   EDs 98-1 to 98-10, 98-43, 98-11 to 98-23, 98-24 (NP), 98-25 to 98-42

567. Wayne   EDs 96-1 to 96-7, 96-12, 96-8 to 96-11, 96-13 to 96-29

White   EDs 97-1 to 97-21

Will   EDs 99-1 to 99-6, 99-67, 99-7 to 99-16

568. Will   EDs 99-17 to 99-45, 99-49, 99-92

569. Will   EDs 99-46 to 99-48, 99-50 to 99-66, 99-68 to 99-91

570. Williamson   EDs 100-7 to 100-9, 100-1 to 100-6, 100-10 to 100-22, 100-48, 100-23 to 100-31, 100-46, 100-32 to 100-34, 100-41, 100-52, 100-42, 100-35 to 100-40, 100-43, 100-47, 100-44 to 100-45, 100-49 to 100-51, 100-53

571. Winnebago   EDs 101-1 to 101-28, 101-35 to 101-43

572. Winnebago   EDs 101-29 to 101-34, 101-50 to 101-56, 101-44 to 101-49, 101-57 to 101-63, 101-73

573. Winnebago   EDs 101-64 to 101-65, 101-67, 101-66, 101-68 to 101-72

Woodford   EDs 102-1 to 102-29

## Indiana

574. Adams   EDs 1-1 to 1-6, 1-17, 1-7, 1-20, 1-8 to 1-16, 1-18, 1-19, 1-21

Brown   EDs 7-1 to 7-6

Allen, Fort Wayne City   EDs 2-1 to 2-17

575. Allen, Fort Wayne City   EDs 2-18 to 2-23, 2-76, 2-24 to 2-27, 2-77, 2-28, 2-78, 2-29, 2-79, 2-30, 2-80, 2-41 to 2-46

576. Allen, Fort Wayne City   EDs 2-31, 2-34, 2-32 to 2-33, 2-35 to 2-40, 2-47, 2-81, 2-48, 2-82, 2-49 to 2-66

577. Allen   EDs 2-67 to 2-75

Benton   EDs 4-1 to 4-17

Bartholomew   EDs 3-1 to 3-27

578. Blackford   EDs 5-1 to 5-10

Crawford   EDs 13-1 to 13-14

Boone   EDs 6-1 to 6-4, 6-23, 6-5 to 6-22

579. Carroll   EDs 8-1 to 8-5, 8-18, 8-6 to 8-17

Cass   EDs 9-1 to 9-8, 9-23 to 9-26, 9-9 to 9-22, 9-27 to 9-33

580. Clark   EDs 10-1 to 10-4, 10-8 to 10-15, 10-5, 10-6 (void), 10-7, 10-16 to 10-17, 10-27, 10-18 to 10-26

Decatur   EDs 16-1 to 16-15, 16-19, 16-16 to 16-18, 16-20

581. Clay   EDs 11-1 to 11-6, 11-13, 11-7 to 11-12, 11-14 to 11-26

Clinton   EDs 12-1 to 12-25

582. Daviess   EDs 14-1 to 14-23

Dearborn   EDs 15-1 to 15-28

Delaware   EDs 18-23 to 18-27

583. Delaware   EDs 18-1 to 18-6, 18-42, 18-7 to 18-22, 18-28 to 18-32

584. Delaware   EDs 18-33 to 18-41

Elkhart   EDs 20-1 to 20-2, 20-5, 20-3 to 20-4, 20-6, 20-25 to 20-26, 20-38 to 20-42, 20-44 to 20-47, 20-7 to 20-21

585. Elkhart   EDs 20-22 to 20-24, 20-27 to 20-36, 20-43, 20-37

De Kalb   EDs 17-1 to 17-28

586. Dubois   EDs 19-1 to 19-21

Fayette   EDs 21-1 to 21-11, 21-16, 21-12 to 21-15, 21-17 to 21-19

Fountain   EDs 23-1 to 23-11

587. Fountain   EDs 23-12 to 23-22

Franklin   EDs 24-1 to 24-13, 24-14 (NP), 24-15 to 24-21

Floyd   EDs 22-1 to 22-6, 22-20 to 22-21, 22-7 to 22-15

588. Floyd   EDs 22-16 to 22-19

Fulton   EDs 25-1 to 25-16

Gibson   EDs 26-1 to 26-31

589. Grant   EDs 27-1 to 27-40, 27-41 (void)

590. Greene   EDs 28-1 to 28-5, 28-7, 28-6, 28-8 to 28-24, 28-28 to 28-29, 28-25 to 28-27

Hamilton   EDs 29-1 to 29-4, 29-6, 29-5, 29-7 to 29-24

591. Hancock   EDs 30-1 to 30-18

Hendricks   EDs 32-1 to 32-15, 32-24, 32-16 to 32-23

Howard   EDs 34-1 to 34-10

592. Howard   EDs 34-11 to 34-30

Harrison   EDs 31-1, 31-24, 31-2 to 31-23

Henry   EDs 33-1 to 33-14

593. Henry   EDs 33-15 to 33-25, 33-32, 33-26 to 33-31, 33-33 to 33-39

Huntington   EDs 35-1 to 35-14, 35-16, 35-18, 35-26, 35-15, 35-17, 35-19 to 35-23

594. Huntington   EDs 35-24 to 35-25, 35-27

Jackson   EDs 36-1 to 36-21

Jasper   EDs 37-1 to 37-18

Jennings   EDs 40-1 to 40-16

595. Jay   EDs 38-1 to 38-22

Lagrange   EDs 44-1 to 44-4, 44-6, 44-5, 44-7 to 44-16

Jefferson   EDs 39-1 to 39-18

596. Johnson   EDs 41-1 to 41-18

Knox   EDs 42-1 to 42-25

597. Knox   EDs 42-26 to 42-35

Lawrence   EDs 47-1 to 47-13, 47-24, 47-14, 47-25, 47-15, 47-26, 47-16 to 47-17, 47-27, 47-18 to 47-23

598. Kosciusko   EDs 43-1 to 43-5, 43-7, 43-6, 43-8 to 43-31

Lake, Gary City   EDs 45-1 to 45-7, 45-20 to 45-27

599. Lake, Gary City   EDs 45-8 to 45-19, 45-34 to 45-41, 45-28 to 45-33, 45-42 to 45-50

600. Lake, Gary City   EDs 45-51 to 45-66, 45-67 to 45-86, 45-93 to 45-97

601. Lake   EDs 45-87 to 45-92, 45-98 to 45-122, 45-131 to 45-133

602. Lake   EDs 45-123 to 45-130, 45-134 to 45-162, 45-167 to 45-169

603. Lake   EDs 45-163 to 45-166, 45-170 to 45-187

La Porte   EDs 46-1 to 46-18

604. La Porte   EDs 46-19 to 46-21, 46-22 (NP), 46-23, 46-51, 46-24, 46-52, 46-25 to 46-30, 46-53, 46-55, 46-31 to 46-42, 46-54, 46-43 to 46-50

Madison   EDs 48-1 to 48-9

605. Madison   EDs 48-10 to 48-17, 48-19, 48-18, 48-20 to 48-38, 48-54, 48-39 to 48-43, 48-63, 48-44 to 48-51

606. Madison   EDs 48-52 to 48-53, 48-55 to 48-62

Marion   EDs 49-226, 49-233, 49-242, 49-251 (NP), 49-227 to 49-230, 49-291, 49-231 to 49-232, 49-234 to 49-235

Marion, Indianapolis City   EDs 49-1, 49-292 to 49-293, 49-2, 49-441, 49-3, 49-442, 49-4, 49-294, 49-5, 49-295 to 49-296, 49-6 to 49-7, 49-297 to 49-298, 49-8 to 49-9, 49-299 to 49-300

607. Marion, Indianapolis City   EDs 49-10 to 49-14, 49-301, 49-15, 49-302, 49-16 to 49-17, 49-303, 49-18 to 49-19, 49-304, 49-20, 49-305, 49-21, 49-306, 49-443, 49-307, 49-22 to 49-23, 49-308 to 49-309, 49-24, 49-310, 49-25, 49-311, 49-26, 49-312, 49-27 to 49-28, 49-313, 49-29

608. Marion, Indianapolis City   EDs 49-30 to 49-31, 49-314, 49-32 to 49-38, 49-315, 49-39, 49-316 to 49-317, 49-40, 49-318, 49-41 to 49-42, 49-319 to 49-320, 49-43 to 49-45, 49-321 to 49-322, 49-46, 49-444, 49-47 to 49-48, 49-323, 49-49 to 49-50, 49-324, 49-51, 49-325, 49-52, 49-326, 49-53

609. Marion, Indianapolis City   EDs 49-54 to 49-58, 49-327 to 49-330, 49-59, 49-331 to 49-332, 49-60, 49-333, 49-61 to 49-62, 49-334, 49-63, 49-335, 49-64 to 49-66, 49-336, 49-67 to 49-68, 49-337, 49-69, 49-338, 49-70 to 49-71, 49-72 (NP), 49-339, 49-73, 49-340, 49-74, 49-341, 49-75, 49-342, 49-445 to 49-446, 49-343

610. Marion, Indianapolis City   EDs 49-76, 49-447 to 49-448, 49-77, 49-449 to 49-450, 49-344 to 49-346, 49-78, 49-451, 49-347, 49-79 to 49-80, 49-348, 49-81, 49-349, 49-452, 49-350, 49-82, 49-351, 49-453, 49-83 to 49-84, 49-352, 49-85, 49-353, 49-86 to 49-88, 49-354, 49-89, 49-355, 49-90, 49-356

611. Marion, Indianapolis City   EDs 49-91 to 49-92, 49-357, 49-93, 49-358, 49-94, 49-359, 49-95 to 49-96, 49-360, 49-97 to 49-98, 49-361, 49-99, 49-362, 49-100 to 49-108, 49-363, 49-109, 49-364 to 49-365, 49-110 to 49-111, 49-366, 49-112, 49-367, 49-113, 49-368 to 49-369, 49-114 to 49-115, 49-370, 49-116, 49-371, 49-117, 49-372, 49-118

612. Marion, Indianapolis City   EDs 49-119, 49-373 to 49-374, 49-120, 49-375 to 49-376, 49-121 to 49-123, 49-377, 49-124, 49-378, 49-125 to 49-126, 49-379, 49-127 to 49-129, 49-380, 49-130, 49-381, 49-131, 49-382, 49-132 to 49-133, 49-383, 49-134, 49-384, 49-135 to 49-136, 49-385 to 49-387, 49-137, 49-388, 49-138 to 49-140, 49-389

613. Marion, Indianapolis City   EDs 49-141, 49-390 to 49-392, 49-142 to 49-145, 49-393, 49-146 to 49-148, 49-394, 49-149 to 49-151, 49-395, 49-152 to 49-155, 49-396, 49-156 to 49-157, 49-397 to 49-398, 49-158 to 49-159, 49-399 to 49-401, 49-160, 49-402

614. Marion, Indianapolis City   EDs 49-161, 49-403, 49-162 to 49-163, 49-404, 49-164, 49-405, 49-165 to 49-166, 49-406, 49-167 to 49-169, 49-407, 49-170 to 49-171, 49-408, 49-172, 49-409, 49-173, 49-410, 49-174, 49-411, 49-175, 49-454, 49-176 to 49-178, 49-412, 49-179, 49-413, 49-180 (NP), 49-414, 49-181 to 49-182, 49-415, 49-183 to 49-184, 49-416, 49-185 to 49-186, 49-417 to 49-419

615. Marion, Indianapolis City   EDs 49-187 (NP), 49-420 to 49-421, 49-188, 49-189 (NP), 49-190 to 49-191, 49-422, 49-192 to 49-195, 49-423, 49-196, 49-424, 49-197, 49-425, 49-198 to 49-199, 49-426, 49-200, 49-427, 49-201, 49-428, 49-202, 49-429, 49-203 to 49-204, 49-430, 49-205, 49-431, 49-206, 49-207 (NP), 49-208, 49-432, 49-209, 49-433, 49-210, 49-434, 49-211, 49-435, 49-212 to 49-213, 49-436 (NP), 49-214

616. Marion, Indianapolis City   EDs 49-215 to 49-217, 49-437, 49-218 to 49-220, 49-438, 49-221, 49-439, 49-222, 49-440, 49-223 to 49-225

Marion   EDs 49-236, 49-455, 49-237 to 49-241, 49-243 to 49-250, 49-252 to 49-262

617. Marion   EDs 49-263 to 49-290

Marshall   EDs 50-1 to 50-20

618. Martin   EDs 51-1 to 51-3, 51-5, 51-4, 51-6 to 51-12

Miami   EDs 52-1 to 52-14, 52-22 to 52-28, 52-15 to 52-21

Monroe   EDs 53-1 to 53-3, 53-12 to 53-20

619. Monroe   EDs 53-4, 53-26, 53-5, 53-27, 53-6 to 53-11, 53-28, 53-21 to 53-25

Morgan   EDs 55-1 to 55-21

Newton   EDs 56-1 to 56-15

620. Montgomery   EDs 54-1, 54-15, 54-26, 54-2 to 54-14, 54-16 to 54-25, 54-27, 54-33 to 54-34, 54-28 to 54-32

Noble   EDs 57-1 to 57-23

Ohio   EDs 58-1 to 58-5

621. Orange   EDs 59-1 to 59-15

Perry   EDs 62-1 to 62-9, 62-17, 62-10 to 62-16

Pike   EDs 63-1 to 63-2, 63-17, 63-3 to 63-16

622. Owen   EDs 60-1 to 60-16

Parke   EDs 61-1 to 61-13, 61-17, 61-14 to 61-16, 61-18 to 61-21

Porter   EDs 64-1 to 64-25

Posey   EDs 65-15 to 65-19

623. Posey   EDs 65-1 to 65-14

Pulaski   EDs 66-1 to 66-16

Putnam   EDs 67-1 to 67-23

Ripley   EDs 69-1 to 69-7

624. Ripley   EDs 69-8, 69-18, 69-9 to 69-17, 69-19

Steuben   EDs 76-1 to 76-15, 76-19, 76-16 to 76-18, 76-20 to 76-21

Randolph   EDs 68-1 to 68-11, 68-22, 68-12 to 68-21, 68-23 to 68-28

625. Rush   EDs 70-1 to 70-18

Scott   EDs 72-1 to 72-6

St. Joseph, South Bend City   EDs 71-1 to 71-18

626. St. Joseph, South Bend City   EDs 71-19 to 71-39, 71-52 to 71-57

627. St. Joseph, South Bend City   EDs 71-40 to 71-51, 71-58 to 71-78

628. St. Joseph   EDs 71-79 to 71-97

Shelby   EDs 73-1 to 73-10, 73-22, 73-11 to 73-16, 73-23, 73-17 to 73-21, 73-24

629. Spencer   EDs 74-1 to 74-17

Starke   EDs 75-1 to 75-4, 75-8, 75-5 to 75-7, 75-9 to 75-13

Sullivan   EDs 77-1 to 77-26

630. Switzerland   EDs 78-1 to 78-9

Tippecanoe   EDs 79-1 to 79-36

631. Tipton   EDs 80-1 to 80-15

Warren   EDs 86-1 to 86-16

Union   EDs 81-1 to 81-8

Washington   EDs 88-1 to 88-13, 88-15, 88-14, 88-16 to 88-27

632. Vanderburgh, Evansville City   EDs 82-1 to 82-2, 82-6, 82-56, 82-7 to 82-11, 82-26 to 82-30, 82-57, 82-31 to 82-47

633. Vanderburgh, Evansville City   EDs 82-12 to 82-16, 82-22 to 82-25, 82-3 to 82-5, 82-58, 82-62, 82-59 to 82-61, 82-17 to 82-21, 82-42 to 82-45, 82-55, 82-46, 82-48 to 82-54

634. Vermillion   EDs 83-1 to 83-20

Vigo   EDs 84-1 to 84-7, 84-36 to 84-43

635. Vigo   EDs 84-8 to 84-19, 84-32 to 84-35, 84-20 to 84-31, 84-44 to 84-48

636. Vigo   EDs 84-49 to 84-70

Wabash   EDs 85-1 to 85-19

637. Warrick   EDs 87-1 to 87-21

Wayne   EDs 89-1 to 89-5, 89-53, 89-6 to 89-25, 89-28 to 89-29, 89-32 to 89-38

638. Wayne   EDs 89-26 to 89-27, 89-30 to 89-31, 89-39 to 89-48, 89-54, 89-49 to 89-52

Wells   EDs 90-1, 90-7, 90-15, 90-2 to 90-6, 90-8 to 90-14, 90-16 to 90-19, 90-21, 90-20, 90-22

White   EDs 91-1 to 91-10

639. White   EDs 91-11 to 91-19

Whitley   EDs 92-1 to 92-17

## Iowa

640. Adair   EDs 1-1 to 1-25

Audubon   EDs 5-1 to 5-4, 5-14, 5-5 to 5-13, 5-15 to 5-18

Adams   EDs 2-1 to 2-6, 2-14, 2-7 to 2-13, 2-15 to 2-18

Allamakee   EDs 3-1 to 3-24

641. Appanoose   EDs 4-1, 4-28, 4-2, 4-16, 4-3 to 4-15, 4-17 to 4-27, 4-29 to 4-31, 4-33, 4-32, 4-34

Benton   EDs 6-1 to 6-19, 6-26, 6-20 to 6-25, 6-27 to 6-39

642. Black Hawk   EDs 7-1 to 7-15, 7-32 to 7-43, 7-22 to 7-31

643. Black Hawk   EDs 7-16 to 7-21, 7-44 to 7-46

Boone   EDs 8-1 to 8-3, 8-34, 8-4 to 8-7, 8-36, 8-8 to 8-17, 8-31, 8-38, 8-18 to 8-19, 8-21, 8-20, 8-22 to 8-27

644. Boone   EDs 8-28, 8-39, 8-29 to 8-30, 8-32 to 8-33, 8-35, 8-37, 8-40

Bremer   EDs 9-1 to 9-26

Buchanan   EDs 10-1, 10-18, 10-2 to 10-17, 10-19 to 10-33

645. Buena Vista   EDs 11-1 to 11-29

Butler   EDs 12-1, 12-19, 12-2 to 12-7, 12-14, 12-8 to 12-13, 12-28, 12-15 to 12-18, 12-20 to 12-21, 12-29, 12-22 to 12-27, 12-30

Calhoun   EDs 13-1 to 13-2, 13-25, 13-3 to 13-8, 13-27, 13-9 to 13-24, 13-26, 13-28 to 13-31

646. Carroll   EDs 14-1 to 14-7, 14-8 (void), 14-9 to 14-15, 14-29, 14-16 to 14-18, 14-19 (NP), 14-35, 14-20 to 14-28, 14-30 to 14-34, 14-36

Cass   EDs 15-1 to 15-27

Cedar   EDs 16-1 to 16-9, 16-18, 16-10 to 16-11

647. Cedar   EDs 16-12 to 16-17, 16-19 to 16-26

Cherokee   EDs 18-1 to 18-27

Cerro Gordo   EDs 17-1 to 17-13, 17-35, 17-14 to 17-18, 17-22 to 17-27

648. Cerro Gordo   EDs 17-19 to 17-21, 17-28 to 17-34, 17-36 to 17-38

Chickasaw   EDs 19-1 to 19-6, 19-14, 19-7 to 19-9, 19-11, 19-10, 19-12 to 19-13, 19-15 to 19-22

Clarke   EDs 20-1 to 20-16

Clay   EDs 21-1 to 21-28

649. Clayton   EDs 22-1 to 22-9, 22-39, 22-10 to 22-12, 22-41, 22-13 to 22-20, 22-24, 22-21 to 22-23, 22-25 to 22-38, 22-40, 22-42 to 22-43

Clinton   EDs 23-1 to 23-7, 23-10, 23-8 to 23-9, 23-11 to 23-18

650. Clinton   EDs 23-19 to 23-46

Crawford   EDs 24-1 to 24-23, 24-29, 24-24 to 24-28, 24-30 to 24-36

Dallas   EDs 25-1 to 25-3, 25-24, 25-4 to 25-12, 25-13 (NP), 25-14 to 25-19

651. Dallas   EDs 25-20 to 25-23, 25-25 to 25-35

Dickinson   EDs 30-1 to 30-3, 30-20, 30-4 to 30-11, 30-13, 30-12, 30-14 to 30-15, 30-22, 30-16 to 30-19, 30-21, 30-23 to 30-24

Davis   EDs 26-1, 26-20, 26-2 to 26-19

Emmet   EDs 32-1 to 32-13, 32-20, 32-14 to 32-19, 32-21

652. Decatur   EDs 27-1 to 27-2, 27-23, 27-3 to 27-22, 27-24 to 27-27

Delaware   EDs 28-1, 28-17, 28-2 to 28-16, 28-18 to 28-32

Des Moines   EDs 29-1 to 29-2, 29-18 to 29-20, 29-22, 29-21, 29-23 to 29-33

653. Des Moines   EDs 29-3 to 29-17

Dubuque   EDs 31-1, 31-59, 31-2 to 31-6, 31-53, 31-7 to 31-27

654. Dubuque   EDs 31-28 to 31-52, 31-54 to 31-58, 31-60

Fayette   EDs 33-1 to 33-26

655. Fayette   EDs 33-27 to 33-34, 33-36, 33-35, 33-37 to 33-38

Floyd   EDs 34-1 to 34-11, 34-14 to 34-15, 34-12 to 34-13, 34-16 to 34-22

Franklin   EDs 35-1 to 35-5, 35-10, 35-13, 35-25 (NP), 35-6 to 35-9, 35-11 to 35-12, 35-14 to 35-24, 35-26 to 35-29

Fremont   EDs 36-1 to 36-10

656. Fremont   EDs 36-11 to 36-21

Greene   EDs 37-1 to 37-25

Grundy   EDs 38-1 to 38-23

Guthrie   EDs 39-1 to 39-6, 39-18, 39-7 to 39-17, 39-19 to 39-20

657. Guthrie   EDs 39-21 to 39-28

Hamilton   EDs 40-1 to 40-28

Hancock   EDs 41-1 to 41-3, 41-25, 41-4 to 41-7, 41-22, 41-8 to 41-21, 41-23 to 41-24, 41-26

Hardin   EDs 42-1 to 42-10, 42-30, 42-11 to 42-14

658. Hardin   EDs 42-16, 42-15, 42-17 to 42-29

Harrison   EDs 43-1 to 43-32

Henry   EDs 44-1 to 44-5, 44-27, 44-6 to 44-26

659. Howard   EDs 45-1, 45-8, 45-2 to 45-7, 45-9 to 45-21

Humboldt   EDs 46-1 to 46-2, 46-25, 46-3 to 46-11, 46-20, 46-12 to 46-19, 46-21 to 46-24, 46-26 to 46-27

Ida   EDs 47-1 to 47-17

Iowa   EDs 48-1 to 48-8, 48-19, 48-9 to 48-16, 48-23, 48-17 to 48-18

660. Iowa   EDs 48-20 to 48-22, 48-24 to 48-25

Jackson   EDs 49-1 to 49-5, 49-35, 49-6 to 49-8, 49-33, 49-9 to 49-24, 49-26, 49-25, 49-27 to 49-32, 49-34, 49-36 to 49-38

Jasper   EDs 50-1 to 50-3, 50-19, 50-4 to 50-18, 50-37, 50-20 to 50-28

661. Jasper   EDs 50-29 to 50-36, 50-38

Jefferson   EDs 51-1 to 51-22

Johnson   EDs 52-1 to 52-26

662. Johnson   EDs 52-27 to 52-35

Jones   EDs 53-1 to 53-13, 53-26, 53-14 to 53-25, 53-27 to 53-28

Keokuk   EDs 54-1 to 54-32

663. Kossuth   EDs 55-1 to 55-8, 55-13, 55-9 to 55-12, 55-14 to 55-44

Lee   EDs 56-1 to 56-2, 56-6, 56-3 to 56-5, 56-7 to 56-10, 56-18 to 56-19, 56-11 to 56-17

664. Lee   EDs 56-20 to 56-25, 56-36, 56-26 to 56-35

Linn   EDs 57-1 to 57-27, 57-31, 57-28 to 57-30, 57-32 to 57-40

665. Linn   EDs 57-41 to 57-72

666. Louisa   EDs 58-1 to 58-21

Lucas   EDs 59-1 to 59-19

Lyon   EDs 60-1 to 60-15, 60-28, 60-16 to 60-23, 60-25, 60-24, 60-26 to 60-27, 60-29

Madison   EDs 61-13, 61-18, 61-14 to 61-17, 61-19 to 61-26

667. Madison   EDs 61-1 to 61-12

Mahaska   EDs 62-1 to 62-31

668. Marion   EDs 63-1 to 63-32

Marshall   EDs 64-1 to 64-13, 64-33, 64-14 to 64-31

669. Marshall   EDs 64-32, 64-34 to 64-40

Mills   EDs 65-1 to 65-24

Mitchell   EDs 66-1 to 66-26

Monona   EDs 67-1, 67-15, 67-17, 67-31, 67-2 to 67-5, 67-13, 67-6 to 67-12, 67-14, 67-16, 67-18 to 67-30, 67-32 to 67-33

670. Monroe   EDs 68-1 to 68-20

Montgomery   EDs 69-1 to 69-4, 69-16, 69-5 to 69-15, 69-17 to 69-21

Muscatine   EDs 70-1 to 70-18

671. Muscatine   EDs 70-19 to 70-28

O'Brien   EDs 71-1 to 71-9, 71-11, 71-26, 71-10, 71-12 to 71-21, 71-30, 71-22 to 71-25, 71-27 to 71-29, 71-31

Osceola   EDs 72-1 to 72-16

Palo Alto   EDs 74-1 to 74-3, 74-9, 74-4 to 74-8, 74-10 to 74-26

672. Page   EDs 73-1, 73-4, 73-2 to 73-3, 73-5 to 73-7, 73-18, 73-8 to 73-17, 73-19 to 73-24, 73-29, 73-25 to 73-28, 73-30 to 73-34

Plymouth   EDs 75-1 to 75-37

673. Pocahontas   EDs 76-1 to 76-13, 76-16, 76-14 to 76-15, 76-17 to 76-28

Polk, Des Moines City   EDs 77-89 to 77-95, 77-1 to 77-2, 77-130, 77-3, 77-131 to 77-132, 77-4 to 77-7

674. Polk, Des Moines City   EDs 77-8 to 77-29

675. Polk, Des Moines City   EDs 77-30 to 77-54

676. Polk, Des Moines City   EDs 77-55 to 77-68, 77-79, 77-133

677. Polk, Des Moines City   EDs 77-80 to 77-88, 77-69 to 77-78

678. Polk   EDs 77-96 to 77-103, 77-108, 77-104 to 77-107, 77-109 to 77-110, 77-127, 77-111 to 77-113, 77-119, 77-114 to 77-118, 77-120 to 77-126, 77-128 to 77-129

Pottawattamie   EDs 78-1 to 78-13, 78-37, 78-58, 78-38 to 78-50, 78-52, 78-51, 78-53 to 78-57, 78-59 to 78-65

679. Pottawattamie   EDs 78-14 to 78-30, 78-66, 78-31 to 78-36, 78-67

680. Poweshiek   EDs 79-1 to 79-29

Ringgold   EDs 80-1 to 80-9, 80-30, 80-10 to 80-16, 80-26, 80-17 to 80-25, 80-27, 80-31, 80-28 to 80-29

Sac   EDs 81-1 to 81-16, 81-22, 81-17 to 81-21, 81-23 to 81-26

681. Scott   EDs 82-1, 82-54, 82-2 to 82-5, 82-58, 82-6, 82-9, 82-7 to 82-8, 82-10 to 82-15, 82-50 to 82-53, 82-55 to 82-57, 82-59 to 82-66, 82-16 to 82-36

682. Scott   EDs 82-37 to 82-49

Shelby   EDs 83-1 to 83-9, 83-17, 83-10 to 83-16, 83-18 to 83-26, 83-30, 83-27 to 83-29, 83-31 to 83-32

Sioux   EDs 84-1, 84-18, 84-2 to 84-7

683. Sioux   EDs 84-8 to 84-13, 84-22, 84-14 to 84-17, 84-19 to 84-21, 84-23 to 84-36, 84-38, 84-37, 84-39

Story   EDs 85-1 to 85-7, 85-8 (NP), 85-9 to 85-23

684. Story   EDs 85-24 to 85-27, 85-37, 85-28 to 85-36, 85-38

Union   EDs 88-1 to 88-24

Tama   EDs 86-1 to 86-7, 86-35, 86-8 to 86-14, 86-36, 86-15 to 86-28, 86-37, 86-29 to 86-31, 86-38, 86-32 to 86-34

685. Taylor   EDs 87-1 to 87-26

Van Buren   EDs 89-1 to 89-3, 89-18, 89-4 to 89-6, 89-12, 89-7 to 89-11, 89-13 to 89-15, 89-17, 89-16, 89-19 to 89-25

Wapello   EDs 90-1 to 90-6, 90-19, 90-7 to 90-11, 90-33, 90-12, 90-34, 90-13 to 90-14

686. Wapello   EDs 90-15 to 90-18, 90-20 to 90-32

Warren   EDs 91-1 to 91-3, 91-19, 91-4 to 91-5, 91-17, 91-6 to 91-15, 91-36, 91-16, 91-18, 91-20 to 91-32, 91-34 to 91-35, 91-33

Wayne   EDs 93-1 to 93-6, 93-11, 93-7 to 93-10, 93-12 to 93-25

687. Washington   EDs 92-1 to 92-27, 92-28 (NP)

Webster   EDs 94-1 to 94-5, 94-44, 94-6 to 94-15, 94-24, 94-16 to 94-23, 94-25 to 94-32, 94-46, 94-48 (NP), 94-33, 94-45, 94-47, 94-49, 94-34 to 94-37

688. Webster   EDs 94-38 to 94-43

Winnebago   EDs 95-1 to 95-15, 95-19, 95-16 to 95-18, 95-20

Winneshiek   EDs 96-1 to 96-32

689. Woodbury   EDs 97-1 to 97-9, 97-19, 97-10, 97-25, 97-72, 97-11 to 97-18, 97-20 to 97-24, 97-26 to 97-34, 97-80, 97-35 to 97-38, 97-81, 97-39, 97-82, 97-40 to 97-45

690. Woodbury   EDs 97-46 to 97-50, 97-83, 97-51 to 97-55, 97-84, 97-56 to 97-63, 97-85, 97-64 to 97-67

691. Woodbury   EDs 97-68 to 97-69, 97-86, 97-70 to 97-71, 97-73 to 97-79

Worth   EDs 98-1 to 98-5, 98-9, 98-6 to 98-8, 98-10 to 98-20

Wright   EDs 99-1, 99-23, 99-2 to 99-7, 99-30 to 99-32, 99-8 to 99-13, 99-19, 99-14 to 99-18, 99-20 to 99-22, 99-24 to 99-29

### *Kansas*

692. Allen   EDs 1-1 to 1-26

Anderson   EDs 2-1 to 2-11, 2-22, 2-12 to 2-21

Barber   EDs 4-1 to 4-21, 4-26, 4-22 to 4-25

693. Atchison   EDs 3-1 to 3-24

Barton   EDs 5-1 to 5-17, 5-27, 5-18 to 5-26, 5-28 to 5-29, 5-33, 5-30 to 5-32

Chase   EDs 9-1 to 9-14

694. Bourbon   EDs 6-1 to 6-24

Clark   EDs 13-1 to 13-13

Brown   EDs 7-1 to 7-2, 7-19, 7-3 to 7-18, 7-20 to 7-28

Cheyenne   EDs 12-1 to 12-19

695. Butler   EDs 8-1 to 8-49

Chautauqua   EDs 10-1 to 10-18

696. Cherokee   EDs 11-1 to 11-9, 11-10 (NP), 11-11 to 11-35

Cloud   EDs 15-1 to 15-27

697. Clay   EDs 14-1 to 14-29

Coffey   EDs 16-1 to 16-20

Comanche   EDs 17-1 to 17-13

Cowley   EDs 18-1 to 18-12

698. Cowley   EDs 18-13 to 18-45

Crawford   EDs 19-1 to 19-19, 19-29 to 19-36

699. Crawford   EDs 19-20 to 19-28, 19-37 to 19-44

Decatur   EDs 20-1 to 20-30

Doniphan   EDs 22-1 to 22-17

700. Dickinson   EDs 21-1 to 21-20, 21-40, 21-21 to 21-39

Douglas   EDs 23-1 to 23-25

701. Edwards   EDs 24-1 to 24-14

Ellis   EDs 26-1 to 26-22

Elk    EDs 25-1 to 25-15

Ellsworth    EDs 27-1 to 27-24

702.  Finney    EDs 28-1 to 28-5, 28-11, 28-6 to 28-10

Geary    EDs 31-1 to 31-15

Ford    EDs 29-1 to 29-4, 29-10, 29-5 to 29-9, 29-11 to 29-25

Gove    EDs 32-1 to 32-13

703.  Franklin    EDs 30-1 to 30-28

Grant    EDs 34-2 to 34-4, 34-1

Graham    EDs 33-1 to 33-15

Greenwood    EDs 37-1 to 37-24

704.  Gray    EDs 35-1 to 35-5, 35-11, 35-6, 35-12, 35-7 to 35-10

Greeley    EDs 36-1 to 36-5

Jackson    EDs 43-1 to 43-3, 43-9, 43-4 to 43-8, 43-10 to 43-25

Hamilton    EDs 38-1 to 38-10

Harper    EDs 39-1 to 39-27

Haskell    EDs 41-1 to 41-5

Hodgeman    EDs 42-1 to 42-4, 42-11, 42-5 to 42-10

705.  Harvey    EDs 40-1 to 40-24

Kearny    EDs 47-1 to 47-5, 47-7, 47-6, 47-8

Jefferson    EDs 44-1 to 44-20

Kingman    EDs 48-1 to 48-9, 48-25, 48-10 to 48-11, 48-31, 48-12 to 48-24, 48-26 to 48-30

706.  Jewell    EDs 45-1 to 45-32

Kiowa    EDs 49-1 to 49-19

Johnson    EDs 46-1 to 46-24

707.  Labette    EDs 50-1 to 50-21, 50-32 to 50-33, 50-22 to 50-31

Lane    EDs 51-1 to 51-10

Leavenworth    EDs 52-1 to 52-14, 52-15 (NP), 52-16 to 52-18

708.  Leavenworth    EDs 52-19 to 52-34

Logan    EDs 55-1 to 55-14

Lincoln    EDs 53-1 to 53-20, 53-22, 53-21, 53-23 to 53-25

Linn    EDs 54-1 to 54-17

709.  Lyon    EDs 56-1 to 56-12, 56-19, 56-13 to 56-18, 56-20 to 56-29

McPherson    EDs 57-1 to 57-36

710.  Marion    EDs 58-1 to 58-35

Meade    EDs 60-1 to 60-12

Marshall    EDs 59-1 to 59-29, 59-32, 59-30 to 59-31, 59-33 to 59-39

711.  Miami    EDs 61-26, 61-1 to 61-25

Mitchell    EDs 62-1 to 62-30

Morris    EDs 64-1, 64-25, 64-2 to 64-24

712.  Montgomery    EDs 63-1 to 63-6, 63-25, 63-7 to 63-24, 63-26 to 63-40

713.  Morton    EDs 65-1 to 65-9

Neosho    EDs 67-1 to 67-23

Nemaha    EDs 66-1 to 66-28

Ness    EDs 68-1 to 68-2, 68-4 to 68-9, 68-3, 68-10 to 68-15

714.  Norton    EDs 69-1 to 69-28

Osborne    EDs 71-1 to 71-28

Osage    EDs 70-1 to 70-24

Ottawa    EDs 72-1 to 72-25

715.  Pawnee    EDs 73-1 to 73-5, 73-28, 73-6 to 73-27

Phillips    EDs 74-1 to 74-32

Pottawatomie    EDs 75-1 to 75-20, 75-22, 75-21, 75-23 to 75-35

Pratt    EDs 76-1, 76-27, 76-2 to 76-5, 76-21, 76-6 to 76-20, 76-22 to 76-26, 76-28 to 76-31

716.  Rawlins    EDs 77-1 to 77-23

Republic    EDs 79-1 to 79-4, 79-31, 79-5 to 79-6, 79-28, 79-7 to 79-12, 79-23, 79-13 to 79-22, 79-24 to 79-27, 79-29 to 79-30

Reno    EDs 78-1 to 78-16, 78-35 to 78-62

717.  Reno    EDs 78-17 to 78-34

Rice    EDs 80-1 to 80-28

Rooks    EDs 82-1 to 82-27

718.  Riley    EDs 81-1 to 81-26

Seward    EDs 88-1 to 88-7

Rush    EDs 83-1, 83-11, 83-2 to 83-10, 83-12 to 83-21

Russell    EDs 84-1 to 84-20

Scott    EDs 86-1 to 86-5, 86-7, 86-6, 86-8

719.  Saline    EDs 85-1 to 85-14, 85-32, 85-15 to 85-20, 85-31, 85-21 to 85-30

Sedgwick    EDs 87-1 to 87-10, 87-36, 87-11 to 87-16, 87-82, 87-17 to 87-35, 87-37 to 87-40

720.  Sedgwick, Wichita City    EDs 87-41 to 87-61

721.  Sedgwick, Wichita City    EDs 87-62 to 87-77, 87-81 (NP), 87-78 to 87-80

722.  Shawnee    EDs 89-1 to 89-18, 89-49, 89-23 to 89-27, 89-19 to 89-22, 89-28 to 89-34

723.  Shawnee    EDs 89-35 to 89-48

Sheridan    EDs 90-1 to 90-16

Smith    EDs 92-1 to 92-31

Stanton    EDs 94-1 to 94-6

724.  Sherman    EDs 91-1 to 91-17

Stafford    EDs 93-1 to 93-25

Stevens    EDs 95-1, 95-3 to 95-4, 95-2, 95-8, 95-5 to 95-7

Sumner    EDs 96-1 to 96-8, 96-36, 96-9 to 96-35, 96-37 to 96-47

725.  Thomas    EDs 97-1 to 97-18

Trego    EDs 98-1 to 98-10

Wabaunsee    EDs 99-1 to 99-20

Wallace    EDs 100-1 to 100-8

Washington    EDs 101-1 to 101-26, 101-36, 101-27 to 101-35

Wichita    EDs 102-1 to 102-5

726.  Wilson    EDs 103-1 to 103-28

Woodson    EDs 104-1 to 104-13

Wyandotte, Kansas City    EDs 105-65 to 105-76, 105-1 to 105-3

727.  Wyandotte, Kansas City    EDs 105-4 to 105-21

728.  Wyandotte, Kansas City    EDs 105-22 to 105-24, 105-33 to 105-44

729.  Wyandotte, Kansas City    EDs 105-25 to 105-32, 105-45 to 105-52

730.  Wyandotte, Kansas City    EDs 105-53 to 105-64

### Kentucky

731.  Adair    EDs 1-1 to 1-14

Ballard    EDs 4-1 to 4-14

Allen    EDs 2-1 to 2-13

Bath    EDs 6-1 to 6-10, 6-13, 6-11 to 6-12, 6-14 to 6-15

732. Anderson   EDs 3-1 to 3-9

   Bourbon   EDs 9-1 to 9-14

   Barren   EDs 5-1 to 5-2, 5-23, 5-3 to 5-22

733. Bell   EDs 7-1 to 7-14, 7-20 to 7-22, 7-15 to 7-19, 7-23 to 7-24

   Butler   EDs 16-1 to 16-14

734. Boone   EDs 8-1 to 8-13

   Boyd   EDs 10-1 to 10-9, 10-23 to 10-26, 10-27 (NP), 10-10 to 10-12, 10-30, 10-13 to 10-14, 10-29, 10-15 to 10-17, 10-28, 10-18 to 10-22

735. Boyle   EDs 11-1, 11-4, 11-2 to 11-3, 11-5 to 11-7, 11-17, 11-8 to 11-16

   Bullitt   EDs 15-1 to 15-10

   Bracken   EDs 12-1 to 12-14

   Breckinridge   EDs 14-1 to 14-20

736. Breathitt   EDs 13-1 to 13-7, 13-8 (void), 13-9 to 13-13

   Carlisle   EDs 20-1 to 20-11

   Caldwell   EDs 17-1 to 17-13

   Crittenden   EDs 28-1 to 28-15

737. Calloway   EDs 18-1, 18-18, 18-2 to 18-17

   Carroll   EDs 21-1 to 21-12

   Campbell   EDs 19-1 to 19-14

738. Campbell   EDs 19-15 to 19-28, 19-55, 19-29, 19-46 to 19-50, 19-30 to 19-45, 19-51 to 19-54

   Clinton   EDs 27-1 to 27-10

739. Carter   EDs 22-1 to 22-17

   Casey   EDs 23-1 to 23-15

   Christian   EDs 24-1 to 24-6

740. Christian   EDs 24-7 to 24-9, 24-12, 24-10 to 24-11, 24-13 to 24-31

   Clark   EDs 25-1 to 25-15

   Cumberland   EDs 29-1 to 29-10

741. Clay   EDs 26-1 to 26-17

   Elliott   EDs 32-1 to 32-7

   Daviess   EDs 30-1 to 30-33

742. Daviess   EDs 30-34 to 30-50

   Edmonson   EDs 31-1 to 31-11

   Estill   EDs 33-1 to 33-6, 33-14, 33-7 to 33-13

   Grant   EDs 41-1 to 41-12

743. Fayette   EDs 34-1 to 34-11, 34-24 to 34-26, 34-12, 34-42, 34-13, 34-41, 34-14 to 34-23

744. Fayette   EDs 34-27 to 34-28, 34-43, 34-29 to 34-40

   Gallatin   EDs 39-1 to 39-6

   Fleming   EDs 35-1 to 35-16

   Floyd   EDs 36-1 to 36-13

745. Floyd   EDs 36-14 to 36-28

   Franklin   EDs 37-1 to 37-17

   Hancock   EDs 46-1 to 46-10

746. Fulton   EDs 38-1 to 38-13

   Garrard   EDs 40-1 to 40-11

   Graves   EDs 42-1 to 42-20, 42-26, 42-30, 42-21 to 42-25, 42-27 to 42-29, 42-31 to 42-32

747. Graves   EDs 42-33 to 42-39

   Hardin   EDs 47-1, 47-12, 47-21, 47-2 to 47-11, 47-13 to 47-20, 47-22 to 47-24

   Grayson   EDs 43-2, 43-17, 43-1, 43-3 to 43-16, 43-18 to 43-19

   Green   EDs 44-1 to 44-11

748. Greenup   EDs 45-1 to 45-19

   Harlan   EDs 48-1 to 48-7, 48-31 to 48-34

749. Harlan   EDs 48-8 to 48-30

   Hart   EDs 50-1 to 50-3, 50-17, 50-4 to 50-16

750. Harrison   EDs 49-1 to 49-20

   Henry   EDs 52-1 to 52-5, 52-12, 52-6 to 52-11, 52-13 to 52-21

   Henderson   EDs 51-1 to 51-24

751. Hickman   EDs 53-1 to 53-9

   Hopkins   EDs 54-1 to 54-30

   Jackson   EDs 55-1 to 55-12

752. Jefferson   EDs 56-178 to 56-185, 56-213, 56-186 to 56-187, 56-188 (NP), 56-189 to 56-212

753. Jefferson, Louisville City   EDs 56-1 to 56-2, 56-84, 56-3 to 56-25

754. Jefferson, Louisville City   EDs 56-26 to 56-52

755. Jefferson, Louisville City   EDs 56-53 to 56-78

756. Jefferson, Louisville City   EDs 56-79 to 56-83, 56-85 to 56-109

757. Jefferson, Louisville City   EDs 56-110 to 56-128

758. Jefferson, Louisville City   EDs 56-129 to 56-151

759. Jefferson, Louisville City   EDs 56-152 to 56-170

760. Jefferson, Louisville City   EDs 56-171 to 56-177

   Jessamine   EDs 57-1 to 57-9

   Knott   EDs 60-1 to 60-10

761. Johnson   EDs 58-1 to 58-15

   Kenton   EDs 59-1 to 59-13, 59-27 to 59-38

762. Kenton   EDs 59-14 to 59-26, 59-39 to 59-58

763. Knox   EDs 61-1, 61-16, 61-2 to 61-15, 61-17 to 61-18

   Larue   EDs 62-1 to 62-12

   Lawrence   EDs 64-1, 64-18, 64-2 to 64-8, 64-11, 64-9 to 64-10, 64-12 to 64-17, 64-19 to 64-20

764. Laurel   EDs 63-1 to 63-17

   Lyon   EDs 72-1 to 72-10

   Lee   EDs 65-1 to 65-11

   Lincoln   EDs 69-1 to 69-12

765. Leslie   EDs 66-1 to 66-11

   McCreary   EDs 74-1 to 74-10

   Letcher   EDs 67-1, 67-20, 67-2 to 67-19, 67-21

766. Letcher   EDs 67-22 to 67-26

   Mason   EDs 81-1 to 81-22

   Lewis   EDs 68-1 to 68-18

   McLean   EDs 75-1 to 75-8, 75-14, 75-9 to 75-13, 75-15

767. Livingston   EDs 70-1 to 70-12

   Magoffin   EDs 77-1 to 77-12

   Logan   EDs 71-1 to 71-27

   Menifee   EDs 83-1 to 83-7

768. McCracken   EDs 73-1 to 73-8, 73-12 to 73-14, 73-9 to 73-11, 73-15 to 73-22

   Meade   EDs 82-1 to 82-4, 82-9, 82-5 to 82-8, 82-10 to 82-12

769. Madison   EDs 76-1 to 76-24

   Marion   EDs 78-1 to 78-21

   Martin   EDs 80-1 to 80-8

770. Marshall   EDs 79-1 to 79-19

   Montgomery   EDs 87-1 to 87-13

   Mercer   EDs 84-1 to 84-17

   Monroe   EDs 86-1 to 86-9, 86-12, 86-10 to 86-11, 86-13 to 86-16

771. Metcalfe    EDs 85-1 to 85-9

    Morgan    EDs 88-1, 88-6, 88-11, 88-15, 88-2 to 88-5, 88-7 to 88-10, 88-12 to 88-14, 88-16 to 88-18

    Muhlenberg    EDs 89-1 to 89-15, 89-19, 89-16 to 89-18

772. Muhlenberg    EDs 89-20 to 89-27

    Nelson    EDs 90-1 to 90-19

    Nicholas    EDs 91-1 to 91-7, 91-9, 91-8, 91-10 to 91-11

    Oldham    EDs 93-1 to 93-11

    Owen    EDs 94-1 to 94-16

773. Ohio    EDs 92-1 to 92-25

    Owsley    EDs 95-1 to 95-8

    Robertson    EDs 101-1, 101-3, 101-2, 101-4 to 101-7

    Rockcastle    EDs 102-1 to 102-4, 102-15, 102-5 to 102-14, 102-16 to 102-17

774. Pendleton    EDs 96-1 to 96-14

    Perry    EDs 97-1 to 97-4, 97-22 to 97-27, 97-5 to 97-21

    Powell    EDs 99-1 to 99-7

775. Pike    EDs 98-1 to 98-31

776. Pike    EDs 98-32 to 98-35

    Rowan    EDs 103-1 to 103-10

    Spencer    EDs 108-1 to 108-9

    Pulaski    EDs 100-1 to 100-9, 100-34, 100-10 to 100-11, 100-13 to 100-16, 100-12, 100-17 to 100-22, 100-31 to 100-33

777. Pulaski    EDs 100-23 to 100-30

    Russell    EDs 104-1 to 104-10

    Trimble    EDs 112-1 to 112-8

    Scott    EDs 105-1 to 105-19

    Simpson    EDs 107-1 to 107-12

778. Shelby    EDs 106-1 to 106-10, 106-20, 106-11 to 106-19

    Taylor    EDs 109-1 to 109-10

    Todd    EDs 110-1 to 110-16

    Trigg    EDs 111-1 to 111-14

779. Union    EDs 113-1 to 113-13

    Wolfe    EDs 119-1 to 119-10

    Warren    EDs 114-1 to 114-22

780. Warren    EDs 114-23 to 114-31

    Wayne    EDs 116-1 to 116-14

    Washington    EDs 115-1 to 115-8, 115-11, 115-16, 115-9 to 115-10, 115-12 to 115-15, 115-17 to 115-18

    Woodford    EDs 120-1 to 120-4, 120-6, 120-5, 120-7 to 120-9

781. Webster    EDs 117-1 to 117-24

    Whitley    EDs 118-1, 118-16, 118-2 to 118-15, 118-17 to 118-25

## Louisiana

782. Acadia    EDs 1-1 to 1-27

    Allen    EDs 2-1 to 2-12

783. Ascension    EDs 3-1 to 3-15

    Caldwell    EDs 11-1 to 11-14

    Assumption    EDs 4-1 to 4-9

    Catahoula    EDs 13-1 to 13-11

784. Avoyelles    EDs 5-1 to 5-13, 5-29, 5-14 to 5-28

    Beauregard    EDs 6-1 to 6-14

785. Bienville    EDs 7-1 to 7-21

    Bossier    EDs 8-1 to 8-19

786. Caddo    EDs 9-1 to 9-9, 9-64, 9-10 to 9-26

787. Caddo    EDs 9-27 to 9-56, 9-75, 9-57 to 9-63

788. Caddo    EDs 9-65 to 9-74

    Cameron    EDs 12-1 to 12-6

    Calcasieu    EDs 10-1 to 10-14, 10-19 to 10-20, 10-29 to 10-30

789. Calcasieu    EDs 10-15 to 10-16, 10-31, 10-17 to 10-18, 10-21 to 10-28

    Concordia    EDs 15-1 to 15-13

    Claiborne    EDs 14-1 to 14-15, 14-19 to 14-22

790. Claiborne    EDs 14-16, 14-23, 14-17 to 14-18

    East Feliciana    EDs 19-1 to 19-14

    De Soto    EDs 16-1 to 16-15, 16-19 to 16-23

791. De Soto    EDs 16-16 to 16-18

    Lincoln    EDs 31-1 to 31-19

    East Baton Rouge    EDs 17-1 to 17-14, 17-35

792. East Baton Rouge    EDs 17-15 to 17-16, 17-36, 17-17 to 17-23, 17-31 to 17-34, 17-24 to 17-30

    East Carroll    EDs 18-1 to 18-5, 18-6 (void), 18-7 to 18-13

793. Evangeline    EDs 20-1 to 20-18

    Franklin    EDs 21-22, 21-1 to 21-21, 21-23

794. Grant    EDs 22-1 to 22-14

    La Salle    EDs 30-1 to 30-13

    Iberia    EDs 23-1 to 23-18, 23-19 (void), 23-20

795. Iberville    EDs 24-1 to 24-22

    Jackson    EDs 25-1 to 25-2, 25-16, 25-3 to 25-15

    Madison    EDs 33-1 to 33-11

796. Jefferson    EDs 26-1 to 26-6, 26-7 (NP), 26-8, 26-15 to 26-18, 26-9 to 26-14, 26-19 to 26-21, 26-22 (NP), 26-23

797. Jefferson    EDs 26-24 to 26-26

    Jefferson Davis    EDs 27-1 to 27-14

    Lafayette    EDs 28-1 to 28-17

798. Lafayette    EDs 28-18 to 28-25

    Livingston    EDs 32-1 to 32-16

    Lafourche    EDs 29-1 to 29-11, 29-15 to 29-18

799. Lafourche    EDs 29-12 to 29-14

    Morehouse    EDs 34-1 to 34-5, 34-21, 34-6 to 34-20

    Natchitoches    EDs 35-1 to 35-22

800. Natchitoches    EDs 35-23 to 35-27

    Red River    EDs 41-1 to 41-10

    Orleans, New Orleans City    EDs 36-1 to 36-12

801. Orleans, New Orleans City    EDs 36-13 to 36-38

802. Orleans, New Orleans City    EDs 36-39 to 36-60

803. Orleans, New Orleans City    EDs 36-61 to 36-91

804. Orleans, New Orleans City    EDs 36-92 to 36-105

805. Orleans, New Orleans City    EDs 36-106 to 36-124

806. Orleans, New Orleans City    EDs 36-125 to 36-140

807. Orleans, New Orleans City    EDs 36-141 to 36-152

808. Orleans, New Orleans City    EDs 36-153 to 36-179

809. Orleans, New Orleans City    EDs 36-180, 36-181 (void), 36-182 to 36-202

810. Orleans, New Orleans City    EDs 36-203 to 36-226

811. Orleans, New Orleans City   EDs 36-227 to 36-246
812. Orleans, New Orleans City   EDs 36-247 to 36-265
813. Orleans, New Orleans City   EDs 36-266 to 36-277
814. Ouachita   EDs 37-1 to 37-4, 37-21 to 37-33, 37-5 to 37-20
815. Plaquemines   EDs 38-1 to 38-8
    Saint James   EDs 47-1 to 47-10
    Pointe Coupee   EDs 39-1 to 39-14
    St. Bernard   EDs 44-1 to 44-8
816. Rapides   EDs 40-1 to 40-18, 40-51, 40-19 to 40-37
817. Rapides   EDs 40-38 to 40-45, 40-52, 40-46 to 40-50
    St. John the Baptist   EDs 48-1 to 48-6
    Richland   EDs 42-1 to 42-16
818. Sabine   EDs 43-1 to 43-20
    St. Charles   EDs 45-1 to 45-6
    Tensas   EDs 54-1 to 54-12
819. St. Helena   EDs 46-1 to 46-7
    Union   EDs 56-1 to 56-18
    St. Landry   EDs 49-1 to 49-9, 49-32 to 49-38
820. St. Landry   EDs 49-10 to 49-14, 49-19 to 49-31, 49-15 to 49-18
    St. Tammany   EDs 52-1 to 52-20
821. St. Martin   EDs 50-1 to 50-15
    St. Mary   EDs 51-1 to 51-14, 51-15 (NP), 51-16 to 51-18
822. Tangipahoa   EDs 53-1 to 53-17, 53-26, 53-18 to 53-25
    West Baton Rouge   EDs 61-1 to 61-10
823. Terrebonne   EDs 55-1 to 55-14
    Vermilion   EDs 57-1 to 57-18, 57-20 to 57-21
824. Vermilion   EDs 57-19, 57-22 to 57-23
    Vernon   EDs 58-1 to 58-10, 58-19, 58-11 to 58-18
    Washington   EDs 59-1 to 59-17
825. Washington   EDs 59-18 to 59-22
    Webster   EDs 60-1 to 60-12, 60-20 to 60-21, 60-13 to 60-19
    West Carroll   EDs 62-1 to 62-8
826. West Feliciana   EDs 63-1 to 63-12
    Winn   EDs 64-1 to 64-14

### Maine

827. Androscoggin   EDs 1-1 to 1-12, 1-14 to 1-15, 1-39 to 1-41, 1-16 to 1-33
828. Androscoggin   EDs 1-34 to 1-38, 1-13, 1-42 to 1-47
    Aroostook   EDs 2-1 to 2-7, 2-13 to 2-17, 2-8 to 2-12, 2-191 (NP), 2-18 to 2-37
* 829. Aroostook   EDs 2-38 to 2-89, 2-93, 2-98 to 2-99, 2-101 to 2-105, 2-113, 2-120 to 2-121, 2-131, 2-145, 2-148, 2-160, 2-164, 2-169 to 2-170, 2-178 to 2-179
830. Cumberland   EDs 3-1 to 3-25, 3-26 (NP), 3-27 to 3-29, 3-30 (NP), 3-31 to 3-46
831. Cumberland   EDs 3-47 to 3-51, 3-56 to 3-72, 3-52 to 3-55, 3-73 to 3-86, 3-87 (NP), 3-88 to 3-91, 3-110 to 3-111
832. Cumberland   EDs 3-92 to 3-100, 3-102 to 3-109, 3-101, 3-112 to 3-113

Franklin   EDs 4-1 to 4-19, 4-20 (NP), 4-21 to 4-37, 4-38 (NP), 4-39, 4-40 to 4-42 (NP), 4-43 to 4-46, 4-47 (NP), 4-48 to 4-50, 4-51 (NP), 4-52 to 4-53, 4-54 (NP)
Hancock   EDs 5-1 to 5-4
833. Hancock   EDs 5-5 to 5-43, 5-44 to 5-45 (NP), 5-46 to 5-47, 5-48 (NP), 5-49, 5-50 to 5-52 (NP), 5-53, 5-54 to 5-58 (NP)
    Kennebec   EDs 6-1 to 6-16
834. Kennebec   EDs 6-17 to 6-56
835. Knox   EDs 7-1 to 7-29
    Lincoln   EDs 8-1 to 8-20
    Oxford   EDs 9-1 to 9-2, 9-3 (NP), 9-4 to 9-14, 9-15 (NP), 9-16 to 9-24
836. Oxford   EDs 9-25 to 9-32, 9-33 (NP), 9-34 to 9-38, 9-39 (NP), 9-40 to 9-42, 9-43 (NP), 9-44 to 9-55, 9-56 (NP), 9-57 to 9-59, 9-60 to 9-64 (NP)
    Penobscot   EDs 10-1 to 10-16
837. Penobscot   EDs 10-17 to 10-75
** 838. Penobscot   EDs 10-76 to 10-110, 10-111 (NP), 10-112 to 10-113, 10-114 (NP), 10-115 to 10-116, 10-117 to 10-119 (NP), 10-120 to 10-122, 10-123 to 10-128 (NP), 10-129
    Piscataquis   EDs 11-1 to 11-5, 11-8 to 11-9, 11-11 to 11-17, 11-20 to 11-28, 11-30 to 11-31, 11-33 to 11-37, 11-39 to 11-42, 11-44 to 11-45, 11-47, 11-55 to 11-57, 11-59 to 11-60, 11-65, 11-73 to 11-74, 11-76
    Sagadahoc   EDs 12-1 to 12-5
839. Sagadahoc   EDs 12-6 to 12-17
    Somerset   EDs 13-1 to 13-2, 13-3 (NP), 13-4 to 13-7, 13-8 (NP), 13-9 to 13-11, 13-12 to 13-14 (NP), 13-15 to 13-18, 13-19 to 13-21 (NP), 13-22 to 13-33, 13-34 to 13-35 (NP), 13-36 to 13-38, 13-40, 13-42 to 13-44, 13-46 to 13-47, 13-49, 13-52 to 13-59, 13-61 to 13-64, 13-68 to 13-74, 13-76 to 13-81, 13-83, 13-85, 13-87, 13-89, 13-95
840. Waldo   EDs 14-1 to 14-30
    Washington   EDs 15-1 to 15-26, 15-27 (NP), 15-28 to 15-50
841. Washington   EDs 15-51 to 15-66, 15-67 (NP), 15-68, 15-69 to 15-72 (NP), 15-73, 15-74 (NP), 15-75, 15-76 to 15-82 (NP), 15-83, 15-84 (NP), 15-85, 15-86 to 15-89 (NP)
    York   EDs 16-1 to 16-41
842. York   EDs 16-42 to 16-61

### Maryland

843. Allegany   EDs 1-1 to 1-12, 1-28, 1-13 to 1-25, 1-69, 1-26 to 1-27, 1-29 to 1-37, 1-48, 1-38
844. Allegany   EDs 1-39 to 1-47, 1-49 to 1-68
    Anne Arundel   EDs 2-3, 2-4 (NP), 2-5 to 2-8, 2-37, 2-11 to 2-13, 2-38, 2-14 to 2-21, 2-22 (void), 2-34
845. Anne Arundel   EDs 2-1 to 2-2, 2-23 to 2-27, 2-28 (NP), 2-9 to 2-10, 2-29 to 2-33, 2-35 to 2-36
    Baltimore   EDs 3-1 to 3-18, 3-29 to 3-30
846. Baltimore   EDs 3-19 to 3-28, 3-32 to 3-36, 3-50 to 3-52, 3-31, 3-37 to 3-49, 3-62 to 3-64
847. Baltimore   EDs 3-53 to 3-61, 3-65 to 3-72, 3-75 to 3-77, 3-73 to 3-74
848. Baltimore City   EDs 4-1 to 4-2, 4-526, 4-3 to 4-5, 4-453, 4-6, 4-527, 4-7 to 4-8, 4-528, 4-9 to 4-21

---

*Roll 829, Aroostook County—The following EDs, which have no population, do not appear on the microfilm: 2-90 to 2-92, 2-94 to 2-97, 2-100, 2-106 to 2-112, 2-114 to 2-119, 2-122 to 130, 2-132 to 2-144, 2-146 to 147, 2-149 to 2-159, 2-161 to 163, 2-165 to 2-168, 2-171 to 2-177, 2-180 to 2-190.

**Roll 838, Piscataquis County—The following EDs, which have no population, do not appear on the microfilm: 11-6 to 11-7, 11-10, 11-18 to 11-19, 11-29, 11-32, 11-38, 11-43, 11-46, 11-48 to 11-54, 11-58, 11-61 to 11-64, 11-66 to 11-72, 11-75, 11-77 to 11-114.

849. Baltimore City   EDs 4-22 to 4-41, 4-454, 4-42 to 4-45

850. Baltimore City   EDs 4-529, 4-46 to 4-67

851. Baltimore City   EDs 4-68, 4-530, 4-69 to 4-71, 4-531, 4-72, 4-532, 4-73, 4-533, 4-74, 4-534, 4-75, 4-535, 4-76 to 4-78, 4-455, 4-79 to 4-80, 4-536, 4-81, 4-537, 4-82, 4-538, 4-83, 4-539, 4-84 to 4-85, 4-540, 4-86 to 4-87

852. Baltimore City   EDs 4-88 to 4-94, 4-456 to 4-457, 4-541 (NP), 4-95 to 4-97, 4-542, 4-98, 4-543, 4-99, 4-544, 4-100, 4-545, 4-101 to 4-106, 4-546, 4-107, 4-547, 4-108 to 4-109

853. Baltimore City   EDs 4-548, 4-110, 4-549, 4-111 to 4-112, 4-550, 4-113, 4-551 to 4-552, 4-458 to 4-459, 4-487, 4-114 to 4-115, 4-460, 4-116 to 4-117, 4-553, 4-118, 4-461, 4-119, 4-554, 4-120 to 4-121, 4-555, 4-122, 4-556, 4-123, 4-462, 4-557, 4-124, 4-558, 4-125, 4-488 to 4-490, 4-559 to 4-560

854. Baltimore City   EDs 4-126, 4-561, 4-127, 4-562, 4-128, 4-563, 4-129, 4-564, 4-130, 4-565, 4-131, 4-491 to 4-492, 4-132 to 4-133, 4-493 to 4-494, 4-134 to 4-138, 4-566, 4-139 to 4-140, 4-567, 4-141 to 4-150

855. Baltimore City   EDs 4-151 to 4-152, 4-463, 4-153, 4-568, 4-154, 4-464, 4-155, 4-569, 4-156 to 4-165, 4-465, 4-166 to 4-171, 4-570 to 4-571, 4-173, 4-172 (void)

856. Baltimore City   EDs 4-495 to 4-496, 4-174 to 4-177, 4-572, 4-178 to 4-179, 4-573, 4-180, 4-574, 4-181, 4-575, 4-182, 4-576 to 4-577, 4-183, 4-578, 4-184, 4-579, 4-185 to 4-186, 4-580, 4-187 to 4-188, 4-581, 4-189 to 4-190, 4-582, 4-191, 4-583, 4-192 to 4-194, 4-584, 4-195 to 4-196

857. Baltimore City   EDs 4-585 to 4-586, 4-197, 4-587, 4-198, 4-588, 4-199, 4-589, 4-200, 4-590, 4-201, 4-591, 4-202, 4-592, 4-203, 4-593, 4-204 to 4-208, 4-594, 4-209, 4-595, 4-210, 4-596, 4-211 to 4-212, 4-597, 4-213, 4-598

858. Baltimore City   EDs 4-214, 4-599, 4-215 to 4-221, 4-600, 4-222 to 4-223, 4-466, 4-224 to 4-227, 4-601, 4-228 to 4-237

859. Baltimore City   EDs 4-467, 4-602, 4-238, 4-603 to 4-604, 4-239, 4-497 to 4-499, 4-605, 4-240 to 4-243, 4-500 to 4-501, 4-244, 4-502 to 4-505, 4-245, 4-606 to 4-608, 4-468

860. Baltimore City   EDs 4-246, 4-609, 4-247 to 4-248, 4-469, 4-610, 4-249, 4-611 to 4-612, 4-250 to 4-251, 4-613 to 4-615, 4-252, 4-616, 4-253, 4-617, 4-254 to 4-263

861. Baltimore City   EDs 4-264 to 4-267, 4-618, 4-268 to 4-270, 4-506 to 4-508, 4-271, 4-470, 4-272, 4-619, 4-273, 4-620, 4-274, 4-621, 4-471, 4-275 to 4-276, 4-622, 4-472, 4-277 to 4-284

862. Baltimore City   EDs 4-285 to 4-289, 4-623, 4-290 to 4-300, 4-624, 4-301 to 4-312

863. Baltimore City   EDs 4-313, 4-625, 4-314, 4-626, 4-315 to 4-317, 4-627, 4-318 to 4-319, 4-628, 4-320 to 4-321, 4-629, 4-322 to 4-324, 4-630, 4-325 to 4-328, 4-631, 4-329, 4-632, 4-330 to 4-331, 4-633, 4-332 to 4-333, 4-634, 4-334, 4-635, 4-335, 4-636

864. Baltimore City   EDs 4-336 to 4-337, 4-509 to 4-510, 4-338 to 4-340, 4-637, 4-341, 4-638, 4-342 to 4-344, 4-473, 4-345 to 4-354, 4-474 (NP), 4-355 to 4-356, 4-475, 4-357

865. Baltimore City   EDs 4-358 to 4-367, 4-639, 4-368, 4-640, 4-369 to 4-378, 4-641, 4-379 to 4-380, 4-642, 4-381 to 4-383

866. Baltimore City   EDs 4-384 to 4-387, 4-643, 4-388, 4-476 to 4-477, 4-389, 4-644, 4-390, 4-645, 4-391 to 4-393, 4-478, 4-394 to 4-395, 4-479, 4-396 to 4-399, 4-647, 4-400 to 4-401, 4-648

867. Baltimore City   EDs 4-402, 4-649, 4-403, 4-650, 4-404 to 4-407, 4-651, 4-408 to 4-414, 4-652, 4-415 to 4-417, 4-480, 4-418 to 4-653

868. Baltimore City   EDs 4-419, 4-654, 4-420 to 4-421, 4-655, 4-422, 4-511 to 4-512, 4-481, 4-423, 4-656 to 4-657, 4-424, 4-513 to 4-514, 4-425, 4-515 to 4-516, 4-426

869. Baltimore City   EDs 4-517, 4-658 to 4-659, 4-427, 4-660, 4-482 (NP), 4-428 to 4-429, 4-518 to 4-519, 4-430, 4-661 to 4-662, 4-431, 4-663, 4-432 to 4-435, 4-483, 4-436, 4-664, 4-437, 4-665

870. Baltimore City   EDs 4-438 to 4-439, 4-666, 4-440, 4-520 to 4-521, 4-441 to 4-444, 4-667, 4-445, 4-668, 4-446, 4-669, 4-484 (NP), 4-447, 4-485, 4-448 to 4-449

871. Baltimore City   EDs 4-670 to 4-671, 4-450, 4-522 to 4-525, 4-451, 4-486, 4-672, 4-452, 4-673

   Calvert   EDs 5-1 to 5-8

   Caroline   EDs 6-1 to 6-18

872. Carroll   EDs 7-1 to 7-19, 7-23, 7-20 to 7-22, 7-24 to 7-30

   Charles   EDs 9-1 to 9-12, 9-15, 9-13 to 9-14

873. Cecil   EDs 8-1 to 8-20

   Dorchester   EDs 10-1 to 10-28

874. Frederick   EDs 11-1 to 11-54

875. Garrett   EDs 12-1 to 12-9, 12-12, 12-23, 12-10 to 12-11, 12-13 to 12-22, 12-24 to 12-25

   Harford   EDs 13-17 to 13-19, 13-1 to 13-2, 13-9, 13-22, 13-3 (NP), 13-4 to 13-8, 13-10 to 13-13, 13-23, 13-14 to 13-16, 13-20 to 13-21

876. Howard   EDs 14-1 to 14-8, 14-9 (void), 14-10 to 14-15

   Kent   EDs 15-1 to 15-8, 15-12, 15-9 to 15-11

   Montgomery   EDs 16-1 to 16-6, 16-14, 16-7 to 16-13, 16-23 to 16-31

877. Montgomery   EDs 16-15 to 16-22, 16-32 to 16-38

   Prince George's   EDs 17-1 to 17-19, 17-21 to 17-26

878. Prince George's   EDs 17-20, 17-27 to 17-46, 17-55 to 17-56, 17-47 to 17-54

   Queen Anne's   EDs 18-1 to 18-14

879. St. Mary's   EDs 19-1 to 19-13

   Somerset   EDs 20-1, 20-19, 20-2 to 20-8, 20-13, 20-9 to 20-10, 20-21, 20-11 to 20-12, 20-14 to 20-18, 20-20

   Talbot   EDs 21-1 to 21-8, 21-15 to 21-16

880. Talbot   EDs 21-9 to 21-14

   Worcester   EDs 24-1 to 24-7, 24-17, 24-8 to 24-16, 24-18 to 24-19

   Washington   EDs 22-5 to 22-15, 22-20 to 22-26

881. Washington   EDs 22-16 to 22-19, 22-1 to 22-4, 22-27 to 22-57

   Wicomico   EDs 23-1 to 23-6, 23-13 to 23-14

882. Wicomico   EDs 23-7 to 23-12, 23-15 to 23-27

## *Massachusetts*

883. Barnstable   EDs 1-1 to 1-20

   Berkshire   EDs 2-1 to 2-11

884. Berkshire   EDs 2-12 to 2-49

885. Berkshire   EDs 2-50 to 2-53, 2-62 to 2-72, 2-54 to 2-61, 2-73 to 2-85

886. Bristol   EDs 3-159 to 3-190

887. Bristol, Fall River City   EDs 3-1 to 3-24

888. Bristol, Fall River City   EDs 3-25 to 3-59

889. Bristol, Fall River City   EDs 3-60 to 3-73, 3-243, 3-74 to 3-83

890. Bristol, New Bedford City   EDs 3-191 to 3-195, 3-84 to 3-89, 3-91, 3-90, 3-92 to 3-99

891. Bristol, New Bedford City   EDs 3-100 to 3-128, 3-130

892. Bristol, New Bedford City   EDs 3-129, 3-131 to 3-158

893. Bristol   EDs 3-196 to 3-221, 3-244, 3-222 to 3-225

894. Bristol   EDs 3-226 to 3-242

Dukes   EDs 4-1 to 4-8

Essex   EDs 5-1 to 5-11

895. Essex   EDs 5-12 to 5-35, 5-50, 5-285, 5-51, 5-80 to 5-82

896. Essex   EDs 5-36 to 5-49, 5-52 to 5-57, 5-61 to 5-69

897. Essex   EDs 5-58 to 5-60, 5-70 to 5-79, 5-83 to 5-100

898. Essex   EDs 5-101 to 5-108, 5-116 to 5-125, 5-109 to 5-115, 5-126 to 5-134

899. Essex, Lynn City   EDs 5-135 to 5-136, 5-141 to 5-151, 5-137 to 5-140, 5-152 to 5-161

900. Essex, Lynn City   EDs 5-162 to 5-173, 5-187 to 5-189, 5-174 to 5-186, 5-190 to 5-192

901. Essex   EDs 5-193 to 5-197, 5-211 to 5-222, 5-198 to 5-210

902. Essex   EDs 5-223 to 5-256

903. Essex   EDs 5-257 to 5-268, 5-282 to 5-284, 5-269 to 5-281

904. Franklin   EDs 6-1 to 6-8, 6-11 to 6-18, 6-9 to 6-10, 6-19 to 6-40

905. Hampden   EDs 7-97 to 7-110, 7-117 to 7-118, 7-111 to 7-116, 7-119 to 7-122

906. Hampden   EDs 7-123, 7-127 to 7-140, 7-142 to 7-163

907. Hampden   EDs 7-164 to 7-167, 7-124 to 7-126, 7-168 to 7-187, 7-197 to 7-205

908. Hampden   EDs 7-206, 7-141, 7-207 to 7-209, 7-188 to 7-196, 7-210

Hampden, Springfield City   EDs 7-1 to 7-19

909. Hampden, Springfield City   EDs 7-20 to 7-27, 7-211 to 7-212, 7-28 to 7-46

910. Hampden, Springfield City   EDs 7-47 to 7-78

911. Hampden, Springfield City   EDs 7-79 to 7-96

912. Hampshire   EDs 8-1 to 8-18, 8-24 to 8-40

913. Hampshire   EDs 8-19 to 8-23, 8-41 to 8-55

Middlesex   EDs 9-158 to 9-168

914. Middlesex   EDs 9-169 to 9-175, 9-189 to 9-193, 9-176 to 9-188

915. Middlesex, Cambridge City   EDs 9-1 to 9-35

916. Middlesex, Cambridge City   EDs 9-36 to 9-63

917. Middlesex, Cambridge City   EDs 9-64 to 9-76, 9-194 to 9-209

918. Middlesex   EDs 9-210 to 9-211, 9-222 to 9-232, 9-212 to 9-221

919. Middlesex   EDs 9-233 to 9-259, 9-556, 9-260 to 9-261

920. Middlesex, Lowell City   EDs 9-77 to 9-83, 9-95 to 9-99, 9-84 to 9-94, 9-100 to 9-109

921. Middlesex, Lowell City   EDs 9-110 to 9-138

922. Middlesex, Lowell City   EDs 9-139 to 9-157, 9-262 to 9-269, 9-274 to 9-276

923. Middlesex   EDs 9-270 to 9-273, 9-277 to 9-303

924. Middlesex   EDs 9-304 to 9-311, 9-324 to 9-329, 9-312 to 9-319, 9-330 to 9-333

925. Middlesex   EDs 9-320 to 9-323, 9-334 to 9-335, 9-351 to 9-358, 9-336 to 9-350, 9-398 to 9-399

926. Middlesex   EDs 9-359 to 9-367, 9-373 to 9-376, 9-368 to 9-372, 9-377 to 9-385, 9-393 to 9-395

927. Middlesex   EDs 9-386 to 9-392, 9-396 to 9-397, 9-400 to 9-407

Middlesex, Somerville City   EDs 9-408 to 9-421

928. Middlesex, Somerville City   EDs 9-422 to 9-426, 9-435 to 9-441, 9-427 to 9-434, 9-450 to 9-456

929. Middlesex, Somerville City   EDs 9-442 to 9-449, 9-457 to 9-464

Middlesex   EDs 9-465 to 9-469, 9-478 to 9-485

930. Middlesex   EDs 9-470 to 9-477, 9-486 to 9-491, 9-555, 9-492 to 9-508

931. Middlesex   EDs 9-509 to 9-527, 9-543 to 9-554

932. Middlesex   EDs 9-528 to 9-542

Nantucket   EDs 10-1 to 10-2

Norfolk   EDs 11-1 to 11-8

933. Norfolk   EDs 11-9 to 11-33

934. Norfolk   EDs 11-34 to 11-61

935. Norfolk   EDs 11-62 to 11-83, 11-122 to 11-125

936. Norfolk   EDs 11-84 to 11-101, 11-106 to 11-111

937. Norfolk   EDs 11-102 to 11-105, 11-112 to 11-121, 11-126 to 11-135, 11-146 to 11-147

938. Norfolk   EDs 11-136 to 11-145

Plymouth   EDs 12-1 to 12-24

939. Plymouth   EDs 12-25 to 12-57

940. Plymouth   EDs 12-58 to 12-93

941. Plymouth   EDs 12-94 to 12-108

Suffolk, Boston City   EDs 13-1 to 13-13

942. Suffolk, Boston City   EDs 13-14 to 13-30, 13-580 (NP), 13-31 to 13-49

943. Suffolk, Boston City   EDs 13-50 to 13-51, 13-581, 13-52, 13-582, 13-53 to 13-61, 13-583, 13-62 to 13-74, 13-584, 13-75, 13-585, 13-76 to 13-82, 13-586, 13-83 to 13-85

944. Suffolk, Boston City   EDs 13-86 (NP), 13-587, 13-87 to 13-93, 13-588, 13-94 to 13-106, 13-589, 13-107 to 13-111, 13-590, 13-112 to 13-120, 13-591 to 13-592, 13-121 to 13-122, 13-593, 13-123 to 13-126, 13-594

945. Suffolk, Boston City   EDs 13-127 to 13-130, 13-595, 13-131, 13-596, 13-132 to 13-139, 13-597, 13-140 to 13-143, 13-598, 13-144 to 13-146, 13-599, 13-147, 13-600, 13-148 to 13-152, 13-601, 13-153 to 13-155, 13-602, 13-156 to 13-158, 13-603, 13-159, 13-604, 13-160, 13-605

946. Suffolk, Boston City   EDs 13-161, 13-606, 13-162 to 13-163, 13-607, 13-164 to 13-167, 13-267, 13-629, 13-268 to 13-283, 13-630, 13-284 to 13-292

947. Suffolk, Boston City   EDs 13-293 to 13-294, 13-631, 13-295 to 13-300, 13-632, 13-301 to 13-315, 13-168 (NP), 13-608, 13-169 to 13-170, 13-609, 13-171 to 13-173, 13-610, 13-174 to 13-180, 13-611

948. Suffolk, Boston City   EDs 13-181 to 13-182, 13-612, 13-183, 13-613, 13-184 to 13-189, 13-614, 13-190, 13-615, 13-191 to 13-193, 13-616, 13-194 to 13-195, 13-617, 13-196 to 13-199, 13-618, 13-200 to 13-204, 13-619, 13-205 to 13-207, 13-208 (void), 13-209 to 13-216, 13-620, 13-217, 13-621 to 13-622, 13-218

949. Suffolk, Boston City   EDs 13-219 to 13-220, 13-623, 13-221, 13-624, 13-316 to 13-317, 13-633, 13-318 to 13-323, 13-634, 13-324, 13-635, 13-325 to 13-327, 13-636, 13-328, 13-637, 13-329, 13-638 to 13-639, 13-330 to 13-331, 13-640 to 13-641, 13-332 to 13-337, 13-642, 13-338 to 13-341, 13-643, 13-342 to 13-343

950. Suffolk, Boston City   EDs 13-344 to 13-347, 13-644, 13-348 to 13-350, 13-645 (NP), 13-351, 13-646, 13-352, 13-647, 13-353 to 13-359, 13-648, 13-360 to 13-364, 13-649, 13-365 to 13-367, 13-650, 13-368, 13-651, 13-369 to 13-372

951. Suffolk, Boston City   EDs 13-373 to 13-376, 13-652 (NP), 13-377, 13-653, 13-378 to 13-383, 13-654, 13-384 to 13-390, 13-655 to 13-656, 13-391 to 13-394, 13-657, 13-395 to 13-399

952. Suffolk, Boston City   EDs 13-658, 13-400, 13-659, 13-401 to 13-419

953. Suffolk, Boston City   EDs 13-420 to 13-423, 13-660 to 13-661, 13-424 to 13-427, 13-662, 13-428 to 13-429, 13-663, 13-430, 13-664, 13-431, 13-665, 13-432 to 13-436, 13-666, 13-437 to 13-444

954. Suffolk, Boston City   EDs 13-445, 13-667, 13-446 to 13-448, 13-668, 13-449, 13-669, 13-450 to 13-455, 13-670, 13-456 to 13-465, 13-671, 13-466 to 13-467

955. Suffolk, Boston City   EDs 13-672, 13-468 to 13-471, 13-673, 13-472 to 13-476, 13-674, 13-477, 13-675, 13-478 to 13-480, 13-676, 13-481, 13-677 to 13-678, 13-482, 13-679 to 13-680, 13-483

956. Suffolk, Boston City   EDs 13-484 to 13-489, 13-681, 13-490, 13-682, 13-491, 13-683, 13-492 to 13-493, 13-684, 13-494 to 13-501, 13-685 to 13-686, 13-502

957. Suffolk, Boston City   EDs 13-687, 13-503 to 13-504, 13-688, 13-505 to 13-508, 13-689, 13-509 to 13-511, 13-690, 13-512 to 13-520

958. Suffolk, Boston City   EDs 13-521, 13-222 to 13-224, 13-625, 13-225 to 13-235, 13-626, 13-236 to 13-249

959. Suffolk, Boston City   EDs 13-250 to 13-255, 13-627, 13-256 to 13-257, 13-628, 13-258 to 13-266, 13-522 to 13-535

960. Suffolk   EDs 13-536 to 13-563, 13-569 to 13-570

961. Suffolk   EDs 13-564 to 13-568, 13-571 to 13-579
     Worcester   EDs 14-125 to 14-140

962. Worcester   EDs 14-141 to 14-170, 14-181 to 14-186

963. Worcester   EDs 14-171 to 14-180, 14-187 to 14-191, 14-195 to 14-197, 14-192 to 14-194, 14-198 to 14-209, 14-307, 14-210

964. Worcester   EDs 14-211 to 14-212, 14-229 to 14-238, 14-213 to 14-228

965. Worcester   EDs 14-239 to 14-272, 14-276 to 14-277

966. Worcester   EDs 14-273 to 14-275, 14-278, 14-308, 14-279 to 14-288, 14-294 to 14-295, 14-289 to 14-293, 14-296, 14-297 (NP), 14-298 to 14-306

967. Worcester, Worcester City   EDs 14-1 to 14-18

968. Worcester, Worcester City   EDs 14-19 to 14-51

969. Worcester, Worcester City   EDs 14-52 to 14-80

970. Worcester, Worcester City   EDs 14-81 to 14-100

971. Worcester, Worcester City   EDs 14-101 to 14-124

## Michigan

972. Alcona   EDs 1-1 to 1-5, 1-9, 1-6 to 1-8, 1-10 to 1-15
     Alger   EDs 2-1 to 2-11
     Baraga   EDs 7-1 to 7-8
     Allegan   EDs 3-1 to 3-8, 3-23, 3-9 to 3-22, 3-24 to 3-25

973. Allegan   EDs 3-26 to 3-39
     Antrim   EDs 5-1 to 5-9, 5-13, 5-10 to 5-12, 5-14 to 5-20
     Alpena   EDs 4-1 to 4-16
     Arenac   EDs 6-1 to 6-9, 6-17, 6-10 to 6-16, 6-18 to 6-19

974. Barry   EDs 8-1 to 8-4, 8-14, 8-5 to 8-6, 8-17, 8-7 to 8-13, 8-15 to 8-16, 8-18 to 8-26
     Benzie   EDs 10-1 to 10-6, 10-18, 10-7 to 10-17, 10-19
     Bay   EDs 9-1 to 9-4, 9-7 to 9-16

975. Bay   EDs 9-5 to 9-6, 9-17 to 9-45
     Clare   EDs 18-1 to 18-19

976. Barrien   EDs 11-1 to 11-16, 11-46, 11-17 to 11-41

977. Barrien   EDs 11-42 to 11-45, 11-47 to 11-62
     Branch   EDs 12-1 to 12-25

978. Calhoun   EDs 13-1 to 13-33

979. Calhoun   EDs 13-37, 13-34 to 13-36, 13-38 to 13-61
     Cass   EDs 14-1 to 14-23

980. Charlevoix   EDs 15-1 to 15-22
     Cheboygan   EDs 16-1 to 16-28

Chippewa   EDs 17-1 to 17-27

981. Clinton   EDs 19-1 to 19-5, 19-27, 19-6 to 19-26
     Crawford   EDs 20-1 to 20-7
     Emmet   EDs 24-1 to 24-11, 24-13, 24-12, 24-14 to 24-25
     Gladwin   EDs 26-1 to 26-18

982. Delta   EDs 21-1 to 21-17, 21-20 to 21-23, 21-18 to 21-19, 21-24 to 21-27
     Dickinson   EDs 22-1 to 22-5, 22-13 to 22-19

983. Dickinson   EDs 22-6 to 22-12
     Eaton   EDs 23-1 to 23-30
     Iosco   EDs 35-1 to 35-15

984. Genesee, Flint City   EDs 25-1 to 25-23

985. Genesee, Flint City   EDs 25-24 to 25-41, 25-89

986. Genesee, Flint City   EDs 25-62 to 25-68, 25-42 to 25-45, 25-90, 25-46 to 25-50

987. Genesee, Flint City   EDs 25-51 to 25-61, 25-69 to 25-74
     Genesee   EDs 25-75 to 25-77, 25-83, 25-78 to 25-79, 25-91, 25-80 to 25-82, 25-84 to 25-87, 25-92, 25-88

988. Gogebic   EDs 27-1 to 27-26
     Grand Traverse   EDs 28-1 to 28-21

989. Gratiot   EDs 29-1 to 29-16, 29-18, 29-17, 29-19 to 29-30
     Huron   EDs 32-1 to 32-11, 32-20, 32-12 to 32-19, 32-21 to 32-31

990. Huron   EDs 32-32 to 32-40
     Ingham   EDs 33-1 to 33-13, 33-30 to 33-33, 33-43 to 33-49

991. Ingham   EDs 33-18 to 33-23, 33-34 to 33-42, 33-14 to 33-17, 33-24 to 33-29, 33-50

992. Ingham   EDs 33-51 to 33-58, 33-66, 33-59 to 33-65
     Ionia   EDs 34-1 to 34-4, 34-12, 34-5 to 34-11, 34-13 to 34-35

993. Hillsdale   EDs 30-1 to 30-30
     Houghton   EDs 31-1 to 31-4, 31-9, 31-5 to 31-8, 31-10 to 31-22

994. Houghton   EDs 31-23 to 31-41
     Iron   EDs 36-1 to 36-19
     Isabella   EDs 37-1 to 37-6

995. Isabella   EDs 37-7 to 37-21
     Jackson   EDs 38-1 to 38-2, 38-56, 38-34, 38-57, 38-3 to 38-19

996. Jackson   EDs 38-20 to 38-29, 38-33, 38-35 to 38-36, 38-30 to 38-32, 38-37 to 38-48

997. Jackson   EDs 38-49 to 38-55
     Kalamazoo   EDs 39-1 to 39-2, 39-56, 39-3, 39-62, 39-54, 39-4, 39-52, 39-5, 39-9, 39-6 to 39-8, 39-10, 39-60, 39-11 to 39-16, 39-24 to 39-25, 39-43, 39-46, 39-26 to 39-32

998. Kalamazoo   EDs 39-17 to 39-23, 39-33 to 39-38, 39-61, 39-39 to 39-42, 39-44 to 39-45, 39-47 to 39-51, 39-53, 39-55, 39-57 to 39-59

999. Kalkaska   EDs 40-1 to 40-17, 40-18 (NP)
     Kent   EDs 41-102 to 41-103, 41-128, 41-104 to 41-114, 41-147 to 41-148, 41-115, 41-1 to 41-11

1000. Kent, Grand Rapids City   EDs 41-12 to 41-31

1001. Kent, Grand Rapids City   EDs 41-32 to 41-51

1002. Kent, Grand Rapids City   EDs 41-52 to 41-75

1003. Kent, Grand Rapids City   EDs 41-76 to 41-92

1004. Kent, Grand Rapids City   EDs 41-93 to 41-101, 41-116 to 41-121, 41-131, 41-122 to 41-127, 41-129 to 41-130, 41-132 to 41-135

1005. Kent   EDs 41-136 to 41-146

Keweenaw   EDs 42-1 to 42-7

Livingston   EDs 47-1 to 47-24

1006. Lake   EDs 43-1 to 43-6, 43-9, 43-7 to 43-8, 43-10 to 43-13, 43-17, 43-14 to 43-16, 43-18 to 43-19

Leelanau   EDs 45-1 to 45-15

Mackinac   EDs 49-1 to 49-14

Lapeer   EDs 44-1 to 44-11, 44-30, 44-18, 44-12 to 44-17, 44-19 to 44-29

1007. Lenawee   EDs 46-1 to 46-14, 46-49, 46-15 to 46-23, 46-28, 46-24 to 46-27, 46-29 to 46-40, 46-47, 46-41 to 46-46, 46-48

1008. Luce   EDs 48-1 to 48-6

Manistee   EDs 51-1 to 51-25

Macomb   EDs 50-1 to 50-3, 50-50, 50-4 to 50-7, 50-14, 50-8 to 50-13, 50-15 to 50-18

1009. Macomb   EDs 50-19 to 50-24, 50-28 to 50-37, 50-25 to 50-26, 50-39, 50-27, 50-38, 50-40 to 50-41, 50-43, 50-42, 50-44 to 50-49, 50-51

1010. Marquette   EDs 52-1 to 52-17, 52-25 to 52-36, 52-18 to 52-24, 52-37 to 52-41

Mason   EDs 53-1 to 53-10, 53-16 to 53-21

1011. Mason   EDs 53-11 to 53-15, 53-22 to 53-25

Mecosta   EDs 54-1, 54-12, 54-2 to 54-11, 54-13 to 54-26

Menominee   EDs 55-1 to 55-27

1012. Midland   EDs 56-1 to 56-21

Missaukee   EDs 57-1 to 57-9, 57-14, 57-10 to 57-13, 57-15 to 57-18

Monroe   EDs 58-1 to 58-19

1013. Monroe   EDs 58-20 to 58-39

Montcalm   EDs 59-1 to 59-4, 59-13, 59-15, 59-31, 59-5 to 59-12, 59-14, 59-16 to 59-30, 59-32 to 59-34

1014. Montmorency   EDs 60-1 to 60-9

Muskegon   EDs 61-1 to 61-32

1015. Muskegon   EDs 61-33 to 61-46, 61-48 to 61-49, 61-47

Newaygo   EDs 62-1 to 62-7, 62-17, 62-8 to 62-16, 62-18 to 62-31

1016. Oakland   EDs 63-1 to 63-30

1017. Oakland   EDs 63-31 to 63-36, 63-144, 63-37 to 63-56, 63-57 (NP), 63-58 to 63-73, 63-134

1018. Oakland   EDs 63-74 to 63-82, 63-83 (NP), 63-84 to 63-94, 63-145, 63-95 to 63-98, 63-116 to 63-123, 63-143, 63-124

1019. Oakland   EDs 63-99 to 63-108, 63-140, 63-109 to 63-110, 63-113, 63-128, 63-142, 63-114 to 63-115, 63-111 to 63-112, 63-141, 63-125 to 63-127, 63-129 to 63-130, 63-137, 63-131 to 63-133, 63-135 to 63-136, 63-138 to 63-139

1020. Oceana   EDs 64-1 to 64-22

Ontonagon   EDs 66-1 to 66-13

Ogemaw   EDs 65-1 to 65-16

Osceola   EDs 67-1 to 67-4, 67-17, 67-5 to 67-16, 67-18 to 67-23

Otsego   EDs 69-1 to 69-12

1021. Oscoda   EDs 68-1 to 68-6

Presque Isle   EDs 71-1 to 71-18

Saginaw   EDs 73-1 to 73-9, 73-13 (void), 73-10 to 73-12, 73-14 to 73-30

1022. Saginaw   EDs 73-31 to 73-51, 73-53 to 73-56

1023. Saginaw   EDs 73-52, 73-57 to 73-70

Ottawa   EDs 70-1 to 70-14, 70-21 to 70-27, 70-31 to 70-32

1024. Ottawa   EDs 70-15 to 70-20, 70-28 to 70-30, 70-33 to 70-40

Roscommon   EDs 72-1 to 72-11

St. Clair   EDs 74-1 to 74-25

1025. St. Clair   EDs 74-26 to 74-51

St. Joseph   EDs 75-1 to 75-12

1026. St. Joseph   EDs 75-13 to 75-30

Shiawassee   EDs 78-1 to 78-24, 78-35, 78-25 to 78-27

1027. Shiawassee   EDs 78-28 to 78-34

Tuscola   EDs 79-1, 79-16, 79-2 to 79-15, 79-17 to 79-26, 79-28, 79-27, 79-29 to 79-33, 79-35, 79-34, 79-36 to 79-39

Schoolcraft   EDs 77-1 to 77-6, 77-13, 77-7 to 77-12

1028. Sanilac   EDs 76-1 to 76-3, 76-36, 76-4 to 76-35, 76-37 to 76-40

Van Buren   EDs 80-1 to 80-4, 80-6, 80-5, 80-7 to 80-9, 80-25, 80-10 to 80-24, 80-26 to 80-27

1029. Van Buren   EDs 80-28 to 80-32

Washtenaw   EDs 81-1 to 81-5, 81-13 to 81-16, 81-6 to 81-12, 81-17 to 81-23, 81-40, 81-52, 81-24 to 81-25, 81-31, 81-44, 81-26 to 81-30, 81-32 to 81-35

1030. Washtenaw   EDs 81-36 to 81-39, 81-41 to 81-43, 81-45 to 81-51

Wayne   EDs 82-880 to 82-882, 82-1095, 82-883 to 82-893

1031. Wayne   EDs 82-894 to 82-907, 82-1022, 82-908

Wayne, Detroit City   EDs 82-1 to 82-13, 82-1096, 82-14 to 82-18

1032. Wayne, Detroit City   EDs 82-19 to 82-38, 82-40

1033. Wayne, Detroit City   EDs 82-39, 82-41 to 82-58, 82-62, 82-1074, 82-63, 82-1075

1034. Wayne, Detroit City   EDs 82-59 to 82-61, 82-64 to 82-91

1035. Wayne, Detroit City   EDs 82-92 to 82-110, 82-1076, 82-111, 82-1077, 82-112 to 82-117, 82-120

1036. Wayne, Detroit City   EDs 82-118 to 82-119, 82-121 to 82-146

1037. Wayne, Detroit City   EDs 82-147 to 82-164, 82-1078, 82-165 to 82-166, 82-1079, 82-167 to 82-171

1038. Wayne, Detroit City   EDs 82-172 to 82-186, 82-189, 82-187 to 82-188, 82-190 to 82-199, 82-201

1039. Wayne, Detroit City   EDs 82-200, 82-202 to 82-219, 82-222

1040. Wayne, Detroit City   EDs 82-220 to 82-221, 82-223, 82-1080, 82-224, 82-1081, 82-225 to 82-228, 82-1082, 82-229 to 82-242

1041. Wayne, Detroit City   EDs 82-243 to 82-273

1042. Wayne, Detroit City   EDs 82-274 to 82-277, 82-279 to 82-280, 82-278, 82-281 to 82-288

1043. Wayne, Detroit City   EDs 82-289 to 82-301, 82-303, 82-302, 82-304 to 82-311, 82-1083, 82-312

1044. Wayne, Detroit City   EDs 82-313 to 82-315, 82-1084, 82-316, 82-1085, 82-317 to 82-336

1045. Wayne, Detroit City   EDs 82-337 to 82-360

1046. Wayne, Detroit City   EDs 82-361, 82-1086, 82-362, 82-1087, 82-363, 82-1088, 82-364, 82-1089, 82-365 to 82-377

1047. Wayne, Detroit City   EDs 82-378 to 82-403

1048. Wayne, Detroit City   EDs 82-404 to 82-419

1049. Wayne, Detroit City   EDs 82-420 to 82-441

1050. Wayne, Detroit City   EDs 82-442 to 82-443, 82-1090, 82-444, 82-1091, 82-445, 82-1092, 82-446, 82-1093, 82-448, 82-447, 82-449 to 82-461

1051. Wayne, Detroit City   EDs 82-462 to 82-471, 82-473, 82-472, 82-474 to 82-480

1052. Wayne, Detroit City   EDs 82-481 to 82-510

1053. Wayne, Detroit City   EDs 82-511 to 82-532

1054. Wayne, Detroit City   EDs 82-533 to 82-539, 82-1073, 82-540 to 82-541

1055. Wayne, Detroit City   EDs 82-542 to 82-562

1056. Wayne, Detroit City   EDs 82-563 to 82-594

1057. Wayne, Detroit City   EDs 82-595 to 82-624

1058. Wayne, Detroit City   EDs 82-625 to 82-652

1059. Wayne, Detroit City   EDs 82-653 to 82-682

1060. Wayne, Detroit City   EDs 82-683 to 82-713

1061. Wayne, Detroit City   EDs 82-714 to 82-748

1062. Wayne, Detroit City   EDs 82-749 to 82-776

1063. Wayne, Detroit City   EDs 82-777 to 82-800, 82-803

1064. Wayne, Detroit City   EDs 82-801 to 82-802, 82-804 to 82-817, 82-821

1065. Wayne, Detroit City   EDs 82-818, 82-820, 82-825, 82-819, 82-822

1066. Wayne, Detroit City   EDs 82-823 to 82-824, 82-826, 82-828, 82-827, 82-829, 82-831, 82-833

1067. Wayne, Detroit City   EDs 82-830, 82-832, 82-834 to 82-835, 82-838, 82-836 to 82-837, 82-839 to 82-842

1068. Wayne, Detroit City   EDs 82-843 to 82-849, 82-1094, 82-850 to 82-851

1069. Wayne, Detroit City   EDs 82-852 to 82-862, 82-864

1070. Wayne, Detroit City   EDs 82-863, 82-865 to 82-867, 82-870, 82-868 to 82-869, 82-871 to 82-873

1071. Wayne, Detroit City   EDs 82-874 to 82-879, 82-909 to 82-922, 82-927

1072. Wayne   EDs 82-925 to 82-926, 82-928 to 82-934, 82-935 (void), 82-923 to 82-924, 82-936 to 82-952

1073. Wayne   EDs 82-953 to 82-979

1074. Wayne   EDs 82-980 to 82-1003

1075. Wayne   EDs 82-1004 to 82-1013, 82-1016 to 82-1020, 82-1028 to 82-1032, 82-1014 to 82-1015, 82-1021, 82-1023 to 82-1027, 82-1033 to 82-1035

1076. Wayne   EDs 82-1036 to 82-1047, 82-1097, 82-1048 to 82-1049, 82-1054 to 82-1064, 82-1070, 82-1065, 82-1071, 82-1066 to 82-1069, 82-1072

1077. Wayne   EDs 82-1050 to 82-1053

Wexford   EDs 83-1 to 83-2, 83-22, 83-3 to 83-21, 83-23 to 83-27

### Minnesota

1078. Aitkin   EDs 1-1 to 1-61

Anoka   EDs 2-1 to 2-22

Benton   EDs 5-1 to 5-19

1079. Becker   EDs 3-1 to 3-9, 3-13, 3-10 to 3-12, 3-14 to 3-44

Beltrami   EDs 4-1 to 4-44, 4-46, 4-45, 4-47 to 4-64, 4-65 (NP), 4-66, 4-67 (NP), 4-68, 4-69 to 4-71 (NP), 4-72 to 4-73, 4-74 to 4-79 (NP), 4-80 to 4-84, 4-85 to 4-86 (NP), 4-87 to 4-88, 4-89 to 4-97 (NP), 4-98

1080. Big Stone   EDs 6-1 to 6-22

Blue Earth   EDs 7-1 to 7-38

1081. Brown   EDs 8-1 to 8-26

Carlton   EDs 9-1 to 9-37

1082. Carver   EDs 10-1 to 10-17, 10-19, 10-18, 10-20 to 10-24

Cass   EDs 11-1 to 11-65, 11-66 (NP), 11-67 to 11-72, 11-73 to 11-74 (NP), 11-75 to 11-79

Chippewa   EDs 12-1 to 12-24

1083. Chisago   EDs 13-1 to 13-5, 13-22, 13-6 to 13-21

Clearwater   EDs 15-1 to 15-12, 15-13 (NP), 15-14 to 15-29, 15-30 (NP), 15-31 to 15-37

Clay   EDs 14-1 to 14-37, 14-44, 14-38 to 14-43

Cook   EDs 16-1 to 16-16

1084. Cottonwood   EDs 17-1 to 17-24

Dodge   EDs 20-1 to 20-18

Crow Wing   EDs 18-1 to 18-12, 18-55, 18-13 to 18-54

1085. Dakota   EDs 19-1 to 19-27, 19-32 to 19-34, 19-42, 19-35, 19-28 to 19-31, 19-36 to 19-41

Douglas   EDs 21-1 to 21-26, 21-35, 21-27 to 21-34

1086. Faribault   EDs 22-1 to 22-12, 22-25, 22-13 to 22-24, 22-26 to 22-30, 22-32, 22-31

Fillmore   EDs 23-1 to 23-37

1087. Freeborn   EDs 24-1 to 24-4, 24-32 to 24-33, 24-5 to 24-31

Goodhue   EDs 25-1 to 25-27

1088. Goodhue   EDs 25-28 to 25-35

Grant   EDs 26-1 to 26-23

Hubbard   EDs 29-1 to 29-8, 29-9 (NP), 29-10 to 29-33

Hennepin   EDs 27-267 to 27-291

1089. Hennepin, Minneapolis City   EDs 27-1 to 27-28

1090. Hennepin, Minneapolis City   EDs 27-29 to 27-40, 27-318, 27-41, 27-319, 27-42 to 27-52, 27-320

1091. Hennepin, Minneapolis City   EDs 27-53, 27-321, 27-54, 27-322, 27-84 to 27-113

1092. Hennepin, Minneapolis City   EDs 27-55 to 27-69, 27-323, 27-70, 27-324, 27-71 to 27-83

1093. Hennepin, Minneapolis City   EDs 27-114 to 27-130

1094. Hennepin, Minneapolis City   EDs 27-131 to 27-158

1095. Hennepin, Minneapolis City   EDs 27-159 to 27-181

1096. Hennepin, Minneapolis City   EDs 27-182 to 27-192, 27-325, 27-193, 27-326, 27-194 to 27-196

1097. Hennepin, Minneapolis City   EDs 27-197 to 27-198, 27-327, 27-199, 27-328, 27-200 to 27-219

1098. Hennepin, Minneapolis City   EDs 27-220 to 27-233

1099. Hennepin, Minneapolis City   EDs 27-234 to 27-250

1100. Hennepin, Minneapolis City   EDs 27-251 to 27-256, 27-257 (NP), 27-258 to 27-266

1101. Hennepin   EDs 27-292 to 27-317

Houston   EDs 28-1 to 28-23

Isanti   EDs 30-1 to 30-17

1102. Itasca   EDs 31-1 to 31-77, 31-78 (NP), 31-79 to 31-85, 31-86 (NP), 31-87 to 31-88, 31-89 to 31-90 (NP), 31-91 to 31-92, 31-93 (NP), 31-94

Koochiching   EDs 36-1 to 36-51, 36-52 to 36-54 (NP), 36-55 to 36-58, 36-59 (NP), 36-60, 36-61 to 36-62 (NP), 36-63 to 36-66, 36-67 to 36-68 (NP), 36-69 to 36-70, 36-71 to 36-72 (NP), 36-73 to 36-80

1103. Jackson   EDs 32-1 to 32-25

Kittson   EDs 35-1 to 35-38

Kanabec   EDs 33-1 to 33-18

Lac Qui Parle   EDs 37-1 to 37-30

1104. Kandiyohi   EDs 34-1 to 34-36

Lake  EDs 38-1 to 38-11

Le Sueur  EDs 40-1 to 40-24

1105.  Lake of the Woods  EDs 39-1 to 39-35, 39-36 (NP), 39-37 to 39-38, 39-39 (NP)

Lyon  EDs 42-1 to 42-30

Lincoln  EDs 41-1 to 41-20

McLeod  EDs 43-1 to 43-16

1106.  McLeod  EDs 43-17 to 43-25

Marshall  EDs 45-1 to 45-60

Mahnomen  EDs 44-1 to 44-19

Meeker  EDs 47-1 to 47-17, 47-27, 47-18 to 47-19, 47-25 to 47-26, 47-20 to 47-24

1107.  Martin  EDs 46-1 to 46-32

Mille Lacs  EDs 48-1 to 48-9, 48-11, 48-10, 48-12 to 48-25

Murray  EDs 51-1 to 51-29

1108.  Morrison  EDs 49-1 to 49-48

Mower  EDs 50-1 to 50-37

1109.  Nicollet  EDs 52-1 to 52-20

Nobles  EDs 53-1 to 53-32

Norman  EDs 54-1 to 54-31

1110.  Olmsted  EDs 55-1 to 55-3, 55-19, 55-35, 55-20 to 55-22, 55-34 (NP), 55-23, 55-36, 55-24 to 55-25, 55-29, 55-26 to 55-27, 55-37, 55-28, 55-4 to 55-18, 55-30 to 55-33

Pennington  EDs 57-1 to 57-27

1111.  Otter Tail  EDs 56-1 to 56-53, 56-55, 56-54, 56-56 to 56-85

1112.  Pine  EDs 58-1 to 58-47

Pipestone  EDs 59-1 to 59-22

Polk  EDs 60-1 to 60-21

1113.  Polk  EDs 60-22 to 60-30, 60-80, 60-31 to 60-57, 60-59, 60-58, 60-60 to 60-79

Pope  EDs 61-1 to 61-28

Red Lake  EDs 63-1 to 63-16

1114.  Ramsey, St. Paul City  EDs 62-172 to 62-178, 62-1, 62-179, 62-2 to 62-12

1115.  Ramsey, St. Paul City  EDs 62-180, 62-13 to 62-14, 62-31 to 62-41, 62-15 to 62-16, 62-181, 62-17 to 62-19

1116.  Ramsey, St. Paul City  EDs 62-20, 62-182, 62-21 to 62-30, 62-42 to 62-51

1117.  Ramsey, St. Paul City  EDs 62-52 to 62-58, 62-183, 62-59 to 62-66

1118.  Ramsey, St. Paul City  EDs 62-67 to 62-68, 62-184, 62-69 to 62-95

1119.  Ramsey, St. Paul City  EDs 62-96, 62-185, 62-97 to 62-117

1120.  Ramsey, St. Paul City  EDs 62-118 to 62-126, 62-127, 62-187, 62-128, 62-186, 62-188 to 62-189, 62-129 to 62-131

1121.  Ramsey, St. Paul City  EDs 62-132 to 62-137, 62-190, 62-138 to 62-151, 62-191, 62-152 to 62-153

1122.  Ramsey, St. Paul City  EDs 62-154, 62-192 to 62-196, 62-155 to 62-156, 62-197, 62-157, 62-198, 62-158, 62-199, 62-159, 62-200, 62-160, 62-201 to 62-202, 62-161, 62-203, 62-162 to 62-164

1123.  Ramsey, St. Paul City  EDs 62-165 to 62-170, 62-204, 62-171

Redwood  EDs 64-1 to 64-42

1124.  Renville  EDs 65-1 to 65-37

Rice  EDs 66-1 to 66-31

1125.  Rock  EDs 67-1 to 67-19

Roseau  EDs 68-1 to 68-50, 68-51 to 68-52 (NP), 68-53 to 68-54

St. Louis, Duluth City  EDs 69-1 to 69-35

1126.  St. Louis, Duluth City  EDs 69-36 to 69-64

1127.  St. Louis, Duluth City  EDs 69-65 to 69-97

1128.  St. Louis  EDs 69-98 to 69-176

1129.  St. Louis  EDs 69-177 to 69-202, 69-203 (NP), 69-204 to 69-215, 69-273, 69-216 to 69-225, 69-226 to 69-228 (NP), 69-229 to 69-231, 69-232 to 69-233 (NP), 69-234 to 69-236, 69-237 to 69-241 (NP), 69-242 to 69-243, 69-244 to 69-245 (NP), 69-246, 69-247 (NP), 69-248, 69-249 to 69-251 (NP), 69-252, 69-253 to 69-254 (NP), 69-255, 69-256 (NP), 69-257 to 69-258, 69-259 to 69-260 (NP), 69-261 to 69-264, 69-265 (NP), 69-266 to 69-267, 69-268 to 69-269 (NP), 69-270 to 69-271, 69-272 (NP)

Scott  EDs 70-1 to 70-22

Sherburne  EDs 71-1 to 71-19

1130.  Sibley  EDs 72-1 to 72-24

Stearns  EDs 73-1 to 73-5, 73-24, 73-6 to 73-23, 73-25 to 73-41, 73-76, 73-42 to 73-52, 73-61

1131.  Stearns  EDs 73-53 to 73-60, 73-62 to 73-68, 73-78, 73-69, 73-79, 73-70 to 73-75, 73-77

Steele  EDs 74-1 to 74-21

1132.  Stevens  EDs 75-1 to 75-21

Swift  EDs 76-1 to 76-29

Todd  EDs 77-1 to 77-31, 77-40, 77-32 to 77-39

1133.  Traverse  EDs 78-1 to 78-19

Wabasha  EDs 79-1 to 79-27

Wadena  EDs 80-1 to 80-19

Waseca  EDs 81-1 to 81-18

1134.  Washington  EDs 82-1 to 82-18, 82-20 to 82-21, 82-19, 82-22 to 82-32

Watonwan  EDs 83-1 to 83-20

Wilken  EDs 84-1 to 84-31

1135.  Winona  EDs 85-1 to 85-26, 85-41 to 85-85, 85-27 to 85-40

Yellow Medicine  EDs 87-1 to 87-29

1136.  Wright  EDs 86-1 to 86-36

## Mississippi

1137.  Adams  EDs 1-1 to 1-13

Alcorn  EDs 2-1 to 2-18

1138.  Amite  EDs 3-1 to 3-14

Benton  EDs 5-1 to 5-10

Attala  EDs 4-1 to 4-16

1139.  Bolivar  EDs 6-1 to 6-29, 6-43 to 6-48

1140.  Bolivar  EDs 6-30 to 6-42

Calhoun  EDs 7-1 to 7-6, 7-9, 7-7 to 7-8, 7-10 to 7-18

Carroll  EDs 8-1 to 8-13

1141.  Chickasaw  EDs 9-1 to 9-20

Choctaw  EDs 10-1 to 10-2, 10-12, 10-3 to 10-11

Clarke  EDs 12-1 to 12-14

1142.  Claiborne  EDs 11-1 to 11-10

Clay  EDs 13-1 to 13-15

Coahoma  EDs 14-1 to 14-3, 14-13 to 14-23

1143.  Coahoma  EDs 14-4 to 14-12, 14-24 to 14-25

Franklin  EDs 19-1 to 19-14

Copiah  EDs 15-1 to 15-10, 15-14 to 15-18

1144.  Copiah  EDs 15-11 to 15-13

Covington  EDs 16-1 to 16-14

George  EDs 20-1 to 20-6

De Soto   EDs 17-1 to 17-16

1145.  Forrest   EDs 18-1 to 18-14

Greene   EDs 21-1 to 21-8

Grenada   EDs 22-1 to 22-11

1146.  Hancock   EDs 23-1 to 23-10

Harrison   EDs 24-1 to 24-24

1147.  Hinds   EDs 25-1 to 25-28

1148.  Hinds   EDs 25-29 to 25-50

Holmes   EDs 26-1 to 26-18

1149.  Holmes   EDs 26-19 to 26-24

Jasper   EDs 31-1 to 31-13

Humphreys   EDs 27-1 to 27-16

1150.  Issaquena   EDs 28-1 to 28-6

Itawamba   EDs 29-1 to 29-12

Jackson   EDs 30-1 to 30-11, 30-12 (void), 30-13 to 30-15

Jefferson   EDs 32-1 to 32-11

Jefferson Davis   EDs 33-1 to 33-3

1151.  Jefferson Davis   EDs 33-4 to 33-11

Jones   EDs 34-1 to 34-3, 34-15 to 34-24, 34-4 to 34-14

1152.  Kemper   EDs 35-1 to 35-16

Lafayette   EDs 36-1 to 36-15

Lamar   EDs 37-1 to 37-9

1153.  Lauderdale   EDs 38-1 to 38-28

Lawrence   EDs 39-1 to 39-2, 39-4 to 39-5

1154.  Lawrence   EDs 39-3, 39-6 to 39-11

Leake   EDs 40-1 to 40-14

Lee   EDs 41-1 to 41-9, 41-10 (NP), 41-11 to 41-21

1155.  Lee   EDs 41-22 to 41-25

Marion   EDs 46-1 to 46-13

Leflore   EDs 42-1 to 42-5, 42-15 to 42-19

1156.  Leflore   EDs 42-6 to 42-7, 42-20 to 42-21, 42-8, 42-22, 42-9 to 42-14

Lincoln   EDs 43-1 to 43-17

1157.  Lowndes   EDs 44-1 to 44-22

Madison   EDs 45-1 to 45-11, 45-16 to 45-20

1158.  Madison   EDs 45-12 to 45-15

Oktibbeha   EDs 53-1 to 53-15

Marshall   EDs 47-1 to 47-15

1159.  Monroe   EDs 48-1 to 48-4, 48-29, 48-5 to 48-28

Pearl River   EDs 55-1 to 55-11

1160.  Montgomery   EDs 49-1 to 49-12

Perry   EDs 56-1 to 56-7

Neshoba   EDs 50-1 to 50-16

1161.  Newton   EDs 51-1 to 51-3, 51-6, 51-10, 51-4 to 51-5, 51-7 to 51-9, 51-11 to 51-19

Stone   EDs 66-1 to 66-6

Noxubee   EDs 52-1 to 52-18

1162.  Panola   EDs 54-1 to 54-22

Pike   EDs 57-1 to 57-7, 57-13 to 57-14, 57-11 to 57-12, 57-9 to 57-10, 57-8, 57-15 to 57-17

1163.  Pike   EDs 57-18 to 57-20

Quitman   EDs 60-1 to 60-18

Pontotoc   EDs 58-1 to 58-16

Prentiss   EDs 59-1 to 59-3

1164.  Prentiss   EDs 59-4 to 59-13

Sharkey   EDs 63-1, 63-12, 63-2 to 63-11

Rankin   EDs 61-1 to 61-18

Scott   EDs 62-1 to 62-3

1165.  Scott   EDs 62-4 to 62-14

Simpson   EDs 64-1, 64-8, 64-2 to 64-7, 64-11 to 64-15, 64-9 to 64-10, 64-16 to 64-17

Smith   EDs 65-1 to 65-14

1166.  Sunflower   EDs 67-1 to 67-4, 67-22 to 67-29, 67-10 to 67-21

1167.  Sunflower   EDs 67-5 to 67-9

Tippah   EDs 70-1 to 70-13

Tallahatchie   EDs 68-1 to 68-2, 68-10 to 68-24

1168.  Tallahatchie   EDs 68-3 to 68-9

Tate   EDs 69-1 to 69-12, 69-16, 69-13 to 69-15

Tishomingo   EDs 71-1 to 71-16

Tunica   EDs 72-1 to 72-7

1169.  Tunica   EDs 72-8 to 72-11

Union   EDs 73-1 to 73-18

Walthall   EDs 74-1 to 74-6

Warren   EDs 75-1 to 75-5, 75-20 to 75-22

1170.  Warren   EDs 75-6 to 75-19

Washington   EDs 76-1 to 76-4, 76-14 to 76-26

1171.  Washington   EDs 76-5, 76-6 (void), 76-7 to 76-10, 76-11 (void), 76-12 to 76-13

Wayne   EDs 77-1 to 77-10

Winston   EDs 80-1 to 80-12

1172.  Webster   EDs 78-1 to 78-18

Wilkinson   EDs 79-1 to 79-12

Yalobusha   EDs 81-1 to 81-20

Yazo   EDs 82-1 to 82-4, 82-20 to 82-21

1173.  Yazoo   EDs 82-5 to 82-19


*Missouri*

1174.  Adair   EDs 1-1 to 1-22

Andrew   EDs 2-1 to 2-18

Audrain   EDs 4-1 to 4-5, 4-11, 4-6 to 4-10, 4-12 to 4-22

1175.  Atchison   EDs 3-1 to 3-17

Barry   EDs 5-1 to 5-32

Barton   EDs 6-1 to 6-13, 6-16, 6-19, 6-14 to 6-15, 6-17 to 6-18, 6-20 to 6-21

1176.  Bates   EDs 7-1 to 7-3, 7-17, 7-4 to 7-16, 7-18 to 7-39

Benton   EDs 8-1, 8-15, 8-2 to 8-3, 8-16, 8-4 to 8-7, 8-17, 8-8 to 8-14

Bollinger   EDs 9-1 to 9-15

Boone   EDs 10-1 to 10-9

1177.  Boone   EDs 10-10 to 10-33

Buchanan   EDs 11-1 to 11-24

1178.  Buchanan   EDs 11-25 to 11-50

1179.  Buchanan   EDs 11-51 to 11-59

Caldwell   EDs 13-1 to 13-19

Butler    EDs 12-1, 12-23, 12-2 to 12-22

Callaway    EDs 14-1 to 14-4

1180.  Callaway    EDs 14-5 to 14-27

Camden    EDs 15-1, 15-14, 15-2 to 15-13

Cape Girardeau    EDs 16-1 to 16-24, 16-36, 16-25 to 16-27

1181.  Cape Girardeau    EDs 16-28 to 16-35

Carroll    EDs 17-1 to 17-35

Carter    EDs 18-1 to 18-10

Cass    EDs 19-1 to 19-3, 19-5, 19-15, 19-4, 19-6 to 19-14, 19-16 to 19-34

1182.  Cedar    EDs 20-1 to 20-13

Chariton    EDs 21-1 to 21-27

Christian    EDs 22-1 to 22-23

Clark    EDs 23-1 to 23-15, 23-18, 23-16 to 23-17, 23-19

1183.  Clay    EDs 24-1 to 24-26

Clinton    EDs 25-1 to 25-21

Crawford    EDs 28-1 to 28-14

1184.  Cole    EDs 26-1 to 26-24

Cooper    EDs 27-1 to 27-26

1185.  Dade    EDs 29-1 to 29-21

Dent    EDs 33-1 to 33-14

Dallas    EDs 30-1 to 30-6, 30-10, 30-7 to 30-9, 30-11 to 30-13

Daviess    EDs 31-1 to 31-11, 31-12 (NP), 31-14, 31-13, 31-15 to 31-24

1186.  De Kalb    EDs 32-1 to 32-10, 32-19, 32-11 to 32-18

Douglas    EDs 34-1 to 34-24

Dunklin    EDs 35-1 to 35-23

1187.  Dunklin    EDs 35-24 to 35-31

Franklin    EDs 36-1 to 36-34

Gasconade    EDs 37-1 to 37-17

1188.  Gentry    EDs 38-1 to 38-17

Greene    EDs 39-1 to 39-6, 39-7 (NP), 39-8 to 39-19, 39-20 (void), 39-21, 39-22 (void), 39-23, 39-24 (void), 39-25, 39-26 (void), 39-27, 39-28 (void), 39-29 to 39-30

1189.  Greene    EDs 39-31 to 39-64

Holt    EDs 44-1 to 44-20

1190.  Grundy    EDs 40-1 to 40-22

Hickory    EDs 43-1 to 43-11

Harrison    EDs 41-1 to 41-6, 41-8, 41-21, 41-30, 41-7, 41-9 to 41-14, 41-22, 41-15 to 41-20, 41-23 to 41-29, 41-31 to 41-34

Henry    EDs 42-1 to 42-10

1191.  Henry    EDs 42-11 to 42-30

Howard    EDs 45-1 to 45-14

Howell    EDs 46-1 to 46-20

Iron    EDs 47-1 to 47-10

1192.  Jackson    EDs 48-251 to 48-261, 48-242 to 48-250, 48-262 to 48-268

1193.  Jackson, Kansas City    EDs 48-1 to 48-16, 48-21 to 48-26, 48-17 to 48-20, 48-27 to 48-32

1194.  Jackson, Kansas City    EDs 48-33 to 48-66

1195.  Jackson, Kansas City    EDs 48-67 to 48-90

1196.  Jackson, Kansas City    EDs 48-91, 48-92 (void), 48-93 to 48-102, 48-104, 48-103, 48-105 to 48-112

1197.  Jackson, Kansas City    EDs 48-113 to 48-120

1198.  Jackson, Kansas City    EDs 48-121 to 48-124, 48-130, 48-125 to 48-129, 48-131 to 48-147

1199.  Jackson, Kansas City    EDs 48-148 to 48-173

1200.  Jackson, Kansas City    EDs 48-174 to 48-191, 48-192 (void), 48-193 to 48-194

1201.  Jackson, Kansas City    EDs 48-195 to 48-218

1202.  Jackson, Kansas City    EDs 48-219 to 48-230

1203.  Jackson, Kansas City    EDs 48-231 to 48-239

1204.  Jackson    EDs 48-240 to 48-241, 48-269 to 48-283

1205.  Jasper    EDs 49-1, 49-47, 49-2 to 49-5, 49-63, 49-6 to 49-7, 49-62, 49-8 to 49-39

1206.  Jasper    EDs 49-40 to 49-46, 49-48 to 49-61

Jefferson    EDs 50-1 to 50-25

1207.  Johnson    EDs 51-1 to 51-27

Knox    EDs 52-1 to 52-18

Laclede    EDs 53-1 to 53-18

1208.  Lafayette    EDs 54-3, 54-29, 54-32, 54-1 to 54-2, 54-4 to 54-7, 54-12, 54-8 to 54-11, 54-13 to 54-28, 54-30 to 54-31, 54-33 to 54-34

Lawrence    EDs 55-1 to 55-30

1209.  Lewis    EDs 56-1 to 56-15

Lincoln    EDs 57-1 to 57-24

Linn    EDs 58-1 to 58-29

1210.  Livingston    EDs 59-1 to 59-23

Maries    EDs 63-1 to 63-11

McDonald    EDs 60-1 to 60-20

Madison    EDs 62-1 to 62-12

1211.  Macon    EDs 61-1 to 61-15, 61-17, 61-16, 61-18 to 61-35, 61-37, 61-39, 61-36, 61-38, 61-40

Marion    EDs 64-1 to 64-13

1212.  Marion    EDs 64-14 to 64-21

Miller    EDs 66-1 to 66-4, 66-18, 66-5 to 66-17

Mercer    EDs 65-1 to 65-15

Mississippi    EDs 67-1 to 67-9, 67-18, 67-10 to 67-17

1213.  Moniteau    EDs 68-1 to 68-6, 68-18, 68-7 to 68-17

Montgomery    EDs 70-1 to 70-21

Monroe    EDs 69-1 to 69-18

Morgan    EDs 71-1 to 71-13

New Madrid    EDs 72-1 to 72-2

1214.  New Madrid    EDs 72-3 to 72-4, 72-27, 72-5 to 72-8, 72-28, 72-9 to 72-26

Newton    EDs 73-1 to 73-6, 73-28, 73-7 to 73-21, 73-27, 73-22 to 73-26

1215.  Nodaway    EDs 74-1 to 74-37

Oregon    EDs 75-1 to 75-20

Osage    EDs 76-1 to 76-17

1216.  Ozark    EDs 77-1, 77-19, 77-2 to 77-18

Phelps    EDs 81-1 to 81-16

Pemiscot    EDs 78-1 to 78-6, 78-31, 78-7 to 78-19

1217.  Pemiscot    EDs 78-20 to 78-30

Platte    EDs 83-1 to 83-12, 83-21, 83-13 to 83-20

Perry    EDs 79-1 to 79-21

Pettis    EDs 80-1 to 80-16

1218.  Pettis    EDs 80-17 to 80-31

Pike    EDs 82-1, 82-25, 82-2 to 82-24

Polk    EDs 84-1 to 84-7

1219.  Polk    EDs 84-8 to 84-12, 84-18, 84-13 to 84-17, 84-19 to 84-23

Pulaski    EDs 85-1 to 85-11

Putnam    EDs 86-1 to 86-18

Ralls    EDs 87-1 to 87-12

1220. Randolph    EDs 88-1 to 88-28

Ray    EDs 89-1 to 89-25

Reynolds    EDs 90-1 to 90-8

1221. Ripley    EDs 91-1 to 91-10, 91-17, 91-11 to 91-16

St. Clair    EDs 93-1 to 93-22

St. Charles    EDs 92-1 to 92-5, 92-8, 92-24, 92-6 to 92-7, 92-9 to 92-23, 92-25 to 92-27

1222. St. Francois    EDs 94-1 to 94-24, 94-26, 94-25, 94-27 to 94-33

Ste. Genevieve    EDs 97-1 to 97-10

Schuyler    EDs 99-1 to 99-12

1223. St. Louis    EDs 95-2 to 95-5, 95-13, 95-37, 95-6, 95-1, 95-7 to 95-12, 95-35, 95-14, 95-17, 95-144, 95-18, 95-140 to 95-143, 95-19 to 95-33, 95-111

1224. St. Louis    EDs 95-34, 95-90, 95-36, 95-38 to 95-61, 95-112 to 95-113, 95-62 to 95-67

1225. St. Louis    EDs 95-68 to 95-70, 95-15 to 95-16, 95-71 to 95-73, 95-114, 95-74, 95-115 to 95-118, 95-75, 95-119, 95-76, 95-120, 95-77 to 95-78, 95-80, 95-82, 95-121, 95-79, 95-81, 95-83, 95-122, 95-84, 95-123 to 95-125

1226. St. Louis    EDs 95-126 to 95-128, 95-85, 95-129 to 95-131, 95-86, 95-132 to 95-133, 95-87 to 95-89, 95-91 to 95-105, 95-134 to 95-139, 95-106 to 95-110

1227. St. Louis City    EDs 96-1 to 96-3, 96-543, 96-4, 96-544, 96-5, 96-545, 96-6 to 96-7, 96-546, 96-8 to 96-13, 96-14 (void), 96-15 to 96-16, 96-547, 96-17

1228. St. Louis City    EDs 96-258 to 96-289

1229. St. Louis City    EDs 96-290 to 96-310, 96-560, 96-311 to 96-314, 96-353 to 96-364

1230. St. Louis City    EDs 96-365 to 96-397

1231. St. Louis City    EDs 96-315 to 96-329, 96-330 (void), 96-331 to 96-352

1232. St. Louis City    EDs 96-398 to 96-428, 96-561, 96-429 to 96-431

1233. St. Louis City    EDs 96-432 to 96-449, 96-562, 96-450 to 96-452, 96-563 to 96-565, 96-453 to 96-455

1234. St. Louis City    EDs 96-456 to 96-466, 96-566 to 96-567, 96-467, 96-568, 96-468, 96-569, 96-469, 96-570, 96-470 to 96-471, 96-571 to 96-572, 96-472

1235. St. Louis City    EDs 96-473 to 96-484, 96-573, 96-485 to 96-492

1236. St. Louis City    EDs 96-493 to 96-505, 96-574, 96-506, 96-18, 96-576, 96-19 to 96-32

1237. St. Louis City    EDs 96-33 to 96-43, 96-548, 96-44 to 96-59

1238. St. Louis City    EDs 96-60 to 96-68, 96-549, 96-69 to 96-89, 96-103 to 96-105

1239. St. Louis City    EDs 96-106 to 96-112, 96-550, 96-113, 96-577, 96-114 to 96-118, 96-551, 96-119 to 96-134

1240. St. Louis City    EDs 96-135 to 96-143, 96-552, 96-578, 96-553, 96-144, 96-554, 96-145, 96-579, 96-146 to 96-152

1241. St. Louis City    EDs 96-153 to 96-159, 96-160 (void), 96-161 to 96-166, 96-580, 96-555, 96-581, 96-167, 96-582, 96-168 to 96-175

1242. St. Louis City    EDs 96-176 to 96-182, 96-556, 96-183 to 96-192, 96-557, 96-507 to 96-521

1243. St. Louis City    EDs 96-522 to 96-532, 96-575, 96-533 to 96-542, 96-90 to 96-102

1244. St. Louis City    EDs 96-193 to 96-224, 96-583

1245. St. Louis City    EDs 96-225 to 96-232, 96-558, 96-584, 96-233, 96-585, 96-234 to 96-239, 96-559, 96-240 to 96-243

1246. St. Louis City    EDs 96-244 to 96-245, 96-246 (NP), 96-247 to 96-257

Saline    EDs 98-1 to 98-25

1247. Saline    EDs 98-26 to 98-31

Scotland    EDs 100-1 to 100-16

Shannon    EDs 102-1 to 102-23

Scott    EDs 101-1 to 101-28

1248. Shelby    EDs 103-1 to 103-16

Stone    EDs 105-1 to 105-15, 105-22, 105-16 to 105-21

Stoddard    EDs 104-1 to 104-24

1249. Sullivan    EDs 106-1 to 106-14, 106-16, 106-15, 106-17 to 106-19, 106-23, 106-20 to 106-22

Taney    EDs 107-1 to 107-15

Texas    EDs 108-1 to 108-24

Warren    EDs 110-1 to 110-8, 110-10, 110-9, 110-11 to 110-13

1250. Vernon    EDs 109-1 to 109-15, 109-17, 109-32, 109-16, 109-18 to 109-31, 109-33 to 109-41

Washington    EDs 111-1 to 111-16

Worth    EDs 114-1 to 114-12

1251. Wayne    EDs 112-1 to 112-13

Webster    EDs 113-1 to 113-21

Wright    EDs 115-1 to 115-3, 115-20, 115-4 to 115-6, 115-8, 115-7, 115-9 to 115-19

## *Montana*

1252. Beaverhead    EDs 1-1 to 1-11

Big Horn    EDs 2-1 to 2-7, 2-9, 2-15, 2-8, 2-10 to 2-13, 2-16, 2-14

Blaine    EDs 3-1 to 3-19, 3-53, 3-20 to 3-52

Broadwater    EDs 4-1 to 4-33

Carbon    EDs 5-1 to 5-64, 5-65 (NP)

Carter    EDs 6-1 to 6-36

1253. Cascade    EDs 7-1 to 7-9, 7-13 to 7-18, 7-10 to 7-12, 7-19 to 7-60

1254. Cascade    EDs 7-61 to 7-103

Custer    EDs 9-1, 9-42 to 9-43, 9-2, 9-44 to 9-45, 9-3, 9-46, 9-4, 9-47, 9-5 to 9-41

Daniels    EDs 10-1 to 10-2, 10-21, 10-3, 10-23, 10-4 to 10-20, 10-22

Chouteau    EDs 8-1 to 8-12, 8-13 (NP), 8-14 to 8-95

Dawson    EDs 11-1 to 11-52, 11-54 to 11-64, 11-53 (NP), 11-65 to 11-73

1255. Deer Lodge    EDs 12-1 to 12-7, 12-8 (NP), 12-9 to 12-26

Fallon    EDs 13-1 to 13-4, 13-12, 13-6 to 13-11, 13-5, 13-13 to 13-42

Granite    EDs 20-1 to 20-12

Fergus    EDs 14-1, 14-144, 14-2, 14-145, 14-3, 14-146, 14-4 to 14-112, 14-114, 14-113, 14-115 to 14-140, 14-141 (NP), 14-142 to 14-143

* 1256. Flathead   EDs 15-1 to 15-21, 15-27, 15-22 to 15-26

Garfield   EDs 17-1 to 17-52

Gallatin   EDs 16-1 to 16-39

Glacier   EDs 18-1 to 18-4, 18-20 to 18-25, 18-5 to 18-19

1257. Golden Valley   EDs 19-1 to 19-33, 19-34 (NP), 19-35 to 19-36, 19-37 (NP), 19-38 to 19-44, 19-45 to 19-46 (NP), 19-47 to 19-50

Hill   EDs 21-1 to 21-3, 21-4 (NP), 21-5 to 21-70

Jefferson   EDs 22-1 to 22-30

Judith Basin   EDs 23-1 to 23-24, 23-27 (NP), 23-25 to 23-26, 23-36, 23-28 to 23-35, 23-37 to 23-54

Lake   EDs 24-1 to 24-11

Lincoln   EDs 27-1 to 27-27

1258. Lewis & Clark   EDs 25-1 to 25-56

Liberty   EDs 26-1 to 26-26

McCone   EDs 28-55, 28-1 to 28-52, 28-53 (NP), 28-54

Madison   EDs 29-1 to 29-19

Mineral   EDs 31-1 to 31-5

Musselshell   EDs 33-1 to 33-2, 33-57, 33-3 to 33-10, 33-11 (NP), 33-12 to 33-20, 33-21 (NP), 33-22 to 33-36, 33-37 (NP), 33-38, 33-39 (NP), 33-40 to 33-54, 33-55 (NP), 33-56

** 1259. Meagher   EDs 30-1 to 30-23

Missoula   EDs 32-1 to 32-44

Park   EDs 34-1 to 34-2, 34-3 (NP), 34-4 to 34-41, 34-42 (NP), 34-43 to 34-75

Phillips   EDs 36-1 to 36-28, 36-53, 36-29 to 36-39, 36-52, 36-40 to 36-51

1260. Petroleum   EDs 35-1 to 35-26, 35-27 (NP), 35-28 to 35-33

Pondera   EDs 37-1 to 37-14, 37-35, 37-15 to 37-34

Powder River   EDs 38-1 to 38-33

Rosebud   EDs 44-1 to 44-48

Powell   EDs 39-1 to 39-10, 39-11 (NP), 39-12 to 39-13

Prairie   EDs 40-1 to 40-31

Ravalli   EDs 41-1 to 41-16

1261. Richland   EDs 42-1 to 42-55, 42-56 (NP), 42-57 to 42-94

Roosevelt   EDs 43-1 to 43-32

Sanders   EDs 45-1 to 45-11, 45-20, 45-12 to 45-19

Sheridan   EDs 46-1 to 46-59

Silver Bow   EDs 47-1 to 47-6

1262. Silver Bow   EDs 47-7 to 47-65

1263. Stillwater   EDs 48-1 to 48-56, 48-57 (NP), 48-58 to 48-63, 48-64 to 48-65 (NP), 48-66 to 48-78

Valley   EDs 53-1, 53-38, 53-2 to 53-7, 53-36, 53-8 to 53-24, 53-37, 53-25 to 53-35

Sweet Grass   EDs 49-1 to 49-56, 49-57 (NP), 49-58 to 49-63, 49-64 (NP), 49-65 to 49-66

Toole   EDs 51-1 to 51-17, 51-19 (NP), 51-18, 51-20 to 51-57

Wheatland   EDs 54-1 to 54-31, 54-32 (NP), 54-33 to 54-36

*** 1264. Teton   EDs 50-1 to 50-48

Treasure   EDs 52-1 to 52-20

Wibaux   EDs 55-1 to 55-34

Yellowstone   EDs 56-1, 56-16 to 56-40, 56-2 to 56-12, 56-13 (NP), 56-14 to 56-15, 56-41 to 56-73

Yellowstone National Park   EDs 16-40 (NP), 16-41, 16-76 to 16-78 (NP), 16-79

## *Nebraska*

1265. Adams   EDs 1-1, 1-31, 1-2 to 1-30, 1-32

Antelope   EDs 2-1 to 2-32

Arthur   EDs 3-1 to 3-8

Banner   EDs 4-1 to 4-7

Boyd   EDs 8-1 to 8-18

1266. Blaine   EDs 5-1 to 5-9

Brown   EDs 9-1 to 9-17

Burt   EDs 11-1 to 11-16

Boone   EDs 6-1 to 6-19

Box Butte   EDs 7-1 to 7-15

1267. Buffalo   EDs 10-1 to 10-43

Butler   EDs 12-1 to 12-29

Chase   EDs 15-1 to 15-17

1268. Cass   EDs 13-1, 13-33, 13-2 to 13-7, 13-29, 13-8 to 13-28, 13-30 to 13-32, 13-34

Cedar   EDs 14-1 to 14-32

Cherry   EDs 16-1 to 16-48

1269. Cheyenne   EDs 17-1 to 17-16, 17-23, 17-17 to 17-22

Clay   EDs 18-1 to 18-15, 18-26, 18-16 to 18-25, 18-27

Colfax   EDs 19-1 to 19-19

Cuming   EDs 20-1 to 20-20

1270. Custer   EDs 21-1 to 21-41

Dakota   EDs 22-1 to 22-16

Dawson   EDs 24-1 to 24-30

1271. Dawes   EDs 23-1 to 23-19

Deuel   EDs 25-1 to 25-5

Dixon   EDs 26-1 to 26-23

Dodge   EDs 27-1 to 27-5, 27-31 to 27-32, 27-6 to 27-21, 27-29, 27-22 to 27-28, 27-30

1272. Douglas, Omaha City   EDs 28-138 to 28-158, 28-1, 28-161, 28-2 to 28-8

1273. Douglas, Omaha City   EDs 28-9 to 28-12, 28-40 to 28-47, 28-13 to 28-25

1274. Douglas, Omaha City   EDs 28-26 to 28-39, 28-48 to 28-61

1275. Douglas, Omaha City   EDs 28-62 to 28-82

1276. Douglas, Omaha City   EDs 28-83 to 28-86, 28-159, 28-87, 28-160, 28-88 to 28-96

1277. Douglas, Omaha City   EDs 28-97, 28-162, 28-98 to 28-102, 28-163 to 28-164, 28-103 to 28-112

1278. Douglas, Omaha City   EDs 28-113 to 28-124, 28-165, 28-125 to 28-126

1279. Douglas, Omaha City   EDs 28-127 to 28-137

1280. Dundy   EDs 29-1 to 29-17

Franklin   EDs 31-1 to 31-4, 31-18, 31-5 to 31-10, 31-24, 31-11 to 31-17, 31-19 to 31-23, 31-25

Frontier   EDs 32-1 to 32-31

Fillmore   EDs 30-1 to 30-25

Furnas   EDs 33-1 to 33-28

1281. Gage   EDs 34-1 to 34-3, 34-30, 34-4 to 34-20, 34-38, 34-21 to 34-29, 34-31 to 34-37, 34-39 to 34-46

---

* Roll 1256, Gallatin County—For EDs 16-40 to 16-41, see Yellowstone National Park, roll 1264.
** Roll 1259, Park County—For EDs 34-76, 34-77 to 34-78 (NP), 34-79, see Yellowstone National Park, roll 1264
*** Roll 1264, Yellowstone National Park—For EDs 16-1 to 16-39, see Gallatin County, roll 1256. For EDs 34-1 to 34-2, 34-3 (NP), 34-4 to 34-41, 34-42 (NP), and 34-43 to 34-75, see Park County, roll 1259.

Garden    EDs 35-1 to 35-14

Garfield    EDs 36-1 to 36-10

Gosper    EDs 37-1 to 37-14

Grant    EDs 38-1 to 38-4

Greeley    EDs 39-1 to 39-16, 39-17 (NP), 39-18 to 39-21

1282.    Hall    EDs 40-1 to 40-21, 40-24, 40-22 to 40-23, 40-25 to 40-29

Hamilton    EDs 41-1 to 41-5, 41-23, 41-6 to 41-22

Harlan    EDs 42-1 to 42-4, 42-19, 42-5 to 42-18, 42-20 to 42-22, 42-24, 42-23, 42-25

Hayes    EDs 43-1 to 43-9, 43-17, 43-10, 43-12, 43-11, 43-13 to 43-16

1283.    Hitchcock    EDs 44-1 to 44-15, 44-21, 44-16 to 44-20, 44-22 to 44-25

Holt    EDs 45-1 to 45-45

Hooker    EDs 46-1 to 46-6

Howard    EDs 47-1 to 47-22

Jefferson    EDs 48-1 to 48-28

1284.    Johnson    EDs 49-1 to 49-14

Keith    EDs 51-1 to 51-5, 51-7 to 51-9, 51-6, 51-14, 51-10 to 51-13, 51-15 to 51-16

Keya Paha    EDs 52-1 to 52-12

Kimball    EDs 53-1 to 53-9

Kearney    EDs 50-1 to 50-6, 50-9, 50-7 to 50-8, 50-10 to 50-21

Knox    EDs 54-1 to 54-39

1285.    Lancaster    EDs 55-1 to 55-16, 55-79, 55-17, 55-80, 55-18, 55-81, 55-19 to 55-20, 55-78, 55-21 to 55-33

1286.    Lancaster    EDs 55-34 to 55-46, 55-77, 55-47 to 55-76

Logan    EDs 57-1 to 57-9

1287.    Lincoln    EDs 56-1 to 56-34, 56-58, 56-35 to 56-57

Loup    EDs 58-1 to 58-9

McPherson    EDs 59-1 to 59-6

Merrick    EDs 61-2, 61-1, 61-3 to 61-16

Morrill    EDs 62-1 to 62-20

1288.    Madison    EDs 60-1, 60-8, 60-2 to 60-7, 60-9 to 60-31

Nance    EDs 63-1 to 63-15

Otoe    EDs 66-1 to 66-2, 66-33, 66-3 to 66-17, 66-20, 66-32, 66-21, 66-24, 66-18 to 66-19, 66-22, 66-25 to 66-26, 66-30, 66-23, 66-31, 66-27 to 66-29

1289.    Nemaha    EDs 64-1 to 64-2, 64-21 to 64-22, 64-3 to 64-20

Nuckolls    EDs 65-1 to 65-24

Pawnee    EDs 67-1 to 67-4, 67-9, 67-5 to 67-6, 67-8, 67-7, 67-10 to 67-19

Perkins    EDs 68-1 to 68-16

Phelps    EDs 69-1 to 69-6, 69-18, 69-7 to 69-17, 69-19 to 69-22

1290.    Pierce    EDs 70-1 to 70-22

Red Willow    EDs 73-1 to 73-14, 73-23, 73-15 to 73-22, 73-24 to 73-27

Platte    EDs 71-1 to 71-16, 71-18, 71-17, 71-19 to 71-32

Rock    EDs 75-1 to 75-16

1291.    Polk    EDs 72-1 to 72-13

Saline    EDs 76-1 to 76-24

Richardson    EDs 74-1 to 74-28

1292.    Sarpy    EDs 77-1 to 77-17

Seward    EDs 80-1 to 80-23, 80-25 to 80-28, 80-24, 80-29

Saunders    EDs 78-1 to 78-10, 78-39, 78-11 to 78-38

Scotts Bluff    EDs 79-1 to 79-9

1293.    Scotts Bluff    EDs 79-10 to 79-30

Sheridan    EDs 81-1 to 81-32

Sherman    EDs 82-1 to 82-18

Sioux    EDs 83-1 to 83-20, 83-21 (NP)

1294.    Stanton    EDs 84-1 to 84-14

Thayer    EDs 85-1 to 85-27

Thomas    EDs 86-1 to 86-7

Thurston    EDs 87-1 to 87-19

Washington    EDs 89-1 to 89-17

1295.    Valley    EDs 88-1 to 88-18

Wayne    EDs 90-1 to 90-19

Wheeler    EDs 92-1 to 92-14

Webster    EDs 91-1 to 91-22

York    EDs 93-1 to 93-8, 93-15, 93-9 to 93-14, 93-16 to 93-32

## Nevada

1296.    Churchill    EDs 1-1 to 1-16

Clark    EDs 2-1 to 2-14

Elko    EDs 4-1 to 4-8, 4-44, 4-9 to 4-10, 4-45, 4-11 to 4-22, 4-46, 4-23, 4-25, 4-24 (NP), 4-26 to 4-27, 4-29, 4-28, 4-30 to 4-43

Douglas    EDs 3-1 to 3-4

Esmeralda    EDs 5-1 to 5-7

Eureka    EDs 6-1 to 6-6

Humboldt    EDs 7-1 to 7-5, 7-13, 7-6 to 7-12

Lander    EDs 8-1 to 8-2

Lincoln    EDs 9-1 to 9-14

Lyon    EDs 10-1 to 10-13

Mineral    EDs 11-1 to 11-4, 11-13, 11-5 to 11-9, 11-12, 11-10 to 11-11

Ormsby    EDs 13-1 to 13-5

1297.    Nye    EDs 12-1 to 12-23

Pershing    EDs 14-1, 14-5 to 14-7, 14-2 to 14-3, 14-8, 14-4

Storey    EDs 15-1 to 15-2

White Pine    EDs 17-1 to 17-4, 17-20, 17-5 to 17-19

Washoe    EDs 16-1 to 16-2, 16-4, 16-3, 16-5 to 16-6, 16-27, 16-7, 16-28, 16-8 to 16-9, 16-29, 16-10 to 16-15, 16-30 to 16-31, 16-16 (void), 16-17 to 16-24, 16-26, 16-32, 16-25

## New Hampshire

1298.    Belknap    EDs 1-1 to 1-19

Carroll    EDs 2-1 to 2-9, 2-10 (NP), 2-11 to 2-21

Cheshire    EDs 3-1 to 3-8, 3-20

1299.    Cheshire    EDs 3-9 to 3-19, 3-21 to 3-34

Coos    EDs 4-1, 4-2 (NP), 4-3 to 4-15, 4-16 (NP), 4-17 to 4-18, 4-20, 4-19, 4-21 to 4-22 (NP), 4-23 to 4-24, 4-25 (NP), 4-26 to 4-28, 4-29 (NP)

1300.    Coos    EDs 4-30 to 4-31, 4-32 (NP), 4-33, 4-34 (NP), 4-35 to 4-36, 4-37 to 4-38 (NP), 4-39 to 4-41, 4-42 (NP), 4-43 to 4-46, 4-47 (NP), 4-48 to 4-51, 4-52 (NP), 4-53 to 4-56

Grafton    EDs 5-1 to 5-28, 5-31 to 5-32

1301.    Grafton    EDs 5-29 to 5-30, 5-33 to 5-47

Hillsborough   EDs 6-1 to 6-37

1302. Hillsborough   EDs 6-38 to 6-54, 6-60 to 6-62, 6-55 to 6-59, 6-63 to 6-73

1303. Hillsborough   EDs 6-74 to 6-84, 6-85 (void), 6-86 to 6-115

1304. Merrimack   EDs 7-1 to 7-8, 7-31 to 7-47, 7-9 to 7-30

1305. Merrimack   EDs 7-48 to 7-56
Rockingham   EDs 8-1 to 8-28, 8-34 to 8-43, 8-52

1306. Rockingham   EDs 8-29 to 8-33, 8-44 to 8-51
Strafford   EDs 9-1 to 9-37

1307. Sullivan   EDs 10-1 to 10-21

## New Jersey

1308. Atlantic   EDs 1-1 to 1-26

1309. Atlantic   EDs 1-27 to 1-34, 1-78 to 1-80, 1-35 to 1-39, 1-43 to 1-44, 1-40 to 1-42, 1-45 to 1-58

1310. Atlantic   EDs 1-59 to 1-77
Bergen   EDs 2-1 to 2-19

1311. Bergen   EDs 2-20 to 2-50, 2-260, 2-51 to 2-56

1312. Bergen   EDs 2-57 to 2-86, 2-95 to 2-98

1313. Bergen   EDs 2-87 to 2-94, 2-99 to 2-102, 2-122 to 2-130, 2-103 to 2-121

1314. Bergen   EDs 2-131 to 2-133, 2-261, 2-134 to 2-168

1315. Bergen   EDs 2-169 to 2-200, 2-210, 2-258, 2-211 to 2-213

1316. Bergen   EDs 2-201 to 2-209, 2-215 to 2-224, 2-214, 2-225 to 2-238

1317. Bergen   EDs 2-239 to 2-241, 2-259, 2-242 to 2-257
Burlington   EDs 3-1 to 3-16

1318. Burlington   EDs 3-17 to 3-34, 3-40 to 3-43, 3-35 to 3-39, 3-44 to 3-56

1319. Burlington   EDs 3-57 to 3-79
Camden, Camden City   EDs 4-76 to 4-89, 4-1 to 4-5

1320. Camden, Camden City   EDs 4-6 to 4-14, 4-18 to 4-22, 4-15 to 4-17, 4-23 to 4-30

1321. Camden, Camden City   EDs 4-31 to 4-54

1322. Camden, Camden City   EDs 4-55 to 4-75

1323. Camden   EDs 4-90 to 4-116, 4-120, 4-117 to 4-119, 4-121 to 4-124, 4-131 to 4-133

1324. Camden   EDs 4-125 to 4-130, 4-134 to 4-166

1325. Camden   EDs 4-167 to 4-180
Cape May   EDs 5-1 to 5-29

1326. Cumberland   EDs 6-1 to 6-41, 6-56 to 6-57

1327. Cumberland   EDs 6-42 to 6-55, 6-58 to 6-61
Essex   EDs 7-303 to 7-324

1328. Essex   EDs 7-325 to 7-361

1329. Essex   EDs 7-362 to 7-386, 7-401 to 7-427

1330. Essex   EDs 7-387 to 7-400, 7-428 to 7-462

1331. Essex   EDs 7-463 to 7-504

1332. Essex   EDs 7-505 to 7-550

1333. Essex, Newark City   EDs 7-1 to 7-7, 7-647, 7-8 to 7-24, 7-648, 7-25 to 7-28, 7-29 (NP), 7-30 to 7-36

1334. Essex, Newark City   EDs 7-37 to 7-55, 7-649, 7-56 to 7-71

1335. Essex, Newark City   EDs 7-72, 7-650, 7-73 to 7-103

1336. Essex, Newark City   EDs 7-104 to 7-123, 7-651 to 7-656, 7-124 to 7-132

1337. Essex, Newark City   EDs 7-133 to 7-156, 7-657 to 7-664

1338. Essex, Newark City   EDs 7-665 to 7-667, 7-157 to 7-169, 7-170 (NP), 7-171 to 7-190

1339. Essex, Newark City   EDs 7-191, 7-668 to 7-671, 7-192 to 7-217

1340. Essex, Newark City   EDs 7-218 to 7-238, 7-672 to 7-677

1341. Essex, Newark City   EDs 7-239 to 7-240, 7-241 (void), 7-242 to 7-271, 7-678, 7-272 to 7-273

1342. Essex, Newark City   EDs 7-274 to 7-282, 7-679, 7-283 to 7-292, 7-680, 7-293 to 7-302

1343. Essex   EDs 7-551 to 7-552, 7-570 to 7-586, 7-595 to 7-598, 7-587 to 7-594, 7-599 to 7-612

1344. Essex   EDs 7-553 to 7-569, 7-613 to 7-646

1345. Gloucester   EDs 8-1 to 8-27, 8-48, 8-28 to 8-29

1346. Gloucester   EDs 8-30 to 8-35, 8-49, 8-36 to 8-47
Hudson   EDs 9-188 to 9-198

1347. Hudson   EDs 9-211 to 9-220, 9-199 to 9-210, 9-221 to 9-224

1348. Hudson   EDs 9-225 to 9-259

1349. Hudson   EDs 9-260 to 9-299

1350. Hudson, Jersey City   EDs 9-1 to 9-6, 9-7 (NP), 9-8 to 9-31, 9-32 (NP), 9-33 to 9-37

1351. Hudson, Jersey City   EDs 9-38 to 9-70

1352. Hudson, Jersey City   EDs 9-71 to 9-87

1353. Hudson, Jersey City   EDs 9-88 to 9-112

1354. Hudson, Jersey City   EDs 9-113 to 9-132

1355. Hudson, Jersey City   EDs 9-133 to 9-160

1356. Hudson, Jersey City   EDs 9-161 to 9-187

1357. Hudson   EDs 9-300 to 9-304, 9-311 to 9-323, 9-305 to 9-310, 9-352 to 9-359

1358. Hudson   EDs 9-324 to 9-351, 9-360 to 9-365

1359. Hudson   EDs 9-366 to 9-384, 9-441, 9-385 to 9-401, 9-442, 9-402, 9-443, 9-403, 9-444, 9-404, 9-445, 9-405, 9-446

1360. Hudson   EDs 9-406 to 9-440

1361. Hunterdon   EDs 10-1 to 10-36
Mercer   EDs 11-72 to 11-74, 11-37, 11-75 to 11-76, 11-107 to 11-108, 11-91 to 11-95

1362. Mercer, Trenton City   EDs 11-77 to 11-90, 11-96 to 11-98, 11-109 to 11-110, 11-99 to 11-103, 11-1 to 11-5

1363. Mercer, Trenton City   EDs 11-6 to 11-31

1364. Mercer, Trenton City   EDs 11-32 to 11-36, 11-38 to 11-54, 11-56

1365. Mercer, Trenton City   EDs 11-55, 11-57 to 11-71, 11-111, 11-104 to 11-106

1366. Middlesex   EDs 12-1 to 12-12, 12-146, 12-13, 12-19, 12-14 to 12-18, 12-20, 12-147, 12-21 to 12-33

1367. Middlesex   EDs 12-34 to 12-43, 12-47 to 12-57, 12-44 to 12-46, 12-58 to 12-63, 12-148, 12-64 to 12-68, 12-75 to 12-80

1368. Middlesex   EDs 12-69 to 12-74, 12-81 to 12-110

1369. Middlesex   EDs 12-111 to 12-145

1370. Monmouth   EDs 13-1 to 13-13, 13-15 to 13-28, 13-123, 13-29 to 13-46

1371. Monmouth   EDs 13-47 to 13-54, 13-14, 13-74 to 13-82, 13-55 to 13-73

1372. Monmouth   EDs 13-83 to 13-89, 13-121, 13-90 to 13-92, 13-122, 13-93 to 13-94, 13-99 to 13-106, 13-95 to 13-98, 13-107 to 13-120

1373. Morris   EDs 14-1 to 14-13, 14-15 to 14-20, 14-14, 14-21, 14-23 to 14-36, 14-39 to 14-40, 14-22, 14-59

1374. Morris   EDs 14-37 to 14-38, 14-41 to 14-55, 14-60 to 14-61, 14-56 to 14-58, 14-62 to 14-76

1375. Ocean   EDs 15-1 to 15-43

Passaic   EDs 16-89 to 16-94

1376. Passaic   EDs 16-95 to 16-115, 16-188, 16-124 to 16-125

1377. Passaic   EDs 16-116 to 16-123, 16-126 to 16-152

1378. Passaic   EDs 16-153 to 16-169

Passaic, Paterson City   EDs 16-1 to 16-15

1379. Passaic, Paterson City   EDs 16-16 to 16-39

1380. Passaic, Paterson City   EDs 16-40 to 16-67

1381. Passaic, Paterson City   EDs 16-68 to 16-88

1382. Passaic   EDs 16-170, 16-189, 16-171 to 16-187

Salem   EDs 17-1 to 17-14, 17-17 to 17-20

1383. Salem   EDs 17-15 to 17-16, 17-21 to 17-25

Somerset   EDs 18-1 to 18-19, 18-21 to 18-31, 18-38 to 18-39

1384. Somerset   EDs 18-32 to 18-37, 18-20, 18-40 to 18-51

Sussex   EDs 19-1 to 19-31

1385. Union, Elizabeth City   EDs 20-1 to 20-34, 20-55 to 20-58

1386. Union, Elizabeth City   EDs 20-35 to 20-42, 20-48 to 20-54, 20-43 to 20-47, 20-59 to 20-60, 20-178, 20-184, 20-61 to 20-62, 20-185, 20-179, 20-63, 20-180, 20-64, 20-181

1387. Union, Elizabeth City   EDs 20-65 to 20-68, 20-182, 20-69 to 20-71, 20-183, 20-72 to 20-90

1388. Union   EDs 20-91 to 20-118

1389. Union   EDs 20-119 to 20-141, 20-152 to 20-159

1390. Union   EDs 20-142 to 20-147, 20-160, 20-186, 20-161 to 20-167, 20-148 to 20-151, 20-168 to 20-177

1391. Warren   EDs 21-1 to 21-18, 21-33, 21-37, 21-19 to 21-32, 21-34 to 21-36

### New Mexico

1392. Bernalillo   EDs 1-5 to 1-13, 1-52, 1-14 to 1-23, 1-1, 1-47, 1-2 to 1-3, 1-53, 1-51, 1-4, 1-24 to 1-25, 1-48, 1-26 to 1-29, 1-49 (NP), 1-30 to 1-36, 1-37 (NP), 1-38 to 1-45, 1-50 (NP), 1-46

Catron   EDs 2-1 to 2-20

1393. Chaves   EDs 3-1 to 3-24

Guadalupe   EDs 10-1 to 10-27

Colfax   EDs 4-1 to 4-22, 4-46, 4-23 to 4-45

De Baca   EDs 6-1 to 6-17

1394. Curry   EDs 5-1 to 5-20

Harding   EDs 11-1 to 11-22

Hidalgo   EDs 12-1 to 12-2, 12-11, 12-3 to 12-10

Dona Ana   EDs 7-1 to 7-11, 7-12 (NP), 7-13 to 7-21, 7-27, 7-22 to 7-26, 7-28

1395. Eddy   EDs 8-1 to 8-15

Lincoln   EDs 14-1 to 14-20

Grant   EDs 9-1 to 9-27

Lea   EDs 13-1 to 13-10, 13-18, 13-11 to 13-17

1396. Luna   EDs 15-1, 15-13, 15-2 to 15-12

McKinley   EDs 16-1 to 16-18, 16-31, 16-19 to 16-30

Mora   EDs 17-1 to 17-27

Otero   EDs 18-1 to 18-20

1397. Quay   EDs 19-1 to 19-29

Roosevelt   EDs 21-1 to 21-32

Rio Arriba   EDs 20-1 to 20-6, 20-7 (NP), 20-8, 20-47 to 20-48, 20-9 to 20-26, 20-27 (NP), 20-28 to 20-29, 20-35 (NP), 20-36, 20-31 to 20-34, 20-30, 20-37 to 20-41, 20-42 (NP), 20-43 to 20-46

1398. Sandoval   EDs 22-1 to 22-2, 22-33 (NP), 22-35, 22-3, 22-4 (NP), 22-34 (NP), 22-5 to 22-8, 22-9 (NP), 22-10 to 22-11, 22-44, 22-12 to 22-14, 22-15 (NP), 22-16, 22-31, 22-41, 22-17 to 22-18 (NP), 22-36 (NP), 22-42, 22-19, 22-20 (NP), 22-37, 22-39 (NP), 22-43 (NP), 22-21 to 22-22, 22-38 (NP), 22-23, 22-40 (NP), 22-24 to 22-26, 22-27 (NP), 22-28, 22-32, 22-29 to 22-30

Socorro   EDs 27-1 to 27-6, 27-7 (NP), 27-8 to 27-35

San Juan   EDs 23-1 to 23-7, 23-22, 23-8, 23-23, 23-9 to 23-15, 23-24, 23-16 to 23-20, 23-21 (NP)

Sierra   EDs 26-1 to 26-13, 26-20, 26-14 to 26-16, 26-21, 26-17 to 26-19

1399. San Miguel   EDs 24-1 to 24-65

Santa Fe   EDs 25-1 (NP), 25-43, 25-2, 25-47, 25-3 to 25-20, 25-21 (NP), 25-22, 25-44 to 25-45, 25-23 to 25-26, 25-42 (NP), 25-27 to 25-29, 25-46, 25-30 to 25-33, 25-41, 25-48 (NP), 25-34 to 25-40

1400. Taos   EDs 28-1 to 28-4, 28-33, 28-5 to 28-9, 28-29, 28-10 (NP), 28-30, 28-11 to 28-22, 28-31, 28-23 to 28-25, 28-32, 28-26 to 28-28

Union   EDs 30-1 to 30-43

Torrance   EDs 29-1 to 29-22, 29-28 (NP), 29-23 to 29-27

Valencia   EDs 31-1 to 31-8, 31-35, 31-9 to 31-10, 31-40, 31-11, 31-41, 31-12 to 31-14, 31-38, 31-15 to 31-20, 31-36, 31-21 to 31-22, 31-42, 31-39, 31-23, 31-43, 31-37, 31-24 to 31-25, 31-44 (NP), 31-26 to 31-29, 31-45, 31-30 to 31-34

### New York

1401. Albany, Albany City   EDs 1-1 to 1-33

1402. Albany, Albany City   EDs 1-34 to 1-53, 1-54 (void), 1-55, 1-62, 1-56 to 1-58

1403. Albany, Albany City   EDs 1-59 to 1-61, 1-63 to 1-76, 1-78 to 1-94

1404. Albany   EDs 1-95 to 1-106, 1-133 to 1-142, 1-107 to 1-120

1405. Albany   EDs 1-121 to 1-125, 1-77, 1-126 to 1-132, 1-143 to 1-147, 1-160 to 1-161, 1-148 to 1-159

Allegany   EDs 2-1 to 2-15, 2-22

1406. Allegany   EDs 2-17, 2-45, 2-16, 2-18 to 2-21, 2-23 to 2-44, 2-46

Broome   EDs 4-1 to 4-17

1407. Broome   EDs 4-18 to 4-52

1408. Broome   EDs 4-53 to 4-59, 4-74 to 4-98, 4-107, 4-99

1409. Broome   EDs 4-60 to 4-73, 4-100 to 4-106

Cattaraugus   EDs 5-1 to 5-11, 5-65 to 5-66, 5-12 to 5-37, 5-61 to 5-64

1410. Cattaraugus   EDs 5-38 to 5-60, 5-67 to 5-83

Cayuga   EDs 6-1 to 6-6

1411. Cayuga   EDs 6-7 to 6-28, 6-35, 6-29 to 6-34, 6-36 to 6-63

1412. Chautauqua   EDs 7-1 to 7-7, 7-46, 7-8 to 7-15, 7-33 to 7-37, 7-43 to 7-45, 7-47 to 7-49, 7-109, 7-50 to 7-51, 7-16 to 7-32, 7-38 to 7-42

1413. Chautauqua   EDs 7-52 to 7-53, 7-110, 7-54 to 7-85

1414. Chautauqua   EDs 7-86 to 7-108

Chemung   EDs 8-1 to 8-23

1415. Chemung   EDs 8-24 to 8-41, 8-49, 8-42 to 8-48, 8-50 to 8-63

Chenango   EDs 9-1 to 9-7

1416. Chenango   EDs 9-8 to 9-42

Clinton   EDs 10-1 to 10-14, 10-45, 10-15 to 10-17, 10-41, 10-18 to 10-24

1417.   Clinton   EDs 10-25 to 10-33, 10-35 to 10-36, 10-34, 10-37 to 10-40, 10-42 to 10-44

Columbia   EDs 11-1 to 11-6, 11-16, 11-7 to 11-15, 11-17 to 11-33, 11-37 to 11-38

*1418.   Columbia   EDs 11-34 to 11-36, 11-39 to 11-43

Cortland   EDs 12-1 to 12-8, 12-11, 12-12 to 12-13, 12-18 to 12-20, 12-14, 12-21, 12-15 to 12-17, 12-22 to 12-34, 12-9, 12-10

Delaware   EDs 13-1 to 13-21

1419.   Delaware   EDs 13-22 to 13-26, 13-43, 13-27 to 13-31, 13-52, 13-32 to 13-42, 13-44 to 13-51

Dutchess   EDs 14-1 to 14-27

1420.   Dutchess   EDs 14-28 to 14-64, 14-81 to 14-82

1421.   Dutchess   EDs 14-65 to 14-80, 14-83 to 14-90

Erie   EDs 15-353 to 15-373

1422.   Erie, Buffalo City   EDs 15-1 to 15-23

1423.   Erie, Buffalo City   EDs 15-24 to 15-29, 15-74 to 15-90

1424.   Erie, Buffalo City   EDs 15-30 to 15-43, 15-213, 15-44 to 15-55

1425.   Erie, Buffalo City   EDs 15-56 to 15-65, 15-67 to 15-73, 15-91 to 15-107

1426.   Erie, Buffalo City   EDs 15-108 to 15-135

1427.   Erie, Buffalo City   EDs 15-136 to 15-170

1428.   Erie, Buffalo City   EDs 15-171 to 15-193

1429.   Erie, Buffalo City   EDs 15-194 to 15-203, 15-212, 15-214 to 15-217, 15-318, 15-218 to 15-220, 15-222 to 15-225, 15-238 to 15-241

1430.   Erie, Buffalo City   EDs 15-242 to 15-269

1431.   Erie, Buffalo City   EDs 15-204, 15-475 to 15-476, 15-205 to 15-208, 15-477, 15-209 to 15-211, 15-226 to 15-237

1432.   Erie, Buffalo City   EDs 15-270 to 15-293, 15-221, 15-294 to 15-297

1433.   Erie, Buffalo City   EDs 15-298 to 15-305, 15-330, 15-306 to 15-317, 15-319 to 15-329, 15-331 to 15-334

1434.   Erie, Buffalo City   EDs 15-335 to 15-337, 15-338 (void), 15-339 to 15-352, 15-374 to 15-383, 15-66

1435.   Erie   EDs 15-384 to 15-417, 15-436 to 15-444

1436.   Erie   EDs 15-418 to 15-435, 15-445 to 15-453, 15-466

1437.   Erie   EDs 15-454 to 15-465, 15-467 to 15-474

Essex   EDs 16-1 to 16-17

1438.   Essex   EDs 16-18, 16-20, 16-25, 16-19, 16-21 to 16-24, 16-26 to 16-35

Franklin   EDs 17-1 to 17-7, 17-47, 17-8 to 17-28, 17-33 to 17-42

1439.   Franklin   EDs 17-29 to 17-32, 17-43 to 17-46

Fulton   EDs 18-1 to 18-3, 18-24 to 18-36, 18-4 to 18-23

1440.   Fulton   EDs 18-37 to 18-46

Genesee   EDs 19-1 to 19-40

1441.   Greene   EDs 20-1 to 20-28

Hamilton   EDs 21-1 to 21-10

Herkimer   EDs 22-1, 22-62, 22-2 to 22-3, 22-44, 22-4 to 22-8, 22-63, 22-9 to 22-10, 22-19 to 22-29

1442.   Herkimer   EDs 22-11 to 22-17, 22-64, 22-18, 22-65, 22-30 to 22-43, 22-46, 22-51, 22-45, 22-47 to 22-50, 22-52 to 22-61

Jefferson   EDs 23-1 to 23-9

1443.   Jefferson   EDs 23-12, 23-40, 23-10 to 23-11, 23-13 to 23-31, 23-46, 23-32 to 23-39, 23-41 to 23-45, 23-47 to 23-63

1444.   Jefferson   EDs 23-64 to 23-85

Lewis   EDs 25-1, 25-24 to 25-25, 25-2 to 25-3, 25-36, 25-4 to 25-8, 25-37, 25-9 to 25-13, 25-19, 25-14 to 25-18, 25-33, 25-20 to 25-23, 25-26, 25-38, 25-27 to 25-32, 25-34 to 25-35

1445.   Livingston   EDs 26-1 to 26-21, 26-26 to 26-27, 26-22 to 26-25, 26-28 to 26-35

Madison   EDs 27-1 to 27-17

1446.   Madison   EDs 27-18 to 27-31, 27-48, 27-32 to 27-47

Monroe   EDs 28-198 to 28-206, 28-210 to 28-215

1447.   Monroe   EDs 28-207 to 28-209, 28-220 to 28-227, 28-216 to 28-219, 28-228 to 28-243

1448.   Monroe   EDs 28-244 to 28-263

Monroe, Rochester City   EDs 28-1 to 28-15

1449.   Monroe, Rochester City   EDs 28-16 to 28-43, 28-44 (NP)

1450.   Monroe, Rochester City   EDs 28-45 to 28-73

1451.   Monroe, Rochester City   EDs 28-74 to 28-96, 28-264, 28-97 to 28-99

1452.   Monroe, Rochester City   EDs 28-100 to 28-111, 28-127 to 28-145

1453.   Monroe, Rochester City   EDs 28-146 to 28-169

1454.   Monroe, Rochester City   EDs 28-112 to 28-126, 28-170 to 28-182

1455.   Monroe, Rochester City   EDs 28-183 to 28-197

1456.   Montgomery   EDs 29-1 to 29-44

1457.   Montgomery   EDs 29-45 to 29-52

Nassau   EDs 30-1 to 30-8, 30-15 to 30-22, 30-9 to 30-14, 30-38 to 30-46

1458.   Nassau   EDs 30-23 to 30-37, 30-47 to 30-61, 30-74 to 30-81

1459.   Nassau   EDs 30-62 to 30-63, 30-150 to 30-151, 30-64 to 30-73, 30-82 to 30-91, 30-214, 30-92 to 30-102

1460.   Nassau   EDs 30-103 to 30-121, 30-215, 30-122 to 30-134

1461.   Nassau   EDs 30-135 to 30-149, 30-216, 30-152 to 30-173

1462.   Nassau   EDs 30-174 to 30-191, 30-217, 30-192 to 30-213

1463.   Bronx, Bronx Borough   EDs 3-1 (NP), 3-717 to 3-718, 3-719 (NP), 3-2 to 3-7, 3-720 (NP), 3-721, 3-8 to 3-13, 3-970, 3-14 to 3-33

1464.   Bronx, Bronx Borough   EDs 3-34 to 3-50, 3-722, 3-51 to 3-69

1465.   Bronx, Bronx Borough   EDs 3-70 to 3-93, 3-723, 3-94 to 3-98, 3-724, 3-99, 3-725 (NP), 3-726 to 3-727, 3-100 to 3-104, 3-728, 3-105 to 3-107

1466.   Bronx, Bronx Borough   EDs 3-108 to 3-109, 3-729, 3-110 to 3-131

1467.   Bronx, Bronx Borough   EDs 3-132 to 3-133, 3-730, 3-134 to 3-153

1468.   Bronx, Bronx Borough   EDs 3-154 to 3-164, 3-731, 3-165, 3-167 to 3-172, 3-166, 3-173 to 3-177

1469.   Bronx, Bronx Borough   EDs 3-178 to 3-206, 3-732, 3-207, 3-733, 3-208 to 3-210, 3-734, 3-211 to 3-212, 3-213 to 3-214 (NP), 3-735 to 3-736, 3-737 (NP), 3-215

1470.   Bronx, Bronx Borough   EDs 3-216 to 3-227, 3-738, 3-228 to 3-229, 3-739 (NP), 3-740, 3-230, 3-741 to 3-745, 3-746 to 3-747 (NP), 3-748, 3-231 to 3-245

1471.   Bronx, Bronx Borough   EDs 3-246 to 3-279

1472.   Bronx, Bronx Borough   EDs 3-280 to 3-292, 3-293 (NP), 3-749, 3-294 to 3-309

1473.   Bronx, Bronx Borough   EDs 3-310 to 3-333, 3-750, 3-334 to 3-335

---

* Roll 1418, Courtland County—Some of the pages from EDs 12-9 and 12-10 are intermingled with ED 12-11. Beginning with ED 12-12, the pages and EDs are in the correct order.

1474. Bronx, Bronx Borough   EDs 3-336 to 3-363

1475. Bronx, Bronx Borough   EDs 3-364 to 3-368, 3-971, 3-369 to 3-374, 3-972, 3-375, 3-751 to 3-752, 3-376, 3-753 to 3-755, 3-756 to 3-757 (NP), 3-758 to 3-760, 3-377 (void), 3-378, 3-761 to 3-762, 3-763 (NP), 3-379, 3-764 to 3-765, 3-380, 3-766 to 3-767, 3-768 (NP), 3-769 to 3-772, 3-381 (NP), 3-773 to 3-776, 3-382, 3-777 to 3-779, 3-780 (NP), 3-383 (NP), 3-781 to 3-782 (NP), 3-783, 3-784 (NP), 3-785 to 3-790

1476. Bronx, Bronx Borough   EDs 3-791 to 3-795 (NP), 3-384, 3-796 to 3-798, 3-385 to 3-386, 3-799 to 3-800, 3-387, 3-801 to 3-805, 3-388, 3-806 to 3-808, 3-389 to 3-390, 3-809 to 3-810, 3-391 to 3-393, 3-811, 3-394 (NP), 3-812 to 3-814, 3-395 to 3-396, 3-815, 3-397 to 3-405

1477. Bronx, Bronx Borough   EDs 3-406 to 3-407, 3-816, 3-817 (NP), 3-408, 3-818, 3-409 to 3-420, 3-819 (NP), 3-421 to 3-428, 3-820

1478. Bronx, Bronx Borough   EDs 3-429, 3-821, 3-430, 3-822, 3-431 to 3-434, 3-435 (NP), 3-823 to 3-824, 3-436, 3-825, 3-437 to 3-438, 3-826, 3-439 to 3-443

1479. Bronx, Bronx Borough   EDs 3-444 to 3-445, 3-827, 3-446 to 3-450, 3-828 (NP), 3-451, 3-829, 3-452 to 3-459, 3-830 to 3-833, 3-460, 3-834 to 3-836, 3-461, 3-837 to 3-839

1480. Bronx, Bronx Borough   EDs 3-840 to 3-842, 3-462, 3-843 to 3-844, 3-463 to 3-465, 3-845 to 3-846, 3-466, 3-847, 3-467 to 3-468, 3-848, 3-469, 3-849 to 3-851, 3-852 (NP), 3-853, 3-854 (NP), 3-470, 3-855 (NP), 3-856 to 3-862, 3-863 (NP), 3-864 to 3-865, 3-866 to 3-869 (NP), 3-471, 3-870, 3-871 (NP), 3-472 to 3-473, 3-872 to 3-875, 3-474, 3-876 to 3-880, 3-881 (NP), 3-475, 3-882 to 3-887, 3-888 (NP), 3-889 to 3-890, 3-891 to 3-892 (NP), 3-893, 3-894 (NP), 3-895 to 3-897, 3-476

1481. Bronx, Bronx Borough   EDs 3-898 to 3-901, 3-477, 3-902 to 3-905, 3-478, 3-906 to 3-909, 3-479 to 3-480, 3-910, 3-481, 3-911 to 3-914, 3-482, 3-915 to 3-916, 3-483, 3-917, 3-484, 3-918 to 3-919, 3-485, 3-920 to 3-921, 3-486, 3-922, 3-487 to 3-488

1482. Bronx, Bronx Borough   EDs 3-489, 3-923, 3-490, 3-924 to 3-925, 3-491 to 3-509

1483. Bronx, Bronx Borough   EDs 3-510 to 3-520, 3-521 (NP), 3-926, 3-522 to 3-538

1484. Bronx, Bronx Borough   EDs 3-539 to 3-569

1485. Bronx, Bronx Borough   EDs 3-570 to 3-575, 3-927, 3-576 to 3-579, 3-928, 3-580 to 3-589

1486. Bronx, Bronx Borough   EDs 3-590 (NP), 3-929, 3-591 to 3-592, 3-930, 3-593 to 3-599, 3-931 (NP), 3-600 to 3-613

1487. Bronx, Bronx Borough   EDs 3-614 to 3-620, 3-621 (void), 3-622, 3-932, 3-933 (NP), 3-623 to 3-640

1488. Bronx, Bronx Borough   EDs 3-641 to 3-666

1489. Bronx, Bronx Borough   EDs 3-667, 3-668 (NP), 3-669 to 3-670, 3-934 (NP), 3-671 to 3-676, 3-935 to 3-936 (NP), 3-677 to 3-686, 3-937 to 3-939 (NP), 3-687, 3-940, 3-688 to 3-690

1490. Bronx, Bronx Borough   EDs 3-691 to 3-704, 3-941, 3-705 to 3-707, 3-942 to 3-944, 3-708, 3-945 to 3-947, 3-709, 3-948 to 3-955, 3-710, 3-956 to 3-962, 3-963 (NP), 3-711, 3-964, 3-965 to 3-966 (NP), 3-712, 3-967, 3-713 to 3-714, 3-968, 3-715 to 3-716, 3-969

1491. Kings, Brooklyn Borough   EDs 24-903 to 24-921, 24-1704, 24-922 to 24-930, 24-1705, 24-931 to 24-933, 24-1706, 24-934, 24-1707, 24-935 to 24-937

1492. Kings, Brooklyn Borough   EDs 24-938 to 24-939, 24-1708, 24-940 to 24-946, 24-1709, 24-947 to 24-949, 24-1201 to 24-1219

1493. Kings, Brooklyn Borough   EDs 24-1220 to 24-1232, 24-1773 to 24-1775, 24-1233, 24-1776 to 24-1778, 24-1234, 24-1779 to 24-1784, 24-1235 (NP), 24-1785 (NP), 24-1786 to 24-1788, 24-1236, 24-1789, 24-1237, 24-1790 (NP), 24-1238, 24-1791, 24-1239 to 24-1240, 24-1792 (NP), 24-1793 to 24-1794, 24-1241, 24-1795 to 24-1797, 24-1242, 24-1798, 24-1243, 24-1799 to 24-1801 (NP), 24-1802 to 24-1803

1494. Kings, Brooklyn Borough   EDs 24-1804 to 24-1809 (NP), 24-1810, 24-1244, 24-1811, 24-1812 (NP), 24-1813 to 24-1814, 24-1245 to 24-1246, 24-1815, 24-1247, 24-1816 to 24-1817, 24-1818 to 24-1821 (NP), 24-1822, 24-1248 to 24-1249, 24-1823 to 24-1826, 24-1827 to 24-1828 (NP), 24-1250, 24-1829 to 24-1831, 24-1832 (NP), 24-1833 to 24-1841, 24-1842 to 24-1844 (NP), 24-1251, 24-1845 to 24-1846, 24-1252, 24-1847 to 24-1850, 24-1253, 24-1851 to 24-1857, 24-1858 (NP), 24-1859, 24-1860 (NP), 24-1254, 24-1861 to 24-1863, 24-1255, 24-1864 to 24-1868, 24-1256

1495. Kings, Brooklyn Borough   EDs 24-1257, 24-1869, 24-1258, 24-1870, 24-1259 to 24-1260, 24-1871, 24-1261 to 24-1262, 24-1872 to 24-1874, 24-1263, 24-1875, 24-1264, 24-1876 to 24-1878, 24-1265 to 24-1273

1496. Kings, Brooklyn Borough   EDs 24-1274, 24-1879, 24-1275, 24-1880 to 24-1888, 24-1276 to 24-1283, 24-1889, 24-1284 to 24-1285, 24-1890 to 24-1893, 24-1286 to 24-1287

1497. Kings, Brooklyn Borough   EDs 24-1296, 24-1288, 24-1894, 24-1289 to 24-1292, 24-1895 to 24-1897, 24-1293, 24-1898 to 24-1899, 24-1294, 24-1900 to 24-1901, 24-1295 to 24-1298, 24-1902 to 24-1903, 24-1299, 24-1904, 24-1300, 24-1905 to 24-1906, 24-1301, 24-1907, 24-1302 to 24-1303, 24-1908, 24-1304

1498. Kings, Brooklyn Borough   EDs 24-1305 to 24-1306, 24-1909, 24-1307 to 24-1310, 24-1910, 24-1311 to 24-1313, 24-1911, 24-1314 to 24-1320, 24-1912, 24-1321 to 24-1324, 24-1913 to 24-1914, 24-1325, 24-1915, 24-1326 to 24-1329, 24-1916, 24-1330, 24-1917, 24-1331 to 24-1332

1499. Kings, Brooklyn Borough   EDs 24-950 to 24-972, 24-1710 to 24-1711, 24-973, 24-1712, 24-974 to 24-979, 24-980 (NP), 24-1713, 24-981 to 24-982, 24-1714 to 24-1716, 24-983, 24-1717 to 24-1719, 24-984 to 24-985

* 1500. Kings, Brooklyn Borough   EDs 24-986 to 24-987, 24-1720, 24-1722, 24-1723 (NP), 24-988 to 24-991, 24-992 (NP), 24-1724, 24-993 to 24-999, 24-1000 (NP), 24-1725 to 24-1726, 24-1001 to 24-1002, 24-1727 to 24-1728, 24-1729 to 24-1730 (NP), 24-1731, 24-1003, 24-1732 to 24-1733, 24-1, 24-1473, 24-2 to 24-3, 24-1474, 24-4 to 24-8, 24-1475, 24-9 to 24-21

1501. Kings, Brooklyn Borough   EDs 24-22 to 24-23, 24-1476, 24-24 to 24-25, 24-1477, 24-26 to 24-27, 24-1478, 24-28 to 24-30, 24-1479, 24-31 to 24-38, 24-1480, 24-39 to 24-46, 24-1481, 24-47, 24-1482

1502. Kings, Brooklyn Borough   EDs 24-269, 24-1559, 24-270 to 24-300

1503. Kings, Brooklyn Borough   EDs 24-301 to 24-312, 24-1560, 24-313 to 24-330

1504. Kings, Brooklyn Borough   EDs 24-331, 24-1561, 24-332 to 24-336, 24-1562, 24-337 to 24-345, 24-1563, 24-346 to 24-354, 24-1004 to 24-1013

---

* Roll 1500, Kings, Brooklyn Borough—There appears to be no ED 24-1721.

1505. Kings, Brooklyn Borough   EDs 24-1014, 24-1734, 24-1015 to 24-1029, 24-1735 (NP), 24-1030 to 24-1038, 24-1039 (NP), 24-1736, 24-1040 to 24-1041, 24-1737 to 24-1738, 24-1042, 24-1739, 24-1043

1506. Kings, Brooklyn Borough   EDs 24-1740, 24-1044 to 24-1052, 24-1741, 24-1053 to 24-1059, 24-1742, 24-1060 to 24-1080

1507. Kings, Brooklyn Borough   EDs 24-1081 to 24-1091, 24-1743, 24-1092, 24-1744 (NP), 24-1093, 24-1745 to 24-1746, 24-1094 to 24-1099, 24-1100 (NP), 24-1747, 24-1101 to 24-1102, 24-1748, 24-1103 to 24-1110, 24-1749, 24-1111, 24-1750, 24-1112

1508. Kings, Brooklyn Borough   EDs 24-1113 to 24-1114, 24-1751, 24-1115, 24-1752 to 24-1753, 24-1116 to 24-1120, 24-1754, 24-1121 to 24-1122, 24-1755, 24-1123, 24-1756 to 24-1757, 24-1124, 24-1758, 24-1125 to 24-1127, 24-1759 to 24-1760, 24-1128, 24-1761 to 24-1762 (NP), 24-1763, 24-1129 to 24-1130, 24-1764, 24-1131, 24-1765, 24-1132

1509. Kings, Brooklyn Borough   EDs 24-1133 to 24-1135, 24-1766, 24-1136, 24-1767, 24-1137, 24-1768, 24-1138 to 24-1156

1510. Kings, Brooklyn Borough   EDs 24-1157 to 24-1158, 24-1769, 24-1159 to 24-1160, 24-1770, 24-1161 to 24-1175, 24-1771, 24-1176 to 24-1178

1511. Kings, Brooklyn Borough   EDs 24-1179 to 24-1191, 24-1772, 24-1192 to 24-1200

1512. Kings, Brooklyn Borough   EDs 24-48, 24-1483 to 24-1484, 24-49, 24-1485, 24-50 to 24-51, 24-1486, 24-52 to 24-56, 24-1487, 24-57, 24-1488, 24-58 to 24-63, 24-65 to 24-70, 24-1489, 24-71, 24-1490, 24-72 to 24-73, 24-74 (NP), 24-1491, 24-75

1513. Kings, Brooklyn Borough   EDs 24-76 to 24-77, 24-1492 (NP), 24-78, 24-1493, 24-1953, 24-79 to 24-89, 24-1494, 24-90 to 24-93, 24-1495, 24-94 to 24-100, 24-1496, 24-101, 24-1497, 24-102, 24-1498, 24-103

1514. Kings, Brooklyn Borough   EDs 24-104 to 24-106, 24-1499, 24-107 to 24-109, 24-1500, 24-110 to 24-111, 24-1501, 24-112 to 24-113, 24-1502, 24-114 to 24-123, 24-64, 24-124, 24-1503, 24-125 to 24-126, 24-1504 to 24-1506, 24-127, 24-1507, 24-128, 24-1508, 24-129 to 24-133

1515. Kings, Brooklyn Borough   EDs 24-134 to 24-139, 24-1509, 24-140 to 24-141, 24-1510, 24-599 to 24-600, 24-1631, 24-601 to 24-619

1516. Kings, Brooklyn Borough   EDs 24-620 to 24-623, 24-1632, 24-624 to 24-631, 24-1633, 24-632 to 24-636, 24-1634, 24-637, 24-638 (NP), 24-1635 to 24-1636, 24-639, 24-1637, 24-640, 24-1638, 24-641 to 24-646, 24-1639, 24-647 to 24-648, 24-1640, 24-649

1517. Kings, Brooklyn Borough   EDs 24-1641, 24-650, 24-1642, 24-651, 24-1643, 24-142 to 24-145, 24-1511, 24-146, 24-1512 to 24-1515, 24-1516 to 24-1517 (NP), 24-1518 to 24-1519, 24-147 to 24-162, 24-1520, 24-163 to 24-170

1518. Kings, Brooklyn Borough   EDs 24-171, 24-1521, 24-172 (void), 24-173 to 24-175, 24-1522, 24-176 to 24-184, 24-1523 to 24-1524 (NP), 24-1525 to 24-1527, 24-185, 24-1528 to 24-1529, 24-186 to 24-187, 24-1530 to 24-1532, 24-188, 24-1533, 24-189 to 24-199, 24-1534

1519. Kings, Brooklyn Borough   EDs 24-200 to 24-212, 24-1535, 24-213, 24-1536, 24-214, 24-1537, 24-215 to 24-229, 24-1538

1520. Kings, Brooklyn Borough   EDs 24-230, 24-1539, 24-231, 24-1540 to 24-1542, 24-1543 (NP), 24-232 to 24-233, 24-1544 to 24-1545, 24-234 to 24-240, 24-1546 (NP), 24-1547 to 24-1551, 24-241, 24-1552, 24-242 to 24-248, 24-1553 to 24-1555, 24-249 to 24-251, 24-1556, 24-252 to 24-256

1521. Kings, Brooklyn Borough   EDs 24-257, 24-1557, 24-258 to 24-261, 24-1558, 24-262 to 24-268, 24-1333 to 24-1342, 24-1918, 24-1343 to 24-1345, 24-1919 to 24-1920, 24-1346, 24-1921, 24-1922 (NP), 24-1347, 24-1923, 24-1348, 24-1924, 24-1349 to 24-1350

1522. Kings, Brooklyn Borough   EDs 24-1925, 24-1351, 24-1352 (void), 24-1353 to 24-1368, 24-1926, 24-1369, 24-1927, 24-1370 to 24-1372

1523. Kings, Brooklyn Borough   EDs 24-1373 to 24-1390, 24-1928, 24-1391 to 24-1395

1524. Kings, Brooklyn Borough   EDs 24-1396 to 24-1398, 24-1929, 24-1399, 24-1930, 24-1400 to 24-1422

1525. Kings, Brooklyn Borough   EDs 24-1423 to 24-1426, 24-1931, 24-1427, 24-1932 to 24-1933, 24-1428 to 24-1431, 24-1934 to 24-1937, 24-1432 to 24-1435, 24-1436 (NP), 24-1938 to 24-1939, 24-1437 to 24-1441, 24-1940 to 24-1941, 24-1442

1526. Kings, Brooklyn Borough   EDs 24-1443, 24-1942, 24-1444 to 24-1453, 24-1943, 24-1454 to 24-1459, 24-1944 to 24-1945, 24-1460, 24-1946, 24-1947 to 24-1949 (NP), 24-1461 to 24-1462, 24-1950, 24-1463 to 24-1466, 24-1951 (NP), 24-1467 to 24-1472, 24-1952

1527. Kings, Brooklyn Borough   EDs 24-652 to 24-654, 24-1644, 24-655 to 24-656, 24-1645, 24-657 to 24-666, 24-1646, 24-667 to 24-669, 24-1647, 24-670 to 24-673, 24-1648, 24-674 to 24-675, 24-1649, 24-676 to 24-679, 24-1650 (NP), 24-680 to 24-686

1528. Kings, Brooklyn Borough   EDs 24-687 to 24-689, 24-1651, 24-690, 24-1652, 24-691 to 24-693, 24-1653, 24-694 to 24-697, 24-1654, 24-698 to 24-708, 24-1655, 24-709 to 24-714, 24-1656, 24-715 to 24-719

1529. Kings, Brooklyn Borough   EDs 24-720 to 24-748

1530. Kings, Brooklyn Borough   EDs 24-749 to 24-756, 24-1657, 24-757 to 24-758, 24-1658 (NP), 24-759, 24-760 (NP), 24-761 to 24-763, 24-1659, 24-764, 24-1660, 24-765, 24-1661, 24-766 to 24-770

1531. Kings, Brooklyn Borough   EDs 24-1662, 24-771, 24-1663 to 24-1664, 24-772, 24-1665, 24-773 to 24-789, 24-1666, 24-790 to 24-791

1532. Kings, Brooklyn Borough   EDs 24-792 to 24-809, 24-1667 to 24-1670, 24-810, 24-1671, 24-811, 24-1672 to 24-1674, 24-812, 24-1675, 24-813 to 24-814, 24-1676 to 24-1678

1533. Kings, Brooklyn Borough   EDs 24-815 to 24-818, 24-1679, 24-819, 24-1680 to 24-1681, 24-820, 24-1682 to 24-1683, 24-821, 24-1684 to 24-1687, 24-822, 24-1688, 24-823 to 24-826, 24-355 to 24-362, 24-1564, 24-363 to 24-365, 24-1565, 24-366, 24-1566, 24-367 to 24-370

1534. Kings, Brooklyn Borough   EDs 24-371 to 24-380, 24-1567, 24-381 to 24-385, 24-1568, 24-386 to 24-391, 24-1569, 24-392 to 24-394, 24-1570, 24-395 to 24-396, 24-1571, 24-397 to 24-403

1535. Kings, Brooklyn Borough   EDs 24-1572, 24-404 to 24-409, 24-410 (NP), 24-1573, 24-411 to 24-414, 24-1574, 24-415 to 24-418, 24-1575, 24-419 to 24-420, 24-422 to 24-436

1536. Kings, Brooklyn Borough   EDs 24-437 to 24-449, 24-1576, 24-421, 24-450 to 24-451, 24-452 (void), 24-453 to 24-456, 24-827 to 24-828, 24-1689, 24-829 to 24-831, 24-1690, 24-832 to 24-837, 24-1691

1537. Kings, Brooklyn Borough   EDs 24-838 to 24-842, 24-1692, 24-843, 24-1693, 24-844, 24-1694, 24-845, 24-1695, 24-846 to 24-847, 24-1696, 24-848 to 24-849, 24-1697, 24-850 to 24-859

1538. Kings, Brooklyn Borough   EDs 24-860 to 24-871, 24-1698 to 24-1699, 24-872, 24-1700, 24-873 to 24-884

1539. Kings, Brooklyn Borough    EDs 24-885 to 24-891, 24-1701, 24-892 to 24-901, 24-1702 to 24-1703, 24-902, 24-457, 24-1577 to 24-1578, 24-458, 24-1579 (NP), 24-459, 24-1580, 24-460, 24-1581, 24-461 to 24-465, 24-1582, 24-466 to 24-467

1540. Kings, Brooklyn Borough    EDs 24-468 to 24-474, 24-1583, 24-475 to 24-483, 24-1584, 24-484 to 24-487, 24-1585, 24-488, 24-1586, 24-489 to 24-490, 24-1587, 24-491 to 24-496

1541. Kings, Brooklyn Borough    EDs 24-497 to 24-506, 24-1588 to 24-1589, 24-507 to 24-508, 24-509 (NP), 24-1590 to 24-1595, 24-510 to 24-521

1542. Kings, Brooklyn Borough    EDs 24-522 to 24-537, 24-538 (NP), 24-1596 to 24-1598 (NP), 24-1599 to 24-1603, 24-539 (NP), 24-1604 to 24-1616 (NP), 24-1617 to 24-1618, 24-1619 (NP), 24-1620 to 24-1621, 24-1622 (NP), 24-540, 24-1623 to 24-1624, 24-1625 (NP), 24-541, 24-1626, 24-542 to 24-547

1543. Kings, Brooklyn Borough    EDs 24-548 to 24-553, 24-1627, 24-554, 24-1628, 24-555 to 24-558, 24-1629, 24-559 to 24-580

1544. Kings, Brooklyn Borough    EDs 24-581 to 24-591, 24-592 (NP), 24-593 to 24-598, 24-1630

New York, Manhattan Borough    EDs 31-1 to 31-7, 31-1169, 31-8 to 31-19

1545. New York, Manhattan Borough    EDs 31-20 to 31-32, 31-1170 to 31-1171, 31-33, 31-1172, 31-34 to 31-38, 31-1173, 31-39 to 31-40, 31-1174, 31-41, 31-1175, 31-42, 31-1176, 31-43 to 31-47, 31-1177, 31-48 to 31-49

1546. New York, Manhattan Borough    EDs 31-50 to 31-63, 31-1178 to 31-1179, 31-64 to 31-65, 31-1180, 31-66 to 31-74, 31-1181, 31-75 to 31-78, 31-1182, 31-79 to 31-82

1547. New York, Manhattan Borough    EDs 31-83 to 31-102, 31-103 (void), 31-104 to 31-122

1548. New York, Manhattan Borough    EDs 31-277 to 31-279, 31-1203, 31-280 to 31-311

1549. New York, Manhattan Borough    EDs 31-312, 31-1204, 31-313 to 31-316, 31-1205, 31-317, 31-1206, 31-318 to 31-327, 31-123 to 31-142

1550. New York, Manhattan Borough    EDs 31-143 to 31-158, 31-1183, 31-159 to 31-161, 31-328 to 31-346, 31-1184

1551. New York, Manhattan Borough    EDs 31-347 to 31-371, 31-1207, 31-372 to 31-378, 31-162 to 31-167

1552. New York, Manhattan Borough    EDs 31-168 to 31-199

1553. New York, Manhattan Borough    EDs 31-200 to 31-202, 31-379 to 31-385, 31-1208, 31-386 to 31-403

1554. New York, Manhattan Borough    EDs 31-404 to 31-430, 31-203 to 31-205

1555. New York, Manhattan Borough    EDs 31-206 to 31-224, 31-1185, 31-225 to 31-232

1556. New York, Manhattan Borough    EDs 31-233 to 31-241, 31-431 to 31-451

1557. New York, Manhattan Borough    EDs 31-452 to 31-477

1558. New York, Manhattan Borough    EDs 31-242, 31-1186 to 31-1187, 31-243 to 31-254, 31-255 (void), 31-256 to 31-258, 31-1188, 31-259, 31-1189 to 31-1190, 31-260 to 31-262, 31-1191, 31-263 to 31-266, 31-1192 to 31-1194, 31-267 to 31-268, 31-1195, 31-269 (void), 31-270, 31-1196

1559. New York, Manhattan Borough    EDs 31-1197, 31-271, 31-1198, 31-272, 31-1199, 31-273, 31-1200, 31-274 to 31-275, 31-1201, 31-276, 31-1202, 31-478 to 31-492

1560. New York, Manhattan Borough    EDs 31-493 to 31-522, 31-1209, 31-523 to 31-528

1561. New York, Manhattan Borough    EDs 31-577, 31-578 (NP), 31-1216, 31-579 to 31-602, 31-603 (void), 31-604 to 31-611

1562. New York, Manhattan Borough    EDs 31-612 to 31-613, 31-1233, 31-614 to 31-617, 31-1234, 31-618, 31-1217, 31-619, 31-1218, 31-620 to 31-621, 31-1219, 31-622 (NP), 31-623 to 31-639, 31-1235 to 31-1236, 31-1237 (NP), 31-640, 31-854, 31-1222, 31-855 to 31-859

1563. New York, Manhattan Borough    EDs 31-860 to 31-863, 31-868, 31-864 to 31-867, 31-869 to 31-891

1564. New York, Manhattan Borough    EDs 31-892 to 31-899, 31-641 to 31-652, 31-1238, 31-653 to 31-662

1565. New York, Manhattan Borough    EDs 31-663 to 31-700

1566. New York, Manhattan Borough    EDs 31-529 to 31-536, 31-1210 (NP), 31-537 to 31-547, 31-1211, 31-548 to 31-552

1567. New York, Manhattan Borough    EDs 31-553 to 31-568, 31-1212, 31-569, 31-1213, 31-570 to 31-572, 31-1214, 31-573, 31-1215, 31-574 to 31-576

1568. New York, Manhattan Borough    EDs 31-701 to 31-720, 31-1239, 31-721 to 31-737

1569. New York, Manhattan Borough    EDs 31-738 to 31-747, 31-748 (NP), 31-749 to 31-770, 31-1240

1570. New York, Manhattan Borough    EDs 31-771 to 31-777, 31-1241, 31-778 (NP), 31-779 to 31-780, 31-1242, 31-781 to 31-785, 31-1243, 31-786 to 31-794, 31-1220

1571. New York, Manhattan Borough    EDs 31-795 to 31-796, 31-1244, 31-797 to 31-811, 31-1245, 31-812, 31-813 (NP), 31-1221, 31-814 to 31-818, 31-1246, 31-819 to 31-821, 31-1247

1572. New York, Manhattan Borough    EDs 31-822 to 31-824, 31-825 (void), 31-826 to 31-843, 31-1248, 31-844 to 31-853, 31-1249

1573. New York, Manhattan Borough    EDs 31-900 to 31-923

1574. New York, Manhattan Borough    EDs 31-924 to 31-951

1575. New York, Manhattan Borough    EDs 31-952 to 31-959, 31-1223 (NP), 31-960 to 31-978, 31-1224, 31-979 to 31-982

1576. New York, Manhattan Borough    EDs 31-983 to 31-1011

1577. New York, Manhattan Borough    EDs 31-1012 to 31-1022, 31-1225, 31-1023 to 31-1040

1578. New York, Manhattan Borough    EDs 31-1041 to 31-1046, 31-1047 (NP), 31-1226, 31-1048 to 31-1066, 31-1227, 31-1067 to 31-1071

1579. New York, Manhattan Borough    EDs 31-1072 to 31-1082, 31-1228, 31-1083 to 31-1096, 31-1229, 31-1097 to 31-1101

1580. New York, Manhattan Borough    EDs 31-1102 to 31-1123, 31-1124 (NP), 31-1125 to 31-1135

1581. New York, Manhattan Borough    EDs 31-1136 to 31-1141, 31-1230, 31-1143 to 31-1160, 31-1142, 31-1161 to 31-1165, 31-1231, 31-1166, 31-1232, 31-1167 to 31-1168

1582. Queens, Queens Borough    EDs 41-1 (NP), 41-637, 41-2 to 41-5, 41-638, 41-6 to 41-8, 41-639 to 41-640 (NP), 41-9, 41-641, 41-10, 41-642, 41-11, 41-643 to 41-644, 41-12 to 41-13, 41-645 (NP), 41-14 to 41-15, 41-646, 41-16 to 41-19, 41-647, 41-20, 41-648, 41-21 to 41-24

1583. Queens, Queens Borough    EDs 41-25 to 41-27, 41-649, 41-28 to 41-46

1584. Queens, Queens Borough    EDs 41-47, 41-650, 41-48 to 41-53, 41-651 to 41-653, 41-54 to 41-67

1585. Queens, Queens Borough    EDs 41-68, 41-654, 41-655 (NP), 41-69 to 41-76, 41-656 (NP), 41-657 to 41-660, 41-77 to 41-78, 41-661 to 41-668, 41-79, 41-1575, 41-669 to 41-673, 41-674 (NP), 41-80, 41-675, 41-81

1586. Queens, Queens Borough EDs 41-82, 41-676 (NP), 41-83 to 41-84, 41-677, 41-85, 41-678 to 41-679, 41-86, 41-680, 41-681 (NP), 41-87, 41-682, 41-683 to 41-685 (NP), 41-686 to 41-689, 41-690 (NP), 41-691, 41-88, 41-692 to 41-694, 41-89 to 41-90, 41-695, 41-91 to 41-96, 41-696 (NP), 41-97 to 41-106

1587. Queens, Queens Borough EDs 41-107 to 41-109, 41-697, 41-110 to 41-111, 41-698, 41-112 to 41-114, 41-699, 41-115, 41-700, 41-116, 41-117 (NP), 41-701 (NP), 41-702 to 41-703, 41-118 to 41-122, 41-704, 41-705 (NP), 41-706, 41-123 to 41-126, 41-707, 41-127

1588. Queens, Queens Borough EDs 41-708, 41-128, 41-709, 41-129, 41-710 to 41-711, 41-130, 41-712 to 41-714, 41-131, 41-715 to 41-719, 41-132 to 41-133, 41-720, 41-134 to 41-137, 41-721 to 41-723, 41-138 to 41-144, 41-724 to 41-725, 41-145, 41-726 to 41-738, 41-146 (NP), 41-739 to 41-740, 41-741 (NP), 41-742 to 41-748, 41-749 (NP), 41-750 to 41-751, 41-752 (NP), 41-753

1589. Queens, Queens Borough EDs 41-147, 41-754 (NP), 41-755 to 41-756, 41-148 to 41-151, 41-757 to 41-758, 41-759 (NP), 41-152 to 41-154, 41-760 to 41-763 (NP), 41-764, 41-155 to 41-173, 41-765 to 41-766 (NP), 41-767 to 41-768, 41-174

1590. Queens, Queens Borough EDs 41-175 to 41-190, 41-191 (NP), 41-192 to 41-197, 41-769, 41-198 to 41-199

1591. Queens, Queens Borough EDs 41-200 to 41-206, 41-770 to 41-771, 41-772 to 41-774 (NP), 41-775 to 41-776, 41-207, 41-777 to 41-780, 41-208, 41-781, 41-209 to 41-211, 41-782, 41-212 to 41-214, 41-783 to 41-785, 41-215, 41-786 to 41-790, 41-791 (NP), 41-792 to 41-794, 41-216, 41-795 to 41-798, 41-217, 41-799 to 41-802

1592. Queens, Queens Borough EDs 41-803 to 41-806, 41-218 to 41-230, 41-807, 41-231 to 41-232, 41-808, 41-233 to 41-235, 41-809, 41-810 (NP), 41-811, 41-812 to 41-815 (NP), 41-816 to 41-817, 41-236, 41-818 to 41-823, 41-237 to 41-240, 41-824 to 41-831 (NP), 41-832 to 41-836, 41-241, 41-837 to 41-844

1593. Queens, Queens Borough EDs 41-845 to 41-848, 41-849 (NP), 41-850 to 41-851, 41-852 to 41-853 (NP), 41-242 to 41-243, 41-854, 41-244 to 41-252, 41-855, 41-253 to 41-254, 41-856 (NP), 41-857 to 41-859, 41-860 (NP), 41-255 to 41-256, 41-861 to 41-862, 41-257, 41-863 (NP), 41-864 to 41-869, 41-258, 41-870 to 41-873, 41-259, 41-874, 41-260, 41-875, 41-261 to 41-264, 41-876 to 41-886, 41-265 (NP), 41-887 (NP), 41-888 to 41-891, 41-892 to 41-893 (NP), 41-894 to 41-896, 41-897 (NP), 41-898 to 41-899, 41-266

1594. Queens, Queens Borough EDs 41-267, 41-900 to 41-906, 41-268, 41-907 to 41-908, 41-269, 41-909, 41-270, 41-910 to 41-912, 41-271, 41-913 to 41-914, 41-272, 41-915 to 41-918, 41-273, 41-919 to 41-921, 41-922 (NP), 41-274, 41-923 to 41-926, 41-927 (NP), 41-928 to 41-930, 41-275 (NP), 41-931 (NP), 41-932 to 41-933, 41-934 to 41-936 (NP), 41-937, 41-938 to 41-940 (NP), 41-941, 41-942 to 41-948 (NP), 41-949 to 41-950, 41-951 to 41-954 (NP), 41-276, 41-955 to 41-961, 41-962 to 41-963 (NP), 41-277 (NP), 41-964 to 41-971 (NP), 41-972, 41-973 to 41-977 (NP), 41-978, 41-979 (NP), 41-980, 41-981 (NP), 41-982, 41-983 (NP), 41-278 (NP), 41-984 to 41-985, 41-986 to 41-987 (NP), 41-988, 41-989 to 41-992 (NP), 41-993 to 41-1010, 41-279, 41-1011 to 41-1014, 41-1015 (NP), 41-1016 to 41-1017, 41-1018 to 41-1029 (NP), 41-1030 to 41-1031, 41-1032 to 41-1033 (NP), 41-280 (NP), 41-1034 to 41-1035 (NP), 41-1036, 41-1037 to 41-1045 (NP), 41-1046 to 41-1051

1595. Queens, Queens Borough EDs 41-1052 to 41-1054, 41-281, 41-1055, 41-1056 (NP), 41-1057 to 41-1064, 41-282, 41-1065 to 41-1067, 41-283, 41-1068 to 41-1070, 41-284, 41-1071, 41-285, 41-1072, 41-286 to 41-289, 41-1073, 41-290, 41-1074 to 41-1078, 41-291, 41-1079 (NP), 41-1080 to 41-1083, 41-292, 41-1084, 41-293 to 41-295, 41-1085, 41-296, 41-1086

1596. Queens, Queens Borough EDs 41-297 to 41-298, 41-1087, 41-299, 41-1088, 41-300, 41-1089, 41-301, 41-1090, 41-302, 41-1091, 41-303, 41-1092, 41-304 to 41-307, 41-1093 to 41-1094, 41-308, 41-1095 to 41-1096, 41-309 (NP), 41-1097 to 41-1098 (NP), 41-1099 to 41-1104, 41-1105 (NP), 41-1106 to 41-1107, 41-310 (NP), 41-1108 to 41-1118 (NP), 41-1119 to 41-1120, 41-1121 (NP), 41-1122 to 41-1126, 41-1127 (NP), 41-1128, 41-1129 (NP), 41-311 to 41-312, 41-1130 to 41-1137, 41-313, 41-1138 to 41-1146, 41-314, 41-1147, 41-315, 41-1148 to 41-1149

1597. Queens, Queens Borough EDs 41-1150 to 41-1152, 41-316 to 41-320, 41-1153 to 41-1158, 41-321 to 41-328, 41-1159 to 41-1160, 41-329, 41-1161, 41-330 to 41-333, 41-1162, 41-334 to 41-342

1598. Queens, Queens Borough EDs 41-343 to 41-344, 41-1163, 41-345 to 41-346, 41-1164, 41-347 to 41-349, 41-1165 to 41-1171, 41-350 to 41-359, 41-1172, 41-1173 (NP), 41-360 to 41-370

1599. Queens, Queens Borough EDs 41-371 to 41-372, 41-1174 to 41-1176, 41-373, 41-1177 to 41-1180, 41-374, 41-1181 to 41-1184, 41-375 to 41-376, 41-1185 to 41-1188, 41-377, 41-1189 to 41-1190, 41-378, 41-1191, 41-379 to 41-380, 41-1192 to 41-1193, 41-381, 41-1194 to 41-1196, 41-382, 41-1197 to 41-1200

1600. Queens, Queens Borough EDs 41-1201 to 41-1205, 41-383, 41-1206 to 41-1209, 41-384, 41-1210 to 41-1213, 41-385, 41-1214 to 41-1216, 41-386, 41-1217 to 41-1219, 41-1220 (NP), 41-1221 to 41-1222, 41-387, 41-1223, 41-388, 41-1224 to 41-1226, 41-389, 41-1227 to 41-1232, 41-390, 41-1233 to 41-1237, 41-391, 41-1238 to 41-1241, 41-392, 41-1242 to 41-1247

1601. Queens, Queens Borough EDs 41-1248 to 41-1250, 41-393, 41-1251 to 41-1253, 41-394, 41-1254, 41-395, 41-1255, 41-396, 41-1256, 41-397, 41-1257, 41-398 to 41-404, 41-1258, 41-405, 41-1259 to 41-1262, 41-1263 (NP), 41-406, 41-1264, 41-407, 41-1265 to 41-1270, 41-1271 to 41-1272 (NP), 41-1273 to 41-1275

* 1602. Queens, Queens Borough

1603. Queens, Queens Borough EDs 41-1317 to 41-1319, 41-425, 41-1320 to 41-1325, 41-426, 41-1326 to 41-1333, 41-427, 41-1334 to 41-1338, 41-428, 41-1339 to 41-1340, 41-1341 (NP), 41-429, 41-1342 to 41-1343, 41-1344 (NP), 41-1345 to 41-1348, 41-1349 to 41-1351 (NP), 41-1352 to 41-1353, 41-430, 41-1354 to 41-1358, 41-1359 (NP), 41-1360, 41-1361 (NP), 41-1362, 41-1363 (NP), 41-431, 41-1364 (NP), 41-1365, 41-1366 (NP), 41-1367 to 41-1368, 41-1369 to 41-1371 (NP), 41-1372 to 41-1373, 41-1374 (NP), 41-432, 41-1375 to 41-1379, 41-433 to 41-437

1604. Queens, Queens Borough EDs 41-408 to 41-409, 41-1276 to 41-1277, 41-1278 (NP), 41-1279, 41-1280 (NP), 41-1281 to 41-1286, 41-410, 41-1287, 41-411 to 41-418, 41-1288 to 41-1289, 41-419, 41-1290, 41-420 to 41-421, 41-1291 to 41-1292, 41-422, 41-1293 to 41-1295, 41-423, 41-1296 to 41-1297, 41-1298 to 41-1299 (NP), 41-1300 to 41-1303, 41-424, 41-1304 to 41-1310, 41-1311 (NP), 41-1312 to 41-1316

1605. Queens, Queens Borough EDs 41-1380, 41-438, 41-1381 to 41-1383, 41-1384 (NP), 41-1385, 41-1386 (NP), 41-439 to 41-440, 41-1387, 41-441, 41-1388 to 41-1389, 41-442, 41-1390, 41-443 to 41-444, 41-1391 to 41-1393, 41-445 (NP), 41-1394 to 41-1395 (NP), 41-1396 to 41-1402, 41-446, 41-1403, 41-1404 to 41-1405 (NP), 41-1406, 41-447, 41-1407, 41-448 to 41-450, 41-1408 to 41-1410, 41-451 (NP), 41-1411, 41-452 to 41-455, 41-1412, 41-456 to 41-457, 41-1413 to 41-1414, 41-458, 41-1415, 41-459 to 41-461, 41-1416, 41-462, 41-1417, 41-463, 41-1418 to 41-1419, 41-464, 41-465 (NP), 41-1420 to 41-1425

---

* Roll 1602, Queens—There is no roll 1602. Roll number 1602 was skipped during the original filming. The EDs for Queens, however, are complete. See rolls 1582 to 1601 and 1603 to 1612.

1606.   Queens, Queens Borough   EDs 41-1426, 41-466 to 41-467, 41-1427, 41-1428 to 41-1430 (NP), 41-1431, 41-1432 to 41-1435 (NP), 41-1436, 41-1437 (NP), 41-1438 to 41-1441, 41-1442 to 41-1443 (NP), 41-468, 41-1444 (NP), 41-1445 to 41-1448, 41-1449 (NP), 41-1450, 41-1451 to 41-1456 (NP), 41-469, 41-1457 (NP), 41-1458, 41-470 to 41-471, 41-1459 to 41-1460, 41-472 to 41-473, 41-1461 to 41-1467, 41-1468 (NP), 41-1469 to 41-1470, 41-474, 41-1471, 41-475, 41-1472 to 41-1481, 41-476, 41-1482, 41-477, 41-1483, 41-478, 41-1484 to 41-1485, 41-1486 (NP), 41-1487 to 41-1488, 41-1489 (NP), 41-1490, 41-1491 (NP), 41-1492, 41-1493 to 41-1497 (NP), 41-479, 41-1498 to 41-1501, 41-480, 41-1502

1607.   Queens, Queens Borough   EDs 41-481, 41-1503 to 41-1504, 41-1505 (NP), 41-1506, 41-1507 to 41-1508 (NP), 41-1509 to 41-1512, 41-482 to 41-484, 41-1513, 41-485 to 41-489, 41-1514 to 41-1516, 41-490 to 41-511

1608.   Queens, Queens Borough   EDs 41-512 to 41-533, 41-1517 to 41-1518, 41-534, 41-1519 to 41-1520, 41-535 to 41-543

1609.   Queens, Queens Borough   EDs 41-544 to 41-562, 41-1521 to 41-1522, 41-563, 41-1523, 41-564 to 41-566, 41-1524, 41-567 to 41-568, 41-1525 to 41-1526, 41-1527 (NP), 41-1528, 41-569, 41-1529, 41-570, 41-571 (NP), 41-1530, 41-572, 41-1531

1610.   Queens, Queens Borough   EDs 41-1532 to 41-1535, 41-1536 to 41-1537 (NP), 41-573, 41-1538, 41-1539 (NP), 41-1540, 41-1541 to 41-1542 (NP), 41-1543 to 41-1547, 41-1548 to 41-1550 (NP), 41-574, 41-1551 to 41-1557, 41-575, 41-1558, 41-576 to 41-578, 41-1559 to 41-1560, 41-579, 41-1561 to 41-1562, 41-580 to 41-584, 41-1572, 41-585 to 41-586, 41-1587 (NP), 41-1573, 41-588 to 41-592

1611.   Queens, Queens Borough   EDs 41-593, 41-1574, 41-594 to 41-614, 41-1563 to 41-1564, 41-615 to 41-622

1612.   Queens, Queens Borough   EDs 41-623 to 41-636, 41-1565 to 41-1571

Richmond, Richmond Borough   EDs 43-1, 43-101, 43-2 to 43-4, 43-102 to 43-103, 43-5 to 43-7, 43-104, 43-8 to 43-12, 43-105, 43-13 to 43-16

1613.   Richmond, Richmond Borough   EDs 43-17 to 43-18, 43-106 to 43-107, 43-19, 43-108 to 43-111, 43-20 to 43-24, 43-112, 43-25, 43-113 to 43-117, 43-26, 43-118 to 43-125, 43-27, 43-126 to 43-128, 43-28 to 43-29, 43-129, 43-30 to 43-31, 43-130, 43-32, 43-131, 43-33, 43-132 to 43-133, 43-34, 43-134 to 43-136, 43-35, 43-137 to 43-140, 43-36, 43-141 to 43-142, 43-37, 43-143

1614.   Richmond, Richmond Borough   EDs 43-144, 43-38, 43-145 to 43-146, 43-39, 43-147 to 43-150, 43-40 (NP), 43-151 to 43-154, 43-41 (NP), 43-155 (NP), 43-156 to 43-164, 43-42, 43-165, 43-43, 43-166 to 43-170, 43-44, 43-171 to 43-172, 43-45 to 43-46, 43-173 to 43-174, 43-47, 43-175 to 43-176, 43-177 (NP), 43-178 to 43-179, 43-48, 43-180 to 43-182, 43-49, 43-183, 43-50, 43-184, 43-51 to 43-52, 43-185, 43-53 to 43-54, 43-186, 43-55, 43-187, 43-56, 43-188, 43-57 to 43-58, 43-189 to 43-193, 43-59, 43-194 to 43-200, 43-60, 43-201 to 43-207

1615.   Richmond, Richmond Borough   EDs 43-208 to 43-209, 43-61, 43-210 (NP), 43-211 to 43-214, 43-215 (NP), 43-216, 43-62 (NP), 43-63 to 43-64, 43-217 to 43-220, 43-65, 43-221, 43-66 to 43-67, 43-222 to 43-231, 43-68, 43-232 to 43-236, 43-69, 43-237 to 43-240, 43-241 (NP), 43-242, 43-70, 43-243 to 43-246, 43-71, 43-247 to 43-251, 43-72, 43-252 to 43-253, 43-73 to 43-74, 43-254 to 43-256, 43-75, 43-257 to 43-261, 43-76 to 43-77, 43-262 to 43-272, 43-78, 43-273 to 43-275, 43-79, 43-276

1616.   Richmond, Richmond Borough   EDs 43-277 to 43-278, 43-80, 43-279 to 43-280, 43-81, 43-281 to 43-287, 43-82, 43-288, 43-83, 43-289 to 43-291, 43-84, 43-292, 43-293 (NP), 43-294, 43-85, 43-295 (NP), 43-296 to 43-302, 43-303 (NP), 43-86, 43-304 to 43-310, 43-311 (NP), 43-312 to 43-315, 43-87, 43-316, 43-88, 43-317 to 43-321 (NP), 43-322 to 43-326, 43-327 to 43-331 (NP), 43-332 to 43-335, 43-336 to 43-339 (NP), 43-340,

43-89 (NP), 43-341 to 43-344, 43-90, 43-345, 43-91, 43-346 to 43-347, 43-92 to 43-94, 43-348 to 43-349, 43-95, 43-350 to 43-351, 43-96, 43-352 to 43-353, 43-97, 43-354, 43-98, 43-355, 43-99, 43-356, 43-100 (NP), 43-357 (NP), 43-358 to 43-361, 43-362 (NP), 43-363

1617.   Niagara   EDs 32-1 to 32-3, 32-102, 32-4 to 32-20, 32-21 (NP), 32-22 to 32-26, 32-116, 32-27, 32-117, 32-28 to 32-43

1618.   Niagara   EDs 32-44 to 32-46, 32-47 (NP), 32-48 to 32-74

1619.   Niagara   EDs 32-75 to 32-86, 32-89 to 32-92, 32-87 to 32-88, 32-93 to 32-101, 32-103 to 32-105, 32-118, 32-106 to 32-113, 32-114 (NP), 32-115

1620.   Oneida   EDs 33-1 to 33-12, 33-176, 33-13 to 33-24, 33-177, 33-25, 33-65, 33-26 to 33-39, 33-70, 33-40 to 33-46

1621.   Oneida   EDs 33-47 to 33-64, 33-66 to 33-69, 33-71 to 33-73

Oneida, Utica City   EDs 33-74 to 33-97

1622.   Oneida, Utica City   EDs 33-98 to 33-137

1623.   Oneida, Utica City   EDs 33-138 to 33-156, 33-178, 33-157 to 33-159

Oneida   EDs 33-160 to 33-175

Onondaga   EDs 34-125 to 34-127, 34-213, 34-128, 34-132, 34-129 to 34-131

1624.   Onondaga   EDs 34-133 to 34-139, 34-214, 34-140 to 34-153, 34-215, 34-154 to 34-174

1625.   Onondaga   EDs 34-175 to 34-182, 34-216 to 34-217, 34-183 to 34-193

Onondaga, Syracuse City   EDs 34-1 to 34-7, 34-218, 34-8 to 34-13, 34-219 to 34-220, 34-14 to 34-15, 34-194, 34-16

1626.   Onondaga, Syracuse City   EDs 34-17 to 34-20, 34-195, 34-21 to 34-27, 34-196, 34-28 to 34-30, 34-197, 34-31 to 34-33, 34-198 to 34-199, 34-34, 34-200

1627.   Onondaga, Syracuse City   EDs 34-35, 34-201, 34-36 to 34-49, 34-60 to 34-69

1628.   Onondaga, Syracuse City   EDs 34-50 to 34-59, 34-70 to 34-77, 34-202, 34-78 to 34-80, 34-203, 34-81, 34-204, 34-82 to 34-85

1629.   Onondaga, Syracuse City   EDs 34-86, 34-205, 34-222, 34-87, 34-206, 34-223, 34-88, 34-224 to 34-225, 34-89 to 34-90, 34-207, 34-226, 34-91 to 34-92, 34-227, 34-93 to 34-104, 34-208

1630.   Onondaga, Syracuse City   EDs 34-105 to 34-109, 34-209 to 34-210, 34-111 to 34-113, 34-110, 34-211, 34-228, 34-114 to 34-123, 34-212, 34-124, 34-229 to 34-232, 34-221

1631.   Ontario   EDs 35-1 to 35-13, 35-19 to 35-29, 35-14 to 35-18, 35-30 to 35-37, 35-45, 35-38 to 35-44, 35-46 to 35-58

1632.   Orange   EDs 36-1 to 36-46

1633.   Orange   EDs 36-47 to 36-74, 36-113, 36-75 to 36-86, 36-96 to 36-97

1634.   Orange   EDs 36-87 to 36-95, 36-98 to 36-100, 36-112, 36-101 to 36-111

Orleans   EDs 37-1 to 37-28

1635.   Orleans   EDs 37-29 to 37-32

Oswego   EDs 38-1 to 38-23, 38-28, 38-24 to 38-27, 38-29 to 38-43, 38-66, 38-44 to 38-45

1636.   Oswego   EDs 38-46 to 38-57, 38-67, 38-58 to 38-65

Otsego   EDs 39-1, 39-58, 39-2 to 39-18, 39-42 to 39-43, 39-19 to 39-26, 39-59, 39-27 to 39-38

1637. Otsego　EDs 39-39 to 39-41, 39-44 to 39-51, 39-60, 39-52 to 39-57

Putnam　EDs 40-1 to 40-15

Rensselaer　EDs 42-1 to 42-22, 42-42, 42-23 to 42-25

1638. Rensselaer　EDs 42-26 to 42-41, 42-43 to 42-69, 42-85 to 42-89

1639. Rensselaer　EDs 42-70 to 42-84, 42-92 to 42-97, 42-90 to 42-91, 42-98 to 42-111

1640. Rockland　EDs 44-1 to 44-4, 44-49, 44-5 to 44-8, 44-48, 44-9 to 44-13, 44-16, 44-14 to 44-15, 44-17 to 44-19, 44-50, 44-20, 44-51, 44-21 to 44-22, 44-52, 44-23 to 44-26, 44-54, 44-27 to 44-30, 44-47, 44-31 to 44-32, 44-53, 44-33 to 44-36

1641. Rockland　EDs 44-37 to 44-46

St. Lawrence　EDs 45-1 to 45-7, 45-45, 45-8 to 45-33, 45-42 to 45-44, 45-46 to 45-48

1642. St. Lawrence　EDs 45-34 to 45-41, 45-49 to 45-51, 45-55 to 45-66, 45-94, 45-67 to 45-68, 45-52 to 45-78, 45-53 to 45-54, 45-69 to 45-77, 45-79 to 45-93

1643. Saratoga　EDs 46-1 to 46-16, 46-21 to 46-26, 46-17 to 46-20, 46-27 to 46-33, 46-39 to 46-47

1644. Saratoga　EDs 46-34 to 46-38, 46-48 to 46-54

Schenectady　EDs 47-12 to 47-18, 47-1 to 47-11, 47-19 to 47-22

1645. Schenectady　EDs 47-23 to 47-30, 47-37 to 47-44, 47-31 to 47-36, 47-52 to 47-61

1646. Schenectady　EDs 47-45 to 47-51, 47-62 to 47-83

Schoharie　EDs 48-1 to 48-8

1647. Schoharie　EDs 48-9 to 48-11, 48-27, 48-12 to 48-26

Schuyler　EDs 49-1 to 49-4, 49-12, 49-5, 49-16, 49-6 to 49-11, 49-13 to 49-15, 49-17 to 49-18

Seneca　EDs 50-1 to 50-26

1648. Steuben　EDs 51-1 to 51-13, 51-22 to 51-33, 51-14 to 51-21, 51-34 to 51-44, 51-55 to 51-67

1649. Steuben　EDs 51-45 to 51-54, 51-68 to 51-82

Suffolk　EDs 52-1 to 52-18, 52-21 to 52-24

1650. Suffolk　EDs 52-19 to 52-20, 52-25 to 52-45, 52-137, 52-47, 52-114, 52-46, 52-48 to 52-51, 52-75 to 52-88

1651. Suffolk　EDs 52-89 to 52-101, 52-52 to 52-74

1652. Suffolk　EDs 52-102 to 52-112, 52-126 to 52-135, 52-113, 52-115 to 52-125, 52-136

Sullivan　EDs 53-1 to 53-9, 53-14 to 53-16

1653. Sullivan　EDs 53-10 to 53-13, 53-17 to 53-39

Tioga　EDs 54-1 to 54-25

1654. Tompkins　EDs 55-1 to 55-12, 55-17 to 55-30, 55-13 to 55-16, 55-31 to 55-41

Ulster　EDs 56-1 to 56-10, 56-33 to 56-36

1655. Ulster　EDs 56-11 to 56-32, 56-37 to 56-58

1656. Ulster　EDs 56-59 to 56-71

Warren　EDs 57-1 to 57-5, 57-21 to 57-26, 57-6 to 57-20, 57-27 to 57-31

1657. Washington　EDs 58-1 to 58-4, 58-42, 58-5 to 58-8, 58-24, 58-9 to 58-23, 58-25 to 58-41, 58-43 to 58-47

Wayne　EDs 59-1 to 59-6

1658. Wayne　EDs 59-7 to 59-9, 59-46, 59-10 to 59-45, 59-47 to 59-48

Westchester　EDs 60-88 to 60-96, 60-388

1659. Westchester　EDs 60-100 to 60-113, 60-97 to 60-99, 60-114 to 60-115, 60-389 to 60-392, 60-116 to 60-129, 60-137 to 60-138

1660. Westchester　EDs 60-130 to 60-135, 60-393, 60-136, 60-139 to 60-140, 60-141 (NP), 60-142 to 60-168

1661. Westchester　EDs 60-169 to 60-170, 60-394, 60-171 to 60-182, 60-292, 60-183 to 60-186, 60-403, 60-187 to 60-205

1662. Westchester　EDs 60-206 to 60-240

1663. Westchester　EDs 60-241 to 60-242, 60-283, 60-284 to 60-285 (NP), 60-286 to 60-287, 60-243 to 60-278

1664. Westchester　EDs 60-279 to 60-282, 60-288 to 60-291, 60-293 to 60-304, 60-305 (NP), 60-306 to 60-317, 60-334 to 60-340

1665. Westchester　EDs 60-318 to 60-333, 60-341 to 60-346, 60-402, 60-347 to 60-356, 60-399, 60-357

1666. Westchester　EDs 60-358 to 60-373, 60-395 to 60-396

Westchester, Yonkers City　EDs 60-1 to 60-5, 60-397, 60-6 to 60-9, 60-401 (void), 60-10 to 60-14, 60-377

1667. Westchester, Yonkers City　EDs 60-15 to 60-19, 60-378, 60-20 to 60-28, 60-379, 60-39, 60-380, 60-40 to 60-48

1668. Westchester, Yonkers City　EDs 60-29 to 60-38, 60-49 to 60-55, 60-400, 60-56 to 60-62, 60-381, 60-63 to 60-64, 60-398, 60-65 to 60-68

1669. Westchester, Yonkers City　EDs 60-69, 60-382, 60-70 to 60-76, 60-383, 60-77 to 60-78, 60-384, 60-79 to 60-82, 60-385, 60-83 to 60-84, 60-386, 60-85 to 60-86, 60-387, 60-87, 60-374 to 60-376

1670. Wyoming　EDs 61-1 to 61-32

Yates　EDs 62-1 to 62-20

## North Carolina

1671. Alamance　EDs 1-1 to 1-25

Alexander　EDs 2-1 to 2-7

1672. Alexander　EDs 2-8 to 2-11

Alleghany　EDs 3-1 to 3-8

Anson　EDs 4-1 to 4-24

Ashe　EDs 5-1 to 5-15

1673. Ashe　EDs 5-16 to 5-24

Avery　EDs 6-1 to 6-13

Beaufort　EDs 7-1 to 7-26

1674. Bertie　EDs 8-1 to 8-20

Bladen　EDs 9-1 to 9-21

Brunswick　EDs 10-1 to 10-4

1675. Brunswick　EDs 10-5 to 10-8, 10-9 (NP), 10-10 to 10-13

Buncombe　EDs 11-1 to 11-7, 11-25 to 11-26, 11-8 to 11-22, 11-27

1676. Buncombe　EDs 11-23 to 11-24, 11-65, 11-28 to 11-30, 11-52, 11-31 to 11-32, 11-66, 11-33 to 11-36, 11-67, 11-37 to 11-51, 11-53 to 11-62

1677. Buncombe　EDs 11-63 to 11-64

Burke　EDs 12-1 to 12-29

Cabarrus　EDs 13-1 to 13-12

1678. Cabarrus　EDs 13-13 to 13-28

Caldwell　EDs 14-1 to 14-8, 14-15, 14-9 to 14-14, 14-16 to 14-23

1679. Camden　EDs 15-1 to 15-5

Carteret　EDs 16-1 to 16-18

Caswell　EDs 17-1 to 17-10

Catawba　EDs 18-1 to 18-5

1680. Catawba　EDs 18-6 to 18-26

Chatham　EDs 19-1 to 19-16

1681. Chatham　EDs 19-17 to 19-24

Cherokee　EDs 20-1 to 20-14

Chowan　EDs 21-1 to 21-11

Clay　EDs 22-1 to 22-7

Cleveland　EDs 23-1 to 23-6, 23-13 to 23-15

1682.  Cleveland    EDs 23-7 to 23-12, 23-16 to 23-33
Columbus    EDs 24-1 to 24-8

1683.  Columbus    EDs 24-9 to 24-32
Craven    EDs 25-1 to 25-24

1684.  Cumberland    EDs 26-1 to 26-4, 26-5 (NP), 26-6 to 26-35
Currituck    EDs 27-1 to 27-6
Dare    EDs 28-1 to 28-8

1685.  Davidson    EDs 29-1 to 29-35
Davie    EDs 30-1 to 30-2

1686.  Davie    EDs 30-3 to 30-12
Duplin    EDs 31-1 to 31-29
Durham    EDs 32-1 to 32-4

1687.  Durham    EDs 32-5 to 32-11, 32-18 to 32-21, 32-12 to 32-17, 32-22 to 32-26

1688.  Durham    EDs 32-27 to 32-31
Edgecombe    EDs 33-1 to 33-32

1689.  Edgecombe    EDs 33-33 to 33-35
Forsyth    EDs 34-1 to 34-37

1690.  Forsyth    EDs 34-38 to 34-41, 34-52 to 34-66, 34-42 to 34-51

1691.  Franklin    EDs 35-1 to 35-22
Gaston    EDs 36-1 to 36-17

1692.  Gaston    EDs 36-18 to 36-53

1693.  Gates    EDs 37-1 to 37-9
Graham    EDs 38-1 to 38-5
Granville    EDs 39-1 to 39-23
Greene    EDs 40-1 to 40-6

1694.  Greene    EDs 40-7 to 40-15
Guilford    EDs 41-1 to 41-26

1695.  Guilford    EDs 41-27 to 41-59

1696.  Guilford    EDs 41-60 to 41-82
Halifax    EDs 42-1 to 42-11

1697.  Halifax    EDs 42-12 to 42-33
Harnett    EDs 43-1 to 43-14

1698.  Harnett    EDs 43-15 to 43-25
Haywood    EDs 44-1 to 44-21
Henderson    EDs 45-1 to 45-6, 45-18, 45-16 to 45-17

1699.  Henderson    EDs 45-7 to 45-15
Hertford    EDs 46-1 to 46-15
Hoke    EDs 47-1 to 47-4, 47-5 (NP), 47-6 to 47-14
Hyde    EDs 48-1 to 48-11

1700.  Iredell    EDs 49-1 to 49-35
Jackson    EDs 50-1 to 50-8

1701.  Jackson    EDs 50-9 to 50-21
Johnston    EDs 51-1 to 51-10, 51-14 to 51-15, 51-11 to 51-13, 51-16 to 51-31

1702.  Johnston    EDs 51-32 to 51-35, 51-43, 51-36 to 51-42
Jones    EDs 52-1 to 52-11
Lee    EDs 53-1 to 53-15
Lenoir    EDs 54-1 to 54-4, 54-15 to 54-17

1703.  Lenoir    EDs 54-5 to 54-14, 54-18 to 54-27
Lincoln    EDs 55-1 to 55-21
McDowell    EDs 56-1 to 56-6, 56-12 to 56-14

1704.  McDowell    EDs 56-7 to 56-11, 56-15 to 56-16
Macon    EDs 57-1 to 57-14

Madison    EDs 58-1 to 58-20
Martin    EDs 59-1 to 59-7

1705.  Martin    EDs 59-8 to 59-22
Mecklenburg    EDs 60-1 to 60-16

1706.  Mecklenburg    EDs 60-17 to 60-43

1707.  Mecklenburg    EDs 60-44 to 60-76
Mitchell    EDs 61-1 to 61-12

1708.  Montgomery    EDs 62-1 to 62-15
Moore    EDs 63-1 to 63-24
Nash    EDs 64-1 to 64-6

1709.  Nash    EDs 64-7 to 64-41
New Hanover    EDs 65-1 to 65-8

1710.  New Hanover    EDs 65-9 to 65-17, 65-20 to 65-23, 65-18 to 65-19, 65-24 to 65-27
Northampton    EDs 66-1 to 66-17

1711.  Northampton    EDs 66-18 to 66-26
Onslow    EDs 67-1 to 67-12
Orange    EDs 68-1 to 68-15
Pamlico    EDs 69-1 to 69-3

1712.  Pamlico    EDs 69-4 to 69-12
Pasquotank    EDs 70-1 to 70-12
Pender    EDs 71-1 to 71-15
Perquimans    EDs 72-1 to 72-9

1713.  Person    EDs 73-1 to 73-11
Pitt    EDs 74-2, 74-38, 74-1, 74-3 to 74-26

1714.  Pitt    EDs 74-27 to 74-37, 74-39 to 74-43
Polk    EDs 75-1 to 75-10
Randolph    EDs 76-1 to 76-13

1715.  Randolph    EDs 76-14 to 76-34
Richmond    EDs 77-1 to 77-3, 77-7 to 77-10, 77-4 to 77-6, 77-11 to 77-21

1716.  Robeson    EDs 78-1 to 78-46, 78-57

1717.  Robeson    EDs 78-47 to 78-56
Rockingham    EDs 79-1 to 79-2, 79-11 to 79-19, 79-3 to 79-10, 79-20 to 79-24, 79-27

1718.  Rockingham    EDs 79-25 to 79-26, 79-28 to 79-30
Rowan    EDs 80-1 to 80-12, 80-20, 80-13, 80-21, 80-14, 80-24, 80-15 to 80-19, 80-22 to 80-23, 80-25 to 80-26, 80-28 to 80-34

1719.  Rowan    EDs 80-35 to 80-38, 80-27, 80-39 to 80-45
Rutherford    EDs 81-1 to 81-22, 81-27 to 81-29

1720.  Rutherford    EDs 81-23 to 81-26
Sampson    EDs 82-1 to 82-22, 82-27, 82-23 to 82-26, 82-28 to 82-34

1721.  Scotland    EDs 83-1 to 83-12
Stanly    EDs 84-1 to 84-15, 84-20, 84-16 to 84-19, 84-21 to 84-22
Stokes    EDs 85-1 to 85-4

1722.  Stokes    EDs 85-5 to 85-18
Surry    EDs 86-1 to 86-25

1723.  Swain    EDs 87-1 to 87-10
Transylvania    EDs 88-1 to 88-4, 88-7, 88-5 to 88-6, 88-8 to 88-11

Tyrrell    EDs 89-1 to 89-6

Union    EDs 90-14, 90-24, 90-13, 90-15 to 90-23, 90-25 to 90-36

1724. Union    EDs 90-1 to 90-12

Washington    EDs 94-1 to 94-9

Vance    EDs 91-1 to 91-18

1725. Wake    EDs 92-1 to 92-33, 92-35 to 92-38, 92-49 to 92-50, 92-34, 92-51 to 92-52

1726. Wake    EDs 92-39 to 92-48, 92-53 to 92-70

Warren    EDs 93-1 to 93-4, 93-8, 93-5, 93-9, 93-6 to 93-7, 93-10 to 93-11

1727. Warren    EDs 93-12 to 93-20

Watauga    EDs 95-1 to 95-16

Wayne    EDs 96-1 to 96-10, 96-28 to 96-38

1728. Wayne    EDs 96-11 to 96-27

Wilkes    EDs 97-1 to 97-25

1729. Wilkes    EDs 97-26 to 97-31

Wilson    EDs 98-1 to 98-30

Yadkin    EDs 99-1 to 99-4

1730. Yadkin    EDs 99-5, 99-16, 99-6, 99-19, 99-7 to 99-15, 99-17 to 99-18

Yancey    EDs 100-1 to 100-12

## North Dakota

1731. Adams    EDs 1-1 to 1-32

Benson    EDs 3-1 to 3-48

Barnes    EDs 2-1 to 2-58

Billings    EDs 4-1 to 4-29

1732. Bottineau    EDs 5-1 to 5-59

Burke    EDs 7-1 to 7-37

Bowman    EDs 6-1 to 6-39

Burleigh    EDs 8-1 to 8-58

1733. Cass    EDs 9-1 to 9-26, 9-46 to 9-47, 9-84, 9-48 to 9-83, 9-27 to 9-45

1734. Cavalier    EDs 10-1 to 10-16, 10-49, 10-17 to 10-48

Divide    EDs 12-1 to 12-37

Dickey    EDs 11-1 to 11-39

Emmons    EDs 15-1 to 15-43, 15-44 (NP), 15-45 to 15-52

1735. Dunn    EDs 13-1 to 13-53, 13-54 to 13-55 (NP), 13-56 to 13-57, 13-58 to 13-60 (NP), 13-61 to 13-62, 13-63 to 13-65 (NP), 13-66, 13-67 (NP), 13-68 to 13-69, 13-70 to 13-71 (NP)

Eddy    EDs 14-1 to 14-20

Foster    EDs 16-1 to 16-20

Golden Valley    EDs 17-1 to 17-21

Grand Forks    EDs 18-17 to 18-27

1736. Grand Forks    EDs 18-1 to 18-16, 18-28 to 18-39, 18-59, 18-40 to 18-58

Griggs    EDs 20-1 to 20-23

Grant    EDs 19-1 to 19-52

La Moure    EDs 23-1 to 23-40

1737. Hettinger    EDs 21-1 to 21-35

Kidder    EDs 22-1 to 22-21, 22-44, 22-22 to 22-24, 22-26, 22-25, 22-28, 22-27, 22-29 to 22-43

Logan    EDs 24-1 to 24-32

McHenry    EDs 25-1 to 25-66

McIntosh    EDs 26-1 to 26-33

1738. McKenzie    EDs 27-1 to 27-11, 27-13, 27-12, 27-14 to 27-41, 27-80 (NP), 27-42 to 27-67, 27-68 (NP), 27-69, 27-70 to 27-71 (NP), 27-72, 27-73 to 27-76 (NP), 27-77, 27-78 to 27-79 (NP)

Mercer    EDs 29-1 to 29-37, 29-40, 29-38 to 29-39, 29-41, 29-42 (NP), 29-43, 29-44 (NP), 29-45 to 29-46

McLean    EDs 28-1 to 28-63, 28-70 (NP), 28-64 to 28-69, 28-71 to 28-74, 28-75 (NP), 28-76 to 28-83

Oliver    EDs 33-1 to 33-2, 33-4 to 33-18, 33-3, 33-19 to 33-23, 33-24 (NP), 33-25 to 33-26

1739. Morton    EDs 30-1 to 30-23, 30-69, 30-24 to 30-33, 30-34 (NP), 30-35 to 30-68

Mountrail    EDs 31-1 to 31-59, 31-60 (NP), 31-61 to 31-66

Nelson    EDs 32-1 to 32-34

1740. Pembina    EDs 34-1 to 34-35

Pierce    EDs 35-1 to 35-32

Ramsey    EDs 36-1 to 36-48

Renville    EDs 38-1 to 38-30

1741. Ransom    EDs 37-1 to 37-28

Rolette    EDs 40-1 to 40-31

Richland    EDs 39-1 to 39-49

Slope    EDs 44-1 to 44-30, 44-31 (NP), 44-32 to 44-35

1742. Sargent    EDs 41-1 to 41-30

Sheridan    EDs 42-1 to 42-31

Sioux    EDs 43-1 to 43-3, 43-9, 43-19, 43-4 to 43-8, 43-10 to 43-18, 43-20 to 43-21, 43-22 to 43-23 (NP), 43-24 to 43-30, 43-31 (NP), 43-32 to 43-36, 43-37 (NP), 43-38 to 43-42, 43-43 (NP)

Stark    EDs 45-1 to 45-12, 45-14 to 45-15, 45-17 to 45-30, 45-16, 45-31 to 45-36, 45-13, 45-37 to 45-40, 45-46 to 45-47, 45-41 to 45-45, 45-48

Steele    EDs 46-1 to 46-24

1743. Stutsman    EDs 47-1 to 47-79

Towner    EDs 48-1 to 48-37

Traill    EDs 49-1 to 49-31

1744. Walsh    EDs 50-1 to 50-50

Ward    EDs 51-1 to 51-41, 51-48, 51-42 to 51-43, 51-77, 51-44, 51-49, 51-45 to 51-47, 51-76

1745. Ward    EDs 51-50 to 51-75

Wells    EDs 52-1 to 52-43

Williams    EDs 53-1 to 53-71

## Ohio

1746. Adams    EDs 1-1 to 1-5, 1-23, 1-6 to 1-22

Allen    EDs 2-1 to 2-22

1747. Allen    EDs 2-23 to 2-44

Ashtabula    EDs 4-1 to 4-2, 4-17 to 4-29

1748. Ashtabula    EDs 4-10, 4-12 to 4-16, 4-6 to 4-7, 4-11, 4-3 to 4-5, 4-8 to 4-9, 4-30 to 4-60

1749. Ashland    EDs 3-1 to 3-3, 3-6, 3-4 to 3-5, 3-7 to 3-28

Athens    EDs 5-1 to 5-11, 5-38, 5-12 to 5-21

1750. Athens    EDs 5-22 to 5-37

Belmont    EDs 7-1 to 7-13, 7-17 to 7-28

1751. Belmont    EDs 7-14 to 7-16, 7-29 to 7-60

1752. Belmont    EDs 7-61 to 7-66

Carroll    EDs 10-1 to 10-13, 10-16, 10-14 to 10-15, 10-17 to 10-22

Auglaize    EDs 6-1 to 6-29

1753. Brown    EDs 8-1 to 8-6, 8-18, 8-7 to 8-9, 8-29, 8-10 to 8-14, 8-30, 8-15 to 8-17, 8-19 to 8-28

Butler    EDs 9-1 to 9-3, 9-23, 9-48, 9-24, 9-4 to 9-13

1754. Butler    EDs 9-14 to 9-22, 9-25 to 9-29, 9-32 to 9-34, 9-38 to 9-40, 9-57

1755. Butler    EDs 9-30 to 9-31, 9-35 to 9-37, 9-41 to 9-47, 9-49, 9-56, 9-50, 9-54, 9-51 to 9-53, 9-55

Champaign    EDs 11-1 to 11-8, 11-10, 11-9, 11-11 to 11-26

1756. Clark    EDs 12-1 to 12-14, 12-20 to 12-25, 12-39 to 12-52

1757. Clark    EDs 12-26 to 12-38, 12-53 to 12-56, 12-15 to 12-19, 12-57 to 12-60

Clermont    EDs 13-1, 13-14, 13-2 to 13-5, 13-28, 13-6 to 13-10, 13-29

1758. Clermont    EDs 13-11 to 13-13, 13-15 to 13-19, 13-30, 13-20 to 13-27

Coshocton    EDs 16-1 to 16-32

Columbiana    EDs 15-1 to 15-5

1759. Columbiana    EDs 15-6 to 15-36

1760. Columbiana    EDs 15-37 to 15-56

Crawford    EDs 17-1 to 17-2, 17-12 to 17-13, 17-3 to 17-5, 17-40, 17-6 to 17-7, 17-41, 17-8, 17-42, 17-9 to 17-10, 17-43, 17-11, 17-14 to 17-29, 17-38, 17-30

1761. Crawford    EDs 17-31 to 17-37, 17-39

Clinton    EDs 14-1 to 14-24

Cuyahoga    EDs 18-534 to 18-540, 18-781, 18-541 to 18-553

1762. Cuyahoga, Cleveland City    EDs 18-1 to 18-18, 18-782 to 18-785, 18-19, 18-786, 18-20

1763. Cuyahoga, Cleveland City    EDs 18-21 to 18-28, 18-502, 18-29 to 18-33, 18-719, 18-34 to 18-35, 18-720, 18-36 to 18-39, 18-721, 18-40 to 18-45

1764. Cuyahoga, Cleveland City    EDs 18-46 to 18-50, 18-722, 18-723 (NP), 18-51 to 18-55, 18-56 (NP), 18-57 to 18-59, 18-724, 18-60 to 18-62, 18-787 to 18-788, 18-835, 18-63 to 18-65, 18-725, 18-66 to 18-71

1765. Cuyahoga, Cleveland City    EDs 18-72 to 18-74, 18-87 to 18-105, 18-119, 18-727, 18-120, 18-731, 18-121 to 18-123

1766. Cuyahoga, Cleveland City    EDs 18-124 to 18-125, 18-789, 18-126, 18-790 to 18-791, 18-127 to 18-128, 18-792, 18-730, 18-793, 18-129, 18-728 (NP), 18-130, 18-794, 18-131, 18-729, 18-132 to 18-134, 18-732, 18-135 to 18-136

1767. Cuyahoga, Cleveland City    EDs 18-75, 18-726, 18-76 to 18-86, 18-106 to 18-118

1768. Cuyahoga, Cleveland City    EDs 18-137, 18-733, 18-138 to 18-139, 18-734, 18-140, 18-735, 18-141 to 18-176

1769. Cuyahoga, Cleveland City    EDs 18-177 (NP), 18-736 to 18-737, 18-178 to 18-197, 18-198 (void), 18-199, 18-738 (NP), 18-200 to 18-202, 18-203 (NP), 18-204, 18-739 (NP), 18-205, 18-740, 18-206 to 18-207, 18-741 (NP), 18-208 to 18-219

1770. Cuyahoga, Cleveland City    EDs 18-220 to 18-223, 18-742, 18-224 to 18-240, 18-743, 18-241 to 18-243, 18-287 to 18-292

1771. Cuyahoga, Cleveland City    EDs 18-293 to 18-294, 18-752, 18-295, 18-297 to 18-299, 18-795, 18-296, 18-300 to 18-305, 18-753, 18-306, 18-754, 18-307 to 18-316

1772. Cuyahoga, Cleveland City    EDs 18-317 to 18-321, 18-354, 18-839, 18-355 to 18-360, 18-825 to 18-826, 18-361 to 18-370, 18-758, 18-431 to 18-432, 18-837, 18-433

1773. Cuyahoga, Cleveland City    EDs 18-434 to 18-443, 18-798, 18-444, 18-759, 18-445, 18-322 to 18-323, 18-840, 18-324 to 18-326, 18-755, 18-327 to 18-339, 18-756 (void)

1774. Cuyahoga, Cleveland City    EDs 18-340 to 18-345, 18-757, 18-346 to 18-353, 18-371 to 18-378, 18-838, 18-379 to 18-380, 18-796, 18-381 to 18-382, 18-383 (NP)

1775. Cuyahoga, Cleveland City    EDs 18-384 to 18-408, 18-797, 18-409 to 18-412

1776. Cuyahoga, Cleveland City    EDs 18-413 to 18-420, 18-421 (NP), 18-422 to 18-430, 18-446 to 18-455, 18-760, 18-456 to 18-458

1777. Cuyahoga, Cleveland City    EDs 18-459, 18-761, 18-460, 18-762, 18-461 to 18-466, 18-763, 18-467 to 18-471, 18-764, 18-472, 18-799 to 18-800, 18-765, 18-473 to 18-475, 18-820

1778. Cuyahoga, Cleveland City    EDs 18-476, 18-823, 18-477, 18-822, 18-478, 18-821, 18-479 to 18-482, 18-766 to 18-767, 18-483, 18-768, 18-484, 18-769, 18-485, 18-770, 18-486, 18-771, 18-487, 18-772, 18-488 to 18-490, 18-773, 18-830, 18-491

1779. Cuyahoga, Cleveland City    EDs 18-492 to 18-493, 18-827, 18-494 to 18-495, 18-828, 18-496, 18-774 (NP), 18-497 to 18-498, 18-829, 18-499 to 18-500, 18-501 (void), 18-503, 18-801, 18-504 to 18-507, 18-775, 18-508, 18-802

1780. Cuyahoga, Cleveland City    EDs 18-803, 18-509, 18-804, 18-510, 18-805 to 18-806, 18-511 to 18-512, 18-831, 18-807 to 18-808, 18-513, 18-809 to 18-812, 18-514, 18-832 to 18-833, 18-776, 18-515, 18-834, 18-516, 18-813

1781. Cuyahoga, Cleveland City    EDs 18-777, 18-778 (NP), 18-779, 18-244 to 18-252, 18-744, 18-253 to 18-255, 18-745 (NP), 18-256 to 18-264, 18-746, 18-517 to 18-519, 18-814, 18-520 to 18-521, 18-824, 18-522 to 18-527

1782. Cuyahoga, Cleveland City    EDs 18-528, 18-815, 18-529, 18-780, 18-530, 18-816 to 18-817, 18-531 to 18-532, 18-818, 18-533, 18-819, 18-265, 18-747, 18-266, 18-748, 18-267 to 18-278

1783. Cuyahoga, Cleveland City    EDs 18-749, 18-279 to 18-284, 18-750, 18-285, 18-751, 18-286, 18-554 to 18-569

1784. Cuyahoga    EDs 18-570 to 18-594

1785. Cuyahoga    EDs 18-595 to 18-624

1786. Cuyahoga    EDs 18-625 to 18-645, 18-657 to 18-664

1787. Cuyahoga    EDs 18-646 to 18-651, 18-652 (void), 18-653 to 18-656, 18-665 to 18-672, 18-836, 18-673 to 18-684, 18-693 to 18-699

1788. Cuyahoga    EDs 18-685 to 18-692, 18-709 to 18-718, 18-700 to 18-708

Darke    EDs 19-1 to 19-12, 19-22, 19-13 to 19-14

1789. Darke    EDs 19-15 to 19-21, 19-23 to 19-45

Defiance    EDs 20-1 to 20-25

1790. Delaware    EDs 21-1 to 21-29

Erie    EDs 22-1 to 22-2, 22-26, 22-3, 22-14 to 22-18, 22-28 to 22-29, 22-19 to 22-23

1791. Erie    EDs 22-4 to 22-8, 22-27, 22-9 to 22-13, 22-24 to 22-25

Fairfield    EDs 23-1 to 23-26, 23-36, 23-27 to 23-30

1792. Fairfield    EDs 23-31 to 23-35, 23-37 to 23-39

Fayette    EDs 24-1 to 24-20

Franklin    EDs 25-171 to 25-176, 25-241, 25-177 to 25-181, 25-184 to 25-186

1793. Franklin    EDs 25-182 to 25-183, 25-187 to 25-193, 25-194 (NP), 25-199, 25-216, 25-195 to 25-198, 25-200 to 25-203

Franklin, Columbus City    EDs 25-1 to 25-8

1794.   Franklin, Columbus City   EDs 25-9 to 25-10, 25-21 to 25-27, 25-49 to 25-55, 25-224, 25-56

1795.   Franklin, Columbus City   EDs 25-11 to 25-20, 25-28 to 25-39

1796.   Franklin, Columbus City   EDs 25-40 to 25-45, 25-243, 25-46 to 25-48, 25-223, 25-57 to 25-70

1797.   Franklin, Columbus City   EDs 25-71 to 25-85, 25-94 to 25-95, 25-229

1798.   Franklin, Columbus City   EDs 25-96, 25-230, 25-97, 25-244, 25-98, 25-231, 25-99, 25-245, 25-232, 25-100, 25-86, 25-225, 25-87 to 25-88, 25-226, 25-89, 25-227, 25-90 to 25-92, 25-228, 25-93

1799.   Franklin, Columbus City   EDs 25-101 to 25-125

1800.   Franklin, Columbus City   EDs 25-126 to 25-145, 25-233, 25-146, 25-234, 25-147

1801.   Franklin, Columbus City   EDs 25-148, 25-242, 25-149 to 25-164, 25-235 to 25-237, 25-165

1802.   Franklin, Columbus City   EDs 25-238 to 25-239, 25-166, 25-240, 25-167 to 25-170

Franklin   EDs 25-204 to 25-207, 25-222, 25-208 to 25-215, 25-217 to 25-221

Fulton   EDs 26-1 to 26-6

1803.   Fulton   EDs 26-7 to 26-9, 26-19, 26-10 to 26-18, 26-21, 26-20, 26-22

Gallia   EDs 27-1 to 27-25

Geauga   EDs 28-1 to 28-20

1804.   Greene   EDs 29-1 to 29-10, 29-21 to 29-30, 29-11 to 29-20

Guernsey   EDs 30-1 to 30-11, 30-43, 30-17 to 30-18

1805.   Guernsey   EDs 30-12, 30-29, 30-40, 30-13 to 30-16, 30-19 to 30-28, 30-30 to 30-39, 30-41 to 30-42

Hamilton   EDs 31-292 to 31-294

Hamilton, Cincinnati City   EDs 31-1 to 31-2, 31-395, 31-3 to 31-4, 31-396, 31-5 to 31-6, 31-397, 31-7, 31-398 to 31-399, 31-8 to 31-9

1806.   Hamilton, Cincinnati City   EDs 31-10, 31-400 to 31-401, 31-11, 31-402, 31-12 to 31-14, 31-403 to 31-404, 31-15, 31-405 to 31-407, 31-16, 31-408 to 31-409, 31-17 to 31-18, 31-410, 31-19, 31-411, 31-20, 31-412, 31-21 to 31-22, 31-413, 31-23, 31-414, 31-24, 31-415, 31-25, 31-416 to 31-417

1807.   Hamilton, Cincinnati City   EDs 31-26 to 31-27, 31-418, 31-28, 31-419, 31-29, 31-420, 31-30 to 31-35, 31-421, 31-36 to 31-38, 31-422, 31-39 to 31-40, 31-423, 31-41, 31-424, 31-42 to 31-43, 31-425, 31-44, 31-426, 31-45, 31-427, 31-46, 31-428, 31-47 to 31-49, 31-429 to 31-430, 31-50 to 31-51, 31-431, 31-52 to 31-53, 31-432

1808.   Hamilton, Cincinnati City   EDs 31-54 to 31-55, 31-433, 31-56 to 31-59, 31-434, 31-60 to 31-63, 31-435 (NP), 31-436, 31-64 to 31-68, 31-437, 31-69 to 31-70, 31-438, 31-71 to 31-76, 31-439 to 31-441, 31-77, 31-442, 31-78, 31-443, 31-79 to 31-80, 31-444, 31-81 to 31-82, 31-445 to 31-446, 31-83

1809.   Hamilton, Cincinnati City   EDs 31-84, 31-85 (NP), 31-447 to 31-448, 31-86 to 31-89, 31-449 to 31-450, 31-90, 31-451, 31-91 to 31-93, 31-452, 31-94, 31-453, 31-106 to 31-108, 31-464, 31-109, 31-465, 31-110 to 31-114, 31-466, 31-115 to 31-116, 31-467, 31-117 to 31-118, 31-468, 31-119, 31-469, 31-120 to 31-123, 31-470 to 31-471

1810.   Hamilton, Cincinnati City   EDs 31-95, 31-454 to 31-455, 31-96, 31-456, 31-97 to 31-98, 31-457, 31-99, 31-458, 31-100, 31-459 to 31-460, 31-101 to 31-102, 31-461, 31-103, 31-462, 31-104, 31-463, 31-105, 31-124, 31-472, 31-125 to 31-126, 31-473, 31-127 to 31-131, 31-474 to 31-475, 31-132 to 31-133, 31-476 to 31-477, 31-134, 31-478, 31-135 to 31-136, 31-479 to 31-480, 31-137

1811.   Hamilton, Cincinnati City   EDs 31-138 to 31-140, 31-481, 31-141 to 31-142, 31-482 to 31-483, 31-144 to 31-147, 31-484, 31-148, 31-485, 31-149 to 31-150, 31-486 to 31-487, 31-151, 31-488, 31-152 to 31-153, 31-489, 31-154 to 31-155, 31-490

1812.   Hamilton, Cincinnati City   EDs 31-156 to 31-159, 31-491, 31-160 to 31-161, 31-492, 31-162 to 31-163, 31-493, 31-164, 31-494, 31-165 to 31-167, 31-495, 31-168 to 31-173, 31-496, 31-174, 31-497, 31-175, 31-498, 31-176 to 31-179, 31-499, 31-180, 31-500, 31-181 to 31-182, 31-501, 31-183 to 31-184, 31-502, 31-185, 31-503, 31-186 to 31-187, 31-504, 31-188

1813.   Hamilton, Cincinnati City   EDs 31-189 to 31-191, 31-505, 31-192 to 31-195, 31-506, 31-196 to 31-197, 31-507, 31-198, 31-508, 31-199 to 31-202, 31-509, 31-203, 31-510, 31-204 to 31-209, 31-511, 31-210, 31-512, 31-211 to 31-212, 31-513, 31-213 to 31-217, 31-514

1814.   Hamilton, Cincinnati City   EDs 31-218 to 31-219, 31-515, 31-220 to 31-221, 31-516 to 31-517, 31-222, 31-518, 31-223, 31-519 to 31-520, 31-224, 31-521 to 31-522, 31-225 to 31-226, 31-523, 31-227, 31-524, 31-228, 31-525 to 31-526, 31-229 to 31-230, 31-527, 31-340, 31-231 to 31-236, 31-528, 31-237, 31-529, 31-238, 31-530

1815.   Hamilton, Cincinnati City   EDs 31-239 to 31-244, 31-531 to 31-532, 31-245, 31-533, 31-257, 31-543, 31-258 to 31-259, 31-544 to 31-546, 31-260 to 31-261, 31-547, 31-262, 31-548, 31-263, 31-549 to 31-550, 31-264, 31-551, 31-265 to 31-266, 31-552 to 31-553, 31-267, 31-554 to 31-555, 31-268 to 31-269, 31-556

1816.   Hamilton, Cincinnati City   EDs 31-246, 31-534, 31-247, 31-535, 31-248 to 31-253, 31-536 to 31-537, 31-254, 31-538, 31-255, 31-539 to 31-541, 31-256, 31-542, 31-270, 31-557 to 31-558, 31-271 to 31-273, 31-559, 31-274 to 31-275, 31-560 to 31-562, 31-276, 31-563, 31-277 to 31-278, 31-564, 31-279, 31-565, 31-280, 31-566

1817.   Hamilton, Cincinnati City   EDs 31-281 to 31-282, 31-567, 31-283 to 31-284, 31-568, 31-285 to 31-286, 31-569 to 31-570, 31-287 to 31-288, 31-571 to 31-573, 31-289 to 31-291, 31-574 to 31-576

Hamilton   EDs 31-295 to 31-299, 31-308 to 31-314

1818.   Hamilton   EDs 31-300 to 31-306, 31-307 (NP), 31-315, 31-378, 31-316 to 31-318, 31-383, 31-319 to 31-339, 31-341 to 31-350

1819.   Hamilton   EDs 31-351 to 31-358, 31-374, 31-359 to 31-360, 31-377, 31-361 to 31-373, 31-143, 31-375 to 31-376, 31-379 to 31-381

1820.   Hamilton   EDs 31-382, 31-384 to 31-388, 31-338, 31-389 to 31-394

Hancock   EDs 32-1 to 32-11, 32-23 to 32-31, 32-12 to 32-22, 32-32 to 32-36, 32-38, 32-37, 32-39

1821.   Hardin   EDs 33-1 to 33-32

Harrison   EDs 34-1 to 34-25

Henry   EDs 35-1 to 35-6, 35-21, 35-7 to 35-8

1822.   Henry   EDs 35-9, 35-12, 35-18 to 35-19, 35-10 to 35-11, 35-13 to 35-17, 35-20, 35-22 to 35-25

Hocking   EDs 37-1 to 37-18

Holmes   EDs 38-1 to 38-7, 38-19, 38-8 to 38-18, 38-20

1823.   Highland   EDs 36-1 to 36-27

Huron   EDs 39-9 to 39-10, 39-1 to 39-8, 39-11, 39-15, 39-12 to 39-14, 39-34, 39-16 to 39-23

1824.   Huron   EDs 39-24 to 39-33

Jefferson   EDs 41-1 to 41-10, 41-18, 41-11 to 41-12, 41-21, 41-13 to 41-17, 41-19 to 41-20, 41-22 to 41-27, 41-33 to 41-37

1825.   Jefferson   EDs 41-28 to 41-32, 41-38 to 41-45, 41-55 to 41-56, 41-46 to 41-54, 41-57 to 41-58

Knox   EDs 42-1 to 42-5, 42-14 to 42-23

1826.  Knox    EDs 42-6 to 42-13, 42-24 to 42-29, 42-36, 42-30 to 42-35, 42-37

Lake    EDs 43-1 to 43-5, 43-12, 43-6, 43-28, 43-7 to 43-11, 43-13 to 43-24, 43-32

1827.  Lake    EDs 43-25 to 43-27, 43-33, 43-35, 43-29 to 43-31, 43-34

Lawrence    EDs 44-1 to 44-4, 44-10, 44-5 to 44-9, 44-11 to 44-30

1828.  Jackson    EDs 40-1 to 40-7, 40-15, 40-8 to 40-14, 40-16 to 40-23

Licking    EDs 45-1 to 45-22, 45-29 to 45-33

1829.  Licking    EDs 45-23 to 45-28, 45-34 to 45-52

Logan    EDs 46-1 to 46-3, 46-23, 46-4 to 46-16

1830.  Logan    EDs 46-17 to 46-19, 46-25, 46-20 to 46-22, 46-24, 46-26 to 46-33, 46-36, 46-34 to 46-35

Lorain    EDs 47-1, 47-75, 47-2 to 47-20, 47-24 to 47-26

1831.  Lorain    EDs 47-21 to 47-23, 47-27 to 47-33, 47-42 to 47-44, 47-76 to 47-77, 47-34 to 47-41, 47-45 to 47-46, 47-78 to 47-79, 47-47 to 47-50, 47-53, 47-51 to 47-52

1832.  Lorain    EDs 47-54 to 47-61, 47-80, 47-62 to 47-74

Lucas    EDs 48-159 to 48-178

1833.  Lucas, Toledo City    EDs 48-1 to 48-5, 48-197, 48-6 to 48-7, 48-198, 48-8 to 48-12, 48-199, 48-13 to 48-16, 48-200, 48-17 to 48-21, 48-201, 48-22

1834.  Lucas, Toledo City    EDs 48-23 to 48-34, 48-202, 48-35 to 48-37, 48-203, 48-38 to 48-42, 48-204, 48-43, 48-205, 48-44 to 48-45

1835.  Lucas, Toledo City    EDs 48-46 to 48-63, 48-206, 48-64, 48-207, 48-65 to 48-68, 48-101, 48-69 to 48-73, 48-258

1836.  Lucas, Toledo City    EDs 48-74 to 48-75, 48-208, 48-76, 48-209, 48-77, 48-210, 48-78 to 48-81, 48-259, 48-82, 48-211, 48-83, 48-212, 48-84, 48-213 to 48-217, 48-85, 48-218, 48-260 to 48-261, 48-86 to 48-88, 48-219, 48-262, 48-89 to 48-90, 48-220, 48-263

1837.  Lucas, Toledo City    EDs 48-91, 48-221, 48-92, 48-222, 48-93, 48-223 to 48-224, 48-94, 48-225, 48-95 to 48-96, 48-226, 48-264, 48-97 to 48-98, 48-227 to 48-228, 48-99 to 48-100, 48-102 to 48-103, 48-229, 48-104, 48-230, 48-105, 48-231, 48-106, 48-265, 48-107 to 48-109, 48-232, 48-110

1838.  Lucas, Toledo City    EDs 48-111 to 48-113, 48-122, 48-239, 48-123, 48-240, 48-124 to 48-125, 48-241, 48-126 to 48-127, 48-242 , 48-128, 48-243, 48-114, 48-233 to 48-234, 48-115 to 48-117, 48-235, 48-118 to 48-120, 48-236 to 48-237, 48-121, 48-238

1839.  Lucas, Toledo City    EDs 48-129 to 48-131, 48-244, 48-132, 48-245, 48-133, 48-246, 48-134 to 48-135, 48-247, 48-136, 48-248, 48-137, 48-249, 48-138 to 48-141, 48-250, 48-142, 48-251, 48-143 to 48-144, 48-252, 48-145, 48-253, 48-146, 48-254, 48-147 to 48-149

1840.  Lucas, Toledo City    EDs 48-255, 48-150 to 48-156, 48-256, 48-157 to 48-158, 48-257

Lucas    EDs 48-179 to 48-183, 48-191 to 48-196

1841.  Lucas    EDs 48-184 to 48-190

Mahoning    EDs 50-94 to 50-99, 50-132, 50-100 to 50-118

1842.  Mahoning    EDs 50-119 to 50-130, 50-131 (void), 50-133 to 50-142

Mahoning, Youngstown City    EDs 50-1 to 50-16

1843.  Mahoning, Youngstown City    EDs 50-17 to 50-38

1844.  Mahoning, Youngstown City    EDs 50-39 to 50-56

1845.  Mahoning, Youngstown City    EDs 50-57 to 50-62, 50-71 to 50-86

1846.  Mahoning, Youngstown City    EDs 50-87 to 50-93, 50-63 to 50-67, 50-143 to 50-144, 50-68 to 50-70

1847.  Madison    EDs 49-1 to 49-28

Marion    EDs 51-1 to 51-21

1848.  Marion    EDs 51-22 to 51-40

Medina    EDs 52-1 to 52-9, 52-29, 52-10 to 52-28

Miami    EDs 55-1 to 55-2

1849.  Miami    EDs 55-3 to 55-39

1850.  Meigs    EDs 53-1 to 53-26

Mercer    EDs 54-1 to 54-9, 54-23, 54-10 to 54-22, 54-24 to 54-27

1851.  Monroe    EDs 56-1 to 56-11, 56-24, 56-12 to 56-23, 56-25 to 56-29

Montgomery    EDs 57-134 to 57-136, 57-185, 57-137 to 57-141

Montgomery, Dayton City    EDs 57-1 to 57-13

1852.  Montgomery, Dayton City    EDs 57-23 to 57-24, 57-204, 57-25 to 57-28, 57-205, 57-29 to 57-37, 57-48 to 57-56, 57-58 to 57-62

1853.  Montgomery, Dayton City    EDs 57-77 to 57-97, 57-14 to 57-22, 57-38 to 57-40

1854.  Montgomery, Dayton City    EDs 57-41 to 57-44, 57-206, 57-45 to 57-46, 57-207, 57-47, 57-63 to 57-75, 57-76 (NP), 57-114 to 57-123

1855.  Montgomery, Dayton City    EDs 57-98 to 57-104, 57-208, 57-105 to 57-113, 57-124 to 57-133, 57-209, 57-57, 57-210 to 57-214

1856.  Montgomery, Dayton City    EDs 57-178 to 57-179, 57-188, 57-192, 57-215 to 57-224, 57-142 to 57-143, 57-186, 57-144 to 57-147, 57-187, 57-189, 57-148 to 57-149, 57-169, 57-150 to 57-155, 57-190 to 57-191

1857.  Montgomery, Dayton City    EDs 57-156 to 57-158, 57-193, 57-159 to 57-162, 57-194 to 57-197, 57-163 to 57-168, 57-198, 57-170 to 57-174, 57-199, 57-175 to 57-177, 57-200, 57-180 to 57-181, 57-201 to 57-203, 57-182 to 57-184

Morgan    EDs 58-1 to 58-10

1858.  Morgan    EDs 58-11 to 58-19

Morrow    EDs 59-1 to 59-11, 59-23, 59-12 to 59-22

Muskingum    EDs 60-1 to 60-7, 60-55, 60-8 to 60-34

1859.  Muskingum    EDs 60-35 to 60-36, 60-41 to 60-46, 60-53, 60-47 to 60-49, 60-54, 60-37 to 60-40, 60-50 to 60-52

Noble    EDs 61-1 to 61-9, 61-11, 61-10, 61-12 to 61-15, 61-16 (void), 61-17 to 61-23

1860.  Ottawa    EDs 62-1 to 62-11, 62-23, 62-12 to 62-22

Paulding    EDs 63-1 to 63-2, 63-15, 63-3 to 63-14, 63-16 to 63-24

Perry    EDs 64-1, 64-18, 64-2 to 64-9

1861.  Perry    EDs 64-10 to 64-13, 64-31, 64-14 to 64-17, 64-19 to 64-30

Pike    EDs 66-1, 66-6, 66-2 to 66-5, 66-7 to 66-18

Portage    EDs 67-1 to 67-12

1862.  Portage    EDs 67-13 to 67-35

Pickaway    EDs 65-1 to 65-27

1863.  Preble    EDs 68-1 to 68-14, 68-21, 68-15 to 68-20, 68-22 to 68-30

Richland    EDs 70-1 to 70-22

1864.  Richland    EDs 70-23 to 70-47

Ross    EDs 71-1 to 71-18, 71-29 to 71-30

1865.  Ross    EDs 71-19 to 71-28, 71-31

Putnam    EDs 69-1 to 69-30

1866.  Sandusky    EDs 72-1, 72-30 to 72-31, 72-2 to 72-16, 72-25, 72-17 to 72-24, 72-26 to 72-29, 72-32

Scioto    EDs 73-1 to 73-4, 73-9 to 73-11

1867. Scioto   EDs 73-5 to 73-8, 73-12 to 73-24, 73-29 to 73-32, 73-40 to 73-47

1868. Scioto   EDs 73-25 to 73-28, 73-48, 73-33 to 73-35, 73-49, 73-36 to 73-39

Seneca   EDs 74-1 to 74-20

1869. Seneca   EDs 74-21 to 74-39

Stark   EDs 76-1 to 76-2

Stark, Canton City   EDs 76-3 to 76-8, 76-23 to 76-30

1870. Stark, Canton City   EDs 76-31 to 76-41, 76-50 to 76-54, 76-9 to 76-22

1871. Stark, Canton City   EDs 76-42 to 76-48, 76-49 (NP), 76-55 to 76-58, 76-134, 76-136, 76-59 to 76-60, 76-68 to 76-83

1872. Stark   EDs 76-135, 76-61 to 76-67, 76-84 to 76-93, 76-115 to 76-116, 76-121 to 76-123, 76-94 to 76-111

1873. Stark   EDs 76-112 to 76-114, 76-117 to 76-120, 76-124 to 76-133

Shelby   EDs 75-1 to 75-7, 75-10, 75-8 to 75-9, 75-11 to 75-27

1874. Summit, Akron City   EDs 77-1 to 77-2, 77-225, 77-3 to 77-22

1875. Summit, Akron City   EDs 77-23 to 77-54

1876. Summit, Akron City   EDs 77-55 to 77-63, 77-226 to 77-227, 77-64 to 77-73

1877. Summit, Akron City   EDs 77-74 to 77-97

1878. Summit, Akron City   EDs 77-98 to 77-114, 77-228, 77-115 to 77-116, 77-219 to 77-221

1879. Summit, Akron City   EDs 77-222 to 77-224, 77-117 to 77-119, 77-229, 77-120 to 77-134

1880. Summit, Akron City   EDs 77-135 to 77-139, 77-230, 77-140 to 77-153, 77-214, 77-154 to 77-155, 77-215 to 77-218

1881. Summit   EDs 77-156 to 77-158, 77-210, 77-159 to 77-160, 77-211, 77-161 to 77-163, 77-212, 77-164 to 77-165, 77-213, 77-166, 77-168 to 77-169, 77-167, 77-170, 77-231, 77-171 to 77-181

1882. Summit   EDs 77-182 to 77-187, 77-189, 77-188, 77-233, 77-190 to 77-196, 77-203, 77-197 to 77-201, 77-209, 77-202, 77-206, 77-204 to 77-205, 77-207 to 77-208, 77-232

Trumbull   EDs 78-1 to 78-15

1883. Trumbull   EDs 78-19 to 78-36, 78-16 to 78-18, 78-37 to 78-39

1884. Trumbull   EDs 78-40 to 78-55

Trumbull, Youngstown City   EDs 78-56 to 78-69

1885. Tuscarawas   EDs 79-1 to 79-11, 79-59, 79-12 to 79-15, 79-25 to 79-29, 79-39 to 79-41, 79-16 to 79-24, 79-58, 79-42 to 79-54

1886. Tuscarawas   EDs 79-30 to 79-38, 79-55 to 79-57

Union   EDs 80-1 to 80-24

Vinton   EDs 82-1 to 82-16

Washington   EDs 84-1 to 84-5, 84-8 to 84-10

1887. Washington   EDs 84-6 to 84-7, 84-36, 84-11 to 84-27, 84-37, 84-28 to 84-35

Wayne   EDs 85-1, 85-9, 85-2, 85-20, 85-3 to 85-4, 85-13, 85-5 to 85-8, 85-10 to 85-12

1888. Wayne   EDs 85-14 to 85-19, 85-21 to 85-29, 85-32 to 85-38, 85-30 to 85-31

Wood   EDs 87-1 to 87-4, 87-40, 87-5 to 87-15, 87-55, 87-16 to 87-18, 87-22, 87-41, 87-23

1889. Wood   EDs 87-19 to 87-21, 87-24 to 87-39, 87-42 to 87-46, 87-53 to 87-54, 87-47 to 87-52

Wyandot   EDs 88-1, 88-6, 88-2 to 88-5, 88-7 to 88-8, 88-12, 88-9 to 88-11, 88-13 to 88-26

1890. Van Wert   EDs 81-1 to 81-4, 81-26, 81-5 to 81-25, 81-27

1890. Warren   EDs 83-1 to 83-10, 83-23, 83-11 to 83-22, 83-24 to 83-28

1891. Williams   EDs 86-1 to 86-25

## Oklahoma

1892. Adair   EDs 1-1 to 1-12

Beaver   EDs 4-1 to 4-21

Alfalfa   EDs 2-1 to 2-30

Atoka   EDs 3-1 to 3-10

1893. Atoka   EDs 3-11 to 3-18

Blaine   EDs 6-1 to 6-6, 6-7 (NP), 6-8 to 6-29

Beckham   EDs 5-1 to 5-26

1894. Bryan   EDs 7-1 to 7-35

Caddo   EDs 8-1 to 8-25

1895. Caddo   EDs 8-26 to 8-55

Canadian   EDs 9-1 to 9-23, 9-24 (NP), 9-25 to 9-32

1896. Carter   EDs 10-1 to 10-21, 10-26, 10-22 to 10-25, 10-27 to 10-34

Cotton   EDs 17-1 to 17-16

1897. Cherokee   EDs 11-1 to 11-7, 11-16, 11-21, 11-8 to 11-15, 11-17 to 11-20, 11-22 to 11-24

Cimarron   EDs 13-1 to 13-11

Choctaw   EDs 12-1 to 12-27

1898. Cleveland   EDs 14-1 to 14-25

Coal   EDs 15-1 to 15-18

Dewey   EDs 22-1 to 22-27

1899. Comanche   EDs 16-1 to 16-23, 16-37, 16-24 to 16-36

Craig   EDs 18-1 to 18-24

1900. Creek   EDs 19-1 to 19-11, 19-22 to 19-26, 19-28 to 19-33, 19-16 to 19-21, 19-35 to 19-53

1901. Creek   EDs 19-12 to 19-15, 19-27, 19-34, 19-54 to 19-59

Ellis   EDs 23-1 to 23-25

Custer   EDs 20-1 to 20-29

1902. Delaware   EDs 21-1 to 21-20

Harper   EDs 30-1 to 30-18

Garfield   EDs 24-9 to 24-30

1903. Garfield   EDs 24-1 to 24-8, 24-31 to 24-65

Garvin   EDs 25-1 to 25-30

1904. Grady   EDs 26-1 to 26-5, 26-40, 26-6 to 26-39

1905. Grant   EDs 27-1 to 27-33

Greer   EDs 28-1 to 28-8, 28-14, 28-9 to 28-13, 28-21, 28-15 to 28-20

Harmon   EDs 29-1 to 29-14

1906. Haskell   EDs 31-1 to 31-18

Love   EDs 43-1 to 43-14

Hughes   EDs 32-1 to 32-27

1907. Hughes   EDs 32-28 to 32-32

Jefferson   EDs 34-1 to 34-24

Jackson   EDs 33-1 to 33-29

1908. Johnson   EDs 35-1 to 35-25

Latimer   EDs 39-1 to 39-13

Kay   EDs 36-1 to 36-27

1909. Kay   EDs 36-28 to 36-55

Kingfisher   EDs 37-1 to 37-15, 37-29, 37-16 to 37-28

Kiowa   EDs 38-1 to 38-5

1910.  Kiowa   EDs 38-6 to 38-31

Le Flore   EDs 40-1 to 40-25

1911.  Le Flore   EDs 40-26 to 40-42

Lincoln   EDs 41-1 to 41-49

1912.  Logan   EDs 42-1 to 42-37

McClain   EDs 44-1 to 44-5, 44-16, 44-6 to 44-10, 44-17, 44-11 to 44-15

1913.  McCurtain   EDs 45-1 to 45-26, 45-36 to 45-37, 45-27 to 45-35

Mayes   EDs 49-1 to 49-23

1914.  McIntosh   EDs 46-1 to 46-26

Major   EDs 47-1 to 47-19

Murray   EDs 50-1 to 50-17

1915.  Marshall   EDs 48-1 to 48-14

Noble   EDs 52-1 to 52-29

Muskogee   EDs 51-1 to 51-26, 51-48 to 51-50

1916.  Muskogee   EDs 51-31 to 51-47, 51-27 to 51-30, 51-51 to 51-61

Nowata   EDs 53-1 to 53-17

1917.  Okfuskee   EDs 54-1 to 54-29

Oklahoma   EDs 55-1 to 55-22

1918.  Oklahoma, Oklahoma City   EDs 55-23 to 55-28, 55-145 to 55-148, 55-161 to 55-162, 55-149 to 55-151, 55-29 to 55-54, 55-152 to 55-153

1919.  Oklahoma, Oklahoma City   EDs 55-55 to 55-68, 55-73, 55-69 to 55-72, 55-74 to 55-79, 55-154 to 55-156, 55-80 to 55-85, 55-92

1920.  Oklahoma, Oklahoma City   EDs 55-86 to 55-91, 55-93 to 55-118, 55-157, 55-119 to 55-132, 55-134

1921.  Oklahoma, Oklahoma City   EDs 55-133, 55-135 to 55-144, 55-158 to 55-160

Okmulgee   EDs 56-1 to 56-22, 56-43

1922.  Okmulgee   EDs 56-23 to 56-42, 56-44

Osage   EDs 57-1 to 57-22

1923.  Osage   EDs 57-23 to 57-44

Ottawa   EDs 58-1 to 58-30

1924.  Ottawa   EDs 58-31 to 58-38

Pawnee   EDs 59-1 to 59-21, 59-27 to 59-28, 59-22 to 59-26, 59-29 to 59-32

Rogers   EDs 66-1 to 66-23

1925.  Payne   EDs 60-1 to 60-5, 60-19, 60-6 to 60-18, 60-20 to 60-27, 60-33, 60-28 to 60-32, 60-34

Texas   EDs 70-1 to 70-29

1926.  Pittsburg   EDs 61-1 to 61-50

1927.  Pontotoc   EDs 62-1 to 62-33

Woods   EDs 76-1 to 76-32

1928.  Pottawatomie   EDs 63-1 to 63-16, 63-56, 63-17 to 63-33, 63-40, 63-58, 63-41 to 63-53

1929.  Pottawatomie   EDs 63-34 to 63-38, 63-57, 63-39, 63-54 to 63-55

Woodward   EDs 77-1 to 77-27

Pushmataha   EDs 64-1 to 64-18

Roger Mills   EDs 65-1 to 65-15, 65-22, 65-16 to 65-21

1930.  Seminole   EDs 67-1 to 67-24, 67-30 to 67-33

1931.  Seminole   EDs 67-25 to 67-29, 67-34 to 67-40

Sequoyah   EDs 68-1 to 68-28

Stephens   EDs 69-1 to 69-3, 69-8 to 69-9, 69-12 to 69-13

1932.  Stephens   EDs 69-4 to 69-5, 69-28, 69-6 to 69-7, 69-10 to 69-11, 69-14 to 69-23, 69-29, 69-24 to 69-27

Tillman   EDs 71-1 to 71-28

1933.  Tulsa   EDs 72-1 to 72-21, 72-29 to 72-31, 72-22, 72-183, 72-23, 72-184 (NP), 72-24 to 72-28, 72-32 to 72-39, 72-185, 72-40 to 72-42, 72-179 to 72-180, 72-186, 72-181 to 72-182

1934.  Tulsa, Tulsa City   EDs 72-43 to 72-78

1935.  Tulsa, Tulsa City   EDs 72-79 to 72-123

1936.  Tulsa, Tulsa City   EDs 72-124 to 72-156

1937.  Tulsa, Tulsa City   EDs 72-157 to 72-177, 72-178 (NP)

Wagoner   EDs 73-1 to 73-25

1938.  Washington   EDs 74-1 to 74-22

Washita   EDs 75-1 to 75-32

## *Oregon*

1939.  Baker   EDs 1-1 to 1-15, 1-18 to 1-42, 1-16, 1-43, 1-17, 1-44 to 1-48

Crook   EDs 7-1 to 7-20

Curry   EDs 8-1 to 8-16

Benton   EDs 2-1 to 2-34

Grant   EDs 12-1 to 12-5, 12-16, 12-6 to 12-15, 12-17 to 12-30

1940.  Clackamas   EDs 3-1 to 3-18, 3-19 (void), 3-20 to 3-104, 3-105 (NP)

Jefferson   EDs 16-1 to 16-14, 16-16 (NP), 16-15 (NP), 16-19, 16-17 to 16-18

1941.  Clatsop   EDs 4-1 to 4-46

Columbia   EDs 5-1 to 5-7, 5-42, 5-8 to 5-19, 5-21, 5-23, 5-20, 5-22, 5-24 to 5-34, 5-36, 5-35, 5-37 to 5-41

Gilliam   EDs 11-1 to 11-7, 11-16, 11-21, 11-8 to 11-15, 11-17 to 11-20, 11-22 to 11-24

1942.  Coos   EDs 6-1 to 6-40, 6-42 to 6-43, 6-41, 6-44 to 6-60

Deschutes   EDs 9-1 to 9-33

Hood River   EDs 14-1 to 14-14

1943.  Douglas   EDs 10-1, 10-66, 10-2 to 10-13, 10-46, 10-49, 10-14 to 10-26, 10-60, 10-27 to 10-28, 10-63, 10-29 to 10-44, 10-55, 10-45, 10-47 to 10-48, 10-70, 10-50 to 10-54, 10-56 to 10-57, 10-58 (NP), 10-59, 10-61 to 10-62, 10-68, 10-64 to 10-65, 10-69, 10-67

Harney   EDs 13-1 to 13-2, 13-17 to 13-18, 13-23 to 13-24, 13-19, 13-3 to 13-10, 13-25, 13-11 to 13-14, 13-29 to 13-30, 13-15 to 13-16, 13-20 to 13-22, 13-26 to 13-28

Josephine   EDs 17-1 to 17-26

Lake   EDs 19-2 to 19-3, 19-1 (NP), 19-4 to 19-9, 19-11, 19-22, 19-10, 19-12 to 19-21

1944.  Jackson   EDs 15-1 to 15-16, 15-18, 15-17, 15-19 to 15-31, 15-33, 15-32, 15-34 to 15-52, 15-54, 15-53, 15-55 to 15-62, 15-64, 15-63, 15-65 to 15-70

Lincoln   EDs 21-1 to 21-20, 21-22, 21-24, 21-21, 21-23, 21-25 to 21-37

Morrow   EDs 25-1 to 25-15, 25-18, 25-16 to 25-17, 25-19

1945.  Klamath   EDs 18-1 to 18-7, 18-61, 18-8 to 18-9, 18-10 (NP), 18-11 to 18-44, 18-59, 18-45 to 18-58, 18-60, 18-62, 18-64 to 18-67, 18-63

Malheur   EDs 23-1 to 23-25, 23-37, 23-26, 23-38, 23-27 to 23-36, 23-39

1946.  Lane   EDs 20-1 to 20-25, 20-63 to 20-86, 20-88, 20-87, 20-89 to 20-105, 20-26 to 20-62, 20-106 to 20-121

1947. Linn   EDs 22-1 to 22-16, 22-29, 22-47, 22-63, 22-17 to 22-18, 22-65, 22-19 to 22-27, 22-33, 22-51, 22-28, 22-30 to 22-31, 22-49, 22-32, 22-34, 22-52, 22-35 to 22-46, 22-48, 22-50, 22-53 to 22-62, 22-64, 22-66

Marion   EDs 24-1 to 24-15, 24-90, 24-16 to 24-17, 24-92, 24-18 to 24-20, 24-94, 24-21 to 24-25, 24-80, 24-26 to 24-27, 24-98, 24-28 to 24-46, 24-86, 24-47 to 24-51

1948. Marion   EDs 24-52 to 24-79, 24-81 to 24-85, 24-87 to 24-89, 24-91, 24-93, 24-96, 24-95, 24-97, 24-99

Polk   EDs 27-1 to 27-7, 27-18, 27-36, 27-38, 27-8 to 27-9, 27-23, 27-31, 27-33, 27-10 to 27-17, 27-19 to 27-22, 27-24 to 27-25, 27-27, 27-26, 27-28 to 27-30, 27-32, 27-34 to 27-35, 27-37, 27-39 to 27-45

1949. Multnomah, Portland City   EDs 26-1 to 26-85

1950. Multnomah, Portland City   EDs 26-86 to 26-98, 26-99 (NP), 26-100 to 26-167

1951. Multnomah, Portland City   EDs 26-168 to 26-219, 26-271 to 26-304

1952. Multnomah, Portland City   EDs 26-305 to 26-391

1953. Multnomah, Portland City   EDs 26-392 to 26-474

1954. Multnomah, Portland City   EDs 26-475 to 26-553

1955. Multnomah   EDs 26-220 to 26-242, 26-244, 26-246, 26-243, 26-245, 26-247 to 26-270

Sherman   EDs 28-1 to 28-11

Tillamook   EDs 29-1 to 29-40

1956. Umatilla   EDs 30-1 to 30-6, 30-8, 30-7, 30-9 to 30-10, 30-12 to 30-14, 30-16, 30-11, 30-15, 30-17 to 30-21, 30-23, 30-25, 30-22, 30-24, 30-26 to 30-27, 30-29, 30-31, 30-28, 30-30, 30-32 to 30-37, 30-95, 30-38 to 30-46, 30-47 (NP), 30-48 to 30-55, 30-57 to 30-66, 30-56, 30-67 to 30-70, 30-72, 30-71, 30-73 to 30-74, 30-76, 30-75, 30-77 to 30-78, 30-80, 30-79, 30-81 to 30-87, 30-89, 30-88, 30-90 to 30-94

Union   EDs 31-1 to 31-3, 31-4 (NP), 31-5, 31-7, 31-6, 31-8 to 31-9, 31-11, 31-13, 31-15, 31-10, 31-12, 31-14, 31-16 to 31-38, 31-40, 31-39, 31-41 to 31-45, 31-47, 31-49, 31-51, 31-46, 31-48, 31-50, 31-52

Wallowa   EDs 32-1 to 32-3, 32-5, 32-7, 32-9, 32-11, 32-4, 32-6, 32-8, 32-10, 32-12, 32-13 to 32-17, 32-19, 32-18, 32-20 to 32-34, 32-36, 32-38, 32-35, 32-37, 32-39

1957. Wasco   EDs 33-1 to 33-9, 33-48, 33-10 to 33-47, 33-49, 33-50, 33-51 (NP), 33-52

Washington   EDs 34-1 to 34-4, 34-6, 34-61, 34-5, 34-7 to 34-14, 34-16, 34-15, 34-17 to 34-19, 34-21, 34-23, 34-25, 34-20, 34-22, 34-24, 34-26 to 34-29, 34-31, 34-30, 34-32 to 34-60

Wheeler   EDs 35-1 to 35-17

1958. Yamhill   EDs 36-1 to 36-12, 36-14, 36-13, 36-15 to 36-17, 36-19, 36-18, 36-20 to 36-31, 36-37, 36-32 to 36-33, 36-35, 36-34, 36-36, 36-38 to 36-43, 36-45, 36-55, 36-44, 36-46 to 36-48, 36-50, 36-49, 36-51 to 36-54, 36-56 to 36-58

## Pennsylvania

1959. Adams   EDs 1-1 to 1-11, 1-35, 1-12 to 1-18, 1-36, 1-19 to 1-25, 1-37, 1-26, 1-38, 1-27 to 1-34

Allegheny   EDs 2-489 to 2-496, 2-505 to 2-507

1960. Allegheny   EDs 2-497 to 2-504, 2-511 to 2-515, 2-508 to 2-510, 2-889, 2-516 to 2-525

1961. Allegheny   EDs 2-526 to 2-537, 2-890, 2-541, 2-538 to 2-540, 2-543 to 2-544, 2-891, 2-545 to 2-548, 2-892, 2-549 to 2-550, 2-893, 2-551 to 2-552, 2-894

1962. Allegheny   EDs 2-542, 2-553 to 2-557, 2-564, 2-895, 2-565, 2-896, 2-566, 2-897, 2-567, 2-898, 2-558 to 2-563, 2-568, 2-579 to 2-586

1963. Allegheny   EDs 2-569 to 2-570, 2-899, 2-571 to 2-575, 2-900, 2-576, 2-901, 2-577 to 2-578, 2-587 to 2-600, 2-602, 2-902

1964. Allegheny   EDs 2-601, 2-603 to 2-615, 2-617, 2-616, 2-618 to 2-624, 2-636 to 2-639

1965. Allegheny   EDs 2-625 to 2-635, 2-640 to 2-654, 2-694 to 2-696, 2-698 to 2-701, 2-916, 2-708, 2-903

1966. Allegheny   EDs 2-655 to 2-665, 2-716 to 2-718, 2-666 to 2-667, 2-671 to 2-673, 2-677 to 2-684

1967. Allegheny   EDs 2-668 to 2-670, 2-674 to 2-676, 2-685 to 2-693, 2-702 to 2-707, 2-724 to 2-731

1968. Allegheny   EDs 2-709, 2-904, 2-710, 2-905, 2-711 to 2-713, 2-906, 2-714, 2-907, 2-715, 2-908, 2-719 to 2-721, 2-697, 2-722 to 2-723, 2-732 to 2-744, 2-745 (NP), 2-746 to 2-747

1969. Allegheny   EDs 2-751 to 2-762

Allegheny, Pittsburgh City   EDs 2-1 to 2-2, 2-879, 2-3 to 2-11, 2-880, 2-12 to 2-18, 2-881

1970. Allegheny, Pittsburgh City   EDs 2-19 to 2-27, 2-882, 2-28 to 2-34, 2-883, 2-35 to 2-51

1971. Allegheny, Pittsburgh City   EDs 2-52 to 2-82

1972. Allegheny, Pittsburgh City   EDs 2-83 to 2-116

1973. Allegheny, Pittsburgh City   EDs 2-117 to 2-134, 2-149 to 2-156

1974. Allegheny, Pittsburgh City   EDs 2-157 to 2-165, 2-135 to 2-148

1975. Allegheny, Pittsburgh City   EDs 2-166 to 2-167, 2-884, 2-168 to 2-170, 2-885, 2-171 to 2-179, 2-180 (void), 2-181 to 2-187

1976. Allegheny, Pittsburgh City   EDs 2-188 to 2-200, 2-886, 2-201 to 2-211

1977. Allegheny, Pittsburgh City   EDs 2-212 to 2-230

1978. Allegheny, Pittsburgh City   EDs 2-231 to 2-248

1979. Allegheny, Pittsburgh City   EDs 2-249 to 2-271

1980. Allegheny, Pittsburgh City   EDs 2-272 to 2-273, 2-887, 2-274 to 2-297

1981. Allegheny, Pittsburgh City   EDs 2-298 to 2-317

1982. Allegheny, Pittsburgh City   EDs 2-318 to 2-332

1983. Allegheny, Pittsburgh City   EDs 2-333 to 2-340, 2-342, 2-341, 2-343 to 2-345, 2-450 to 2-456

1984. Allegheny, Pittsburgh City   EDs 2-457 to 2-468, 2-375 to 2-388

1985. Allegheny, Pittsburgh City   EDs 2-389 to 2-390, 2-424 to 2-436, 2-391 to 2-406

1986. Allegheny, Pittsburgh City   EDs 2-407 to 2-415, 2-417 to 2-418, 2-420 to 2-423, 2-437 to 2-449

1987. Allegheny, Pittsburgh City   EDs 2-469 to 2-472, 2-416, 2-473 to 2-488, 2-356 to 2-357

1988. Allegheny, Pittsburgh City   EDs 2-358 to 2-366, 2-346 to 2-355

1989. Allegheny, Pittsburgh City   EDs 2-367 to 2-374, 2-888, 2-748 to 2-750

Allegheny   EDs 2-763 to 2-775, 2-780

1990. Allegheny   EDs 2-776 to 2-778, 2-419, 2-779, 2-781 to 2-788, 2-798 to 2-799, 2-806, 2-789 to 2-797, 2-800 to 2-801, 2-909, 2-802 to 2-805, 2-910

1991. Allegheny   EDs 2-807 to 2-810, 2-911 to 2-912, 2-811 to 2-812, 2-913, 2-813, 2-914, 2-814, 2-915, 2-833 to 2-834, 2-840 to 2-842, 2-815 to 2-832

1992. Allegheny   EDs 2-835 to 2-839, 2-843 to 2-866

1993. Allegheny   EDs 2-867 to 2-878

Armstrong   EDs 3-1 to 3-18

1994. Armstrong   EDs 3-19 to 3-33, 3-56, 3-34 to 3-55

1995. Beaver   EDs 4-1 to 4-24, 4-26 to 4-28

1996. Beaver   EDs 4-25, 4-29 to 4-66

1997. Beaver   EDs 4-67 to 4-70, 4-101, 4-71 to 4-100

1998. Bedford   EDs 5-1, 5-43, 5-2 to 5-42
Berks   EDs 6-72 to 6-84

1999. Berks   EDs 6-85 to 6-122, 6-123 (NP), 6-124 to 6-126

2000. Berks   EDs 6-127 to 6-140, 6-142 to 6-145
Berks, Reading City   EDs 6-1 to 6-8, 6-14 to 6-21

2001. Berks, Reading City   EDs 6-9 to 6-13, 6-22 to 6-26, 6-47 to 6-51, 6-27 to 6-37, 6-43 to 6-46

2002. Berks, Reading City   EDs 6-38 to 6-42, 6-66 to 6-71, 6-52 to 6-65

2003. Berks   EDs 6-141, 6-146 to 6-156, 6-157 (void), 6-158 to 6-166
Blair   EDs 7-1 to 7-3, 7-42 to 7-44, 7-84, 7-45 to 7-58

2004. Blair, Altoona City   EDs 7-4 to 7-27, 7-33 to 7-34

2005. Blair   EDs 7-28 to 7-32, 7-35 to 7-41, 7-59 to 7-71, 7-85, 7-72 to 7-80

2006. Blair   EDs 7-81 to 7-83
Bradford   EDs 8-1 to 8-32, 8-38 to 8-39, 8-33 to 8-37, 8-40 to 8-63

2007. Bucks   EDs 9-1 to 9-15, 9-18, 9-16 to 9-17, 9-19 to 9-35, 9-67, 9-36 to 9-38

2008. Bucks   EDs 9-39 to 9-66, 9-68 to 9-74, 9-82, 9-75 to 9-81
Butler   EDs 10-1 to 10-5

2009. Butler   EDs 10-6 to 10-16, 10-20 to 10-23, 10-17 to 10-19, 10-24 to 10-41, 10-72, 10-42

2010. Butler   EDs 10-43, 10-73, 10-44 to 10-71
Cambria   EDs 11-1 to 11-18

2011. Cambria   EDs 11-19 to 11-36, 11-42, 11-38 to 11-40, 11-37, 11-41, 11-43 to 11-46, 11-126, 11-47 to 11-48, 11-85 to 11-89, 11-94 to 11-95

2012. Cambria   EDs 11-49 to 11-74, 11-80, 11-82 to 11-83

2013. Cambria   EDs 11-75 to 11-79, 11-81, 11-84, 11-90 to 11-93, 11-100 to 11-101, 11-96 to 11-99, 11-102 to 11-110, 11-113 to 11-114

2014. Cambria   EDs 11-111 to 11-112, 11-115 to 11-125
Cameron   EDs 12-1 to 12-9
Carbon   EDs 13-1 (NP), 13-2 to 13-17, 13-23

2015. Carbon   EDs 13-18 to 13-22, 13-24 to 13-32, 13-36 to 13-37, 13-41 to 13-43, 13-33 to 13-35, 13-38 to 13-40
Centre   EDs 14-1 to 14-11

2016. Centre   EDs 14-12 to 14-36, 14-38 to 14-39, 14-37, 14-40 to 14-47
Clarion   EDs 16-1 to 16-12, 16-37, 16-13 to 16-19

2017. Clarion   EDs 16-20 to 16-36
Clearfield   EDs 17-1 to 17-23

2018. Clearfield   EDs 17-24 to 17-32, 17-70, 17-33 to 17-55, 17-57, 17-56, 17-58 to 17-69

2019. Chester   EDs 15-1 to 15-32, 15-36, 15-33 to 15-35, 15-37 to 15-46

2020. Chester   EDs 15-47 to 15-58, 15-77 to 15-87, 15-59 to 15-76

2021. Chester   EDs 15-91 to 15-93, 15-88 to 15-90, 15-94 to 15-105, 15-108 to 15-109, 15-106 to 15-107, 15-110
Clinton   EDs 18-1 to 18-18, 18-35, 18-19 to 18-21, 18-36, 18-22 to 18-25

2022. Clinton   EDs 18-26 to 18-34
Crawford   EDs 20-1 to 20-38

2023. Crawford   EDs 20-39 to 20-51, 20-53 to 20-68, 20-52, 20-69
Columbia   EDs 19-1 to 19-17

2024. Columbia   EDs 19-18 to 19-43

Cumberland   EDs 21-1 to 21-4, 21-36, 21-5 to 21-17, 21-20 to 21-21

2025. Cumberland   EDs 21-18 to 21-19, 21-22 to 21-35, 21-37 to 21-54
Dauphin   EDs 22-1 to 22-8

2026. Dauphin   EDs 22-9 to 22-19, 22-28 to 22-34, 22-20 to 22-27, 22-35 to 22-38, 22-49 to 22-54

2027. Dauphin   EDs 22-39 to 22-48, 22-55 to 22-61, 22-65, 22-62 to 22-64, 22-66 to 22-67, 22-119, 22-68 to 22-78, 22-83 to 22-85

2028. Dauphin   EDs 22-79 to 22-82, 22-86 to 22-93, 22-95 to 22-99, 22-94, 22-100 to 22-118

2029. Delaware   EDs 23-1 to 23-13, 23-18 to 23-21, 23-14 to 23-17, 23-22 to 23-28, 23-38 to 23-41

2030. Delaware   EDs 23-29 to 23-37, 23-42 to 23-45, 23-52 to 23-53, 23-46 to 23-51, 23-54 to 23-64

2031. Delaware   EDs 23-65, 23-180, 23-97, 23-66 to 23-68, 23-77 to 23-85, 23-95 to 23-96, 23-98 to 23-101, 23-69 to 23-76, 23-102 to 23-104

2032. Delaware   EDs 23-86 to 23-94, 23-105 to 23-110, 23-140, 23-111 to 23-121, 23-124 to 23-125, 23-126 (NP), 23-127 to 23-128, 23-129 (NP)

2033. Delaware   EDs 23-122 to 23-123, 23-130 to 23-139, 23-177 to 23-179, 23-141 to 23-152

2034. Delaware   EDs 23-153 to 23-176
Elk   EDs 24-1 to 24-5, 24-26, 24-6 to 24-20

2035. Elk   EDs 24-21 to 24-25
Erie   EDs 25-1 to 25-14, 25-107 to 25-108, 25-126, 25-109
Erie, Erie City   EDs 25-15 to 25-37

2036. Erie, Erie City   EDs 25-38 to 25-56, 25-69 to 25-89

2037. Erie, Erie City   EDs 25-57 to 25-68, 25-90 to 25-106, 25-110 to 25-120, 25-125, 25-127 to 25-128

2038. Erie   EDs 25-121 to 25-124, 25-129 to 25-147
Fayette   EDs 26-1 to 26-15

2039. Fayette   EDs 26-16 to 26-40, 26-45 to 26-50

2040. Fayette   EDs 26-41 to 26-44, 26-51 to 26-59, 26-85 to 26-87, 26-60 to 26-73, 26-83 to 26-84

2041. Fayette   EDs 26-74 to 26-82, 26-89 to 26-93, 26-97, 26-88, 26-94 to 26-96, 26-98 to 26-108

2042. Fayette   EDs 26-109 to 26-113
Forest   EDs 27-1 to 27-9
Franklin   EDs 28-1 to 28-2, 28-9 to 28-14, 28-3 to 28-8, 28-15 to 28-21, 28-23 to 28-25

2043. Franklin   EDs 28-22, 28-26 to 28-43
Fulton   EDs 29-1 to 29-12
Greene   EDs 30-1 to 30-10

2044. Greene   EDs 30-11 to 30-19, 30-35, 30-20 to 30-28, 30-32 to 30-33, 30-29 to 30-31, 30-34
Huntingdon   EDs 31-1 to 31-35

2045. Huntingdon   EDs 31-36 to 31-55
Indiana   EDs 32-1 to 32-23, 32-28 to 32-29

2046. Indiana   EDs 32-24 to 32-27, 32-30 to 32-55
Juniata   EDs 34-1 to 34-17

2047. Jefferson   EDs 33-1 to 33-15, 33-24 to 33-29, 33-16 to 33-23, 33-30 to 33-49

2048. Lackawanna   EDs 35-96 to 35-104, 35-118 to 35-123, 35-105 to 35-117

2049. Lackawanna   EDs 35-124 to 35-131, 35-147 to 35-159, 35-161 to 35-162, 35-132 to 35-146, 35-160

2050. Lackawanna   EDs 35-163 to 35-191, 35-194 to 35-199, 35-203

2051. Lackawanna, Scranton City   EDs 35-1 to 35-7, 35-15 to 35-17, 35-8 to 35-14, 35-18 to 35-22

2052. Lackawanna, Scranton City   EDs 35-23 to 35-40, 35-57 to 35-59, 35-69 to 35-72

2053. Lackawanna, Scranton City   EDs 35-41 to 35-44, 35-60 to 35-68, 35-45 to 35-54

2054. Lackawanna, Scranton City   EDs 35-55 to 35-56, 35-82 to 35-86, 35-73 to 35-81

2055. Lackawanna, Scranton City   EDs 35-87 to 35-95
Lackawanna   EDs 35-192, 35-210, 35-193, 35-200 to 35-202, 35-204 to 35-209
Lancaster   EDs 36-1 to 36-6

2056. Lancaster   EDs 36-7 to 36-25, 36-29 to 36-30, 36-26 to 36-28, 36-31 to 36-46

2057. Lancaster   EDs 36-47 to 36-54, 36-60 to 36-65, 36-55 to 36-59, 36-66 to 36-71

2058. Lancaster   EDs 36-72 to 36-85, 36-89 to 36-91, 36-86 to 36-88, 36-92 to 36-105

2059. Lancaster   EDs 36-106 to 36-131
Lawrence   EDs 37-1 to 37-14

2060. Lawrence   EDs 37-15 to 37-23, 37-65 to 37-70, 37-28 to 37-30, 37-71, 37-31, 37-72, 37-24 to 37-27, 37-32 to 37-42

2061. Lawrence   EDs 37-43 to 37-54, 37-73, 37-55 to 37-64
Lebanon   EDs 38-1 to 38-5, 38-48, 38-6 to 38-13, 38-27 to 38-36

2062. Lebanon   EDs 38-14 to 38-26, 38-37 to 38-47
Lehigh   EDs 39-1 to 39-5, 39-8 to 39-9

2063. Lehigh   EDs 39-6 to 39-7, 39-10 to 39-16, 39-31 to 39-34, 39-17 to 39-26, 39-35 to 39-36, 39-43

2064. Lehigh   EDs 39-27 to 39-30, 39-37 to 39-42, 39-44, 39-98, 39-45 to 39-62

2065. Lehigh   EDs 39-63 to 39-97

2066. Luzerne   EDs 40-1 to 40-37, 40-42 to 40-44, 40-94

2067. Luzerne   EDs 40-38 to 40-41, 40-45 to 40-65, 40-95 to 40-100

2068. Luzerne   EDs 40-66 to 40-93

2069. Luzerne   EDs 40-101 to 40-121, 40-180 to 40-192

2070. Luzerne   EDs 40-122 to 40-127, 40-143 to 40-156, 40-195, 40-128 to 40-142

2071. Luzerne   EDs 40-157 to 40-171, 40-196 to 40-198, 40-172 to 40-179, 40-203 to 40-208

2072. Luzerne   EDs 40-193 to 40-194, 40-199 to 40-202, 40-209, 40-211 to 40-219, 40-210, 40-220 to 40-231, 40-233 to 40-234

2073. Luzerne   EDs 40-232, 40-235 to 40-241, 40-244 to 40-247, 40-254 to 40-259, 40-242 to 40-243, 40-248 to 40-253, 40-260 to 40-263, 40-270 to 40-271

2074. Luzerne   EDs 40-264 to 40-269, 40-272 to 40-281
Lycoming   EDs 41-1 to 41-16, 41-85, 41-17 to 41-33, 41-36

2075. Lycoming   EDs 41-34 to 41-35, 41-37, 41-86, 41-39 to 41-40, 41-38, 41-41 to 41-58, 41-75, 41-59 to 41-70, 41-73 to 41-74

2076. Lycoming   EDs 41-71 to 41-72, 41-76 to 41-84
Mercer   EDs 43-1 to 43-7, 43-28 to 43-31, 43-8 to 43-27, 43-35

2077. Mercer   EDs 43-32 to 43-34, 43-36 to 43-53, 43-71 to 43-75, 43-54 to 43-70

2078. Mercer   EDs 43-76 to 43-87
Mifflin   EDs 44-1 to 44-25

2079. McKean   EDs 42-1 to 42-15, 42-17, 42-16, 42-18 to 42-34

2080. Monroe   EDs 45-1 to 45-18, 45-20 to 45-25, 45-19, 45-26
Montgomery   EDs 46-1 to 46-15, 46-19

2081. Montgomery   EDs 46-16 to 46-18, 46-20 to 46-30, 46-37 to 46-38, 46-31 to 46-36, 46-39 to 46-40, 46-111, 46-160, 46-41 to 46-43, 46-45 to 46-46

2082. Montgomery   EDs 46-44, 46-53 to 46-54, 46-51 to 46-52, 46-55 to 46-57, 46-59 to 46-66, 46-168, 46-67 to 46-70, 46-169, 46-71 to 46-74, 46-79, 46-75 to 46-77, 46-170, 46-78, 46-80, 46-175, 46-81 to 46-82

2083. Montgomery   EDs 46-47 to 46-50, 46-58, 46-83 to 46-95, 46-176, 46-96 to 46-107, 46-171, 46-108, 46-172, 46-109, 46-173, 46-110

2084. Montgomery   EDs 46-112 to 46-113, 46-127 to 46-135, 46-174, 46-136 to 46-141, 46-145, 46-114 to 46-126

2085. Montgomery   EDs 46-142 to 46-144, 46-146 to 46-159, 46-161 to 46-167
Montour   EDs 47-1 to 47-17

2086. Northampton   EDs 48-1 to 48-11, 48-112 (NP), 48-12 to 48-16, 48-23, 48-17 to 48-22, 48-24 to 48-31

2087. Northampton   EDs 48-32, 48-107, 48-33 to 48-41, 48-108, 48-42 to 48-46, 48-53 to 48-54, 48-47 to 48-52, 48-55 to 48-66, 48-68

2088. Northampton   EDs 48-67, 48-69 to 48-75, 48-77 to 48-80, 48-83 to 48-86, 48-76, 48-81 to 48-82, 48-87 to 48-97, 48-101 to 48-103, 48-109, 48-104, 48-110, 48-105, 48-111

2089. Northampton   EDs 48-98 to 48-100, 48-106
Perry   EDs 50-1 to 50-30
Northumberland   EDs 49-1 to 49-17

2090. Northumberland   EDs 49-18 to 49-20, 49-21 (void), 49-22 to 49-32, 49-44 to 49-47, 49-33 to 49-43, 49-48

2091. Northumberland   EDs 49-49 to 49-85

2092. Philadelphia, Philadelphia City   EDs 51-1 to 51-20

2093. Philadelphia, Philadelphia City   EDs 51-21 to 51-43

2094. Philadelphia, Philadelphia City   EDs 51-44 to 51-52, 51-1142, 51-53 to 51-59, 51-262 to 51-264

2095. Philadelphia, Philadelphia City   EDs 51-265 to 51-270, 51-272 to 51-273, 51-1153 to 51-1154, 51-274 to 51-285

2096. Philadelphia, Philadelphia City   EDs 51-286 to 51-289, 51-1155, 51-290 to 51-304

2097. Philadelphia, Philadelphia City   EDs 51-305 to 51-306, 51-307 (NP), 51-308 to 51-309, 51-310 (NP), 51-311 to 51-332

2098. Philadelphia, Philadelphia City   EDs 51-333 to 51-357

2099. Philadelphia, Philadelphia City   EDs 51-358 to 51-360, 51-362 to 51-367, 51-368 (NP), 51-1156, 51-539 to 51-554, 51-826 to 51-827

2100. Philadelphia, Philadelphia City   EDs 51-828 to 51-853

2101. Philadelphia, Philadelphia City   EDs 51-854 to 51-8751, 51-555 to 51-564

2102. Philadelphia, Philadelphia City   EDs 51-565 to 51-582, 51-1161, 51-583, 51-1162 to 51-1163, 51-584, 51-1164 to 51-1166, 51-585, 51-1167 to 51-1169, 51-586 to 51-589

2103. Philadelphia, Philadelphia City   EDs 51-590 to 51-605, 51-361, 51-606 to 51-610, 51-1170, 51-611

2104.	Philadelphia, Philadelphia City　EDs 51-612 to 51-616, 51-1171, 51-617 to 51-618, 51-1172 to 51-1175, 51-619, 51-1176, 51-1177 (NP), 51-620 to 51-621, 51-1178, 51-622 to 51-630

2105.	Philadelphia, Philadelphia City　EDs 51-631 to 51-659

2106.	Philadelphia, Philadelphia City　EDs 51-660 to 51-672, 51-871 to 51-873, 51-1182, 51-874 to 51-877

2107.	Philadelphia, Philadelphia City　EDs 51-878 to 51-893, 51-369 to 51-376

2108.	Philadelphia, Philadelphia City　EDs 51-377 to 51-397

2109.	Philadelphia, Philadelphia City　EDs 51-398 to 51-406, 51-894 to 51-909

2110.	Philadelphia, Philadelphia City　EDs 51-910 to 51-919, 51-60 to 51-75

2111.	Philadelphia, Philadelphia City　EDs 51-76 to 51-95, 51-407 to 51-413

2112.	Philadelphia, Philadelphia City　EDs 51-414 to 51-422, 51-673 to 51-684

2113.	Philadelphia, Philadelphia City　EDs 51-685 to 51-706, 51-707 (NP), 51-1179, 51-708

2114.	Philadelphia, Philadelphia City　EDs 51-709 to 51-718, 51-96 to 51-109

2115.	Philadelphia, Philadelphia City　EDs 51-110 to 51-115, 51-920 to 51-936

2116.	Philadelphia, Philadelphia City　EDs 51-719 to 51-741

2117.	Philadelphia, Philadelphia City　EDs 51-742 to 51-744, 51-1180, 51-937, 51-1183, 51-938 to 51-954

2118.	Philadelphia, Philadelphia City　EDs 51-955 to 51-977

2119.	Philadelphia, Philadelphia City　EDs 51-423 to 51-428, 51-1157, 51-429, 51-1158, 51-430 to 51-439

2120.	Philadelphia, Philadelphia City　EDs 51-440 to 51-448, 51-1159, 51-449 to 51-459

2121.	Philadelphia, Philadelphia City　EDs 51-460 to 51-469, 51-978, 51-1184, 51-979 to 51-981, 51-1185 to 51-1186, 51-982, 51-1187 to 51-1188, 51-983, 51-1189, 51-984, 51-1190, 51-985 to 51-986, 51-1191 to 51-1192, 51-987, 51-1193 to 51-1195, 51-988, 51-1196 to 51-1199, 51-989, 51-1200 to 51-1202

2122.	Philadelphia, Philadelphia City　EDs 51-990 to 51-992, 51-1203 to 51-1204, 51-993, 51-1205, 51-994, 51-1206 to 51-1207, 51-995, 51-1208 to 51-1209, 51-996, 51-1210 to 51-1211, 51-997, 51-1212 to 51-1213, 51-998, 51-1214, 51-999 to 51-1000, 51-1215

2123.	Philadelphia, Philadelphia City　EDs 51-1216, 51-1001, 51-1217 to 51-1218, 51-1002, 51-1219, 51-116 to 51-132

2124.	Philadelphia, Philadelphia City　EDs 51-133 to 51-145, 51-745 to 51-756

2125.	Philadelphia, Philadelphia City　EDs 51-757 to 51-764, 51-1181, 51-765 to 51-779

2126.	Philadelphia, Philadelphia City　EDs 51-780 to 51-783, 51-784 (void), 51-785 to 51-786, 51-271, 51-787 to 51-801, 51-146 to 51-149

2127.	Philadelphia, Philadelphia City　EDs 51-150 to 51-174

2128.	Philadelphia, Philadelphia City　EDs 51-175 to 51-185, 51-1143, 51-186 to 51-187, 51-188 (NP), 51-189 to 51-190, 51-191 (NP), 51-1144, 51-192 to 51-199

2129.	Philadelphia, Philadelphia City　EDs 51-200 to 51-218, 51-1145, 51-219 to 51-220

2130.	Philadelphia, Philadelphia City　EDs 51-221 to 51-223, 51-225, 51-224, 51-1146 to 51-1147, 51-226 to 51-233, 51-1148, 51-234 to 51-237

2131.	Philadelphia, Philadelphia City　EDs 51-238 to 51-242, 51-1149, 51-243 to 51-245, 51-1150, 51-246 to 51-247, 51-1003 to 51-1004, 51-1220, 51-1005, 51-1221 to 51-1223, 51-1006, 51-1224, 51-1007, 51-1225, 51-1226 (NP), 51-1008, 51-1227, 51-1009 to 51-1010

2132.	Philadelphia, Philadelphia City　EDs 51-1011 to 51-1027, 51-1228, 51-1028

2133.	Philadelphia, Philadelphia City　EDs 51-1029 to 51-1031, 51-1229, 51-1032, 51-1230 to 51-1232, 51-1033, 51-1233 to 1-1234, 51-1034 to 51-1037, 51-1235, 51-1038

2134.	Philadelphia, Philadelphia City　EDs 51-1039 to 51-1041, 51-1042 (void), 51-1043 to 51-1058

2135.	Philadelphia, Philadelphia City　EDs 51-1059 to 51-1063, 51-1236, 51-1064 to 51-1074

2136.	Philadelphia, Philadelphia City　EDs 51-1075 to 51-1097

2137.	Philadelphia, Philadelphia City　EDs 51-1098 to 51-1112, 51-470 to 51-480

2138.	Philadelphia, Philadelphia City　EDs 51-481 to 51-495, 51-1113 to 51-1120

2139.	Philadelphia, Philadelphia City　EDs 51-1121 to 51-1141, 51-496 to 51-499

2140.	Philadelphia, Philadelphia City　EDs 51-500 to 51-517, 51-1160 (NP), 51-518 to 51-519

2141.	Philadelphia, Philadelphia City　EDs 51-520 to 51-538, 51-802 to 51-804

2142.	Philadelphia, Philadelphia City　EDs 51-805 to 51-825, 51-248 to 51-253

2143.	Philadelphia, Philadelphia City　EDs 51-254 to 51-261, 51-1151, 51-1152 (NP)

　　　Pike　EDs 52-1 to 52-13

　　　Potter　EDs 53-1 to 53-6, 53-8 to 53-9, 53-7, 53-10 to 53-32

2144.	Schuylkill　EDs 54-1 to 54-15, 54-155, 54-16, 54-20, 54-17 to 54-19, 54-21 to 54-31, 54-152, 54-32, 54-39

2145.	Schuylkill　EDs 54-33 to 54-38, 54-40 to 54-48, 54-75 to 54-76, 54-49 to 54-60, 54-71 to 54-74

2146.	Schuylkill　EDs 54-61 to 54-70, 54-79 to 54-85, 54-77, 54-86 to 54-98

2147.	Schuylkill　EDs 54-78, 54-151, 54-99 to 54-103, 54-105, 54-104, 54-106, 54-153, 54-107, 54-154, 54-109, 54-108, 54-110 to 54-111, 54-136 to 54-137, 54-112 to 54-125, 54-138 to 54-139

2148.	Schuylkill　EDs 54-126 to 54-135, 54-143, 54-146 to 54-150, 54-144, 54-140 to 54-142, 54-145, 54-156

　　　Snyder　EDs 55-1 to 55-20

2149.	Somerset　EDs 56-1 to 56-21, 56-25 to 56-26, 56-22 to 56-24, 56-27 to 56-43, 56-49 to 56-51

2150.	Somerset　EDs 56-44 to 56-48, 56-52 to 56-67

　　　Sullivan　EDs 57-1 to 57-14

　　　Union　EDs 60-1 to 60-18

2151.	Susquehanna　EDs 58-1 to 58-47

　　　Tioga　EDs 59-1 to 59-24, 59-26

2152.	Tioga　EDs 59-25, 59-27 to 59-44

　　　Venango　EDs 61-1 to 61-20, 61-33 to 61-40, 61-45 to 61-46, 61-49 to 61-50

2153.	Venango　EDs 61-21 to 61-32, 61-41 to 61-44, 61-47 to 61-48

Warren   EDs 62-1 to 62-5, 62-42, 62-6 to 62-29

2154.   Warren   EDs 62-30 to 62-41

Wayne   EDs 64-1 to 64-10, 64-11 (void), 64-13, 64-12, 64-14 to 64-15, 64-33, 64-16 to 64-32

Westmoreland   EDs 65-1 to 65-3, 65-8 to 65-11

2155.   Westmoreland   EDs 65-4 to 65-7, 65-13 to 65-21, 65-12, 65-22 to 65-31, 65-57 to 65-61, 65-81

2156.   Westmoreland   EDs 65-32 to 65-45, 65-82 to 65-89, 65-46 to 65-56, 65-90, 65-122 to 65-123, 65-129

2157.   Westmoreland   EDs 65-62 to 65-80, 65-91 to 65-106, 65-113

2158.   Westmoreland   EDs 65-107 to 65-112, 65-114, 65-130 to 65-135, 65-141, 65-115 to 65-119, 65-185, 65-120 to 65-121, 65-186, 65-124 to 65-128

2159.   Westmoreland   EDs 65-136 to 65-140, 65-145 to 65-156, 65-142 to 65-144, 65-157 to 65-162, 65-166 to 65-172

2160.   Westmoreland   EDs 65-163 to 65-165, 65-173 to 65-176, 65-187, 65-177 to 65-184

Washington   EDs 63-1 to 63-17

2161.   Washington   EDs 63-18 to 63-31, 63-47 to 63-48, 63-32 to 63-46, 63-76 to 63-77

2162.   Washington   EDs 63-49 to 63-75, 63-80 to 63-84

2163.   Washington   EDs 63-78 to 63-79, 63-85 to 63-105, 63-131, 63-108 to 63-110, 63-124 to 63-130

2164.   Washington   EDs 63-106 to 63-107, 63-111 to 63-123

Wyoming   EDs 66-1 to 66-24

York   EDs 67-1 to 67-8, 67-129

2165.   York   EDs 67-9 to 67-27, 67-33 to 67-36, 67-131, 67-37 to 67-41, 67-47, 67-28 to 67-32, 67-42 to 67-46, 67-48 to 67-56

2166.   York   EDs 67-57 to 67-71, 67-75, 67-72 to 67-74, 67-76 to 67-86, 67-130, 67-87 to 67-92, 67-125 to 67-126, 67-128, 67-127

2167.   York   EDs 67-93 to 67-97, 67-99 to 67-110, 67-98, 67-111 to 67-124

## Rhode Island

2168.   Bristol   EDs 1-1 to 1-13

Kent   EDs 2-1 to 2-7, 2-19 to 2-27

2169.   Kent   EDs 2-8 to 2-18

Newport   EDs 3-1 to 3-4, 3-38, 3-5 to 3-7, 3-9 to 3-11, 3-12 (NP), 3-13 to 3-14, 3-39, 3-15 to 3-22

2170.   Newport   EDs 3-23 to 3-31, 3-8, 3-32 to 3-37

Providence   EDs 4-155 to 4-172

2171.   Providence   EDs 4-173 to 4-206

2172.   Providence   EDs 4-207 to 4-219, 4-222 to 4-231

2173.   Providence   EDs 4-220 to 4-221, 4-232 to 4-237, 4-273 to 4-276, 4-238 to 4-243, 4-256 to 4-261

2174.   Providence   EDs 4-244 to 4-249, 4-268 to 4-272, 4-250 to 4-255, 4-262 to 4-267

2175.   Providence, Providence City   EDs 4-126 to 4-148

2176.   Providence, Providence City   EDs 4-149 to 4-154, 4-1 to 4-13

2177.   Providence, Providence City   EDs 4-14 to 4-32

2178.   Providence, Providence City   EDs 4-33 to 4-58

2179.   Providence, Providence City   EDs 4-59 to 4-77

2180.   Providence, Providence City   EDs 4-78 to 4-102

2181.   Providence, Providence City   EDs 4-277 to 4-282, 4-299 to 4-304, 4-283 to 4-298

Washington   EDs 5-1 to 5-3

2182.   Washington   EDs 5-4 to 5-23

2183.   Providence, Providence City   EDs 4-103 to 4-125

## South Carolina

2184.   Abbeville   EDs 1-1 to 1-24

Aiken   EDs 2-1 to 2-17

2185.   Aiken   EDs 2-18 to 2-36

Allendale   EDs 3-3, 3-7, 3-1 to 3-2, 3-4 to 3-6, 3-8 to 3-14

Anderson   EDs 4-1 to 4-11

2186.   Anderson   EDs 4-12 to 4-32, 4-43, 4-33 to 4-42, 4-44, 4-47, 4-45 to 4-46, 4-48 to 4-50

2187.   Anderson   EDs 4-57, 4-51 to 4-53, 4-56, 4-54 to 4-55

Bamberg   EDs 5-1, 5-11, 5-2 to 5-10, 5-12 to 5-17

Barnwell   EDs 6-1 to 6-3, 6-14, 6-4 to 6-13, 6-15 to 6-20

2188.   Beaufort   EDs 7-1 to 7-22

Berkeley   EDs 8-1 to 8-4, 8-15, 8-5 to 8-10, 8-19, 8-11 to 8-14, 8-16 to 8-18

Calhoun   EDs 9-1 to 9-4

2189.   Calhoun   EDs 9-5 to 9-14

Charleston   EDs 10-1 to 10-8, 10-73, 10-9 to 10-32

2190.   Charleston   EDs 10-33 to 10-50, 10-64, 10-51 to 10-69

2191.   Charleston   EDs 10-70 to 10-72

Cherokee   EDs 11-1 to 11-17, 11-24, 11-18 to 11-20, 11-22, 11-21, 11-23

Chester   EDs 12-1 to 12-15

2192.   Chester   EDs 12-16 to 12-27

Chesterfield   EDs 13-1 to 13-31

Clarendon   EDs 14-1 to 14-3, 14-28, 14-4 to 14-6, 14-11, 14-7 to 14-8

2193.   Clarendon   EDs 14-9 to 14-10, 14-12 to 14-27, 14-29 to 14-32

Colleton   EDs 15-1 to 15-10, 15-15, 15-11 to 15-14, 15-16 to 15-23

2194.   Dillon   EDs 17-1 to 17-21, 17-23, 17-22

Darlington   EDs 16-1 to 16-25

2195.   Darlington   EDs 16-26 to 16-38

Dorchester   EDs 18-1 to 18-3, 18-13, 18-4 to 18-12, 18-14 to 18-19

Edgefield   EDs 19-1 to 19-11, 19-19, 19-12 to 19-18, 19-20 to 19-21

2196.   Fairfield   EDs 20-1 to 20-10, 20-12, 20-11, 20-13 to 20-24

Florence   EDs 21-1 to 21-17

2197.   Florence   EDs 21-18 to 21-24, 21-29, 21-25 to 21-28, 21-30 to 21-40

Georgetown   EDs 22-1 to 22-12

2198.   Greenville   EDs 23-1, 23-19, 23-2 to 23-18, 23-20 to 23-29, 23-32 to 23-33, 23-39 to 23-40

2199.   Greenville   EDs 23-30 to 23-31, 23-34 to 23-38, 23-41 to 23-66, 23-76

2200.   Greenville   EDs 23-67 to 23-75

Greenwood   EDs 24-1 to 24-34

2201.   Hampton   EDs 25-1, 25-5, 25-2 to 25-4, 25-6 to 25-18

Horry   EDs 26-1 to 26-4, 26-11 to 26-13, 26-5 to 26-10, 26-14 to 26-27

2202.   Jasper   EDs 27-1, 27-4, 27-2 to 27-3, 27-9 to 27-10, 27-5 to 27-8

Kershaw   EDs 28-1 to 28-6, 28-13 to 28-17, 28-7 to 28-12, 28-18 to 28-27

Laurens   EDs 30-22 to 30-30

2203.   Laurens   EDs 30-1 to 30-18, 30-20 to 30-21, 30-19, 30-31 to 30-41

Lee    EDs 31-1 to 31-7, 31-14, 31-8 to 31-13, 31-15 to 31-24

2204.    Lancaster    EDs 29-1 to 29-6, 29-17, 29-7 to 29-16, 29-18 to 29-21

Lexington    EDs 32-1 to 32-24

2205.    Lexington    EDs 32-25 to 32-34

McCormick    EDs 33-1 to 33-17

Marlboro    EDs 35-1 to 35-44

2206.    Marion    EDs 34-1 to 34-23

Newberry    EDs 36-1 to 36-17, 36-23, 36-18 to 36-22, 36-24 to 36-26, 36-30, 36-36 to 36-37

2207.    Newberry    EDs 36-27 to 36-29, 36-31 to 36-35

Oconee    EDs 37-1 to 37-20

Orangeburg    EDs 38-1 to 38-9

2208.    Orangeburg    EDs 38-10 to 38-54

Pickens    EDs 39-18 to 39-20

2209.    Pickens    EDs 39-1 to 39-17, 39-24 to 39-26, 39-21 to 39-23

Richland    EDs 40-32 to 40-47

2210.    Richland    EDs 40-1 to 40-31

2211.    Richland    EDs 40-48 to 40-79

Saluda    EDs 41-3 to 41-5, 41-8 to 41-10, 41-1 to 41-2, 41-6 to 41-7, 41-11 to 41-19

Spartanburg    EDs 42-23 to 42-33

2212.    Spartanburg    EDs 42-1 to 42-11, 42-74, 42-34, 42-43, 42-35 to 42-37, 42-75, 42-38 to 42-42, 42-61 to 42-64, 42-76, 42-65 to 42-69

2213.    Spartanburg    EDs 42-12 to 42-22, 42-70, 42-77, 42-71 to 42-73, 42-44 to 42-60

Sumter    EDs 43-1 to 43-5, 43-7 to 43-9

2214.    Sumter    EDs 43-6, 43-20 to 43-35, 43-10 to 43-19

Union    EDs 44-1 to 44-9, 44-14 to 44-15

2215.    Union    EDs 44-10 to 44-13, 44-16 to 44-23

Williamsburg    EDs 45-1 to 45-7, 45-15, 45-8 to 45-14, 45-16 to 45-33

2216.    York    EDs 46-1 to 46-12, 46-15 to 46-26, 46-13 to 46-14, 46-27, 46-44, 46-28 to 46-43

### South Dakota

2217.    Armstrong    EDs 1-1 to 1-2, 1-3 to 1-7 (NP), 1-8 to 1-11, 1-12 to 1-16 (NP), 1-17, 1-18 to 1-22 (NP), 1-23, 1-24 (NP)

Aurora    EDs 2-1 to 2-24

Bon Homme    EDs 5-1 to 5-21

Beadle    EDs 3-1 to 3-49

2218.    Bennett    EDs 4-1 to 4-38

Brookings    EDs 6-1 to 6-34

Brown    EDs 7-1 to 7-16

2219.    Brown    EDs 7-17 to 7-58

Brule    EDs 8-1 to 8-26

Buffalo    EDs 9-1 to 9-5, 9-10 to 9-11, 9-6, 9-12, 9-7 (NP), 9-13 (NP), 9-14 to 9-15, 9-16 (NP), 9-8 to 9-9, 9-17 to 9-19

Butte    EDs 10-1 to 10-34, 10-35 (NP), 10-36 to 10-40, 10-41 (NP), 10-42 to 10-69

Clark    EDs 13-1 to 13-34

2220.    Campbell    EDs 11-1 to 11-28

Charles Mix    EDs 12-1 to 12-31

Clay    EDs 14-1 to 14-19

Corson    EDs 16-1 to 16-66, 16-67 (NP)

2221.    Codington    EDs 15-1 to 15-26

Custer    EDs 17-1 to 17-60

Davison    EDs 18-1 to 18-7, 18-19, 18-8 to 18-18

2222.    Day    EDs 19-1 to 19-37

Deuel    EDs 20-1 to 20-24

Dewey    EDs 21-1 to 21-4, 21-6, 21-5, 21-7 to 21-8, 21-30 to 21-31, 21-32 to 21-34 (NP), 21-35, 21-36 to 21-37 (NP), 21-9, 21-38 to 21-41, 21-42 to 21-43 (NP), 21-44, 21-10 to 21-12, 21-45 to 21-49, 21-50 (NP), 21-51, 21-13 to 21-14, 21-52 to 21-56, 21-57 (NP), 21-58, 21-15 to 21-29

Douglas    EDs 22-1 to 22-17

Edmunds    EDs 23-1 to 23-37

2223.    Fall River    EDs 24-1 to 24-52

Gregory    EDs 27-1 to 27-15, 27-35 to 27-36, 27-16 to 27-34

Faulk    EDs 25-1 to 25-35

Grant    EDs 26-1 to 26-26

Haakon    EDs 28-1 to 28-56

2224.    Hamlin    EDs 29-1 to 29-19

Hand    EDs 30-1 to 30-44

Hanson    EDs 31-1 to 31-16

Harding    EDs 32-1 to 32-16, 32-18 to 32-36, 32-37 (NP), 32-38 to 32-45, 32-17, 32-46, 32-47 (NP), 32-48 to 32-60

Hughes    EDs 33-1 to 33-19, 33-20 (NP), 33-21 to 33-30, 33-31 (NP), 33-32 to 33-33

Hyde    EDs 35-1 to 35-21, 35-24 to 35-26, 35-22 to 35-23

Jackson    EDs 36-1 to 36-25

2225.    Hutchinson    EDs 34-1 to 34-28

Jerauld    EDs 37-1 to 37-18

Jones    EDs 38-1 to 38-38

Kingsbury    EDs 39-1 to 39-5, 39-8, 39-6 to 39-7, 39-9 to 39-23

Lake    EDs 40-1 to 40-24

2226.    Lawrence    EDs 41-1 to 41-13, 41-14 to 41-15 (NP), 41-16 to 41-23, 41-24 (NP), 41-25 to 41-38

Lyman    EDs 43-1 to 43-44, 43-45 to 43-46 (NP), 43-47 to 43-58

Lincoln    EDs 42-1 to 42-25

McCook    EDs 44-1 to 44-22

2227.    McPherson    EDs 45-1 to 45-36

Marshall    EDs 46-1 to 46-10, 46-12, 46-11, 46-13 to 46-31

Mellette    EDs 48-1 to 48-31

Meade    EDs 47-1 to 47-38, 47-39 (NP), 47-40 to 47-49, 47-50 (NP), 47-51 to 47-80, 47-81 (NP), 47-82 to 47-109

Miner    EDs 49-1 to 49-21

2228.    Minnehaha    EDs 50-24 to 50-28, 50-53, 50-29 to 50-40, 50-54, 50-41 to 50-42, 50-1 to 50-23, 50-43 to 50-52

2229.    Moody    EDs 51-1 to 51-21

Perkins    EDs 53-1 to 53-47, 53-61, 53-48 to 53-60

Potter    EDs 54-1 to 54-24, 54-25 (NP), 54-26 to 54-31

Pennington    EDs 52-1 to 52-20, 52-90, 52-21 to 52-41, 52-42 to 52-43 (NP), 52-44 to 52-59, 52-60 (NP), 52-61 to 52-81, 52-82 (NP), 52-83 to 52-84, 52-85 (NP), 52-86 to 52-89

2230.    Roberts    EDs 55-1 to 55-40

Sanborn   EDs 56-1 to 56-19

Shannon   EDs 57-1 to 57-5, 57-6 (NP), 57-7, 57-8 (NP), 57-9 to 57-28, 57-29 (NP), 57-30 to 57-31, 57-32 (NP)

Spink   EDs 58-1 to 58-48

2231.   Stanley   EDs 59-1 to 59-24, 59-25 (NP), 59-26 to 59-31, 59-32 (NP), 59-33 to 59-50, 59-54, 59-51 (NP), 59-52, 59-53 (NP)

Sully   EDs 60-1 to 60-33, 60-34 to 60-35 (NP)

Tripp   EDs 62-1 to 62-2, 62-47, 62-3 to 62-21, 62-49, 62-22 to 62-24, 62-50 to 62-51, 62-54 to 62-55, 62-25 to 62-46, 62-48, 62-52 to 62-53, 62-56 (NP)

Todd   EDs 61-1 to 61-45

Turner   EDs 63-1 to 63-28

2232.   Union   EDs 64-1 to 64-17

Walworth   EDs 65-1, 65-32, 65-2 to 65-31

Washabaugh   EDs 66-1 to 66-16, 66-17 (NP), 66-18 to 66-24, 66-25 (NP), 66-26 to 66-36

Washington   EDs 67-1 to 67-7, 68-8 (NP), 67-9 to 67-13, 67-14 to 67-15 (NP), 67-16 to 67-17, 67-18 (NP), 67-19 to 67-23, 67-24 (NP), 67-25 to 67-28, 67-29 (NP), 67-30 to 67-36, 67-37 (NP), 67-38 to 67-39

Yankton   EDs 68-1 to 68-28

Ziebach   EDs 69-1 to 69-5, 69-51 to 69-54, 69-55 (NP), 69-56 to 69-61, 69-62 to 69-63 (NP), 69-64 to 69-70, 69-6 (NP), 69-7 to 69-31, 69-32 (NP), 69-33 to 69-36, 69-37 (NP), 69-38 to 69-50

## Tennessee

2233.   Anderson   EDs 1-1 to 1-17

Bedford   EDs 2-1 to 2-29

Benton   EDs 3-1 to 3-18

2234.   Bledsoe   EDs 4-1 to 4-7

Blount   EDs 5-1 to 5-28

Bradley   EDs 6-1 to 6-7

2235.   Bradley   EDs 6-8 to 6-12

Campbell   EDs 7-1 to 7-20

Cannon   EDs 8-1 to 8-16

Cheatham   EDs 11-1 to 11-9

2236.   Carroll   EDs 9-1 to 9-5, 9-27, 9-6 to 9-26, 9-28 to 9-30

Carter   EDs 10-1 to 10-24

2237.   Chester   EDs 12-1 to 12-15

Claiborne   EDs 13-1 to 13-17

Clay   EDs 14-1 to 14-8

Cumberland   EDs 18-1 to 18-13

2238.   Cocke   EDs 15-1 to 15-20

Coffee   EDs 16-1 to 16-21

Crockett   EDs 17-1 to 17-19

2239.   Davidson, Nashville City   EDs 19-1, 19-84, 19-2, 19-85, 19-3, 19-86, 19-4 to 19-5, 19-87 to 19-92, 19-6, 19-93 to 19-94, 19-7, 19-95 to 19-98, 19-8, 19-99 to 19-100, 19-9, 19-101 to 19-105, 19-10, 19-106, 19-11, 19-107 to 19-109, 19-12, 19-110, 19-13, 19-111, 19-14, 19-112 to 19-113, 19-15, 19-114, 19-16, 19-115 to 19-116, 19-17, 19-117, 19-18, 19-118, 19-19 to 19-20, 19-119, 19-21 to 19-22, 19-120, 19-23, 19-121, 19-24, 19-122

2240.   Davidson, Nashville City   EDs 19-25, 19-123, 19-26, 19-124, 19-27, 19-125, 19-28, 19-30, 19-126, 19-31, 19-127 to 19-128, 19-32, 19-129, 19-33, 19-130, 19-34, 19-131 to 19-132, 19-35, 19-133 to 19-134, 19-36, 19-135 to 19-140, 19-37, 19-141, 19-38, 19-142, 19-39, 19-143, 19-40 to 19-41, 19-144, 19-42, 19-145 to 19-146

2241.   Davidson, Nashville City   EDs 19-43, 19-147 to 19-148, 19-44, 19-149, 19-45, 19-150, 19-46 to 19-47, 19-151 to 19-152, 19-48, 19-153 to 19-154, 19-49, 19-155 to 19-156, 19-50, 19-157, 19-51, 19-158, 19-52, 19-159, 19-53, 19-160, 19-54, 19-161, 19-55 to 19-56, 19-162 to 19-163, 19-57, 19-164 to 19-165, 19-58, 19-166, 19-59, 19-167 to 19-168, 19-60, 19-169 to 19-170, 19-61, 19-171

2242.   Davidson, Nashville City   EDs 19-62, 19-172, 19-63 to 19-64, 19-173, 19-65, 19-174, 19-66, 19-175, 19-67 to 19-68, 19-176, 19-69 to 19-70, 19-177, 19-71, 19-178 to 19-179, 19-29, 19-180 to 19-181, 19-72, 19-182, 19-73, 19-183, 19-74, 19-184 to 19-187, 19-75, 19-188, 19-76, 19-189 to 19-192, 19-77, 19-193

2243.   Davidson, Nashville City   EDs 19-194 to 19-195, 19-78, 19-196, 19-79 to 19-80, 19-197, 19-81, 19-198, 19-82, 19-199, 19-83, 19-200 to 19-201

Davidson   EDs 19-202 to 19-210, 19-244, 19-211 to 19-213, 19-219 to 19-221

2244.   Davidson   EDs 19-214 to 19-218, 19-222 to 19-240, 19-245, 19-241, 19-246, 19-242 to 19-243

De Kalb   EDs 21-1 to 21-27

2245.   Decatur   EDs 20-1 to 20-8, 20-16, 20-9 to 20-15

Dickson   EDs 22-1 to 22-23

Dyer   EDs 23-1 to 23-21

2246.   Dyer   EDs 23-22 to 23-26

Franklin   EDs 26-1 to 26-25

Fayette   EDs 24-1 to 24-28

2247.   Fentress   EDs 25-1 to 25-9

Grainger   EDs 29-1 to 29-12

Gibson   EDs 27-1 to 27-20

2248.   Gibson   EDs 27-21 to 27-43

Giles   EDs 28-1 to 28-32

2249.   Greene   EDs 30-1 to 30-14, 30-20, 30-15 to 30-19, 30-21 to 30-30

Hamblen   EDs 32-1 to 32-13

2250.   Grundy   EDs 31-1 to 31-11

Hardin   EDs 36-1 to 36-18

Hamilton, Chattanooga City   EDs 33-1 to 33-10, 33-86, 33-11 to 33-12, 33-87, 33-13 to 33-18

2251.   Hamilton, Chattanooga City   EDs 33-19 to 33-42

2252.   Hamilton, Chattanooga City   EDs 33-43 to 33-52, 33-91, 33-53 to 33-57, 33-88, 33-58 to 33-61, 33-89, 33-62 to 33-65, 33-92, 33-66 to 33-68, 33-90, 33-69 to 33-70, 33-83 to 33-85

2253.   Hamilton   EDs 33-71 to 33-82

Hancock   EDs 34-1 to 34-12

Hardeman   EDs 35-1 to 35-12

2254.   Hardeman   EDs 35-13 to 35-23

Henderson   EDs 39-1 to 39-4, 39-18, 39-5 to 39-10, 39-19, 39-11, 39-17, 39-12 to 39-13, 39-16, 39-14 to 39-15

Hawkins   EDs 37-1 to 37-18

2255.   Haywood   EDs 38-1 to 38-24

Henry   EDs 40-1 to 40-8, 40-28, 40-9 to 40-19, 40-29, 40-20 to 40-23, 40-30, 40-24 to 40-27

2256.   Hickman   EDs 41-1 to 41-5, 41-18, 41-6 to 41-17

Humphreys   EDs 43-1 to 43-9

Houston   EDs 42-1 to 42-9

Jefferson   EDs 45-1 to 45-16

2257.   Jackson   EDs 44-1 to 44-16

Johnson   EDs 46-1 to 46-12

Knox, Knoxville City   EDs 47-1 to 47-10, 47-12 to 47-19

2258. Knox, Knoxville City   EDs 47-20 to 47-26, 47-11, 47-27 to 47-46

2259. Knox, Knoxville City   EDs 47-47 to 47-78

2260. Knox   EDs 47-79 to 47-96
      Lake   EDs 48-1 to 48-10
      Lauderdale   EDs 49-1 to 49-16

2261. Lauderdale   EDs 49-17 to 49-22
      Lewis   EDs 51-1 to 51-14
      Loudon   EDs 53-1 to 53-12
      Lawrence   EDs 50-1 to 50-22

2262. Lincoln   EDs 52-1 to 52-29
      McMinn   EDs 54-1 to 54-4, 54-12, 54-5 to 54-11, 54-13 to 54-19

2263. McNairy   EDs 55-1 to 55-26
      Meigs   EDs 61-1 to 61-7
      Macon   EDs 56-1 to 56-14
      Morgan   EDs 65-1 to 65-15

2264. Madison   EDs 57-1 to 57-2, 57-35, 57-3 to 57-11, 57-29 to 57-34, 57-12 to 57-28

2265. Marion   EDs 58-1 to 58-5, 58-7 to 58-11, 58-6, 58-12 to 58-13
      Montgomery   EDs 63-1 to 63-35
      Moore   EDs 64-1 to 64-12

2266. Marshall   EDs 59-1 to 59-16
      Maury   EDs 60-1 to 60-25

2267. Monroe   EDs 62-1 to 62-17
      Pickett   EDs 69-1 to 69-7
      Obion   EDs 66-1 to 66-28

2268. Overton   EDs 67-1 to 67-17
      Perry   EDs 68-1 to 68-9
      Polk   EDs 70-1 to 70-11
      Putnam   EDs 71-1, 71-26, 71-2 to 71-10

2269. Putnam   EDs 71-11 to 71-25
      Rhea   EDs 72-1 to 72-6, 72-10, 72-7 to 72-9, 72-11 to 72-13
      Roane   EDs 73-1 to 73-16

2270. Robertson   EDs 74-1 to 74-27
      Rutherford   EDs 75-1 to 75-24

2271. Rutherford   EDs 75-25 to 75-33
      Scott   EDs 76-1 to 76-7, 76-10, 76-8 to 76-9
      Sequatchie   EDs 77-1 to 77-8
      Sevier   EDs 78-1 to 78-20
      Trousdale   EDs 85-1 to 85-11

2272. Shelby   EDs 79-155 to 79-182, 79-250, 79-183 to 79-191

2273. Shelby, Memphis City   EDs 79-1 to 79-3, 79-210, 79-4 to 79-18, 79-216, 79-19, 79-242, 79-20 to 79-32, 79-225, 79-33 to 79-35

2274. Shelby, Memphis City   EDs 79-36 to 79-53, 79-192, 79-54 to 79-56, 79-235, 79-57 to 79-58, 79-227, 79-59

2275. Shelby, Memphis City   EDs 79-226, 79-236, 79-60 to 79-63, 79-224, 79-228, 79-64 to 79-75, 79-231, 79-218, 79-76, 79-211, 79-77 to 79-78, 79-193, 79-79, 79-194, 79-80, 79-217

2276. Shelby, Memphis City   EDs 79-81 to 79-86, 79-246, 79-87 to 79-90, 79-212, 79-91 to 79-102, 79-195

2277. Shelby, Memphis City   EDs 79-103, 79-220, 79-104, 79-244, 79-105 to 79-107, 79-196, 79-209, 79-108, 79-232, 79-109, 79-233, 79-214, 79-110, 79-248 to 79-249, 79-111, 79-241, 79-215, 79-112 to 79-115, 79-223, 79-219, 79-116, 79-230, 79-117, 79-197, 79-118 to 79-120

2278. Shelby, Memphis City   EDs 79-121, 79-198, 79-234, 79-122 to 79-123, 79-200, 79-213, 79-201, 79-124, 79-237, 79-202, 79-125, 79-199, 79-126 to 79-131, 79-203, 79-132 to 79-133, 79-221 to 79-222, 79-134 to 79-137

* 2279. Shelby, Memphis City   EDs 79-138 to 79-139, 79-204 to 79-205, 79-140 to 79-144, 79-240, 79-206, 79-145, 79-207, 79-243, 79-247, 79-146 to 79-148, 79-229, 79-149, 79-208, 79-150 to 79-154

2280. Smith   EDs 80-1 to 80-26
      Union   EDs 87-1 to 87-12
      Stewart   EDs 81-1 to 81-16
      Unicoi   EDs 86-1 to 86-14

2281. Sullivan   EDs 82-1 to 82-33
      Van Buren   EDs 88-1 to 88-9

2282. Sumner   EDs 83-1 to 83-27
      Tipton   EDs 84-1 to 84-20, 84-22, 84-21, 84-23 to 84-29

2283. Warren   EDs 89-1 to 89-21
      Washington   EDs 90-1 to 90-20

2284. Washington   EDs 90-21 to 90-30
      Wayne   EDs 91-1 to 91-11
      Weakley   EDs 92-1 to 92-19, 92-31, 92-20 to 92-26

2285. Weakley   EDs 92-27 to 92-30, 92-32 to 92-34
      White   EDs 93-1 to 93-20
      Williamson   EDs 94-1 to 94-29

2286. Wilson   EDs 95-1 to 95-30

### Texas

2287. Anderson   EDs 1-1 to 1-7, 1-28, 1-8 to 1-27
      Andrews   EDs 2-1 to 2-4
      Austin   EDs 8-1 to 8-19

2288. Angelina   EDs 3-1 to 3-19
      Aransas   EDs 4-1 to 4-7
      Archer   EDs 5-1 to 5-11
      Atascosa   EDs 7-1 to 7-15

2289. Armstrong   EDs 6-1 to 6-5
      Baylor   EDs 12-1 to 12-7
      Bee   EDs 13-1 to 13-13
      Bailey   EDs 9-1 to 9-5
      Blanco   EDs 16-1 to 16-6
      Borden   EDs 17-1 to 17-5
      Bosque   EDs 18-1 to 18-19

2290. Bandera   EDs 10-1 to 10-5
      Bastrop   EDs 11-1 to 11-21
      Bell   EDs 14-1 to 14-16, 14-31 to 14-34

2291. Bell   EDs 14-17 to 14-30
      Bexar, San Antonio City   EDs 15-1 to 15-10

2292. Bexar, San Antonio City   EDs 15-11 to 15-13, 15-196, 15-14, 15-197, 15-15 to 15-34

---

* Roll 2279, Shelby County, Memphis, TN—ED 79-245 was consolidated with ED 79-1; ED 79-238 was consolidated into ED 79-140; ED 79-239 was consolidated into ED 79-140.

2293.  Bexar, San Antonio City   EDs 15-35 to 15-54, 15-206

2294.  Bexar, San Antonio City   EDs 15-55 to 15-61, 15-207 to 15-210, 15-62 to 15-75

2295.  Bexar, San Antonio City   EDs 15-76 to 15-82, 15-214 to 15-216, 15-83 to 15-90, 15-91 (NP), 15-92 to 15-93

2296.  Bexar, San Antonio City   EDs 15-94 to 15-112

2297.  Bexar, San Antonio City   EDs 15-113 to 15-134

2298.  Bexar, San Antonio City   EDs 15-135 to 15-146

Bexar   EDs 15-147 to 15-154, 15-202, 15-155, 15-211 to 15-213, 15-217 to 15-220, 15-222 to 15-223, 15-164 to 15-165

2299.  Bexar   EDs 15-156 to 15-163, 15-224 to 15-227, 15-166 to 15-170, 15-184 to 15-191, 15-228 to 15-231, 15-171 to 15-173, 15-174 (NP), 15-175 to 15-183, 15-198 to 15-201, 15-203, 15-204 (NP), 15-205, 15-192 to 15-193, 15-194 (NP), 15-195, 15-221

2300.  Bowie   EDs 19-1 to 19-10, 19-34, 19-11 to 19-12, 19-25 to 19-27, 19-13 to 19-24, 19-28 to 19-33

Briscoe   EDs 23-1 to 23-6

2301.  Brazoria   EDs 20-1 to 20-13, 20-14 (NP), 20-15 to 20-18, 20-19 (NP), 20-20 to 20-23

Brazos   EDs 21-1 to 21-16

Brooks   EDs 24-1 to 24-5

2302.  Brewster   EDs 22-1 to 22-9

Burleson   EDs 26-1 to 26-15

Brown   EDs 25-1 to 25-23

2303.  Burnet   EDs 27-1 to 27-71

Calhoun   EDs 29-1 to 29-8

Camp   EDs 32-1 to 32-8

Caldwell   EDs 28-1 to 28-16

2304.  Caldwell   EDs 28-17 to 28-18

Callahan   EDs 30-1 to 30-13

Carson   EDs 33-1 to 33-9

Cameron   EDs 31-1 to 31-3, 31-20 to 31-29, 31-42 to 31-43

2305.  Cameron   EDs 31-4 to 31-9, 31-10 (NP), 31-11 to 31-19, 31-30 to 31-37, 31-44, 31- 38 to 31-41

2306.  Cass   EDs 34-1 to 34-28

Castro   EDs 35-1 to 35-8

Chambers   EDs 36-1 to 36-8

Childress   EDs 38-1 to 38-15

2307.  Cherokee   EDs 37-1 to 37-12, 37-24 to 37-27, 37-36, 37-28 to 37-31, 37-33 to 37-35, 37-13 to 37-23, 37-32

Comal   EDs 46-1 to 46-12

2308.  Clay   EDs 39-1 to 39-16

Crosby   EDs 54-1 to 54-11

Cochran   EDs 40-1 to 40-4

Coleman   EDs 42-1 to 42-19

2309.  Coke   EDs 41-1 to 41-8

Coryell   EDs 50-1 to 50-17

Collin   EDs 43-1 to 43-5

2310.  Collin   EDs 43-6 to 43-40

Collingsworth   EDs 44-1 to 44-12

2311.  Colorado   EDs 45-1 to 45-16

Concho   EDs 48-1 to 48-6

Comanche   EDs 47-1 to 47-17

Cottle   EDs 51-1 to 51-7

2312.  Cooke   EDs 49-1 to 49-25

Crane   EDs 52-1 to 52-5

Crockett   EDs 53-1 to 53-4

Culberson   EDs 55-1 to 55-4

Dallam   EDs 56-1 to 56-10

Dawson   EDs 58-1 to 58-14

2313.  Dallas, Dallas City   EDs 57-1 to 57-17

2314.  Dallas, Dallas City   EDs 57-18 to 57-30

2315.  Dallas, Dallas City   EDs 57-31 to 57-45

2316.  Dallas, Dallas City   EDs 57-46 to 57-57

2317.  Dallas, Dallas City   EDs 57-58 to 57-66

2318.  Dallas, Dallas City   EDs 57-67 to 57-76

2319.  Dallas, Dallas City   EDs 57-77 to 57-84

2320.  Dallas, Dallas City   EDs 57-85 to 57-95

2321.  Dallas, Dallas City   EDs 57-145 to 57-149

Dallas   EDs 57-96 to 57-100

2322.  Dallas   EDs 57-101 to 57-125, 57-126 (NP), 57-127 to 57-144

2323.  Deaf Smith   EDs 59-1 to 59-17

Delta   EDs 60-1 to 60-13

Dickens   EDs 63-1 to 63-8

Denton   EDs 61-1 to 61-23

2324.  Denton   EDs 61-24 to 61-30

Dimmit   EDs 64-1 to 64-10

Donley   EDs 65-1 to 65-8

DeWitt   EDs 62-1 to 62-24

2325.  Duval   EDs 66-1 to 66-9

Eastland   EDs 67-1 to 67-5, 67-6 (NP), 67-7 to 67-9, 67-18 to 67-22, 67-10 to 67-17, 67-23 to 67-36

Ector   EDs 68-1 to 68-8

2326.  Edwards   EDs 69-1 to 69-7

Erath   EDs 72-1 to 72-22

Ellis   EDs 70-1 to 70-17, 70-31 to 70-33

2327.  Ellis   EDs 70-18 to 70-30, 70-34 to 70-44

El Paso, El Paso City   EDs 71-1 to 71-19

2328.  El Paso, El Paso City   EDs 71-20 to 71-42, 71-90, 71-43 to 71-52

2329.  El Paso, El Paso City   EDs 71-53 to 71-87, 71-88 (NP), 71-89

2330.  Falls   EDs 73-1 to 73-28

Fannin   EDs 74-1 to 74-11, 74-29 to 74-30

2331.  Fannin   EDs 74-12 to 74-28, 74-31 to 74-40

Fayette   EDs 75-1 to 75-5, 75-29, 75-6 to 75-24

2332.  Fayette   EDs 75-25 to 75-28

Freestone   EDs 81-1 to 81-21

Fisher   EDs 76-1 to 76-12

Floyd   EDs 77-1 to 77-9

2333.  Foard   EDs 78-1 to 78-8

Franklin   EDs 80-1 to 80-11

Frio   EDs 82-1 to 82-9

Fort Bend   EDs 79-1 to 79-20

2334.  Gaines   EDs 83-1 to 83-3

Grimes   EDs 93-1 to 93-17

Galveston   EDs 84-1 to 84-4, 84-46, 84-5 to 84-16, 84-26 to 84-29

2335.  Galveston   EDs 84-17 to 84-25, 84-30 to 84-45

Gillespie   EDs 86-1 to 86-10

Glasscock   EDs 87-1 to 87-4

2336. Garza   EDs 85-1 to 85-5

Gray   EDs 90-14, 90-1 to 90-13

Goliad   EDs 88-1 to 88-9

Gregg   EDs 92-1 to 92-13

2337. Gonzales   EDs 89-1 to 89-24

Grayson   EDs 91-1 to 91-16, 91-52 to 91-55, 91-58 to 91-60

2338. Grayson   EDs 91-17 to 91-39, 91-56 to 91-57, 91-40 to 91-51

Hall   EDs 96-1 to 96-16, 96-17 (NP)

2339. Guadalupe   EDs 94-1 to 94-25

Hale   EDs 95-1 to 95-16

Hansford   EDs 98-1 to 98-5

2340. Hamilton   EDs 97-1 to 97-12

Hays   EDs 105-1 to 105-2, 105-13, 105-3 to 105-12

Hardeman   EDs 99-1 to 99-11

Hardin   EDs 100-1 to 100-11

2341. Harris, Houston City   EDs 101-1 to 101-11, 101-217, 101-12, 101-218, 101-13

2342. Harris, Houston City   EDs 101-14 to 101-28

2343. Harris, Houston City   EDs 101-29 to 101-40

2344. Harris, Houston City   EDs 101-41 to 101-47, 101-210 to 101-211, 101-48, 101-212 to 101-214, 101-49, 101-215 to 101-216

2345. Harris, Houston City   EDs 101-50 to 101-59

2346. Harris, Houston City   EDs 101-219, 101-60 to 101-75, 101-201

2347. Harris, Houston City   EDs 101-202, 101-76, 101-203, 101-77, 101-204 to 101-206, 101-78, 101-207, 101-79 to 101-83

2348. Harris, Houston City   EDs 101-84 to 101-99

2349. Harris, Houston City   EDs 101-100, 101-208, 101-101, 101-209, 101-102 to 101-116

2350. Harris, Houston City   EDs 101-117, 101-220, 101-118 to 101-129

2351. Harris, Houston City   EDs 101-130 to 101-136, 101-141 to 101-144

2352. Harris   EDs 101-137 to 101-140, 101-145 to 101-165, 101-166 (NP), 101-167 to 101-188

2353. Harris   EDs 101-189 to 101-200

Hemphill   EDs 106-1 to 106-5, 106-6 (NP), 106-7

Harrison   EDs 102-1 to 102-4, 102-18 to 102-31

2354. Harrison   EDs 102-5 to 102-17

Hartley   EDs 103-1 to 103-6

Haskell   EDs 104-1 to 104-15

Henderson   EDs 107-1 to 107-7

2355. Henderson   EDs 107-8 to 107-28

Hood   EDs 111-1 to 111-10

Hidalgo   EDs 108-1 to 108-9, 108-27 to 108-36

2356. Hidalgo   EDs 108-10 to 108-26, 108-65, 108-56 to 108-62, 108-63 (NP), 108-64, 108-37 to 108-55

2357. Hill   EDs 109-1 to 109-24, 109-40, 109-25 to 109-39

Hockley   EDs 110-1 to 110-8

2358. Hopkins   EDs 112-1 to 112-29

Houston   EDs 113-1 to 113-7, 113-28, 113-8 to 113-27

2359. Howard   EDs 114-1 to 114-6, 114-9, 114-7 to 114-8

Hudspeth   EDs 115-1 to 115-4

Hunt   EDs 116-1 to 116-21

2360. Hunt   EDs 116-22 to 116-41

Irion   EDs 118-1 to 118-5

Hutchinson   EDs 117-1 to 117-13

Jack   EDs 119-1 to 119-5, 119-11, 119-6 to 119-10

Jeff Davis   EDs 122-1 to 122-4

2361. Jackson   EDs 120-1 to 120-12

Jasper   EDs 121-1 to 121-12

Jefferson   EDs 123-1 to 123-26

2362. Jefferson   EDs 123-27 to 123-44, 123-46 to 123-60

* 2363. Jefferson   EDs 123-61 to 123-70, 123-84, 123-45, 123-71 to 123-83

2364. Jim Hogg   EDs 124-1 to 124-5

Jim Wells   EDs 125-1 to 125-9

Kendall   EDs 130-1 to 130-7

Kenedy   EDs 131-1 to 131-4

Johnson   EDs 126-1 to 126-24

2365. Johnson   EDs 126-25 to 126-30

Jones   EDs 127-1 to 127-13, 127-19, 127-14 to 127-18

Karnes   EDs 128-1 to 128-17

Kent   EDs 132-1 to 132-9

2366. Kaufman   EDs 129-1 to 129-27

Kleberg   EDs 137-1 to 137-7

2367. Kerr   EDs 133-1, 133-7, 133-2, 133-8, 133-3 to 133-6

Kimble   EDs 134-1 to 134-5

Knox   EDs 138-1 to 138-15

King   EDs 135-1 to 135-5

Kinney   EDs 136-1 to 136-8

Lamar   EDs 139-1 to 139-15

2368. Lamar   EDs 139-16 to 139-39

Lamb   EDs 140-13, 140-1 to 140-12

Lampasas   EDs 141-1 to 141-9

2369. La Salle   EDs 142-1 to 142-3, 142-9, 142-4 to 142-8

Lee   EDs 144-1 to 144-14

Lipscomb   EDs 148-1 to 148-9

Lavaca   EDs 143-1 to 143-22

2370. Leon   EDs 145-20, 145-1 to 145-19

Llano   EDs 150-1 to 150-9

Liberty   EDs 146-1 to 146-14

Live Oak   EDs 149-1 to 149-9

2371. Limestone   EDs 147-1 to 147-29

Loving   EDs 151-1

Lynn   EDs 153-1 to 153-10

2372. Lubbock   EDs 152-1 to 152-31

McCulloch   EDs 154-1 to 154-11

McMullen   EDs 156-1 to 156-4

2373. McLennan   EDs 155-1 to 155-22

2374. McLennan   EDs 155-23 to 155-61

Martin   EDs 159-1 to 159-7

2375. Madison   EDs 157-1 to 157-12

Marion   EDs 158-1 to 158-7

---

* Roll 2363, Jefferson County—There appears to be no ED 123-84.

Mason   EDs 160-1 to 160-8

Matagorda   EDs 161-1 to 161-9, 161-15, 161-10 to 161-14

Maverick   EDs 162-1 to 162-6, 162-7 (NP), 162-8 to 162-9

2376.   Medina   EDs 163-1 to 163-4, 163-11, 163-5 to 163-10

Menard   EDs 164-1 to 164-6

Midland   EDs 165-1 to 165-6

Milam   EDs 166-1 to 166-17

2377.   Milam   EDs 166-18 to 166-25, 166-28, 166-26 to 166-27

Mitchell   EDs 168-1 to 168-13

Mills   EDs 167-1 to 167-10

Montague   EDs 169-1 to 169-20

2378.   Montgomery   EDs 170-1 to 170-14

Moore   EDs 171-1 to 171-4

Morris   EDs 172-1 to 172-12

Motley   EDs 173-1 to 173-7

Nolan   EDs 177-1 to 177-14

2379.   Nacogdoches   EDs 174-1 to 174-22

Navarro   EDs 175-1 to 175-17, 175-43 to 175-46

2380.   Navarro   EDs 175-18 to 175-42

Newton   EDs 176-1 to 176-9

Orange   EDs 181-1 to 181-9

2381.   Nueces   EDs 178-1 to 178-6, 178-24, 178-7 to 178-23

2382.   Ochiltree   EDs 179-1 to 179-6

Oldham   EDs 180-1 to 180-5

Palo Pinto   EDs 182-1 to 182-19

Panola   EDs 183-1 to 183-19

2383.   Parker   EDs 184-1 to 184-20

Parmer   EDs 185-1 to 185-5

Pecos   EDs 186-1 to 186-9

Polk   EDs 187-1 to 187-15

2384.   Potter   EDs 188-1 to 188-23

Rains   EDs 190-1 to 190-7

2385.   Presidio   EDs 189-1 to 189-6, 189-13, 189-7 to 189-12

Randall   EDs 191-1 to 191-6

Reagan   EDs 192-1 to 192-6

Real   EDs 193-1 to 193-4

Roberts   EDs 197-1 to 197-5

Red River   EDs 194-1 to 194-26

2386.   Red River   EDs 194-27 to 194-29

Reeves   EDs 195-1 to 195-9

Refugio   EDs 196-1 to 196-11

Rockwall   EDs 199-1 to 199-8

Robertson   EDs 198-1 to 198-19

2387.   Runnels   EDs 200-1 to 200-13

Swisher   EDs 219-1 to 219-7

Rusk   EDs 201-1 to 201-24

2388.   Rusk   EDs 201-25 to 201-28

San Patricio   EDs 205-1 to 205-10, 205-13, 205-11 to 205-12

Sabine   EDs 202-1 to 202-11

San Augustine   EDs 203-1 to 203-9

Sherman   EDs 211-1 to 211-6

2389.   San Jacinto   EDs 204-1 to 204-10

San Saba   EDs 206-1 to 206-3, 206-8, 206-4 to 206-7

Shackelford   EDs 209-1 to 209-7

Schleicher   EDs 207-1 to 207-5

Scurry   EDs 208-1 to 208-11

Somervell   EDs 213-1 to 213-5

Sterling   EDs 216-1 to 216-4

Stonewall   EDs 217-1 to 217-9

Sutton   EDs 218-1 to 218-5

2390.   Shelby   EDs 210-1 to 210-25

Smith   EDs 212-1 to 212-18, 212-42 to 212-46

2391.   Smith   EDs 212-19 to 212-41, 212-47 to 212-49

Starr   EDs 214-1 to 214-4, 214-5 (NP), 214-6 to 214-13

Stephens   EDs 215-1 to 215-12

2392.   Tarrant, Fort Worth City   EDs 220-1 to 220-18

2393.   Tarrant, Fort Worth City   EDs 220-19 to 220-34

2394.   Tarrant, Fort Worth City   EDs 220-35 to 220-50

2395.   Tarrant, Fort Worth City   EDs 220-51 to 220-68

2396.   Tarrant, Fort Worth City   EDs 220-69 to 220-78

2397.   Tarrant, Fort Worth City   EDs 220-79 to 220-81, 220-85 to 220-86, 220-82 to 220-84, 220-87, 220-128

2398.   Tarrant, Fort Worth City   EDs 220-88 to 220-103, 220-104 (void), 220-105 to 220-119

2399.   Tarrant   EDs 220-120 to 220-127

Terrell   EDs 222-1 to 222-4

Titus   EDs 225-1 to 225-14

Taylor   EDs 221-1 to 221-17, 221-35, 221-18 to 221-20

2400.   Taylor   EDs 221-21 to 221-26, 221-34, 221-27, 221-32, 221-28, 221-33, 221-29 to 221-31

Terry   EDs 223-1 to 223-7

Throckmorton   EDs 224-1 to 224-5

Tom Green   EDs 226-1 to 226-10

* 2401.   Tom Green   EDs 226-11 to 226-18

Wheeler   EDs 242-1 to 242-12, 242-13 (NP), 242-14 to 242-15

Travis   EDs 227-1 to 227-7, 227-42 to 227-44, 227-45 (NP), 227-46 to 227-57

2402.   Travis   EDs 227-8 to 227-41

2403.   Trinity   EDs 228-1 to 228-13

Tyler   EDs 229-1 to 229-9

Upshur   EDs 230-1 to 230-21

Upton   EDs 231-1 to 231-7

2404.   Uvalde   EDs 232-1 to 232-2, 232-11, 232-3 to 232-10

Val Verde   EDs 233-1 to 233-3, 233-13, 233-4 to 233-12

Van Zandt   EDs 234-1 to 234-23

2405.   Van Zandt   EDs 234-24 to 234-29

Victoria   EDs 235-1 to 235-16

Walker   EDs 236-1 to 236-15

Waller   EDs 237-1 to 237-7

2406.   Ward   EDs 238-1 to 238-8

Wise   EDs 249-1 to 249-19

Washington   EDs 239-1 to 239-19

2407.   Webb   EDs 240-1, 240-26, 240-2 to 240-25

Zavala   EDs 254-1 to 254-4, 254-7, 254-5 to 254-6

2408.   Wharton   EDs 241-1 to 241-2, 241-22, 241-3, 241-23, 241-4 to 241-20, 241-24, 241-21

Wichita   EDs 243-1 to 243-12

---

* Roll 2401, Travis County—There appears to be no ED 227-58.

2409.  Wichita   EDs 243-13 to 243-40

2410.  Wichita   EDs 243-41 to 243-55

      Wilbarger   EDs 244-1 to 244-16

2411.  Willacy   EDs 245-1 to 245-11

      Williamson   EDs 246-1 to 246-30

2412.  Wilson   EDs 247-1 to 247-12, 247-16, 247-13 to 247-15

      Winkler   EDs 248-1 to 248-6

      Wood   EDs 250-1 to 250-24

2413.  Yoakum   EDs 251-1 to 251-4

      Young   EDs 252-1, 252-16, 252-2 to 252-15

      Zapata   EDs 253-1 to 253-4

## *Utah*

2414.  Beaver   EDs 1-1 to 1-2, 1-11, 1-3, 1-12, 1-4 to 1-6, 1-10, 1-7 to 1-9

      Box Elder   EDs 2-1 to 2-7, 2-49, 2-8 to 2-22, 2-23 (NP), 2-24 to 2-34, 2-35 (NP), 2-36 to 2-48

      Cache   EDs 3-45, 3-1 to 3-10, 3-46, 3-11 to 3-18, 3-47 to 3-54, 3-19 to 3-39, 3-55, 3-40 to 3-44

2415.  Carbon   EDs 4-1 to 4-2, 4-3 (NP), 4-4 to 4-6, 4-7 (NP), 4-8 to 4-9, 4-10 (NP), 4-11 to 4-38, 4-39 (NP), 4-40

      Emery   EDs 8-1 to 8-22

      Daggett   EDs 5-1 to 5-5

      Davis   EDs 6-1, 6-19, 6-2 to 6-18

      Duchesne   EDs 7-1, 7-2 to 7-3 (NP), 7-4 to 7-12, 7-13 (NP), 7-14 to 7-20, 7-21 to 7-22 (NP), 7-23 to 7-24, 7-25 to 7-26 (NP), 7-27, 7-28 to 7-29 (NP), 7-30, 7-31 (NP), 7-32 to 7-34, 7-35 to 7-38 (NP), 7-39 to 7-40, 7-41 (NP), 7-42 to 7-46, 7-47 to 7-48 (NP)

2416.  Garfield   EDs 9-1 to 9-12, 9-14, 9-13, 9-15

      Grand   EDs 10-1 to 10-12

      Iron   EDs 11-1 to 11-15

      Juab   EDs 12-1, 12-16, 12-2 to 12-12, 12-17, 12-13 to 12-15

      Kane   EDs 13-1, 13-2 (NP), 13-3 to 13-7

      Millard   EDs 14-1 to 14-32

      Morgan   EDs 15-1 to 15-4, 15-7, 15-5 to 15-6

      Piute   EDs 16-1 to 16-8

      Rich   EDs 17-1 to 17-7

      Salt Lake   EDs 18-96 to 18-100, 18-101 (NP)

2417.  Salt Lake   EDs 18-102 to 18-134

      San Juan   EDs 19-1 to 19-2, 19-13, 19-11 to 19-12, 19-3 to 19-6, 19-14, 19-7 to 19-10

2418.  Salt Lake, Salt Lake City   EDs 18-1 to 18-11, 18-135 to 18-136, 18-12 to 18-21

2419.  Salt Lake, Salt Lake City   EDs 18-22 to 18-44

2420.  Salt Lake, Salt Lake City   EDs 18-45 to 18-49, 18-137, 18-50, 18-77 to 18-95

2421.  Salt Lake, Salt Lake City   EDs 18-51 to 18-76

2422.  Sanpete   EDs 20-1 to 20-28

      Summit   EDs 22-1 to 22-22

      Sevier   EDs 21-1 to 21-22, 21-28, 21-23 to 21-27

      Tooele   EDs 23-1 to 23-10, 23-24 (NP), 23-11 to 23-12, 23-13 (NP), 23-14 to 23-23

      Wayne   EDs 28-1 to 28-13

2423.  Utah   EDs 25-1 to 25-29, 25-30 (void), 25-31 to 25-39, 25-50 to 25-54, 25-40 to 25-49, 25-55 to 25-69

2424.  Uintah   EDs 24-1 to 24-14, 24-15 (NP), 24-16 to 24-19, 24-20 (NP), 24-21 to 24-24, 24-25 (NP)

      Wasatch   EDs 26-1 to 26-13

      Washington   EDs 27-1 to 27-5, 27-31 (NP), 27-6, 27-29 (NP), 27-7 to 27-10, 27-11 (NP), 27-12 to 27-15, 27-16 (NP), 27-17, 27-32 (NP), 27-18 to 27-21, 27-30, 27-22, 27-33, 27-23 to 27-26, 27-34 (NP), 27-27 to 27-28

      Weber   EDs 29-14 to 29-17, 29-49, 29-18 to 29-26, 29-50, 29-27 to 29-32, 29-51

2425.  Weber   EDs 29-33, 29-52 to 29-53, 29-34 to 29-36, 29-54 to 29-58, 29-1 to 29-13, 29-37 to 29-48

## *Vermont*

2426.  Addison   EDs 1-1 to 1-27

      Essex   EDs 5-1, 5-2 (NP), 5-3 to 5-13, 5-14 (NP), 5-15 to 5-18, 5-19 (NP), 5-20

      Bennington   EDs 2-1 to 2-11, 2-29, 2-12 to 2-28

      Grand Isle   EDs 7-1 to 7-6

2427.  Caledonia   EDs 3-1 to 3-30

      Chittenden   EDs 4-1 to 4-25

2428.  Chittenden   EDs 4-26 to 4-47

      Franklin   EDs 6-1 to 6-28

2429.  Lamoille   EDs 8-1 to 8-16

      Orange   EDs 9-1 to 9-22

      Orleans   EDs 10-1 to 10-24, 10-31, 10-25 to 10-30

2430.  Rutland   EDs 11-1 to 11-27, 11-43, 11-28, 11-53, 11-29 to 11-39, 11-54, 11-40 to 11-42, 11-44 to 11-52

2431.  Washington   EDs 12-1 to 12-21, 12-29 to 12-31, 12-22 to 12-28, 12-32 to 12-41

      Windsor   EDs 14-1 to 14-11

2432.  Windsor   EDs 14-12 to 14-34, 14-40, 14-35 to 14-39

      Windham   EDs 13-1 to 13-6, 13-38, 13-7 to 13-37

## * *Virginia*

2433.  Accomack   EDs 1-1 to 1-21

      Alleghany   EDs 3-1 to 3-14

2434.  Albemarle   EDs 2-1 to 2-16

      Amelia   EDs 4-1 to 4-6

      Amherst   EDs 5-1 to 5-13

2435.  Appomattox   EDs 6-1 to 6-8

      Augusta   EDs 8-1 to 8-8, 8-21, 8-12 to 8-14, 8-9 to 8-11, 8-15 to 8-20

      Bath   EDs 9-1 to 9-4

2436.  Arlington   EDs 7-1, 7-17, 7-2 to 7-16, 7-18 to 7-21

      Bedford   EDs 10-1 to 10-20

2437.  Bland   EDs 11-1 to 11-4

      Brunswick   EDs 13-1 to 13-6, 13-15, 13-7 to 13-14

      Botetourt   EDs 12-1, 12-8, 12-2 to 12-7, 12-9 to 12-11

      Buckingham   EDs 15-12, 15-1 to 15-11

---

* Virginia—Rolls 2465 to 2483 comprise the independent cities in Virginia, which have the status of counties.

2438. Buchanan   EDs 14-1 to 14-5, 14-14, 14-6 to 14-13

Campbell   EDs 16-1 to 16-2, 16-17, 16-7 to 16-10, 16-3 to 16-6, 16-11 to 16-16

Caroline   EDs 17-1 to 17-13

2439. Carroll   EDs 18-1 to 18-3, 18-7, 18-12, 18-16, 18-4 to 18-6, 18-10, 18-8 to 18-9, 18-11, 18-13 to 18-15, 18-17 to 18-19

Charles City   EDs 19-1 to 19-3

Charlotte   EDs 20-1 to 20-5, 20-9, 20-12, 20-6 to 20-8, 20-10 to 20-11, 20-13 to 20-15

Clarke   EDs 22-1, 22-7, 22-2 to 22-3, 22-5, 22-4, 22-6, 22-8

2440. Chesterfield   EDs 21-1 to 21-8, 21-19, 21-9 to 21-18

Craig   EDs 23-1 to 23-4

Culpeper   EDs 24-1 to 24-9

Cumberland   EDs 25-1 to 25-6

2441. Dickenson   EDs 26-1 to 26-10

Floyd   EDs 32-1 to 32-12

Dinwiddie   EDs 27-1 to 27-12

Essex   EDs 29-1 to 29-7

* 2442. Elizabeth City   EDs 28-1 to 28-11, 28-15 to 28-19

Fairfax   EDs 30-1 to 30-9, 30-22, 30-10 to 30-21, 30-23 to 30-25

2443. Fauquier   EDs 31-1 to 31-16

Fluvanna   EDs 33-1 to 33-10

Franklin   EDs 34-1 to 34-20

2444. Frederick   EDs 35-1 to 35-12

Giles   EDs 36-1 to 36-10

Gloucester   EDs 37-1 to 37-7

Greensville   EDs 41-1, 41-4, 41-7, 41-2 to 41-3, 41-5 to 41-6, 41-8 to 41-9

2445. Goochland   EDs 38-1 to 38-7

Grayson   EDs 39-1 to 39-14

Greene   EDs 40-1 to 40-7

Hanover   EDs 43-1 to 43-12

2446. Halifax   EDs 42-1 to 42-29

Henrico   EDs 44-11 to 44-16

2447. Henrico   EDs 44-1 to 44-10

Henry   EDs 45-1 to 45-7, 45-13 to 45-19

Highland   EDs 46-1 to 46-5

Isle of Wight   EDs 47-1 to 47-9

2448. James City   EDs 48-1 to 48-3

King and Queen   EDs 49-1 to 49-6

King George   EDs 50-1 to 50-6

King William   EDs 51-1 to 51-8

Lancaster   EDs 52-1 to 52-6

Loudoun   EDs 54-1 to 54-20

2449. Lee   EDs 53-1 to 53-7, 53-19, 53-8 to 53-18

Louisa   EDs 55-1 to 55-12

Lunenburg   EDs 56-1 to 56-13

2450. Madison   EDs 57-1 to 57-6

Mathews   EDs 58-1 to 58-6

Mecklenburg   EDs 59-3 to 59-8, 59-1 to 59-2, 59-9 to 59-24

2451. Middlesex   EDs 60-1 to 60-7

Montgomery   EDs 61-1 to 61-14

Nansemond   EDs 62-1 to 62-14

New Kent   EDs 64-1 to 64-4

2452. Nelson   EDs 63-1 to 63-11

Northumberland   EDs 67-1 to 67-7

Norfolk   EDs 65-1 to 65-8, 65-14 to 65-19, 65-20 to 65-21 (void), 65-22 to 65-23

2453. Norfolk   EDs 65-24 to 65-26

Northampton   EDs 66-1 to 66-8

Nottoway   EDs 68-1 to 68-10

Orange   EDs 69-1 to 69-10

2454. Page   EDs 70-1 to 70-11

Patrick   EDs 71-1, 71-6, 71-2 to 71-5, 71-7 to 71-13

Pittsylvania   EDs 72-8, 72-18, 72-7, 72-9 to 72-12, 72-19 to 72-24

2455. Pittsylvania   EDs 72-25 to 72-33, 72-1 to 72-6, 72-13 to 72-17

Powhatan   EDs 73-1 to 73-6

2456. Prince Edward   EDs 74-1 to 74-13

Prince George   EDs 75-1 to 75-7

Prince William   EDs 76-1 to 76-13

Princess Anne   EDs 77-2 to 77-8

2457. Princess Anne   EDs 77-1, 77-9 to 77-13

Pulaski   EDs 78-1 to 78-15

Rappahannock   EDs 79-1 to 79-7

Richmond   EDs 80-1 to 80-5

Roanoke   EDs 81-5 to 81-10

2458. Roanoke   EDs 81-1 to 81-4, 81-11 to 81-14

Rockbridge   EDs 82-1 to 82-16

Rockingham   EDs 83-8 to 83-9

2459. Rockingham   EDs 83-1 to 83-7, 83-10 to 83-24

Russell   EDs 84-1 to 84-19

2460. Scott   EDs 85-1 to 85-20

Shenandoah   EDs 86-1 to 86-9, 86-21, 86-10, 86-22, 86-11 to 86-20, 86-23 to 86-25

Spotsylvania   EDs 89-1 to 89-4

2461. Spotsylvania   EDs 89-5 to 89-9

Stafford   EDs 90-1 to 90-7

Sussex   EDs 92-1 to 92-10

Smyth   EDs 87-1 to 87-6, 87-15, 87-7 to 87-14

2462. Southampton   EDs 88-1 to 88-14, 88-22, 88-15 to 88-21

Surry   EDs 91-1 to 91-8

Tazewell   EDs 93-1 to 93-11

2463. Tazewell   EDs 93-12 to 93-17

Warren   EDs 94-1 to 94-12

Washington   EDs 96-1 to 96-21

** 2464. Warwick   EDs 95-1 to 95-8

Westmoreland   EDs 97-1 to 97-8

York   EDs 100-1 to 100-6

Wise   EDs 98-1 to 98-17

2465. Wise   EDs 98-18 to 98-29

Wythe   EDs 99-1 to 99-14

Buena Vista City   EDs 103-1 to 103-2

2466. Alexandria City   EDs 101-1 to 101-12

* Roll 2442, Elizabeth City—EDs 28-12 to 28-14 are on roll 2467, the independent city of Elizabeth City, now Hampton.

** Roll 2464, York County—ED 100-7 is on roll 2483, Williamsburg City.

Bristol City   EDs 102-1 to 102-6

Charlottesville City   EDs 104-1 to 104-10

2467.   Clifton Forge City   EDs 105-1 to 105-4

Danville City   EDs 106-1 to 106-15

Fredericksburg City   EDs 107-1 to 107-4

Hampton City   EDs 28-12 to 28-14

Harrisonburg City   EDs 108-1 to 108-4

Martinsville City   EDs 45-8 to 45-12

2468.   Hopewell City   EDs 109-1 to 109-5

Lynchburg City   EDs 110-1 to 110-10, 110-24, 110-11 to 110-23

2469.   Newport News City   EDs 111-5 to 111-24, 111-1 to 111-4

Norfolk City   EDs 112-1 to 112-15

2470.   Norfolk City   EDs 112-16 to 112-59

2471.   Norfolk City   EDs 112-60 to 112-90

2472.   Norfolk City   EDs 112-91 to 112-116

2473.   Petersburg City   EDs 113-1 to 113-20

Portsmouth City   EDs 114-1 to 114-19, 114-34

2474.   Portsmouth City   EDs 114-20 to 114-23, 114-33, 114-24 to 114-32

Radford City   EDs 115-1 to 115-4

Richmond City   EDs 116-1, 116-104 to 116-105, 116-2, 116-106, 116-3, 116-107 to 116-108

2475.   Richmond City   EDs 116-4, 116-109, 116-5, 116-110, 116-6 to 116-7, 116-111 to 116-112, 116-8, 116-113, 116-9 to 116-15

2476.   Richmond City   EDs 116-114 to 116-115, 116-16 to 116-19, 116-116, 116-20, 116-117 to 116-118, 116-21 to 116-27, 116-119, 116-28 to 116-29, 116-120 to 116-121

2477.   Richmond City   EDs 116-30 to 116-47, 116-122, 116-48 to 116-49

2478.   Richmond City   EDs 116-50, 116-123, 116-51, 116-124, 116-52 to 116-53, 116-125, 116-54 to 116-56, 116-126, 116-57 to 116-69, 116-127 to 116-128

2479.   Richmond City   EDs 116-70, 116-129 to 116-130, 116-71 to 116-76, 116-131, 116-77 to 116-79

2480.   Richmond City   EDs 116-132, 116-80 to 116-84, 116-133, 116-85 to 116-94

2481.   Richmond City   EDs 116-95 to 116-103

Roanoke City   EDs 117-1 to 117-9

2482.   Roanoke City   EDs 117-10 to 117-34

* 2483.   Roanoke City   EDs 117-35 to 117-39

South Norfolk City   EDs 65-9 to 65-13

Suffolk City   EDs 119-1 to 119-7

Staunton City   EDs 118-1 to 118-6

Williamsburg City   EDs 48-4 to 48-5, 100-7

Winchester City   EDs 120-1 to 120-4

### Washington

2484.   Adams   EDs 1-1 to 1-16, 1-18, 1-17, 1-19 to 1-22

Asotin   EDs 2-1 to 2-17

Benton   EDs 3-1 to 3-29

Chelan   EDs 4-1 to 4-17, 4-19 to 4-20, 4-18, 4-21 to 4-30, 4-34, 4-31 to 4-33, 4-35 to 4-42

2485.   Chelan   EDs 4-43 to 4-49

Clark   EDs 6-1 to 6-14, 6-56, 6-15 to 6-24, 6-61, 6-25 to 6-32, 6-40, 6-33 to 6-39, 6-41 to 6-55, 6-57 to 6-60

** 2486.   Clallam   EDs 5-1 to 5-21, 5-37, 5-22 to 5-33, 5-34 (void), 5-35 to 5-36

Ferry   EDs 10-1 to 10-7, 10-18, 10-8 to 10-17, 10-19

Columbia   EDs 7-1 to 7-2, 7-6, 7-15 to 7-16, 7-20, 7-25, 7-3 to 7-5, 7-7 to 7-10, 7-11 (void), 7-12 to 7-14, 7-17 to 7-19, 7-21 to 7-24, 7-26 to 7-28

Douglas   EDs 9-1 to 9-32

Franklin   EDs 11-1 to 11-3, 11-5 to 11-16

Garfield   EDs 12-1, 12-9 to 12-10, 12-13, 12-2 to 12-8, 12-11 to 12-12, 12-14

2487.   Cowlitz   EDs 8-1 to 8-36, 8-53, 8-37 to 8-38, 8-55, 8-39 to 8-40, 8-57, 8-41 to 8-52, 8-54 (NP), 8-56, 8-58 to 8-62

Grant   EDs 13-1 to 13-24

Jefferson   EDs 16-1 to 16-2, 16-33, 16-3 to 16-7, 16-34, 16-8 to 16-15, 16-32, 16-16 to 16-31

2488.   Grays Harbor   EDs 14-1 to 14-5, 14-80 to 14-81, 14-6 to 14-7, 14-82 (void), 14-8 to 14-19, 14-83, 14-20 to 14-43, 14-75 (NP), 14-44 to 14-48, 14-76 (NP), 14-49 to 14-53, 14-77, 14-54 to 14-58

2489.   Grays Harbor   EDs 14-59 to 14-60, 14-78, 14-61 to 14-64, 14-65 (NP), 14-79, 14-66 to 14-74

Island   EDs 15-1 to 15-21

Klickitat   EDs 20-1 to 20-23, 20-30, 20-24 to 20-29, 20-31 to 20-40, 20-41 (NP)

King   EDs 17-226 to 17-227, 17-394, 17-228 to 17-244, 17-247, 17-245 to 17-246, 17-248 to 17-271

2490.   King   EDs 17-272 to 17-276, 17-278, 17-277, 17-279 to 17-308, 17-397, 17-309 to 17-333, 17-395, 17-334 to 17-350

2491.   King, Seattle City   EDs 17-351 to 17-363, 17-398, 17-364 to 17-365, 17-1 to 17-8, 17-399

2492.   King, Seattle City   EDs 17-9 to 17-24

2493.   King, Seattle City   EDs 17-400, 17-25 to 17-38, 17-401

2494.   King, Seattle City   EDs 17-39 to 17-55

2495.   King, Seattle City   EDs 17-56 to 17-61, 17-402, 17-62 to 17-66, 17-403, 17-67 to 17-71

2496.   King, Seattle City   EDs 17-404 to 17-405, 17-72 to 17-74, 17-406, 17-75 to 17-84

2497.   King, Seattle City   EDs 17-85, 17-407, 17-86, 17-408, 17-87 to 17-103

2498.   King, Seattle City   EDs 17-104 to 17-126

2499.   King, Seattle City   EDs 17-127 to 17-132, 17-409, 17-133, 17-134 (NP), 17-135, 17-136 (NP), 17-137 to 17-157

2500.   King, Seattle City   EDs 17-158 to 17-160, 17-410, 17-161 to 17-163, 17-164 (NP), 17-165 to 17-177

2501.   King, Seattle City   EDs 17-178 to 17-181, 17-411, 17-182 to 17-183, 17-412, 17-184 to 17-185, 17-413, 17-186, 17-414, 17-187, 17-415

2502.   King, Seattle City   EDs 17-188 to 17-191, 17-192 to 17-197

2503.   King, Seattle City   EDs 17-198 to 17-208

2504.   King, Seattle City   EDs 17-209 to 17-211, 17-416, 17-212 to 17-219

2505.   King, Seattle City   EDs 17-220 to 17-225, 17-366 to 17-378, 17-396, 17-379 to 17-389, 17-390 (NP), 17-391, 17-392 to 17-393 (NP)

** Roll 2486, Franklin County, Washington—There appears to be no ED 11-4.

* Roll 2483, Williamsburg City—EDs 100-1 to 100-6 are on roll 2464, York County.

2506. Kitsap   EDs 18-1 to 18-28, 18-54, 18-29 to 18-32, 18-55, 18-33 to 18-53

Kittitas   EDs 19-1, 19-31, 19-2 to 19-22, 19-32, 19-23 to 19-30

2507. Lewis   EDs 21-1 to 21-90

San Juan   EDs 28-1 to 28-16

2508. Lincoln   EDs 22-1 to 22-11, 22-35, 22-56, 22-12 to 22-13, 22-58, 22-14 to 22-15, 22-60, 22-16 to 22-34, 22-36 to 22-37, 22-47, 22-38 to 22-39, 22-49, 22-40 to 22-46, 22-48, 22-50 to 22-55, 22-57, 22-59, 22-61 to 22-63

Mason   EDs 23-1 to 23-20, 23-22 to 23-26, 23-21, 23-27 to 23-31

Okanogan   EDs 24-1 to 24-28, 24-67, 24-29 to 24-30, 24-33, 24-31 to 24-32, 24-34 to 24-35, 24-37, 24-65, 24-68, 24-36, 24-38 to 24-39, 24-66, 24-40, 24-42, 24-41, 24-43 to 24-50, 24-51 (NP), 24-52 to 24-54, 24-69 to 24-70, 24-55 to 24-58, 24-60, 24-59, 24-61 to 24-64

Skamania   EDs 30-1 to 30-11

2509. Pacific   EDs 25-1 to 25-22, 25-41, 25-23 to 25-33, 25-35, 25-37, 25-34, 25-36, 25-38 to 25-40

Pend Orielle   EDs 26-1 to 26-7, 26-27, 26-8 to 26-18, 26-23, 26-19 to 26-22, 26-24 to 26-26, 26-28

Pierce   EDs 27-1 to 27-10, 27-13, 27-11 to 27-12, 27-14 to 27-27, 27-29, 27-28, 27-30 to 27-42

2510. Pierce   EDs 27-43 to 27-63, 27-65, 27-64, 27-66 to 27-74, 27-207, 27-75 to 27-78

Pierce, Tacoma City   EDs 27-79 to 27-88, 27-90, 27-92, 27-89, 27-91, 27-93, 27-123 to 27-134

2511. Pierce, Tacoma City   EDs 27-94 to 27-122, 27-135 to 27-156

2512. Pierce, Tacoma City   EDs 27-157 to 27-172, 27-190 to 27-196, 27-173 to 27-189, 27-197 to 27-206

2513. Skagit   EDs 29-1 to 29-17, 29-68, 29-18 to 29-19, 29-70, 29-20 to 29-21, 29-72, 29-22 to 29-38, 29-41, 29-43, 29-61, 29-63, 29-42, 29-39, 29-59, 29-40, 29-78, 29-44 to 29-50, 29-52 to 29-53, 29-51, 29-54 to 29-58, 29-62, 29-60, 29-64 to 29-67, 29-69, 29-71, 29-73 to 29-74, 29-75 to 29-76 (NP), 29-77

Spokane   EDs 32-109 to 32-128

2514. Spokane, Spokane City   EDs 32-129 to 32-145, 32-174, 32-146 to 32-165, 32-1 to 32-8

2515. Spokane, Spokane City   EDs 32-9 to 32-28

2516. Spokane, Spokane City   EDs 32-29 to 32-35, 32-36 (NP), 32-37 to 32-57

2517. Spokane, Spokane City   EDs 32-58 to 32-84

2518. Spokane, Spokane City   EDs 32-85 to 32-108, 32-166 to 32-173

2519. Snohomish   EDs 31-2, 31-1, 31-3 to 31-90

2520. Snohomish   EDs 31-91 to 31-132, 31-138, 31-133 to 31-137

Stevens   EDs 33-1 to 33-12, 33-14, 33-16, 33-13, 33-15, 33-17 to 33-20, 33-22, 33-24, 33-21, 33-23, 33-25 to 33-81

2521. Thurston   EDs 34-1 to 34-41, 34-43, 34-42, 34-44 to 34-46, 34-48, 34-47, 34-49 to 34-54

Wahkiakum   EDs 35-1 to 35-12

Whatcom   EDs 37-1 to 37-5, 37-104, 37-6, 37-18 to 37-20

2522. Whatcom   EDs 37-7 to 37-17, 37-21 to 37-28, 37-107, 37-29 to 37-30, 37-105, 37-31 to 37-42, 37-106, 37-43 to 37-56, 37-57 to 37-58 (NP), 37-59, 37-60 to 37-61 (NP), 37-62 to 37-63, 37-64 (NP), 37-65, 37-66 to 37-78 (NP), 37-79, 37-80 to 37-86 (NP), 37-87 to 37-88, 37-89 to 37-102 (NP), 37-103

2523. Walla Walla   EDs 36-1 to 36-39, 36-58, 36-40 to 36-57

Whitman   EDs 38-1 to 38-43, 38-75 to 38-76, 38-44 to 38-46, 38-55, 38-67, 38-73, 38-47, 38-79, 38-48 to 38-49, 38-56, 38-74, 38-50 to 38-54, 38-57 to 38-62

2524. Whitman   EDs 38-63 to 38-66, 38-68 to 38-72, 38-77 to 38-78, 38-80

2525. Yakima   EDs 39-1 to 39-50, 39-51 (NP), 39-52 to 39-78

2525. Yakima   EDs 39-79 to 39-92, 39-93 (NP), 39-94 to 39-101, 39-126, 39-102 to 39-117, 39-118 (NP), 39-127 (NP), 39-119 to 39-125

## *West Virginia*

2526. Berkeley   EDs 2-1 to 2-19

Boone   EDs 3-1 to 3-19

2527. Braxton   EDs 4-1 to 4-5, 4-16, 4-6, 4-11, 4-7 to 4-10, 4-12 to 4-15, 4-17 to 4-19

Brooke   EDs 5-1 to 5-14

2528. Barbour   EDs 1-1 to 1-8, 1-15, 1-9 to 1-11, 1-16, 1-12 to 1-14

Cabell   EDs 6-1 to 6-15

2529. Cabell   EDs 6-16 to 6-46

2530. Cabell   EDs 6-47 to 6-50

Calhoun   EDs 7-1 to 7-8

Doddridge   EDs 9-1 to 9-10

Clay   EDs 8-1 to 8-8

Gilmer   EDs 11-1 to 11-11

2531. Fayette   EDs 10-1 to 10-5, 10-18 to 10-25, 10-10 to 10-17

2532. Fayette   EDs 10-6 to 10-9, 10-26 to 10-37

Grant   EDs 12-1 to 12-7

Greenbrier   EDs 13-1 to 13-8, 13-29, 13-9 to 13-13, 13-30, 13-14 to 13-15

2533. Greenbrier   EDs 13-16 to 13-20, 13-31, 13-21 to 13-28

Hampshire   EDs 14-1, 14-3, 14-2, 14-4 to 14-13

Hancock   EDs 15-1 to 15-15

2534. Harrison   EDs 17-1 to 17-15, 17-46, 17-16, 17-45, 17-17 to 17-25, 17-42 to 17-44

2535. Harrison   EDs 17-26 to 17-41

Hardy   EDs 16-1 to 16-10

Jackson   EDs 18-1 to 18-14

2536. Jefferson   EDs 19-1 to 19-10

Kanawha   EDs 20-1 to 20-22

2537. Kanawha   EDs 20-23 to 20-34, 20-37, 20-35 to 20-36, 20-38 to 20-48, 20-52

2538. Kanawha   EDs 20-49 to 20-51, 20-53 to 20-61, 20-77 to 20-78, 20-62 to 20-73, 20-86 to 20-87

2539. Kanawha   EDs 20-74 to 20-76, 20-79 to 20-85

Lewis   EDs 21-1 to 21-2, 21-10 to 21-11, 21-3 to 21-9, 21-12 to 21-18

Lincoln   EDs 22-1 to 22-8

2540. Lincoln   EDs 22-9 to 22-14

Logan   EDs 23-1 to 23-9, 23-11 to 23-23, 23-10, 23-24 to 23-28

2541. Logan   EDs 23-29 to 23-38

Mason   EDs 27-1 to 27-9, 27-24, 27-10, 27-27, 27-11 to 27-20, 27-22 to 27-23, 27-25 to 27-26, 27-21

Marion   EDs 25-31 to 25-33, 25-40, 25-34 to 25-39

2542. Marion   EDs 25-1 to 25-13, 25-16, 25-20, 25-14 to 25-15, 25-17 to 25-19, 25-21 to 25-30

2543. Marshall   EDs 26-1 to 26-29

McDowell   EDs 24-44 to 24-48

2544. McDowell   EDs 24-1 to 24-9, 24-34 to 24-38, 24-10 to 24-19, 24-22 to 24-26

2545. McDowell   EDs 24-20 to 24-21, 24-27 to 24-33, 24-39 to 24-43

Mercer   EDs 28-26 to 28-29, 28-38, 28-30 to 28-34

2546. Mercer   EDs 28-1, 28-35, 28-2 to 28-4, 28-36, 28-40, 28-37, 28-5 to 28-7, 28-39, 28-8 to 28-25
Mineral   EDs 29-1 to 29-6

2547. Mineral   EDs 29-7 to 29-14
Mingo   EDs 30-1 to 30-4, 30-10 to 30-16, 30-5 to 30-9, 30-17 to 30-26

2548. Monongalia   EDs 31-1, 31-28, 31-2 to 31-3, 31-29 to 31-30, 31-4 to 31-26, 31-32, 31-27, 31-31

2549. Monroe   EDs 32-1 to 32-12
Morgan   EDs 33-1 to 33-8
Nicholas   EDs 34-1 to 34-16
Ohio   EDs 35-1 to 35-6, 35-10 to 35-11

2550. Ohio   EDs 35-7 to 35-9, 35-12 to 35-33, 35-34 (void), 35-35 to 35-42

2551. Ohio   EDs 35-43 to 35-47
Pendleton   EDs 36-1 to 36-7
Pleasants   EDs 37-1 to 37-7
Pocahontas   EDs 38-1 to 38-12
Preston   EDs 39-1 to 39-12

2552. Preston   EDs 39-13 to 39-15, 39-26, 39-16, 39-27, 39-17, 39-28, 39-18 to 39-25
Putnam   EDs 40-1 to 40-16
Raleigh   EDs 41-1 to 41-5

2553. Raleigh   EDs 41-6 to 41-14, 41-27 to 41-29, 41-15 to 41-26

2554. Randolph   EDs 42-1 to 42-26
Ritchie   EDs 43-1 to 43-14
Roane   EDs 44-1 to 44-9, 44-16 to 44-17

2555. Roane   EDs 44-10 to 44-15
Summers   EDs 45-1 to 45-19
Taylor   EDs 46-1 to 46-11, 46-17, 46-12 to 46-16
Tucker   EDs 47-1 to 47-3, 47-14, 47-4 to 47-7

2556. Tucker   EDs 47-8 to 47-13
Tyler   EDs 48-1 to 48-16
Upshur   EDs 49-3 to 49-5, 49-9 to 49-10, 49-1 to 49-2, 49-6 to 49-8, 49-11 to 49-13
Wayne   EDs 50-1 to 50-11, 50-15 to 50-16

2557. Wayne   EDs 50-12 to 50-14, 50-17 to 50-22
Webster   EDs 51-1 to 51-11
Wetzel   EDs 52-1 to 52-18

2558. Wood   EDs 54-5 to 54-20, 54-1 to 54-4, 54-21 to 54-34

2559. Wirt   EDs 53-1 to 53-8
Wyoming   EDs 55-1, 55-14, 55-2 to 55-13

## Wisconsin

2560. Adams   EDs 1-1 to 1-19
Bayfield   EDs 4-1 to 4-34
Ashland   EDs 2-1 to 2-25
Barron   EDs 3-1 to 3-2, 3-5

2561. Barron   EDs 3-3 to 3-4, 3-6 to 3-20, 3-22 to 3-25, 3-21, 3-26 to 3-35, 3-42, 3-36 to 3-41
Brown   EDs 5-1 to 5-5, 5-11, 5-6 to 5-10, 5-12 to 5-13, 5-38 to 5-43

2562. Brown   EDs 5-14 to 5-28, 5-30, 5-29, 5-31 to 5-37, 5-44 to 5-59

2563. Buffalo   EDs 6-1 to 6-22
Burnett   EDs 7-1 to 7-23
Calumet   EDs 8-1 to 8-18

Clark   EDs 10-1 to 10-15

2564. Clark   EDs 10-16 to 10-46
Chippewa   EDs 9-1 to 9-28

2565. Chippewa   EDs 9-29 to 9-42
Columbia   EDs 11-1 to 11-38
Crawford   EDs 12-1 to 12-12

2566. Crawford   EDs 12-13 to 12-24
Dane   EDs 13-1 to 13-19, 13-21 to 13-22, 13-20, 13-23 to 13-27, 13-92, 13-28 to 13-32, 13-39, 13-33 to 13-38

2567. Dane   EDs 13-40 to 13-45, 13-48 to 13-49, 13-89, 13-46 to 13-47, 13-50 to 13-51, 13-90 to 13-91, 13-52 to 13-61

2568. Dane   EDs 13-62 to 13-88
Dodge   EDs 14-1 to 14-26

2569. Dodge   EDs 14-27 to 14-55, 14-57, 14-56, 14-58 to 14-59
Door   EDs 15-1 to 15-20
Douglas   EDs 16-1 to 16-15

2570. Douglas   EDs 16-16 to 16-33, 16-37 to 16-38, 16-34 to 16-36, 16-39 to 16-44
Forest   EDs 21-1 to 21-16

2571. Dunn   EDs 17-1 to 17-35
Eau Claire   EDs 18-7 to 18-19

2572. Eau Claire   EDs 18-1 to 18-6, 18-20 to 18-31
Fond Du Lac   EDs 20-1 to 20-10, 20-13 to 20-29

2573. Fond Du Lac   EDs 20-11 to 20-12, 20-30 to 20-54
Florence   EDs 19-1 to 19-8
Iowa   EDs 25-1 to 25-20, 25-29, 25-21 to 25-28

2574. Grant   EDs 22-1 to 22-59
Green   EDs 23-1 to 23-13

2575. Green   EDs 23-14 to 23-27
Green Lake   EDs 24-1 to 24-19
Iron   EDs 26-1 to 26-17
Jackson   EDs 27-1 to 27-28

2576. Jefferson   EDs 28-1 to 28-44
Kewaunee   EDs 31-1 to 31-14

2577. Juneau   EDs 29-1 to 29-28
Kenosha   EDs 30-1 to 30-2, 30-28 to 30-32, 30-3 to 30-5, 30-16 to 30-17, 30-20 to 30-27

2578. Kenosha   EDs 30-6 to 30-15, 30-18 to 30-19, 30-33 to 30-35
La Crosse   EDs 32-1 to 32-20

2579. La Crosse   EDs 32-21 to 32-41
Lafayette   EDs 33-1 to 33-26

2580. Langlade   EDs 34-1 to 34-24
Lincoln   EDs 35-1 to 35-25
Manitowoc   EDs 36-1 to 36-7

2581. Manitowoc   EDs 36-8 to 36-11, 36-28 to 36-42, 36-12 to 36-27

2582. Marathon   EDs 37-1 to 37-36, 37-55 to 37-69

2583. Marathon   EDs 37-37 to 37-54, 37-70 to 37-72
Marinette   EDs 38-1 to 38-32

2584. Marinette   EDs 38-33 to 38-35
Marquette   EDs 39-1 to 39-18

Milwaukee    EDs 40-338 to 40-356

2585. Milwaukee, Milwaukee City    EDs 40-1 to 40-8, 40-408, 40-9 to 40-19, 40-412, 40-20 to 40-28

2586. Milwaukee, Milwaukee City    EDs 40-29 to 40-33, 40-413, 40-34 to 40-49, 40-51 to 40-52, 40-50, 40-53 to 40-65

2587. Milwaukee, Milwaukee City    EDs 40-66 to 40-74, 40-295, 40-75 to 40-96

2588. Milwaukee, Milwaukee City    EDs 40-97 to 40-125

2589. Milwaukee, Milwaukee City    EDs 40-126 to 40-134, 40-314, 40-135 to 40-154

2590. Milwaukee, Milwaukee City    EDs 40-155 to 40-179

2591. Milwaukee, Milwaukee City    EDs 40-180 to 40-199

2592. Milwaukee, Milwaukee City    EDs 40-200 to 40-213

2593. Milwaukee, Milwaukee City    EDs 40-214 to 40-215, 40-409 to 40-411, 40-216 to 40-225, 40-407, 40-226 to 40-238

2594. Milwaukee, Milwaukee City    EDs 40-239 to 40-256, 40-417

2595. Milwaukee, Milwaukee City    EDs 40-257 to 40-258, 40-416, 40-259, 40-414, 40-260 to 40-264

2596. Milwaukee, Milwaukee City    EDs 40-265 to 40-287

2597. Milwaukee, Milwaukee City    EDs 40-288 to 40-294, 40-296 to 40-307

2598. Milwaukee, Milwaukee City    EDs 40-308 to 40-313, 40-315 to 40-330

2599. Milwaukee, Milwaukee City    EDs 40-331 to 40-337, 40-357 to 40-358, 40-370 to 40-373, 40-415, 40-374 to 40-379

2600. Milwaukee    EDs 40-359 to 40-369, 40-380 to 40-385, 40-386 (void), 40-387 to 40-392

2601. Milwaukee    EDs 40-393 to 40-406

Monroe    EDs 41-1 to 41-26, 41-35 to 41-38

2602. Monroe    EDs 41-27 to 41-34, 41-39 to 41-43

Oneida    EDs 43-1 to 43-25

Oconto    EDs 42-1 to 42-40

2603. Outagamie    EDs 44-1 to 44-39

2604. Outagamie    EDs 44-40 to 44-51

Pierce    EDs 47-1 to 47-27

Price    EDs 50-1 to 50-26

2605. Ozaukee    EDs 45-1 to 45-20

Pepin    EDs 46-1 to 46-11

Polk    EDs 48-1 to 48-35

2606. Portage    EDs 49-1 to 49-15, 49-27 to 49-34, 49-16 to 49-26, 49-35 to 49-36

Racine    EDs 51-1 to 51-10, 51-12, 51-53, 51-11

2607. Racine    EDs 51-13 to 51-17, 51-54, 51-18 to 51-19, 51-56, 51-20 to 51-35, 51-57, 51-36

2608. Racine    EDs 51-37 to 51-38, 51-55, 51-39 to 51-48, 51-49 (void), 51-50 to 51-52

Richland    EDs 52-1 to 52-23

Sauk    EDs 56-1 to 56-5

2609. Sauk    EDs 56-6 to 56-41

Rock    EDs 53-1 to 53-14

2610. Rock    EDs 53-15 to 53-18, 53-24 to 53-35, 53-19, 53-53, 53-20 to 53-23, 53-36 to 53-52

Rusk    EDs 54-1 to 54-7

2611. Rusk    EDs 54-8 to 54-40

Sawyer    EDs 57-1, 57-21, 57-2, 57-22, 57-3 to 57-17, 57-23, 57-18 to 57-20

St. Croix    EDs 55-1 to 55-36

2612. Shawano    EDs 58-1 to 58-45

Sheboygan    EDs 59-1 to 59-22

2613. Sheboygan    EDs 59-23 to 59-51

2614. Taylor    EDs 60-1 to 60-27

Vilas    EDs 63-1 to 63-15

Trempealeau    EDs 61-1 to 61-26

Vernon    EDs 62-1 to 62-3

2615. Vernon    EDs 62-4 to 62-37

Walworth    EDs 64-1 to 64-29

2616. Walworth    EDs 64-30 to 64-34

Washburn    EDs 65-1 to 65-25

Waukesha    EDs 67-1 to 67-13, 67-52, 67-14 to 67-34, 67-51, 67-35 to 67-37

2617. Waukesha    EDs 67-38 to 67-45, 67-49, 67-46 to 67-48, 67-50

Waupaca    EDs 68-1 to 68-47

2618. Washington    EDs 66-1 to 66-30

Waushara    EDs 69-1 to 69-25

Wood    EDs 71-1 to 71-12, 71-23 to 71-25

2619. Wood    EDs 71-13 to 71-22, 71-26 to 71-45

Winnebago    EDs 70-1 to 70-20

2620. Winnebago    EDs 70-21 to 70-55

## Wyoming

2621. Albany    EDs 1-1 to 1-32

Big Horn    EDs 2-1 to 2-12, 2-14, 2-13, 2-15 to 2-23, 2-25, 2-24, 2-26 to 2-35

Campbell    EDs 3-1 to 3-30

Converse    EDs 5-1 to 5-28

Crook    EDs 6-1 to 6-27

2622. Carbon    EDs 4-1 to 4-31

Fremont    EDs 7-1 to 7-5, 7-17 (NP), 7-18 to 7-19, 7-6 to 7-16, 7-20

Goshen    EDs 8-1 to 8-24

Hot Springs    EDs 9-1 to 9-14

Johnson    EDs 10-1 to 10-11

2623. Laramie    EDs 11-1 to 11-26

Lincoln    EDs 12-1 to 12-10, 12-13, 12-11 to 12-12

Platte    EDs 16-1 to 16-26

Sublette    EDs 18-1 to 18-8, 18-9 (NP)

2624. Natrona    EDs 13-1 to 13-17, 13-22, 13-18 to 13-21, 13-23 to 13-26

Niobrara    EDs 14-1 to 14-19

Sheridan    EDs 17-1 to 17-2, 17-33, 17-3 to 17-4, 17-34, 17-5 to 17-32

2625. Park    EDs 15-1 to 15-10, 15-24, 15-12 to 15-15, 15-17 to 15-23

Teton    EDs 20-1 to 20-4, 20-7 (NP), 20-5, 20-8, 20-6

Uinta    EDs 21-1 to 21-17

Weston    EDs 23-1 to 23-20

Park    EDs 15-11 (NP), 15-16 (NP)

Sweetwater    EDs 19-1 to 19-25, 19-26 (NP), 19-27 to 19-33

Washakie    EDs 22-1 to 22-8

Yellowstone National Park    EDs 24-1

## Alaska

2626. First Judicial Division    EDs 1-1 to 1-43

2627.   Second Judicial Division   EDs 2-1 to 2-13
        Third Judicial Division   EDs 3-1 to 3-19
2628.   Third Judicial Division   EDs 3-20 to 3-28
        Fourth Judicial Division   EDs 4-1 to 4-46

## American Samoa and Guam

* 2629.   American Samoa   EDs 11 to 15, 1 to 10, 16
          Guam   EDs 7 to 10, 1 to 6, 11 to 13

## Consular Services

** 2630.   Consular Services   Danzig, Poland to Zurich, Switzerland

## Hawaii

2631.   Hawaii   EDs 1-1 to 1-10, 1-45 to 1-49, 1-11 to 1-15, 1-50 to 1-61, 1-23 to 1-34
2632.   Hawaii   EDs 1-35 to 1-44, 1-16 to 1-22, 1-62 to 1-71
        Honolulu   EDs 2-93 to 2-115
2633.   Honolulu   EDs 2-1 to 2-35
2634.   Honolulu   EDs 2-36 to 2-52, 2-56 to 2-70, 2-72, 2-71, 2-73 to 2-75
2635.   Honolulu   EDs 2-76 to 2-92, 2-116 to 2-121, 2-124 to 2-136
2636.   Honolulu   EDs 2-53 to 2-55, 2-122 to 2-123, 2-137 to 2-146
        Kauai   EDs 4-1 to 4-2, 4-5, 4-4, 4-6, 4-3, 4-7 to 4-9, 4-25, 4-10 to 4-22, 4-24, 4-23
2637.   Maui   EDs 5-1 to 5-3, 5-5 to 5-7, 5-29 to 5-40, 5-43, 5-41 to 5-42, 5-44 to 5-46
        Kalawao   ED 3-1
        Maui, Lahaina District   EDs 5-8 to 5-19, 5-4, 5-20, 5-25, 5-21 to 5-24, 5-26 to 5-28

## Panama Canal and Consular Services

*** 2638.   Balboa District   EDs 1-21, 1-1, 1-23, 1-4, 1-2, 1-20, 1-10, 1-18, 1-5, 1-22, 1-24, 1-12, 1-6, 1-16, 1-14 to 1-15, 1-13, 1-19, 1-17, 1-7, 1-9, 1-8, 1-11, 1-3
            Cristobal District   EDs 1-42 to 1-43, 1-34, 1-39, 1-28, 1-26, 1-36, 1-32, 1-31, 1-30, 1-29, 1-40, 1-25, 1-41, 1-33, 1-45, 1-38, 1-27, 1-37, 1-47, 1-46, 1-35, 1-44
            Consular Services   Acapulco, Mexico to Darien, Manchuria and continuation of Danzig (Free State), Danzig, Poland, to Zurich, Switzerland

## Puerto Rico

2639.   Adjuntas Municipality   EDs 44-1 to 44-17
        Arroyo Municipality   EDs 54-1 to 54-8
        Aguada Municipality   EDs 21-1 to 21-19
        Aguas Buenas Municipality   EDs 52-1 to 52-10
2640.   Aguadilla Municipality   EDs 22-1 to 22-20
        Albonito Municipality   EDs 53-1 to 53-10
        Anasco Municipality   EDs 23-1 to 23-26
2641.   Arecibo Municipality   EDs 12-1 to 12-29
2642.   Barceloneta Municipality   EDs 13-1 to 13-8

        Barranquitas Municipality   EDs 55-1 to 55-8
        Bayamon Municipality   EDs 1-1 to 1-15
2643.   Cabo Rojo Municipality   EDs 34-1 to 34-12
        Caguas Municipality   EDs 56-1 to 56-11
2644.   Caguas Municipality   EDs 56-12 to 56-19
        Camuy Municipality.   EDs 24-1 to 24-13
        Carolina Municipality   EDs 2-1 to 2-13
2645.   Catano Municipality   EDs 3-1 to 3-4
        Ciales Municipality   EDs 14-1 to 14-13
        Cayey Municipality   EDs 57-1 to 57-15, 57-17 to 57-25, 57-16
2646.   Ceiba Municipality   EDs 64-1 to 64-8
        Cidra Municipality   EDs 58-1 to 58-13
        Coamo Municipality   EDs 45-1 to 45-12
        Comerio Municipality   EDs 59-1 to 59-6
2647.   Comerio Municipality   EDs 59-7 to 59-9
        Corozal Municipality   EDs 4-1 to 4-12
        Dorado Municipality   EDs 15-1 to 15-6
        Culebra Municipality   EDs 65-1 to 65-5
        Fajardo Municipality   EDs 66-1 to 66-12
        Gúanica Municipality   EDs 35-1 to 35-8
2648.   Guayama Municipality   EDs 60-1 to 60-13
        Guaynilla Municipality   EDs 36-1 to 36-16
        Gurabo Municipality   EDs 67-1 to 67-10
2649.   Guaynabo Municipality   EDs 5-1 to 5-10
        Hatillo Municipality   EDs 25-1 to 25-12
        Hormigueros Municipality   EDs 37-1 to 37-5
        Isabela Municipality   EDs 26-1 to 26-16
2650.   Humacao Municipality   EDs 68-1 to 68-16
        Jayuya Municipality   EDs 46-1 to 46-11
        Juncos Municipality   EDs 69-1 to 69-11
2651.   Juana Diaz Municipality   EDs 47-1 to 47-19
        Las Marias Municipality   EDs 28-1 to 28-13
        Lajas Municipality   EDs 38-1 to 38-11
        Las Piedras Municipality   EDs 70-1 to 70-9
2652.   Lares Municipality   EDs 27-1 to 27-14
        Loiza Municipality   EDs 71-1 to 71-11
        Luquillo Municipality   EDs 72-1 to 72-6
2653.   Manati Municipality   EDs 16-1 to 16-10
        Maricao Municipality   EDs 29-1 to 29-7
        Morovis Municipality   EDs 17-1 to 17-14
2654.   Maunabo Municipality   EDs 61-1 to 61-10
        Moca Municipality   EDs 30-1 to 30-12
        Mayaguez Municipality   EDs 39-1 to 39-9
2655.   Mayaguez Municipality   EDs 39-10 to 39-32
        Naguabo Municipality   EDs 73-1 to 73-11
        Quebradillas Municipality   EDs 31-1 to 31-8
2656.   Naranvito Municipality   EDs 6-1 to 6-8
        Orocovis Municipality   EDs 48-1 to 48-17
        Patillas Municipality   EDs 62-1 to 62-16

---

* Roll 2629, American Samoa and Guam—These two jurisdictions use the traditional ED numbering system; they do not have county numbers.
** Roll 2630 for Consular Services—See roll 2638 for a continuation of Danzig (Free State), Danzig, Poland, to Zurich, Switzerland.
*** Roll 2638, Consular Service—See roll 2630 for a continuation of Danzig, Poland.

Peñuelas Municipality   EDs 40-1 to 40-4, 40-13, 40-5 to 40-9, 40-11, 40-10, 40-12

2657.  Ponce Municipality   EDs 49-1 to 49-9, 49-12 to 49-14, 49-10 to 49-11, 49-15 to 49-25

2658.  Ponce Municipality   EDs 49-26 to 49-43

Rincón Municipality   EDs 32-1 to 32-9

Salinas Municipality   EDs 63-1 to 63-8

* 2659.  Rio Grande Municipality   EDs 74-1 to 74-9

Rio Piedras Municipality   EDs 7-1 to 7-11, 7-12 (void), 7-13 to 7-17

2660.  Sabana Grande Municipality   EDs 41-1 to 41-9

Toa Alta Municipality   EDs 9-1 to 9-9

San German Municipality   EDs 42-1 to 42-23

2661.  San Juan Municipality   EDs 8-1 to 8-3, 8-40 (1a-1b), 8-4, 8-43, 8-40 (2a-15b), 8-5 to 8-6, 8-40 (16a-16b), 8-7 to 8-11, 8-12 to 8-14 (NP), 8-40 (17a-20b), 8-15 to 8-16, 8-40 (21a- 21b), 8-17 to 8-18, 8-40 (22a-22b), 8-19 to 8-23, 8-40 (23a-39)

2662.  San Juan Municipality   EDs 8-24 to 8-37

2663.  San Juan Municipality   EDs 8-38 to 8-39, 8-41 to 8-42

Vega Alta Municipality   EDs 19-1 to 19-8

San Lorenzo Municipality   EDs 75-1 to 75-13

2664.  San Sebastian Municipality   EDs 33-1 to 33-25

Santa Isabel Municipality   EDs 50-1 to 50-8

Toa Baja Municipality   EDs 10-1 to 10-5

Trujillo Alta Municipality   EDs 11-1 to 11-8

2665.  Utuado Municipality   EDs 18-1 to 18-27

Villalbo Municipality   EDs 51-1 to 51-8

2666.  Vega Baja Municipality   EDs 20-1 to 20-16

Vieques Municipality   EDs 76-1 to 76-8

Yabucoa Municipality   EDs 77-1 to 77-11

2667.  Vauco Municipality   EDs 43-1 to 43-22, 43-24, 43-23

## Virgin Islands

2668.  St. Croix Island   EDs 1 to 13

St. John Island   EDs 14 to 18

St. Thomas Island   EDs 19 to 22, 24, 23, 25, 26 (NP), 27 to 29, 30 (NP), 31 to 32

---

* Roll 2659, Rio Grande Municipality—There appears to be no ED 74-10.

# MICROFILM ORDER

Microfilm publication numbers (preceded by an "M" or "T") are assigned to each microfilm publication. Please enter the microfilm publication number and roll number(s) in the proper columns. Because we accept orders for individual rolls, as well as for complete microfilm publications, we must know which rolls you wish to purchase.

Effective May 15, 1996, the price for each roll of microfilm is $34 for U.S. orders. The price is $39 per roll for foreign orders. Shipping is included. These prices are subject to change without notice. For current price information, write to National Archives Customer Service Center (NWCC2), 8601 Adelphi Road, College Park, MD 20740; or call 1-800-234-8861 (in the Washington, DC, metropolitan area, 301-713-6800).

*Sample of correctly completed form.*

| MICRO. PUB. NUMBER | ROLL NUMBER(S) | PRICE |
|---|---|---|
| T624 | 1138 | $34. |
| T1270 | 88 - 89 | $68. |

*Additional order forms are available upon request.*

| ORDERED BY *(Include organization if shipping to a business address.)* | Name |
| | Organization *(if applicable)* |
| | Address *(Number and Street)* |
| | City, State & ZIP Code |
| | Daytime Telephone Number *(Include area code)* |

## PAYMENT TYPE

**SEND YOUR ORDER TO:**

*CREDIT CARD*

Check one and enter card number below.  ☐ VISA  ☐ MasterCard  ☐ American Express  ☐ Discover

Exp. Date

*Signature*

National Archives Trust Fund
Cashier (NAT)
8601 Adelphi Road
College Park, MD 20740
(Credit card orders may be faxed to 301-713-6169)

*OTHER*

☐ Check  ☐ Money Order
*Make payable to: National Archives Trust Fund.*

Amount Enclosed  $

National Archives Trust Fund
P.O. Box 100793
Atlanta, GA 30384-0793

## IDENTIFY THE ROLLS YOU WISH TO ORDER

| MICRO. PUB. NUMBER | ROLL NUMBER(S) | PRICE | | MICRO. PUB. NUMBER | ROLL NUMBER(S) | PRICE |
|---|---|---|---|---|---|---|
| | | | | | | |
| | | | | | | |
| | | | | | | |
| | | | | | | |
| | | | | | | |
| | | | | | | |
| | | | | | *Subtotal (this column)* | |
| | | | | | *Subtotal from first column* | |
| *Subtotal (this column)* | | | | | **TOTAL PRICE** | |

**Privacy Act and Paperwork Reduction Act Public Burden statements
are on the back of this page.**

**PRIVACY ACT STATEMENT**

Collection of this information is authorized by 44 U.S.C. 2108. Disclosure of the information is voluntary; however, we will be unable to respond to your request if you do not furnish your name and address and the minimum required information about the records. The information is used by NARA employees to search for the record; to respond to you; to maintain control over information requests received and answered; and to facilitate preparation of internal statistical reports. If you provide credit card information, that information is used to bill you for copies.

**PAPERWORK REDUCTION ACT PUBLIC BURDEN STATEMENT**

A Federal agency may not conduct or sponsor, and a person is not required to respond to a collection of information unless it displays a current valid OMB control number. The OMB Control No. for this information collection is 3095-0046. Public burden reporting for this collection of information is estimated to be 10 minutes per response. Send comments regarding the burden estimate or any other aspect of the information collection, including suggestions for reducing this burden, to National Archives and Records Administration (NHP), 8601 Adelphi Road, College Park MD 20740. DO NOT SEND COMPLETED FORMS TO THIS ADDRESS. SEND COMPLETED FORMS TO THE ADDRESS INDICATED ON THE FORM ITSELF.

NATIONAL ARCHIVES TRUST FUND BOARD    NATF Form 36 (rev. 2-2001)

# MICROFILM ORDER

Microfilm publication numbers (preceded by an "M" or "T") are assigned to each microfilm publication. Please enter the microfilm publication number and roll number(s) in the proper columns. Because we accept orders for individual rolls, as well as for complete microfilm publications, we must know which rolls you wish to purchase.

Effective May 15, 1996, the price for each roll of microfilm is $34 for U.S. orders. The price is $39 per roll for foreign orders. Shipping is included. These prices are subject to change without notice. For current price information, write to National Archives Customer Service Center (NWCC2), 8601 Adelphi Road, College Park, MD 20740; or call 1-800-234-8861 (in the Washington, DC, metropolitan area, 301-713-6800).

*Sample of correctly completed form.*

| MICRO. PUB. NUMBER | ROLL NUMBER(S) | PRICE |
|---|---|---|
| T624 | 1138 | $34. |
| T1270 | 88 - 89 | $68. |

*Additional order forms are available upon request.*

**ORDERED BY** *(Include organization if shipping to a business address.)*

| | |
|---|---|
| Name | |
| Organization *(if applicable)* | |
| Address *(Number and Street)* | |
| City, State & ZIP Code | |
| Daytime Telephone Number *(Include area code)* | |

## PAYMENT TYPE

**SEND YOUR ORDER TO:**

*CREDIT CARD*

Check one and enter card number below.  ☐ VISA  ☐ MasterCard  ☐ American Express  ☐ Discover

Exp. Date

*Signature*

National Archives Trust Fund
Cashier (NAT)
8601 Adelphi Road
College Park, MD 20740
(Credit card orders may be faxed to 301-713-6169)

*OTHER*

☐ Check  ☐ Money Order
*Make payable to: National Archives Trust Fund.*

Amount Enclosed  $

National Archives Trust Fund
P.O. Box 100793
Atlanta, GA  30384-0793

## IDENTIFY THE ROLLS YOU WISH TO ORDER

| MICRO. PUB. NUMBER | ROLL NUMBER(S) | PRICE | MICRO. PUB. NUMBER | ROLL NUMBER(S) | PRICE |
|---|---|---|---|---|---|
| | | | | | |
| | | | | | |
| | | | | | |
| | | | | | |
| | | | | | |
| | | | | | |
| | | | | *Subtotal (this column)* | |
| | | | | *Subtotal from first column* | |
| | *Subtotal (this column)* | | | **TOTAL PRICE** | |

NATIONAL ARCHIVES TRUST FUND BOARD    NATF Form 36 (rev. 2-2001)

**Privacy Act and Paperwork Reduction Act Public Burden statements
are on the back of this page.**